FOREWORD

*by Alan Geyer**

Once upon a time, a national church conference in the United States deplored "the growing tendency" of the armed forces to influence foreign policy, rejected the idea of a "war economy" as a "possible solution for unemployment," highlighted the relationship between "economic injustice" and the causes of war, declared that "it is impossible wholly to divorce foreign policy from domestic policy," and emphasized the role of local congregations in peacemaking.

That conference did not take place in the 1980s. It was held in Philadelphia in February of 1940: the first of six world order study conferences sponsored by the Federal Council of Churches and the National Council of Churches between 1940 and 1958. Not the least striking feature of that Philadelphia conference's 1940 message on "The Churches and the International Situation" is its clear consciousness of the imperatives of world ecumenism for peacemaking, noting especially the landmark 1937 Oxford Conference on Church, Community, and State and the subsequent work of the Provisional Committee of the World Council of Churches ("in-process-of-becoming").

In March 1942, 377 delegates met for a second study conference at Ohio Wesleyan University. The message of that conference might also surprise some folks today by its declarations that "peace is much more than the cessation or absence of conflict" and that racial justice is "a primary factor in the maintenance of a just and durable peace." So they were talking about "peace with justice" 'way back then!

This volume is an invaluable account of those six American ecumenical conferences, together with a treasury of documents, not only from the conferences themselves but from a variety of special commissions and governing bodies—all on the issues of war and peace.

It may be wondered (indeed I did wonder myself) whether the publication of such a volume now would perform any important service decades after the conferences were held and after almost all their leaders had passed

---

*Dr. Alan Geyer is Professor of Political Ethics and Ecumenics at Wesley Theological Seminary in Washington, DC, and concurrently Senior Scholar of the Churches' Center for Theology and Public Policy. Formerly, he served as Dag Hammarskjold Professor of Peace Studies at Colgate University and editor of *The Christian Century*.

from the scene. Not only the passing of the generations but also a widespread skepticism about the efficacy of most church pronouncements certainly suggests that such a publication may not make it to the top of the best sellers. And the messages from these conferences were not even official policy statements—an arrangement which allowed some church leaders to distance themselves from them.

But the more I read through these pages and pondered their significance, the more I was impelled to recognize what a vital service they do perform for our churches, our society, the guild of historians, and the growing host of would-be peacemakers.

One of the worst habits bred by American culture is the lack of attention to our own modern history, especially what columnist Richard Cohen calls the "near history" of the most recent generations. That very bad habit has led to one disaster after another in US relations with many other nations. This nation has plunged into almost every international crisis with a sense of righteous innocence that is oblivious to our own past involvements with other nations — Iran, Nicaragua, Cuba, the Philippines, the Soviet Union, for examples.

Our churches are hardly exempt from this cultural trait. One of the chronic troubles of American churches and councils since the 1960s, a trouble that has particularly affected relationships with Christians in other countries, has been the lack of institutional memory. Partly that is due to changing programs and priorities, budget pressures, and discontinuities of leadership and staff. But the uses of the past for present mission and ministry have seldom received the attention that they not only deserve but absolutely require.

Nor are the cadres of the peace movement exempt from this habit of historical forgetfulness, if not ignorance. Again and again, fresh spurts of messianic utterance from religious and other peace movements pretend to a prophetic novelty that is unwarranted by any decent respect for the saints of previous generations.

What Harold Lunger has done is to put together a volume which helps greatly to overcome these bad cultural and ecclesiastical habits, not least in the field of international affairs. By assembling these documents and contextualizing them historically, he has provided a solid grounding in the roots of ecumenical ministry in peacemaking. He has offered a precious gift to the American churches in helping to restore their institutional memory.

Among the most interesting features of this book is the procession of prominent clergy and laity addressing these issues through the years, such as John Foster Dulles, Henry P. VanDusen, G. Bromley Oxnam, Reinhold Niebuhr, Harold Stassen, Eugene Carson Blake, Georgia Harkness, Paul Nitze, John C. Bennett, Ernest Gross.

The dominant role of Dulles, as several of his biographers have recounted, was a mixed blessing to church leaders in the 1940s and 1950s.

Chairman of the FCC Commission on a Just and Durable Peace during World War Two — widely heralded for its "Six Pillars of Peace" and its effective campaign for the United Nations Charter — Dulles was regarded by many as the model Christian layman in world affairs. But, as Lunger notes, Dulles's keynote address at a world order conference in Cleveland in 1949 was largely devoted to the promotion of NATO — and was resented by many delegates who succeeded in sidetracking conference approval of that new anti-Soviet alliance. The foreign policies espoused by Secretary of State Dulles in the 1950s received increasing repudiation in these conferences and other church bodies.

The 1958 Cleveland conference, last in the series reported by Lunger, is remembered today primarily for its then-audacious appeal to the US government to "reconsider" its policy of non-recognition of China. That appeal evoked shrill attacks on the NCC from the right: *Christianity Today*, the National Association of Evangelicals, Carl McIntire, Norman Vincent Peale, and others. Perhaps more remarkable is the rediscovery of the 1958 critique of nuclear deterrence, "massive retaliation," "limited war," and "the power to win a war" — topics freshly prominent in the 1980s — combined with strong advocacy of disarmament. The ecumenical establishment's dependence on Dulles as the chief foreign policy adviser obviously had ended.

Two passages in FCC documents from World War Two, published in the appendices, have hardly been overtaken by more recent events. We must be grateful to Lunger for preserving them.

One of these came from an FCC commission of theologians who reported in 1944 on "The Theology and Ethics of War: The Relation of the Church to the War in the Light of the Christian Faith." That commission combined ecclesiology and ethics in an especially felicitous way, as these words reveal:

> In a word, the Church and its gospel must be at every moment both in the midst of human history and beyond it.
>
> This means that to every historic situation, the Church has a dual word to speak. On the one hand, it must try to bring clearly into view the distinctive character of each new situation, neither blurring its uniqueness with generalities, nor losing sight of its continuity with other historic events, past and future. The Church must try to speak directly to the actual needs of each new time. On the other hand, it must try to hold clearly before every age, with changing detailed insights but with steady central conviction, what the Christian faith believes to be abiding truth concerning God and man, sin and salvation. The Church must try to speak steadily a word of faith that is for all times.
>
> These two phases of its preaching and teaching involve a third. From the effort thus to apprehend a new situation in the light of an abiding

faith, specific guiding judgments should emerge that illuminate Christian action. Such judgments are not a code of rules, but a body of working insights in which the meaning of Christian faith for individual and social conduct in the existing historic crisis is made more explicit....

There are thus three phases of the word that the Church must speak to our time: diagnostic, doctrinal, and practical.

Then we may go back to the month of Pearl Harbor, with its bitter public mood of vengeance against Japan and Japanese-Americans in the first weeks of the war, to recover a notably irenic statement from the FCC executive committee, December 30, 1941:

We do not disclaim our own share in the events, economic, political and moral, which made it possible for these evil forces [totalitarianism] to be released....

When bitterness and hatred may easily overwhelm us, the Church is still the stronghold of goodwill. It counts dear all basic human rights. It befriends loyal minorities, including those of alien birth or those descended from peoples with whose governments our country is now at war. The Church cannot abrogate its Gospel of Eternal Love.

The confessional and charitable spirit of that statement, in those circumstances, is worthy of emulation as long as this nation finds itself in hostilities with any other.

We are in debt to Harold Lunger and Friendship Press for helping our churches recall their pilgrimage of peacemaking in those mid-century decades. Of course, the ecumenical witness of those years was inadequate and sometimes shortsighted. The study conferences gave way to more activist styles in the 1960s under the pressure of the civil rights struggle and the war in Indochina. The very word "study" became suspect to many impatient persons who wanted "peace now!" Since the late 1970s peacemaking has been restored as an ecumenical priority, most visibly in the creation of an International Affairs Commission in the National Council of Churches.

It is to be hoped that the best marks of those earlier years may now be reclaimed: a depth of theological discussion, an openness to diverse ethical and political view points, and a special respect for the ministry of the laity, among whom are many who are true professionals in the things that make for peace.

PREFACE

Out of Cleveland, Ohio, in November, 1958, came a plea to the American churches to lead the world from the brink of annihilation to the achievement of lasting peace. Beginning with a statement of some of the basic principles of Christian theology and ethics, the message went on to deal with such specific issues as the character of nuclear weapons and the nature of nuclear war, the cold war, suspension of nuclear tests, conscription, disarmament, the United Nations, economic aid, human rights, the China question, and the general character of U.S. foreign policy.

The messsage came from a national study conference composed of some 600 delegates officially appointed by thirty-three of the major Protestant and Orthodox bodies in the United States, and convened upon call of the National Council of the Churches of Christ in the United States of America.

Many of the reactions to this message and the accompanying resolutions and reports revealed widespread lack of understanding of what was going on. Some interpreted the action of these churchmen as an unwarranted threat to the separation of church and state. Others saw it simply as an example of clerical naivete in meddling with matters beyond their province and understanding. Some objected that the conference did not accurately represent their own personal views. Others welcomed the reports as evidence that the churches were at last beginning to face up to one of the crucial problems of our age.

Many of those who have commented upon the statements of the conference overlooked one or more of the following facts: (1) that this was a *study* conference and not one designed to lay down official policy either for the individual denominations or for the National Council; (2) that while its members were officially appointed by the denominations they were commissioned to speak not *for* the churches but *to* them; (3) that the message was addressed to the *churches* for their consideration and not as a directive to government; (4) that the major purpose of the conference was to stimulate Christian people to think seriously about their "Christian Responsibility Upon a Changing Planet"; (5) that two thirds of the delegates to the conference were Christian laypersons, many of them statesmen with a wide experience in international affairs; and (6) that this was not a new departure in the life of the church—billed as "The Fifth National Study Conference on the Church and World Order," it was actually the sixth in a period of just less than two decades.

The Cleveland Conference of 1958 can be adequately understood only against a background knowledge of the previous study conferences in this series. For in them was evolved a particular method of seeking to discern the will of God and to encourage Christian study and thought in this area of Christian concern.

The first of these study conferences was sponsored by the Federal Council of Churches, which in 1950 merged with other United States inter-church movements to form the National Council of Churches. It is the purpose of this volume to help fill in some of this background by present-ing the messages of those national study conferences from the early days of World War II through early days of the "Cold War." Most of these have for some time been out of print. The original documents, published as pamphlets, have in many instances been lost, worn out, or discarded. The result is that students of the subject find it difficult—if not impossible—to gain access to these materials which are of prime importance for assess-ing an important chapter in the history of Christian social thought as well as for understanding current Christian attitudes on the subject.

Appended are five other documents. The first is the statement of the Federal Council of Churches executive committee following this nation's entry into World War II. Of continuing importance are three documents—"The Relation of the Church to the War in the Light of the Christian Faith," "Atomic Warfare and the Christian Faith," and "The Christian Conscience and Weapons of Mass Destruction" submitted to the Federal Council and the churches by commissions composed of some of the foremost American theologians of the day. Also of current significance is the "Agenda of Action for Peace," a 1960 Pronouncement of the General Board of the National Council of Churches of Christ in the U.S.A.

Grateful acknowledgement is made of the courtesy of the NCCCUSA, in granting permission to reproduce the texts of these documents.

The editor also expresses his appreciation to his colleagues in the American Society of Christian Ethics who encouraged him to carry through this project; to the officers of the International Convention of Christian Churches (Disciples of Christ) for the appointments which made it possible for him to attend four of the six conferences reported herein as an official delegate of his church; to the Faculty Research Grants Committee of Texas Christian University for the grant which assisted in the preparation of this material; to William Robinson for a preliminary survey of the reactions of the periodical press made in connection with a paper in Christian Ethics; and to Marita Fennimore, Anita Hillman, and Margaret Starbird for their assistance in the preparation and typing of the manuscript.

Special thanks go to Jack and Jane Copeland of Granbury, Texas, and William A. and Jean Estes of Tucson, Arizona, for gifts to the National Council of Churches which made possible the publication of this volume.

Harold L. Lunger

CONTENTS

APPENDICES

INTRODUCTION

In the nuclear age the Christian conscience faces no issue more pregnant with destiny than that of war or peace. This challenge confronts us today in a form more terrifying and baffling than ever before. But the underlying issues are not new. They are ones that the American churches have had to face again and again ever since this nation was born out of the travail of its War of Independence.

Earlier Attitudes of the American Churches

Except for some of the Anglican clergy and the so-called "peace churches," American churchmen generally joined in wholehearted support of the revolutionary war. This was true of the Baptists, the Scotch-Irish Presbyterians, and the New England Congregationalists. In her classic study of one segment of this subject, Miss Alice M. Baldwin details the role of the New England clergy in the revolution.[1] Over the years leading up to 1776 they had helped prepare the minds of the colonists for the revolution by their preaching upon the glories of freedom and constitutional government, the dangers of tyranny, and the justification of war in defense of one's rights and liberties. Following the Stamp Act they preached the duty of resistance to England and, once the war had begun, portrayed it as a holy crusade. Their services to the national cause were many and varied. In addition to maintaining the morale and fighting spirit of the civilian population through their preaching and prayers, they served as recruiting agents, chaplains, fighters in the ranks, makers of munitions, and in many other capacities. Most of the clergy in this period, declared it the Christian's duty to support the revolutionary cause, exemplifying it in their own actions. Their people apparently followed their lead with few questions and with a good conscience.

As for the War of 1812, it appears that support was somewhat more hesitant and divided. In brief reference to the matter, Robert Moats Miller declares that New England clergymen like Lyman Beecher and Timothy Dwight opposed "Mr. Madison's war," while frontier parsons, and evangelists like Charles G. Finney and Peter Cartwright, zealously supported it. "Most of the educated, conservative theocrats of the seaboard area and especially New England opposed the struggle as heartily as their Federalist constituents, while the western evangelists echoed the militant whoops of the 'War Hawks.' "[2]   Merle E. Curti attributes the rise of the peace movements among members of American churches in the period after 1815 in part, at least, to disillusionment and war-weariness following this conflict and the European struggle of which it was a part.[3]

The American Peace Crusade represented a movement of clergy and laity against the follies and horrors of war. It had its beginnings in 1815 with the organization of the Massachusetts and New York Peace Societies. A number of high-ranking leaders in state and national government joined with ministers, merchants, and educators in this voluntary and unofficial movement. Embracing both those who supported defensive war and the absolute pacifists, it had its greatest influence after the organization of the American Peace Society in 1828. In addition to focusing attention upon the pacifist issue, the movement popularized the concepts of a "Congress of Nations" and an international "High Court for the adjustment of disputes." The movement began to lose ground after 1841—partly as a result of internal strife over the pacifist issue. By 1860 its force was largely spent. In its day, however, the movement made quite an impact on the thinking and attitudes of the American churches. Many religious leaders—like Alexander Campbell, for instance—had their thinking on the subject of war permanently influenced by the Peace Crusade.[4]

The Mexican War evoked a variety of reactions from the American churches. On the basis of an extensive study of denominational resolutions, the church press, and the sermons of prominent ministers, Clayton S. Ellsworth divides the churches into three groups.[5] Roman Catholics, Methodists, Southern Baptists, and Old School Presbyterians were quite clear and united in support of the American cause. Congregationalists, Unitarians, and Friends were equally united in opposing the war. Episcopalians, Lutherans, the Reformed churches, Disciples of Christ, Northern Baptists, and New School Presbyterians were non-committal or so divided as to defy classification. While the differing responses of the various religious bodies were partly the result of distinctive church teachings on the subject of war and/or the citizen's duty to the state, Ellsworth's study makes it clear that other factors were also operative and perhaps even more decisive. Among these were sectional interests. Northern and eastern states tended to oppose the war for fear it would lead to the extension of slave territory and loss of the economic domination of New England, while southern and western states supported it for the opposite reasons. It is not surprising, then, to find that Congregationalists and Unitarians, who were largely concentrated in New England, opposed the war, while Southern Baptists supported it in harmony with their sectional interests and also with an eye to new and fruitful fields for evangelization. A significant—and disturbing—finding of Ellsworth's is that "no church with its members concentrated in the Southwest or with a strong stake there opposed the war."[6]

With few exceptions the American churches—North and South—gave enthusiastic support to "their side" in the Civil War.[7] The sectional character of certain religious bodies (e.g., Congregational) made this possible, and the doctrinal positions of others (e.g., Lutheran, Catholic, and Anglican) made it all but inevitable. The way had been prepared for a crusading support among Baptists, Methodists, and Presbyterians by their divisions over the slavery issue which had taken place in 1845 and in following years. Few protests were voiced against the patriotic resolutions by which most of the denominations gave their blessing to the cause of Union or Confederacy as the case might be. Among Disciples of Christ there was considerable pacifist opposition from leading editors and ministers—due not only to the strong New Testament orientation of the movement and the pacifism of Alexander Campbell, but also to the fact that much of the movement's strength lay in the border states where there was less enthusiasm for the War. Quakers and other "peace groups," of course, withheld their endorsement. But, with the exceptions noted, most of the American churches and their leaders vigorously supported their sectional cause, portrayed the struggle as one in which high and holy values were at stake, and sought to maintain morale on the home front or, in the case of chaplains, among the fighting men. The northern churches especially engaged in a number of projects to serve the soldiers and sailors, launched "Freedman's Societies" to minister to the Negroes who were being liberated and sent some of their more eloquent voices abroad to "interpret" the Union cause to the leaders and people of Europe.

According to the studies of Julius W. Pratt, only the Friends and Unitarians raised any significant protest against the Spanish-American War.[8] Protestants saw the war as an opportunity to free Cuba from Spanish oppression and papal superstition. Pratt concludes that missionary-minded churchmen were as eager to discover foreign outlets for their evangelistic energies as were men of trade for their products. Protestants, generally, justified both the war and the subsequent taking over of the Spanish possessions as part of this nation's "manifest destiny" under God. American Catholics also supported the war because their doctrine of obedience to the "powers that be" compelled it and also to prove their "patriotism" to their fellow-Americans.

Second thoughts about the role of the churches in the Civil and Spanish-American wars may have contributed to the emphasis on peace which came to be associated with the so-called "social gospel" movement of the opening decades of the twentieth century. Other influences were certainly operative—among them the seeds planted by the American Peace Crusade, the example of the peace churches and others who had withheld support from the nation's past wars, and also the strong ethical emphasis derived from the new theology and the quest for and discovery of the historical Jesus. The writings of Walter Rauschenbusch and others show a vital concern for world peace, although their major emphasis was in other areas.

The Federal Council and the First World War

The Federal Council of the Churches of Christ in America, established in 1908, was the child of the social gospel movement and soon became its chief organizational arm. At the constituting assembly in Philadelphia, a note of internationalism and world peace was sounded. The Council's historian noted that at this assembly

> Peace was heralded as the harbinger of the bright new day that was dawning...[But] despite a general idealism there was little realistic or consistent thought as to how peace might be maintained....Justice Brewer envisaged it through increased peace education by the churches. Dean Henry W. Rogers pointed to the historical origin of international law in Christian states....He spoke hopefully, confidently of the spread of the arbitration movement and of the Hague conferences. ...Charles Stelzle made perhaps the most radical suggestions in calling workers to undertake a "peace strike" in the event of war.[9]

The Federal Council's concern for peace became increasingly evident. The first commission, appointed in 1910, was the Commission on the Church and Social Service. The following year two more commissions were established—one on Evangelism, and the other on Peace and Arbitration.

In his *We Are Not Divided* John A. Hutchison gives the definitive account of the Federal Council's peace activities from these earliest days to 1940, on the eve of American involvement in World War II.[10] He describes the overly optimistic but earnest and well-intentioned program from 1911 through 1915 which finds expression, for example, in Sidney Gulick's *The Fight for Peace*,[11] and also the futile efforts of American churches or church persons to block American involvement in the war in Europe.

When the United States declared war, the Federal Council called a special conference, which met at Washington, D.C., May 7-9, 1917, to consider the role of the Council and the churches in the war. Acknowledging that "after long patience, and with a solemn sense of responsibility, the government of the United States has been forced to recognize that a state of war exists between this country and Germany," the conference statement on "Our Spirit and Purpose" went on to pledge to the government

> both support and allegiance in unstinted measure...As citizens of a peace-loving nation, we abhor war. We have long striven to secure the judicial settlement of all international disputes. But since, in spite of every effort, war has come, we are grateful that the ends to which we are committed are such as we can approve.

The statement listed some of the "special duties" which the hour laid upon the members of the Church of Christ:

to purge our own hearts clean of arrogance and selfishness... to keep ever before the eyes of ourselves and of our allies the ends for which we fight...to testify to our fellow-Christians in every land...our consciousness of unbroken unity in Christ; to unite in the fellowship of service multitudes who love their enemies and are ready to join with them in rebuilding the waste places as soon as peace shall come; to be diligent in works of relief and mercy...to keep alive the spirit of prayer...to hearten those who go to the front, and to comfort their loved ones at home; to care for the welfare of our young men in the army and navy...to be vigilant against every attempt to arouse the spirit of vengeance and unjust suspicion toward those of foreign birth or sympathies; to protect the rights of conscience against every attempt to invade them; to maintain our Christian institutions and activities unimpaired...to guard the gains of education, and of social progress and economic freedom, won at so great a cost...to keep the open mind and the forward look, that the lessons learned in war may not be forgotten when comes that just and sacred peace for which we all pray; above all, to call men everywhere to new obedience to the will of our Father God[12]

In general the clergy and the churches gave full support to their government, portraying the war as a crusade for democracy and peace. Ray H. Abrams relates the story in *Preachers Present Arms*[13] of the aggressive post-war peace program of the churches, which was, perhaps in part, an effort to atone for their sins of omission during 1917 and 1918. Hutchison's study gives a good brief survey.

The Peace Movement Between the Wars

A document of considerable significance, however, must be noted—the statement of "International Ideals of the Churches of Christ," adopted by the Executive Committee of the Federal Council in December, 1921. Its echoes are to be found, for example, in the Guiding Principles adopted by the Delaware Conference in 1942:

1. We believe that nations no less than individuals are subject to God's immutable moral laws.
2. We believe that nations achieve true welfare, greatness and honor only through just dealing and unselfish service.
3. We believe that nations that regard themselves as Christian have special international obligations.
4. We believe that the spirit of Christian brotherliness can remove every unjust barrier of trade, color, creed and race.
5. We believe that CHRISTIAN patriotism demands the practice of good-will between nations.

6. We believe that international policies should secure equal justice for all races.

7. We believe that all nations should associate themselves permanently for world peace and goodwill.

8. We believe in international law, and in the universal use of international courts of justice and boards of arbitration.

9. We believe in a sweeping reduction of armaments by all nations.

10. We believe in a warless world, and dedicate ourselves to its achievement.[14]

As part perhaps of the general revulsion against war which characterized the 1920's, a rather significant pacifist movement swept through the American churches during the latter part of that decade and the early 1930's.[15] Individuals took the so-called "Oxford pledge," renouncing war, and denominational bodies like the Reformed Church, the Presbyterian General Assembly, the Southern Methodists, the Methodist Ecumenical Conference, the Congregational General Council, and the Disciples of Christ did the same. Several established procedures for the registration of conscientious objectors among their constituents.

By 1933 domestic economic problems had come to occupy the major attention of the churches, as of most other Americans, and the problem of war was allowed to drop somewhat into the background. At the same time reflections upon Japan's invasion of Manchuria and newer theological emphases emanating from Europe began to make some leaders of American Protestantism less optimistic about human nature and less sanguine about the possibilities of "building the kingdom of God" by appeals to reason and brotherhood.[16] Developments attendant upon the rise of Mussolini and Hitler were further factors in the re-education of American liberal thinkers. The World Conference on Church, Community and State met at Oxford, England, in July, 1937. The content of this conference's findings was of even greater significance than its method. It was appropriate that when its report was reissued in 1966 it was under the title *Foundations of Ecumenical Social Thought*.[17] There followed a vigorous debate within American church circles over the relative merits of isolationism and interventionism which Paul A. Carter summarizes rather succinctly and fairly in his *Decline and Revival of the Social Gospel*.[18]

The Second World War and the First National Study Conference

When American church leaders faced the issues of World War II they were in a much better position to do so than they had been in previous periods of international or civil tension.

For one thing, they had a background of experience over a period of a century and two-thirds, in which they had gone through five international conflicts of greater or less intensity and duration plus one agonizing civil war, interspersed with at least three periods of organized and rather aggressive and sustained peace interest and activity.

For another, they had developed a much more realistic theological position—thanks, largely, to the influence of English and Continental thinkers.

Third, and not least important, many of their leaders had had experience— especially at Oxford in 1937—with an appropriately Protestant approach to practical problems of Christian social responsibility—an approach involving the consultation of widely representative Christian leaders, clergy and lay, over a period of days, informed by careful preliminary study and research, in a spirit of prayer and earnest inquiry, seeking the will of God for the Church.

Perhaps on the basis of this experience, the American churches faced up to the outbreak of war in Europe in the late summer of 1939 in what was for them—and for the churches of all the involved nations—a bold, new way.

In previous periods of international tension and war, individual clergy and laypersons had sought to define and state their understandings of the relation of the Christian faith to the issues at hand. Generally it was clerical leaders—preachers and editors of the church papers—who stated the will of God for the whole Church; but they often saw the will of God only through the dark glass of sectional and other secular interests and passions. Voluntary societies of those committed to the cause of peace had issued pronouncements and appeals to the Christian conscience—usually propagandist in character. Denominational and interdenominational church bodies had passed resolutions or made policy statements on particular wars or war in general, endorsing specific courses of action which they felt made for peace, and opposing those that seemed to lead toward war. But when denominational bodies spoke, it was once again chiefly by the voice of the clergy. And the resolutions they offered were usually hastily drawn up while the convention or assembly was in session, often under the influence of emotions newly inflamed by the passions of war itself or by the bitter disillusionment that follows the end of hostilities and the assessment of the heavy costs thereof.

The bold, new approach made by the Protestant churches of America in February of 1940 was to bring together a considerable group of officially appointed delegates from many denominations for a "National Study Conference on The Churches and the International Situation." Their numbers were sufficiently large and their backgrounds sufficiently diverse that sectional, denominational, and other biases and prejudices were able to counteract and in some measure correct each other. Facing the national and world situation within a Christian community and in a context of worship and prayer, the individual members were able to rise above some of the secular pressures and passions that might otherwise have swept them along in the relative isolation of their home communities. At the same time laypersons, with their technical knowledge and practical experience, shared in the deliberations with ministers and professors schooled in the theological and ethical aspects of the issues. Delegates moreover did not have to waste a lot of time floundering about without any guidance. Memoranda had been carefully prepared which focused attention upon some of the major facts and issues at hand.

Meeting at Philadelphia, the delegates spent three days in careful study and discussion of the Christian task in light of the then-existing international situation. Findings hammered out in smaller group meetings were submitted to the whole conference, and the consensus of the larger group set forth in a message submitted to the churches to inform and guide individual Christians and denominations.

The results of this conference proved so significant and the findings so useful to the churches that five more were to be held over the next eighteen years. In the process, the study-conference technique was refined and extended to related areas of Christian concern—the church and economic life, social welfare, and church and state. Church leaders exerted influence upon public opinion and governmental policy during the years in which World War II was being fought and won and the foundation laid for the United Nations. At the same time a significant body of thought and judgment gradually emerged which offered real guidance for the future.

The Form and Editing of the Documents

The original documents which came out of these conferences and are reproduced on the following pages lack uniformity in organization and presentation of material from one conference to another, and even among the different parts of the same report. This is the result of how the documents were produced.

Different portions of the reports came out of different discussion groups, each with its own drafting committee, and each putting its findings together in the best form possible within the time available. The plenary sessions in many cases amended or supplemented the section reports with little attention to literary form or unity.

Pressures of time permitted no overall editing to bring uniformity in even such obvious matters as method of numbering or lettering sub-sections, not to mention the elimination of overlapping material. Moreover, many items were left dangling—supplemental resolutions and additional recommendations being tacked on at the end, rather than incorporated into the text where they obviously belonged.

With the exception of correcting obvious typographical errors, the actual *texts* of the reports are reproduced here. In a few instances the material has been *rearranged*, relegating to the bottom of the page notes or explanatory statements which were originally included in the body of the text—usually in parentheses. Most of the footnotes are exact quotations, or paraphrased from the original published reports. The present editor's comments or additions are in brackets. Five addenda adopted after the original reports had been acted upon are also inserted in relation to the paragraphs they were intended to amplify. In a number of cases, in order to bring more clarity and uniformity into the arrangement of material, letters have been changed to numbers, or vice versa, in the designation of sections or series of correlative points.

Brief introductions to each report have been provided to set the historical context of the conferences. They also indicate the make-up of the conferences, modifications of procedure from one to another, and major concerns or contributions to the emerging consensus.

The tables of contents preceding each document show the scope of the conference's concerns, and guide the reader around in the reports. They are adapted, more or less from the original tables of contents in the published reports and carry the same heading.

The first four conferences were convened by the Federal Council of Churches and the others by the National Council. (In 1950 the Federal Council was merged with other interdenominational bodies working in such fields as missions and Christian education to form the National Council.)

The numbering of the conferences in this series began with the Cleveland Conference of 1949 which was referred to as the "Third National Study Conference on the Churches and World Order." The others had simply been identified as national study conferences on "The Churches and the International Situation" (Philadelphia, 1940) and on "The Churches and a Just and Durable Peace" (Delaware, 1942, and Cleveland, 1945). When it became convenient to begin identifying the conferences by number it was apparently decided to begin numbering with Delaware, where attention was for the first time directed more specifically to the continuing problems of peace and world order. Thus the fifth conference dealt with in this volume is identified as the "fourth" by its sponsors.

As might be expected, reactions to the conferences' reports varied widely, from warm acceptance to outright rejection. Since the documents were designed for study by church groups, introductions to the various conferences include some of the reactions from such interdenominational journals as *Christian Century*, *Christianity and Crisis*, and (later) *Christianity Today*. To give a suggestion of the response of the secular press, reactions of such general weekly publications as *Time* and *Newsweek* are also sometimes given.

---

[1]Alice M. Baldwin, *The New England Clergy and the American Revolution* (Durham, NC: Duke University Press, 1928).

[2]Robert Moats Miller, *American Protestantism and Social Issues: 1919-1939* (Chapel Hill: University of North Carolina Press, 1958), p.5.

[3]Merle E. Curti, *The American Peace Crusade: 1815-1860* (Durham, NC: Duke University Press, 1929).

[4]Harold L. Lunger, *The Political Ethics of Alexander Campbell* (St. Louis: Bethany Press, 1954), Chap. XV.

[5]Clayton S. Ellsworth, "American Churches and the Mexican War," *American Historical Review*, XLV, No. 2 (Jan., 1940), pp. 301-326.

[6]*Ibid.*, p.326.

[7]William Warren Sweet, *The Story of Religion in America* (New York: Harper & Brothers, 1939), Chaps. XVIII and XIX; see also Chester F. Dunham, *The Attitude of the Northern Clergy Toward the South* (Toledo, Ohio: Gray Co., 1942).

[8]Julius W. Pratt, *Expansionists of 1898: The Acquisition of Hawaii and the Spanish Islands* (Baltimore: Johns Hopkins Press, 1936), Chap. VIII.

[9]John A. Hutchison, *We Are Not Divided: A Critical and Historical Study of the Federal Council of the Churches of Christ in America* (New York: Round Table Press, 1941), p.50.

[10]*Ibid.*, Chap. VI.

[11]Sidney L. Gulick, *The Fight for Peace: An Aggressive Campaign for American Churches* (New York: Revell, 1915).

[12]*Report of Special Meeting, Washington, DC, May 7,8,9, 1917,* (New York: Federal Council of Churches, 1917), pp. 22-24; also quoted in Hutchison, *op. cit.*, pp. 176-178.

[13]New York: Round Table Press, 1933.

[14]Quoted in Sidney L. Gulick, *Christian Crusade for a Warless World* (New York: Federal Council of Churches, 1923), p. v.; also in Hutchison, *op. cit.*, p.198.

[15]Paul A. Carter, *The Decline and Revival of the Social Gospel: Social and Political Liberalism in American Protestant Churches: 1920-1940* (Ithaca, NY: Cornell University Press, 1956), pp. 133-140; see also Roland H. Bainton, "The Churches and War: Historic Attitudes Toward Christian Participation: A Survey from Biblical Times to the Present Day," *Social Action*, XI, No.1 (Jan. 15, 1945), Part II; and Miller, *op. cit.*, XXI and XXII.

[16]Carter, *op. cit.*, Chap. XIII.

[17]World Conference on Church, Community and State, Oxford, 1937, *Foundations of Ecumenical Social Thought: The Oxford Conference Report*, ed. J. H. Oldham, with an introduction by Harold L. Lunger. (Philadelphia: Fortress Press, 1966).

[18]Carter, *op. cit.*, Chap. XIV.

Chapter I

ON THE BRINK OF WAR:

"The Churches and the International Situation"

Philadelphia, 1940

INTRODUCTION

In mid-July, 1939, with Europe on the brink of war, thirty-five lay experts and ecumenical leaders met in Geneva, Switzerland, convened by the World Council of Churches, to consider the role of the churches in the deteriorating international situation. The memorandum on "The Churches and the International Crisis," which came out of that conference, helped set the course for much subsequent Christian thought and action on the issues of war and peace.

Some six weeks later, Hitler's armies moved into Poland, and the second World War was under way. Although the United States was not immediately involved militarily, it was profoundly involved in many other ways in the problems of Europe and Asia. Christian people and their churches in America faced grave new responsibilities.

Within a few weeks of the outbreak of war in Europe, leaders of the Department of International Justice and Goodwill of the Federal Council of the Churches of Christ in America joined with the Committee on International Relations of the Foreign Missions Conference of North America in issuing a call for a national study conference on "The Churches and the International Situation" to meet in the First Baptist Church, Philadelphia, Pennsylvania, February 27-29, 1940. As delegates arrived in the "City of Brotherly Love," the daily press was filled with reports of the Russian drive on Viborg and the Finnish resistance, a Russian bombing attack on a Swedish village and incidents on the Turkish border, and the stepping up of artillery fire and night air raids on the western front as the Germans poised for a March offensive.

Twenty-eight American communions sent delegates, as did nine interchurch agencies like the YMCA, the YWCA, and the Church Peach Union. Among the denominations represented were Baptists and Unitarians, Mennonites and Methodists, Congregationalists and Episcopalians, Lutherans and Disciples, Presbyterians and Friends, A.M.E. Zion and the Salvation Army.

The 285 delegates, clergy and lay, came from all parts of the country and represented a substantial cross section of the mind of the churches on the problems of peace and war. The presiding officer was James H. Franklin, President of Crozier Theological Seminary.

Six times the delegates joined in formal services of worship as they sought divine guidance. In three plenary sessions they were addressed by

John Foster Dulles, international lawyer; Henry P. Van Dusen, Professor, Union Theological Seminary; and George A. Buttrick, Minister of New York's Madison Avenue Presbyterian Church and President of the Federal Council of Churches. Other addresses were given by Albert W. Beaven, President, Colgate-Rochester Divinity School; and Roswell P. Barnes, a secretary of the Federal Council of Churches.

Most of the delegates' time, however, was spent in smaller groups discussing some of the concrete problems which confronted the churches. For this purpose they were divided into the following six "seminars": The Ecumenical Movement and the Peace and War Problem, The Churches and American Policy, Missions and the World Crisis, The Conscientious Objector in War Time, The Responsibility of the Churches in Relieving Suffering Caused by War, and the Local Church and the World Crisis. The Chairmen of the seminars (in the order named) were Theodore A. Green, Pastor, New Britain, Connecticut; Luman J. Shafer, Chairman of the Committee on International Relations, Foreign Missions Conference; Leslie B. Moss, Secretary, Foreign Missions Conference; Merrill F. Clarke, Pastor, New Canaan, Connecticut; Wynn C. Fairfield, American Board of Commissioners for Foreign Missions; and W. Emory Hartman, Pastor, Carlisle, Pennsylvania.

Discussion in the seminars was primed, but not limited, by preparatory documents put in the hands of each member. Each group was asked to produce a statement or report of its findings. These were then carefully reviewed and discussed by the conference as a whole in plenary session. After being amended or modified, they were then adopted as the expression of the whole conference.

It was stressed repeatedly that the delegates spoke only for themselves and in no sense either for the communions they represented or for the sponsoring bodies at whose call they had been brought together. Their message was presented not as the voice *of* the churches but as a "Message *to* the Churches" (Italics mine). The published document carried the following note (which was echoed in one form or another in all subsequent conferences): "The Executive Committee of the Federal Council of Churches received with appreciation the Message from the Philadelphia Study Conference, authorized its publication and commended it to the churches for their study and action."

Nevertheless the message had considerable authority—that of obvious Christian insight and truth. It therefore had profound influence upon the thinking and actions of American church members during the years of toil and tears that were to follow. It undoubtedly helps account in part for the more restrained attitude of the churches in World War II as compared with their crusading zeal and belligerence in World War I.

The lines had long been drawn between religious leaders in the United States who felt that the prime concern must be to preserve American

neutrality and "keep America out of war," and those who felt that it was
the nation's duty to throw her influence on the side of freedom even though
this might eventually lead to her involvement in hostilities. The story of
this "great debate" has been well told by Paul S. Carter[1] and Robert Moats
Miller.[2] The largely non-interventionist tone of the Philadelphia Conference
message may be seen at several points, especially in the concluding recommendation for "A United Peace Campaign."

While some portions of the report are now chiefly of historic interest,
many others have a surprisingly contemporary ring. One is impressed
especially by the ecumenical spirit which breathes through it and finds
expression particularly in the first report on "The Ecumenical Movement
and the Peace and War Problem," which makes a fitting introduction to
the whole message. (Note especially the opening paragraphs of Section A
on "Tasks of Churches in Time of War" and the "Dedication" which
appears as Section D.)

Other sections of the message cause one to wonder if things might not
be different in the world today had the United States and her allies
followed the leadings of this conference—for example, in the section calling
for a negotiated rather than a dictated peace. Thanks to the strong stand
taken on support of the conscientious objector, the churches' record in this
regard in World War II was much better than it was in World War I.
Emphasis upon the urgency of supporting "orphaned missions" and relieving suffering caused by war paved the way for two glorious chapters in
the life of the churches during and following the war.

Reaction to the conference in religious circles was generally favorable,
if not warmly appreciative. The *Christian Century*, for example, welcomed
the report of the conference as "profoundly reassuring" and spoke of its
"wise and practical guidance for church action in this present emergency."[3]

---

[1]*Op. cit.*, Chap. XIV.
[2]*Op. cit.*, Chap. XXII.
[3]LVII (Mar. 13, 1940). 339f.

A MESSAGE FROM THE NATIONAL
STUDY CONFERENCE ON THE CHURCHES
AND THE INTERNATIONAL SITUATION

Philadelphia, Pennsylvania   **February 27–29, 1940**

I. The Ecumenical Movement and the Peace and War Problem

   Tasks of Churches in Time of War; Toward a World Fellowship of
   Christians; Churches Urged to Study Bases of Durable Peace;
   Dedication.

II. The Churches and American Policy

   Domestic Policy; A Negotiated Peace; The United States and the
   World Community; International Economic Cooperation; Colonies;
   The Conflict in East Asia.

III. Missions and the World Crisis

   The Forward Movement of Christian Missions; War Versus the
   Christian Gospel; A Blueprint for the Missionary Enterprise.

IV. The Conscientious Objector in War Time

   Declarations of Oxford Conference (1937); Liberty of Conscience;
   The Churches and Conscientious Objectors; Services by Conscientious Objectors; Recommendations to Federal Council of Churches.

V. Responsibility of the Churches in Relieving Suffering Caused by War

VI. The Local Church and the World Crisis

   Principles of Action for the Local Church; Programs of Action for
   the Local Church.

VII. Additional Recommendations

   Transmitting Results of Conference to the Churches; A United
   Peace Campaign

THE CHURCHES AND THE INTERNATIONAL SITUATION[1]

I. The Ecumenical Movement and the Peace and War Problem

We believe that the churches of Jesus Christ as branches of the ecumenical movement, members of the one body, Una Sancta, which transcents nations, races and classes, have in their collective life, work and witness an indispensable contribution to make to the solution of the peace and war problem. This problem is essentially a problem of relationships between groups of human beings. Nations, no less than individuals, subsist under the governance of God; they are subject to moral law. We believe that the Christian Gospel and the Christian way of life are the answers to the world's desperate need in the area of international conflict.

We therefore urge the representatives of the ecumenical movement and of the churches which comprise it to devote themselves prayerfully, and courageously to the fulfillment of a world fellowship of Christians.

A. TASKS OF CHURCHES IN TIME OF WAR

The churches should demonstrate in their own life and relationships a community more closely approximating the ideal of the family of God. This would require that they

1. Maintain the integrity of their essential fellowship in spite of the antagonisms and cleavages which set men over against each other in war. This is first of all a matter of the attitudes with which Christians regard one another—preserving the "unity of the spirit in the bond of peace" which is in Christ. It may find expression in the common prayer life of Christians, in ecumenical groups and in correspondence and visitations of individuals.

2. Seek to create a true ecumenical understanding of the issues which divide the peoples. The distortions resulting from censorship, the pressure of official propaganda and the whole system of psychological mobilization make it difficult to arrive at a just and accurate estimate of the needs, motives and purposes of nations.

3. Make their prayer, preaching and conversation truly Christian. Prayer must not degenerate into a means of national propaganda, but must be for

peace and justice among the nations. God's will is the most important factor in every problem. To seek to know that will and receive power to perform it, Christians must constantly turn to God in prayer. While we may not forget our sense of solidarity with our own people and our respective nations, preaching must not seek to create hatred of other nations, but to cultivate goodwill towards all, not only to those within but also to those without the Christian fellowship; to spread the spirit of forgiveness and trust; to increase the habit of charitable judgment; to widen knowledge and understanding of the causes of conflict—these things help to remove the psychological roots of war and are characteristic fruits of the spirit of Christ. War should not be presented as a holy crusade, but preaching should call men to repentance for a common sin, and urge the righteousness of God's Kingdom. We rejoice that, after six months of war in Europe, the churches in the belligerent countries have not generally become the agents of national policy in propaganda.

4. Bear one another's burdens. Some churches are much more heavily burdened by the war than are others—spiritually, financially and in responsibility for pastoral and preaching service. One of the most difficult strains is that of a sense of loneliness in the face of agonizing perplexities. This loneliness is aggravated by the difficulties of communication resulting from war. The ecumenical movement should therefore promote the exchange of greetings, encourage correspondence and arrange for visitations of deputations and individuals across national frontiers. The churches with available material resources should undergird those that are especially hardpressed by assisting them with their problems at home and on the mission field.

5. The churches as an ecumenical movement should energetically promote their common ministry of preaching and healing to the victims of conflict. They should

(a) Provide an adequate sacramental, pastoral and preaching service to prisoners of war and to interned alien civilians.

(b) Provide practical helpfulness and relief to refugees and other victims dislocated by war.

6. The churches, which have a concern for the welfare of all peoples, have a responsibility to contribute to the establishment of such a world order as will more effectively serve the ends of justice, liberty and right, and promote peace. In addition to demonstrating community in their own life and binding the world together by their ecumenical activity, the churches should, therefore,

(a) Study the bases of a just and durable world order.

(b) induce among their own people and in the wider community in which their influence is felt a willingness to pay the price of justice and peace, which will involve concessions of immediate self-interest in terms of exclusive national sovereignty and economic advantage.

(c) Urge statesmen to apply the principles of reconciliation and good-will in the practical affairs of international relations.

(d) Encourage and facilitate steps toward an early negotiated peace in the wars now in progress.

B. TOWARD A WORLD FELLOWSHIP OF CHRISTIANS

We suggest the following means of practical application of the ecumenical spirit:

1. General use of common prayers in the churches and in family and personal devotions in all nations.

2. Simultaneous observance of the Lord's Supper in various nations.

3. Conferences between Christians of neutral nations and belligerent nations.

4. Visitations between neutrals and belligerents.

5. Correspondence between belligerents and between neutrals and belligerents.

6. Interchange of views concerning the needs, motives and purposes of various nations, including belligerents, cleared through the Study Department of the Provisional Committee of the World Council of Churches or through neutral churchmen.

7. Interchange of sermons and prayers used in various churches.

8. Financial assistance to churches and pastors of hard-pressed churches.

9. Assistance on the mission fields to the missionaries of churches under the burden of war.

10. Release of a few of our most competent pastors for non-military chaplaincy service in prison camps.

11. Financing such chaplaincy service.

12. Financial assistance and Christian social service to refugees, and to civilians suffering from the devastations of war.

13. Organizing groups in local parishes which will accept the discipline of sacrificial giving to the extent of reduced standards of living *now* to provide for the assistance of others suffering in the present tragedy abroad.

14. Study of the bases of a just and durable peace by ecumenical conferences, exchange of memoranda, groups in local churches.

15. Collaboration between church agencies and governments in negotiations for the establishing of peace.

C. CHURCHES OF WORLD URGED TO STUDY BASES OF DURABLE PEACE

With a view to clarifying the mind of our churches in the United States regarding the moral, political and economic bases of a durable peace and to preparing the churches for assuming their appropriate responsibility for establishing those bases, we recommend that the churches distribute and study the findings of this conference and the memoranda available from the Study Department of the Provisional Committee of the World Council of Churches.

At Oxford, in 1937, outstanding leaders of the Evangelical Churches of many nations defined the place and function of the Christian Church in the modern world. Again, in Geneva, in 1939, an International Conference of lay experts and ecumenical leaders, convened by the Provisional Committee of the World Council of Churches, agreed upon a definite statement of guiding principles for the solution of international problems and the development of a just international order.

In view of the existing international crisis, the declarations of the Oxford and Geneva Conferences should now be implemented with specific recommendations looking toward the establishment of a world order of love, justice and freedom. This task is now being undertaken by commissions of inquiry in various belligerent and neutral countries and coordinated by the Study Department in Geneva.

We further recommend that plans be initiated by officers and staff of the Provisional Committee of the World Council of Churches looking toward the assembling of a representative gathering of Christian leaders, clerical and lay, as soon as practicable after an armistice has been declared in any of the wars now being waged. The churches have both the right and the duty to share in the task of establishing peace. Unhindered by considerations of power politics, church leaders will be in a position to define policies expressing the Christian principles of goodwill, reconciliation and justice. If such principles received the support of the great body of Christians in all lands, the likelihood of achieving an enduring peace would be greatly enhanced.

D. DEDICATION

We here and now in the presence of God, who has made of one blood all nations of the world, do hereby dedicate ourselves to a ministry of love, forebearance and reconciliation to the people of all lands. We call upon all our fellow-Christians to join with us and with each other in a common purpose to continue in this ministry by His power in spite of unforeseen contingencies, to the end that Christ may be exalted and His Church stand uncompromised and undivided.

II. The Churches and American Policy

In these tragic hours neither the Church nor the nation dare speak in self-righteousness. We are all implicated and share in the common guilt, though in differing degrees. The Church can only approach its task in the spirit of penitence and humility. A humble and a contrite heart, in men or nations, God will not despise.

Greatness is not measured by economic power, prestige, world imperialism and great navies, but rather, "He who would be great among you, let him be the servant of all." Moral and not material forces must finally prevail.

Justice and a new world order will not be realized by the ruthless use of force. No enduring peace can be built on vengeance. "Ye have heard that it hath been said, Thou shalt love thy neighbor and hate thine enemy.... But I say unto you, Love your enemies." The truth alone can set men free.

We should give to Caesar what belongs to Caesar; but even to Caesars the Church must proclaim a moral order by which they and their rule are judged. Man's supreme loyalty is to God, not to the State.

These principles apply equally to individuals and to nations. They are the foundation on which an enduring and just world order must be built.

A. DOMESTIC POLICY

Since the Church regards mankind as a single spiritual brotherhood, we must come to recognize also that the world has developed into a single economic unit. We, therefore, believe that it is impossible wholly to divorce foreign policy from domestic policy and that any comprehensive program for peace must contain a synthesis of both. Moreover, we are convinced that a constructive, creative foreign policy can stem only from a domestic policy which is firmly rooted in democracy and which provides for adequate social security.

Thus we reject as a possible solution for unemployment the enormous armament program which would gear our country to a war economy. We reject it not only because we consider it false economy, but also because the whole system of competitive armaments is contrary to our Christian ideals.

We deprecate the growing tendency on the part of the army and navy to influence foreign policy. We, therefore, advocate the appointment of a Congressional Committee to consider the question of defense in its relation to foreign policy.

Just and considerate treatment for members of religious, racial and political minorities is required of Christian people. We cannot effectively make proposals for meeting these problems abroad unless our own actions and attitudes are consistent with the policies we support.

It is imperative that the churches, in the presence of growing antisemitism, promote goodwill and cooperation with our Jewish fellow citizens.

We also urge the churches to support effective anti-lynching legislation.

There is an obligation on the Church of Christ to aid and succor those who may be victims of violence and oppression. As a practical step we call for a more enlightened and liberal immigration policy so that our great country can once more serve in its traditional role as a place of refuge. We call on our country to use its utmost resources—financial, industrial, and social—with all our goodwill and fullest understanding to help open the way to new homes for refugees.

We request the Federal Council of Churches to keep the churches informed regarding specific legislative proposals which require study and action.

B. A NEGOTIATED PEACE

Every human instinct revolts against the continuation of the present conflict in Europe, especially as the menace of total war becomes more imminent. We are convinced that there is ground for hope that a just peace is now possible by negotiation. It is important for the welfare of mankind that the conflict end, not in a dictated peace, but in a negotiated peace based on the interests of all the peoples concerned.

We, therefore, urge that the United States in collaboration with other neutral nations use every means available to bring about a negotiated peace consistent with a just and fundamental settlement of the problems of Europe. To this end we urge the government to seek the aid of all nations not involved in the war in the creation among themselves of a permanent body for conference and conciliation.

Every day that hostilities continue brings nearer the threat of doom of civilization through active prosecution of unrestricted warfare which spares neither combatant nor civilian and which engulfs women and children and the aged as well as the prime of youth and manhood. Therefore, our churches are morally bound to use every means within their power to bring to the consciousness of their members the immediate necessity of a negotiaated peace based on justice and the legitimate aspiration of peoples.

Further, we urge that the Churches recognize the urgent necessity of preparing Christian people, and public opinion generally, for such essential sacrifices of national self-interest as may   be required to bring about a just and lasting peace.

C. THE UNITED STATES AND THE WORLD COMMUNITY

The United States must remain out of the present conflicts in Europe and the Far East. Our nation, however, can no longer avoid assuming its due share of responsibility for the establishment of a warless world through organization for effective control of matters of common interest. This demands a departure from our traditional policy of refusing to accept any substantial limitation of our national sovereignty.

It must now be clear that no nation has a right to be a law unto itself, or the sole judge of its own cause. If the peace which comes after the present war is to be anything more than a prelude to another conflict, the United States for its own sake and for the sake of humanity will have to renounce its political and economic isloation and identify itself with other nations in the creation of a world government. Only then will we be freed from the burdens of power politics.

In taking this position we subscribe to the declaration of the Oxford Conference (1937) that "A true conception of international order requires a recognition of the fact that the State, whether it admits it or not, is not autonomous, but is under the ultimate governance of God." If this Christian ideal of the State is to be incorporated in the relations of nations, law must be substituted for anarchy in world affairs.

Modern statism implemented by policies of unfettered national sovereignty, is a form of secularism against which we set ourselves. The State, in one form or another, is deified and made an object of worship. The demonic force engendered by the exercising of national sovereignty can only be mastered as nations are prepared to initiate policies consonant with the Christian world view. Over against the theory of the absolute sovereignty of the secular state there stands the sovereignty of God to which we give our primary allegiance.

We call upon our people to mobilize the spiritual resources of our churches in support of an international system of government. This is not to say that nations can have no place in a Christian world order. Diversity of culture and manners among various peoples enriches the world society. A Christian world order does not presuppose the elimination of differences among peoples. What is required is that nation-states no less than individuals shall be made subject to a world system of law, and to a sense of mutual responsibility.

The churches, which in themselves transcend national frontiers, have a peculiar responsibility to help expand men's loyalties to include the whole number of the children of our Heavenly Father, and the world government required by their common needs.

D. INTERNATIONAL ECONOMIC COOPERATION

A political world community could not of itself secure international goodwill and peace. Economic injustice, no less than political anarchy, breeds war. No system of world government which does not facilitate the easing of economic tension-points can vouchsafe peace to the world. If a permanent peace is to follow the present era of military hostilities, nations will have to renounce the practice of economic warfare. Reparations, embargoes, trade and currency restrictions, quotas and tariffs, no less than cannon and bombing planes, are potential instruments of war. These, too, must be renounced if peace, with justice, is to prevail.It is neither right nor just that a few nations should own or control or exercise political domination over the wealth of the world. It is probably not too much to say that half of the world exists below the subsistence level. This is not because there is any lack of raw materials or of the good things of life. It is because economic nationalism, no less than political nationalism, has bedeviled the relations of nations. The result is that the peoples which possess the preponderance of the world's wealth project armies and navies to maintain their privileged position while at the same time the less fortunate nations employ force or the threat of force to secure for themselves a more equitable share of the world's wealth.

We support the following recommendations of the Washington Conference on World Economic Cooperation convened by the National Peace Conference which call for (a) improving the standards of labor and living by international agreement as is being done by the International Labor Organization, (b) access to raw materials on equal terms, (c) freer access to markets so nations may be able to sell that which they best produce in order to have the exchange with which to purchase raw materials, (d) trading on a basis of equality rather than discrimination, (e) currency stabilization and better coordination of financial policies, (f) an autonomous International Economic Organization similar in structure and function to the International Labor Organization and which would have as its purpose the easing of economic tension points and the development of a world economy in the interest of peace and justice.

We recognize that the close causal relationship existing between unemployment, dire economic need and war is both of domestic and international significance. We, therefore, express the conviction that the Church in its efforts to abolish war, should stress all effective means, both domestic and international whereby basic economic needs may be met and a more equitable distribution of economic goods achieved.

E. COLONIES

Closely related to the problem of world economic cooperation is the question of colonies. The period of pioneer and colonial expansion is passing. We concur in the judgment of the Geneva Conference of lay experts and ecumenical leaders convened by the Provisional Committee of the World Council of Churches (1939) that "the task of colonial government is no longer one of exclusive national concern or national interest, but that it must be regarded as a common task of mankind, to be carried out in the interests of the colonial people by the most appropriate form of organization."

We believe that the principle of eventual freedom for all peoples is not only the recognition of an essential right but is also a prerequisite to the creation of that sense of justice and goodwill without which we cannot hope to rid the world of war.

F. THE CONFLICT IN EAST ASIA

We recognize that the United States must accept its share of responsibility for the crisis in East Asia.

There are two basic principles to which any proposals looking toward a settlement of the conflict in East Asia must conform.

First: They must call for a strong and independent China, sovereign in her recognized territory and strong enough to control her own affairs and destiny. Even assuming that China could be induced to suspend her resistance, a peace which did not respect her sovereignty would only be the prelude to a continuing struggle. An irredentist movement would be inevitable, and at some date in the not distant future would break out again in an open conflict which would destroy the peace of East Asia and threaten that of the world. A truly independent and strong China is essential if she is to avoid encroachments of Russia, of the Western imperialisms and of Japan. No indemnity for American losses in China, or renewal of rights of a strictly commercial character, must be allowed to divert attention from this essential point.

The Japanese Government has itself announced that it desires no territory in China, thus recognizing the principle underlying agreements hitherto entered into by nations concerned in the Pacific area. A further consequence of this principle is seen at once to be the abolition of extra-territoriality and of foreign concessions in China.

Second: They must also provide for a strong Japan, no less in control of her own destiny. A prostrated Japan would inevitably invite encroachments from Russia and possibly retaliation from China. Japan's pressing economic problems and needs must be recognized and adequate provision made to meet them. Probably most important is that Japan be given reasonable assurance that she will not be denied access to her natural market in China, whose economy so well supplements her own, either by Chinese boycott or discriminatory measures, or by interference from outside powers. She should be guaranteed equal terms with other nations in supplying China's needs and in securing from that country raw materials she can use in her industries. With her propinquity and the character of her manufactures she will still have a real advantage over her competitors. Any proposals for a settlement in East Asia must seek to furnish Japan full economic opportunity and provide for her a sense of political and economic security.

1. PROPOSALS LOOKING TOWARD A SETTLEMENT

There are certain essential features of a durable settlement in East Asia which apply particularly to Japan and China, and which must ultimately be decided by them. These are indicated here only as a part of the total situation, which vitally affects America as well as China and Japan. These features are stated in summary form below:

Features affecting China:

(a)The cessation of "anti-Japanese" agitation. This assumes, of course, that Japan will take reciprocal measures.

(b) Negotiation of a general commercial treaty with Japan, giving her the utmost consideration consistent with China's own interests and with her commitments to other powers.

(c) The furnishing to Japan of fair and equal access, through quotas, to certain stipulated raw materials (for example, cotton, minerals, salt), where this can be done without injury to China's own economy, Japan to pay for the same through the ordinary processes of trade and commerce. No arrangement is contemplated here which does not fully safeguard Chinnna's sovereignty and freedom.

(d) Negotiation of a *modus vivendi* in regard to Manchuria, looking toward a permanent settlement of this question.

(e) The facilitation of travel and communication arrangements of all kinds between China, Japan, Mancuria, and Korea, provided, of course, that these arrangements are in no way an embarrassment to China or an infringement of her sovereignty.

Features affecting Japan:

(a) The lifting of the naval blockade.

(b) Withdrawal of her troops from China. The details of withdrawal and subsequent reoccupation by Chinese troops should be worked out by a joint Commission specially designated for the purpose. If desired, neutrals might be requested to act as observers under such a Commission. In regard to this section see also *America's possible contribution,* c. below.

(c) The return of all properties, both public and private, expropriated during the war.

America's possible contribution:

If America could see her way clear to take some or all of the following steps, she would undoubtedly thus do much to facilitate a settlement of the situation in East Asia:

(a) Revise the so-called "Exclusion Act" and place both Japan and China on the quota basis in regard to immigration.

(b) Relinquish extra-territoriality, withdraw our naval and military forces, and surrender our inland navigation rights in China, within a very early period, say, within three to five years from the conclusion of the Sino-Japanese war.

(c) Endeavor to obtain the consent of the other powers now enjoying special privileges in China also to relinquish them, and likewise to withdraw their naval and military forces, within the same period.

(d) Seek further to secure the consent of all interested powers for the return of the concessions and foreign settlements to China. Should a three to five-year limit here seem too short, for example, in the case of Shanghai, a "special administrative" status after the analogy of Hankow might be arranged for a somewhat longer period if desired.

(e) Facilitate the opening of the American capital market to loans both to China and Japan, when peace is reestablished.

(f) Government credits to both China and Japan might also be considered in this connection if there are no legal or other difficulties in the way.

(g) In addition, America might offer reciprocal trade agreements to both Japan and China, or a least some arrangement whereby adjustments in tariff schedules could be accomplished and whereby the exchange of central commodities from both countries could be assured.

Further steps:

The following measures are worthy of consideration by all parties concerned, should they seek together a general settlement of the situation:

(a) The making of a regional agreement among the nations bordering on, or vitally interested in, the Pacific area, designed to contribute to mutual security and lasting peace.

(b) Consideration of a joint program of naval limitation and of possible non-fortifying of outlying possessions which would further promote general confidence.

(c) The negotiation of mutual trade-pacts which would foster and develop international trade and commerce.

(d) The establishment of a Board of Reference, such as that originally contemplated by the Washington Conference resolution dated February 4th, 1922, with provision for regular stated meetings to consider questions which may arise.

(e) In all new treaties that may be made between China, Japan, and America, or between these and other nations bordering on the Pacific, the following principles should be borne in mind: first, a provision for consultation in disputes; second, a provision for altering the treaty in the light of changing conditions. The Board of Reference, referred to in the preceding section, or some such agency, might well be of help in this connection.

(f) Cooperation in the regulation and eventual suppression of the traffic in narcotics.

2. RECOMMENDATIONS FOR IMMEDIATE ACTION BY CHRISTIANS

(a) Urge the United States Government

(1) to make use of every opportunity to explore the possibility of a settlement in East Asia along the lines of the proposals made in the previous section, and

(2) to give primary consideration as far as practicable to the settlement of the whole situation in East Asia in all negotiations looking to the making of a new commercial treaty with Japan.

(b) Seek to develop a public opinion favorable to the contribution to be made by America in facilitating a settlement in East Asia as outlined in the Section on *America's possible contribution* above.

(c) Urge the extension of generous credit to China, both by government and by private capital. All will agree that China needs help in her effort to cope with the staggering problem of relief, in the organization and improvement of her economic life by the establishment of cooperatives, in the rehabilitation and advancement of education, and in the development of industry in all parts of unoccupied China.

(d) Give more active support to relief work in China. In this connection we would especially commend the work of the Church Committee for China Relief, which is the officially recognized agency of the Churches.

(e) Urge the extension of the "moral embargo" to include octane gas, crude oil, trucks, scrap iron, et cetera.

(f) In the event the above steps including the moral embargo prove ineffective we urge the American Government to make plain to Japan our desire to remain on friendly terms with her, but also to say to her that we cannot longer be a party to supplying her with the raw or finished products which she uses in her military campaign in China. As a practical measure for carrying this attitude into effect, we would suggest that the Government offer to renew our trade treaty with Japan, but at the same time put her on a reduced basis so far as the sale of supplies to her is concerned. Such a basis might well be, in our judgment, an average quota for the period 1921-1931. We believe that this basis would effectively dissociate the United States from participation in Japan's attack on China, while it would at the same time show Japan that our attitude towards her is friendly, and that our action is intended only to avoid injury to China with whom also we desire to be friendly.

3. LONG RANGE PROGRAM

(a) *The World Mission of the Church*
The most significant contribution which the Churches can make toward
a solution of ten sions in East Asia is the vigorous prosecution of the
missionary program of the Churches. Christian groups have come into
being in the countries of East Asia as in the rest of the world, and the
potential influence of these groups for international goodwill is a fact
of major importance. The Madras Conference gave undoubted evidence
of this. The World Christian Movement is the one which of all others
offers the most hope of international integration in a world which has
disintegrated into areas of suspicion, hate and fear. It is imperative that
every effort be put forth to strengthen the Christian movement in all
its varied aspects in the countries of East Asia and throughout the
world.

(b) *World Political Organization*[2]
All through our consideration of this complicated problem we have
been aware of the fact of world anarchy. So long as each nation remains
the sole judge of its own cause and so long as there are no instruments
available which function in the no man's land of common interest,
which lies between states, situations such as that which now obtains
in East Asia must recur again and again. We have suggested some sort
of a regional agreement among the nations around the Pacific, and
some provision for revising treaties which may be made in the Pacific
area lest the status quo become fixed in too hard and fast a mould and
no allowance be made for the basic human fact of change. We recognize, however, that the ultimate solution of such problems as these calls
for an organized world government to which certain functions of
national sovereignty shall be delegated, and which shall function in the
area of common interest between states, which is now left unorganized
and in a state of anarchy. We would, therefore, urge that Christian
people in all lands study this aspect of the problem of peace and make
every possible effort to bring about a world political organization.

The Conference recommends that the *Memorandum on the Conflict in East
Asia* originally submitted to the Conference as a study document, be made
available to the Churches throughout the country for such use as they wish
to make of it in their consideration of this problem.

III. Missions and the World Crisis

"The Church is called today to live and to give life in a world shaken to its very foundations." It is confronted, both within and without its membership, with misgivings and with outspoken fears that the forces at conflict across the earth have rendered the Christian witness futile.

This Conference expresses gratitude to God that these misgivings and fears are not grounded in fact. It affirms that the Christian movement is not merely a fair-weather enterprise, but carries with it an all-compelling imperative and is as enduring as the love and purposes of God. It calls the Christians of North America to renewed faith and participation in the historic and continuing witness of a world Christianity which demonstrates the love and power of Christ in the experience of the individual, in the fellowship of the community, in the social and political relationships of the nation, and in the achieving of a just international order and an enduring peace. It testifies that the reality of God in Christ as the Savior of mankind, interpreted in the world Christian movement, has made for the creation of a world community of believers in Christian truth, out of which have emerged certain definite and positive achievements, values, and hopeful trends.

A. THE FORWARD MOVEMENT OF CHRISTIAN MISSIONS

In the past centuries, and particularly since the beginning of the Nineteenth Century, the Gospel has penetrated every land and has influenced every people.

Its paramount achievement is that it has produced men and women of creative spiritual power.

It has brought into being and mightily contributed to the world Christian fellowship which is the ecumenical church.

The Christian message and its messengers have surmounted barriers between races, have interpreted peoples to one another, and have enriched their knowledge, philosophy, and culture.

To the world Christian enterprise men and women of every race and nation have made and are making their own unique and indispensable contribution, bringing the best in the material, the human, and the spiritual values of every land to add to the common heritage of all.

In a day when hatred and warfare are separating the nations and threatening the world with destruction, the Church of Christ in every land is drawing men together and is revealing to them their community of interest and of destiny under one common God and Father.

B. WAR VERSUS THE CHRISTIAN GOSPEL

War, with its scourge of destruction, has disrupted the homes and schools and churches in many parts of China and upset the settled program of missions, but

> *The Christian message has been more widely declared than ever before, and the Chinese church today faces opportunities unprecedented in its history.*

The European war has brought untold difficulties to German, French, Finnish, and other missionaries, but

> *A fresh power of Christian fellowship has developed in the united assistance from other lands.*

Decrease in financial resources and missionary personnel has woefully hampered the carrying forward of the world mission, but

> *The churches in many lands have rallied to the need, and have undertaken burdens that demand real heroism.*

Tensions have grown up between nations, but

> *Christians have exhibited in extraordinary ways fellowship across national boundaries.*

Nationalism and other philosophies are increasingly claiming the complete allegiance of mankind, but

> *The Church with courage and persistence, proclaims its supreme loyalty to the eternal God as revealed by Jesus Christ.*

The world crisis has brought appalling difficulties which would dismay and discourage the stoutest heart, but

> *We find the church and the missionaries pressing forward, convinced that this is a day of amazing opportunity to present Christ—the only sufficient answer to the world's need.*

C. A BLUEPRINT OF ACTION FOR CHRISTIANS TO ADVANCE THE MISSIONARY ENTERPISE

In the face of such testimony and challenge, there is a clear call to the Christians of North America to

1. Maintain energetically the ongoing program of missions, stressing evangelism as the essential task.

2. Be ready to take advantage of the revolutionary changes which the war is bringing in our missionary program, particularly in the field of education, and to give support to new ventures.

3. Realize that the world movement which we call missions is of its very nature identical with the life and mission of the universal church.

4. Summon youth to participate in the missionary enterprise as an effective and immediate means toward the realization of their efforts to build a more Christian world.

5. Restate our fundamental conviction that a universally accepted spiritual basis is essential to the permanence of any reconstructed world order.

6. Emphasize the urgency of a program of economic and social reconstruction as an essential part of missions.

7. Accept as integral to all our Christian witness the relief of human suffering, and demonstrate good will and fellowship through sacrificial participation with those who suffer.

8. Recognize the missionary movement as potentially the most effective agency in existence for the establishment of a peaceful world.

9. Encourage certain qualified missionaries and ministers to be students and interpreters of international affairs.

10. Make increasingly possible visitations of national Christian leaders to North America for work among the churches.

11. Be alert to new opportunities for Christian service, such as the spiritualizing of the cooperative movement, training of leaders in rural reconstruction, ministry to students.

12. Enlist a larger constituency for intelligent participation in this worldwide task.

13. Make clear that the missionary enterprise has demonstrated the possibility for effective Christian cooperation and has greatly advanced the movement for church union.

14. Discover opportunities to promote acquaintance and understanding among races, thus laying the foundations for peace.

IV. The Conscientious Objector in War Time

A. DECLARATIONS OF OXFORD CONFERENCE (1937)

The Oxford Conference, in its report entitled "The Universal Church and the World of Nations," analyzed the varying views within the Church on the peace and war issue as follows:

"Here is the first obligation of the Church, to be in living fact the Church, a society with a unity so deep as to be indestructible by earthly divisions of race or nation or class.

"Wars, the occasions of war, and all situations which conceal the fact of conflict under the guise of outward peace, are marks of a world to which the Church is charged to proclaim the Gospel of redemption. War involves compulsory enmity, diabolical outrage against human personality, and a wanton distortion of the truth. War is a particular demonstration of the power of sin in this world, and a defiance of the righteousness of God as revealed in Jesus Christ and Him crucified. No justification of war must be allowed to conceal or minimize this fact.

"In all situations the Christian has to bear in mind both the absolute command, 'Thou shalt love thy neighbor as thyself,' and the obligation to do what most nearly corresponds to that command in the circumstances confronting him. The search for the will of God is a matter of agonizing perplexity for the Christian whose country is involved in war. We have to recognize two widely divergent views regarding war—along with several that are intermediate. One view hopes for the elimination of war by the power of God working in history through the religious and moral enlightenment of men and the exercise of their free wills; the other view regards man as so bound in the necessities of a sinful world that war will be eliminated only as a consequence of the return of Christ in glory.

"In practice this divergence issues in three main positions, which are sincerely and conscientiously held by Christians:

"(1) Some believe that war, especially in its modern form, is always sin, being a denial of the nature of God as love, of the redemptive way of the Cross, and of the community of the Holy Spirit; that war is always ultimately destructive in its effects, and ends in futility by corrupting even the noblest purpose for which it is waged; and that the Church will become a creative, regenerative, and reconciling instrument for the healing of the nations only as it renounces war absolutely. They are therefore constrained to refuse to take part in war themselves, to plead among their fellows for a similar repudiation of war in favour of a better way, and to replace military force by methods of active peace-making.

"(2) Some would participate only in 'just wars.' Here there are at least two points of view, depending upon the definition of the 'just war':

"(a) Some consider that Christians should participate only in such wars as are justifiable on the basis of international law. They believe that in a sinful world the State has the duty, under God, to use force when law and order are threatened. Wars against transgressors of international agreements and pacts are comparable with police measures, and Christians are obliged to participate in them. But if the State requires its citizens to participate in wars which cannot be thus justified they believe that Christians should refuse, for the State has no right to force its citizens to take part in sinful actions. Many would add that no war should be regarded as 'just' if the government concerned fails to submit the subject of dispute or casus belli to arbitration, conciliation, or judgment of an international authority.

"(b) Some would regard a 'just war' as one waged to vindicate what they believe to be an essential Christian principle: to defend the victims of wanton aggression, or to secure freedom for the oppressed. They would urge that it was a Christian duty, where all other means had failed, to take up arms. In so doing they would look to the verdict of conscience as their ultimate sanction. While recognizing the general importance of supporting civil or international order, the maintenance of such order in the present imperfect state of society cannot be a final obligation. The Christian, though he must be willing to accept martyrdom for himself, cannot expose others to it by refusing to fight for them.

"(3) Some, while also stressing the Christian obligation to work for peace and mutual understanding among the nations, hold nevertheless that no such effort can end war in this world. Moreover, while recognizing that political authority is frequently administered in a selfish and immoral way, they nevertheless believe that the State is the agent divinely appointed to preserve a nation from the detrimental effects of anarchic and criminal tendencies amongst its members, and to maintain its existence against the aggression of its neighbors. It is therefore a Christian's duty to obey the political authority as far as possible, and to refrain from everything that is apt to weaken it. This means that normally a Christian must take up arms for his country. Only when he is absolutely certain that his country is fighting for a wrong cause (e.g., in case of an unjustifiable war of aggression) has the ordinary citizen a right to refuse military service.

"Of those who hold this view, some would admit that individuals may be called directly by God to refuse categorically to take part in any war, and so to draw attention to the perverted nature of a world in which wars are possible.

"In either case the individual must recognize in principle the significance of the State and be willing to accept punishment by the authorities for violating the national law."

B. LIBERTY OF CONSCIENCE

We recognize that modern war has become totalitarian, and enforces its demands not only on men of military age, but upon the lives and conduct of all citizens, the productive machinery and the resources of the country, and that therefore the problems raised by military conscription face all citizens to a lesser or greater degree.

One of these problems is the exercise of Liberty of Conscience.

The Church is only fulfilling its most elemental duty when it seeks to arouse men to use their God-given liberty of conscience to follow the clearest insights they are given with reference to war. When therefore some of its members come in honesty and solemnity to a conscientious repudiation of participation in war, the Church has no recourse but to uphold both their right so to choose, and their freedom to take such action as the choice may involve. If the conscience of some Christians leads them to support and participate in war, and others to refuse such support and participation, then the Church must maintain the freedom of members to hold opposite views, in the spirit of Christian fellowship.

C. THE CHURCHES AND CONSCIENTIOUS OBJECTORS

To respect the rights of conscience is only the beginning of the obligation of the Churches. The Churches should make available machinery for registering conscientious objectors in their local churches and with their national bodies. There is a growing feeling that the Churches should challenge the principle of military conscription, that the exercise of conscience on the part of its citizens may be protected. Minority opinion both within the Church and State is indispensable to the welfare of both.

The Church does not seek special privilege for any persons in upholding the rights of conscientious objectors nor do conscientious objectors take their position as an escape from risk and suffering at a time when tragedy is the common lot of mankind.

In seeking to uphold by legal means the civil rights of conscientious objectors, the Church does so as a means of maintaining the religious freedom which God-fearing men must and will act upon, no matter who seeks to deny it, and the civil rights basic to democracy.

D. SERVICES BY CONSCIENTIOUS OBJECTORS IN PEACE AND WAR

The churches and the individual conscientious objector should not only study and explore the possibilities of services by the conscientious objector in wartime, but should undertake to cooperate in time of peace in activities which are aimed at the creation of a world wherein there shall be no occasion for war and to show him now where he can demonstrate the use of ways other than of violence as a means of solving conflicts both nationally and in the local community.

Many of these peace-time services have enhanced value in time of war and could be extended in such times as crises arise. Any service considered by the conscientious objector in peace time or war time should have value to society and to the individuals taking part in it.

Examples of service in peace time might be classified roughly as follows:

(a) Self education and group education to promote personal discipline, clarity of thought, spiritual integrity, training for social service, and group discipline for thought, prayer and action. Such activities would include study classes, international friendship groups, work camps, institutes of international relations, and efforts to overcome racial prejudices, national hatreds, and other divisive influences.

(b) Political activity, also, to secure legislation on foreign and domestic policies for protection of conscience and civil liberties, for economic and political justice, and disarmament; work against legislation, such as the Exclusion Act, etc., which creates international suspicion and ill will.

(c) Projects of reconciliation, rehabilitation and relief at home and abroad, service to refugees, work with the underprivileged, assistance to foreigners.

In time of war many activities need to be continued and amplified. Efforts should be stressed for mediation and stopping the war; work with refugees, alleviation of suffering, relief and reconstruction, fellowship with other conscientious objectors, care of their families, possible regular and frequent prison visitations, the organization of legal and spiritual advice, and the care of aliens who may be under a cloud of misunderstanding.

In the case of some conscientious objectors their services may take a *non-cooperative form*, such as a refusal to take part in any measures designed to help the war system in any way. In such cases it should be the part of the Church to give understanding and support to the group whose conscience led them to make their protest in these terms.

It should be pointed out that the development of some services in war time may easily become part of the military system. During the last war such work as that conducted by ambulance units, Y.M. and Y.W.C.A., the Red Cross, and food-raising units were so drawn into military services that any protest against the war system by the individuals working in them stood in danger of being lost. Experiences of conscientious objectors in 1914-18 were often tragic stories of finding themselves actually part of the war machine, though their intention had been to protest against it.

E. RECOMMENDATION TO FEDERAL COUNCIL OF CHURCHES

The Conference requests the Federal Council of Churches to take the initiative in setting up a committee comprised of representatives of all interested religious bodies, such representatives to be named by these bodies to consider problems concerning the conscientious objector to war. The functions of this committee should include, among others:

1. The study of the Church's obligation and duties to those of its own fellowship who take the position of conscientious objection to war and to give guidance to the churches concerning their relationship with such members to the end that their fellowship with the Church shall not be broken. This may include the making of recommendations regarding official recognition of objectors through some method of registration in the churches and the providing of forms of service for its conscientious objectors.

2. Conferences with the proper governmental agencies regarding the status of the conscientious objector and the procedures used by the state in dealing with him. This seminar declares its strong conviction that the handling of the conscientious objector should be a matter of civilian control at all times.

V. Responsibility of the Churches in Relieving Suffering Caused by War

Our country lies in peace between two areas of war.

To the west, the conflict in East Asia stretches on into an indefinite future. Millions of victims of war-caused floods have been added to the victims of direct military activity. To the east, while the horrors of modern warfare have not yet reached their impending toll and men look with dread to the future, already other millions have been added by this conflict to those hundreds of thousands oppressed on account of race and creed.

America's own formidable problems of unemployment and economic maladjustment, bring multitudes to the verge of starvation in the midst of national plenty. Yet even so we can give humble thanks that our homeland is free from invasion or the threat of war, and that we have the means to remedy the wrongs if we will. As Christian citizens of our country, we must face the obligations of privilege.. It is for us to be the awakened conscience of its Protestant Churches in the face of the tremendous need and our own comparative prosperity.

We recognize with joy and humility the impressive outpouring of gifts by our Jewish brothers and sisters, not only for refugees of their own race and faith, but also for Christian refugees. We are alike shamed and inspired by the way in which Great Britain, France and many smaller nations of the Continent have carried uncomplainingly their heavy burden of refugee populations, and are still trying to carry the load which has become too heavy for them. We confess with shame that the total recent contributions of our Protestant Churches and church members for the relief of suffering seem pitiably small in comparison.

The time has come to act. It is not necessary that we bear the whole burden, but it is our Christian duty to be in the forefront of all efforts to help the needy, and in certain cases to bear the burden in its entirety. We should be quick to respond to the cry for help from those who are hated for religious or racial reasons, or who are considered politically undesirable. We must not forget the missions of our sister churches, crippled by war conditions. Back of any defects of organization lie the basic facts of ignorance and a spirit which denies the validity of Jesus' teaching that we shall love our neighbors as ourselves.

We must make the situation in Asia and Europe grippingly vital to the rank and file of our membership, clergy as well as laymen. We must bring home to individual Christian men and women concern for individual sufferers. The sum total of even small gifts can work marvels and bear witness to Christ's grace. The essential sin of complacent comfort in the presence of distress must be made even clearer to all of us who bear the name of Christ. Prejudices unworthy of our Master must be dissolved by a fresh incarnation of God's love. Youth must be enlisted in such Christlike ministry. The spirit of Christ must dominate both the presentation of the need and the administration of relief. There can be no more convincing witness of our faith than sacrificial service in Christ's name.

We therefore call upon the Committee on Foreign Relief Appeals, jointly constituted by the Federal Council of the Churches of Christ in America and the Foreign Missions Conference of North America to survey the need and give counsel to the churches, speedily to undertake the full task of coordinating the relief appeals which they have already endorsed and others which may need to be made, in such a way that the tragic total need and our Christian responsibility for meeting it may stir the heart and conscience of every Protestant Church and individual Christian to a response much more nearly commensurate with our favored position. It should lead to other measures that may be necessary, such as approach to our government for cooperation. And we call upon the people of our churches to welcome and cooperate in such a program under its leadership.

VI. The Local Church and the World Crisis

In times of world crisis local churches are in danger of adopting a defeatist attitude. Small bands of Christians are likely to be overwhelmed by a sense of impotence and to ask, What can we do in the face of world movements? How can local churches influence world affairs? Is not the present world situation beyond our province to consider and our power to control?

Our answer to such questions is a challenge to every local church in America. We call the churches to a recognition of their supreme opportunity in the present crisis. In a world suffering the ravages of war the Christian community plays a saving and commanding role. God the Father of all counts all men his children. Christian fellowship transcends all barriers. Christian love is the unfailing power in all human relationships. As centers of worship, love and fellowship local churches are sources of unceasing redemptive activity. There are no limits set upon the healing, leavening and redeeming work the local churches may now do.

Today the world crisis lays upon local churches the inescapable obligation to relieve suffering, create brotherliness, extend the spirit of community, and seek lasting peace. They are under obligation to ward off hatred, pronounce war the evil thing it is, alien to the mind of Christ, promote understanding, create sentiment for and shape the policies of international goodwill, justice and peace.

Let no local church in the land evade its obligation or neglect its opportunity! Let every local church make the Christian solution of the present world crisis the subject of genuine concern, careful study, deep prayer and solemn commitment.

A. PRINCIPLES OF ACTION FOR THE LOCAL CHURCH

It is our conviction that local churches should

1. Through their pulpits proclaim the gospel of universal goodwill, forgiveness and understanding with a revitalized sincerity. This is imperative in a world torn by misunderstanding and griefs occasioned by narrow nationalism, racial hatreds and selfish imperialisms. We believe the pulpit of the smallest church is a mighty factor in creating world-minded attitudes.

2. Learn to regard themselves as part of the universal supra-national fellowship which is the world-wide church and strive to maintain the spirit of true brotherhood with churches of other lands, especially with those which may be involved in war and thus seem to be cut off from their Christian brethren in other belligerent and nonbelligerent nations. Christians in warring nations so cut off from the world-wide fellowship of the church need our sympathy and understanding. In the growing ecumenical movement this sense of fellowship across national boundaries is already a reality which needs to be expanded and developed.

3. Seek to teach their individual members that the unity and universality of the church transcend all differences and barriers of class, social status, race and nation. If ecumenicity is to mean anything anywhere it must be reflected in the relationships which exist between the churches in the local community. This implies not only the fullest possible interdenominational fellowship, but also the largest possible inter-faith cooperation.

4. Teach their individual members to distinguish between nationalism and religion. In the face of the tendency to absolutize state and nation and to put loyalty to the state on the same level as that to God, the churches must fearlessly teach that state and nation belong to the sphere of relative, earthly values and that God alone has claim to our unconditioned loyalty.

5. Study the possibilities of bringing about a just peace and seek to develop among their members a willingness to pay their part of the price of such a peace. In particular, local churches should seek to lead their members to understand that permanent peace involves some sort of world organization to which individual states must be willing to surrender certain aspects of sovereignty, such as was surrendered by the several states of the American Union in the formation of the United States of America.

6. Teach their members to distinguish truth from propaganda and to beware of emotional appeals based on hatred for any class or group or cause. Christians should learn properly to evaluate all appeals deliberately designed to influence opinions or actions with reference to predetermined ends without offering opportunity for independent investigation.

7. Acquaint their members with the plight of refugees in various parts of the world, urge support of worthy agencies for their relief, and where possible, accept responsibility for individual refugees or refugee families.

8. Strive to maintain the integrity of Christian fellowship among those

who differ on conscientious grounds as to the duty of participation in war. They should cultivate mutual understanding and tolerance of divergent judgments and should endeavor to counteract the tendency to identify Christian pacifism with political disloyalty. No person should be denied the right of Christian fellowship because of his convictions upon these matters. The churches should ask the state that no person be debarred from citizenship or denied any exercise of the right of religious liberty because of conscientious refusal to participate in the use of military force.

9. Teach their individual members that war and international ill-will have their roots in individual and community attitudes and prejudices. Selfishness in local church competition, greed in business, economic injustices and assumptions of social and racial superiority are local counterparts of national attitudes which create international friction and war. They should teach their members to distinguish between the Christian and the unChristian elements in the social order and to foster love, brotherhood, goodwill, justice, equality and cooperation as the strongest motivating forces for the good life.

10. Develop the ecumenical spirit through worship. Worship and prayer should be as inclusive as the spirit of Christ. In times of war Christians should be especially careful not to identify the war aims of any nation with the will of God and thus convert war into a holy crusade.

11. Strive to develop an understanding among their members that world missions and world peace are aspects of the same gospel and that financial support should be as freely given for the one as for the other. It is regrettable that in many local churches there is no adequate support for agencies devoted to world peace. As missionaries abroad are coming to be increasingly recognized as effective workers for peace so we must support similar workers at home.

12. Seek to guide their members toward an understanding of the privileges and obligations of Christian citizenship and to prepare them to undertake positions of leadership in constructive community enterprises and to assume positions of responsibility in local and national government.

13. Educate their members to an understanding of the essentials of religious freedom, which in our judgment includes (*a*) freedom of the church to determine its own faith and doctrine; (*b*) freedom of public and private worship, preaching and teaching; (*c*) freedom from the imposition by the state of any religious ceremonies or forms of worship; (*d*) freedom of the church to determine the nature of its government and the qualifications of its ministers and members; (*e*) freedom of the individual to join the church of his choice; (*f*) freedom of the church to control the education of its ministers, to give religious instruction to youth and to provide for the development of their religious life; (*g*) freedom of Christian service and missionary activities at home and abroad; (*h*) freedom of the church to use such facilities as are open to all citizens or associations to accomplish these

ends, for example, the right to own and administer property, the right of incorporation, and the right to collect and disburse funds.

14. Give prayerful thought and take concrete action in dealing with the cause, consequences and cure of anti-Semitism. The wave of anti-semitism that engulfs Europe and the anti-Jewish prejudice in America today are contrary to the mind of Christ and constitute a direct challenge to the local Christian communities of America.

B. PROGRAMS OF ACTION FOR THE LOCAL CHURCH

To achieve these ends, new and more effective means must be developed to gear the peace program into the life and work of the church. The following suggestions are made to implement this purpose.

We realize that there are many types of churches and communities. It is impossible to take cognizance of all local conditions, but it is our hope that the suggestions here made may be used and adapted to widely varying conditions.

1. THE MINISTER AND HIS WORK

The minister should not only hold before his people the ideals of human brotherhood and Christian fellowship, but should also be at the center of the practical peace program of his church. Preaching, worship, and the pastoral office are all vital in this program.

The tremendous problems for Christian people raised by the spread of war and suffering need earnest and repeated consideration in the pulpit. The worship services likewise offer rich opportunities for increasing the world-mindedness of the congregation. Worship has been called "the most ecumenical act," and there are aids to increase the ecumenical spirit. More worship material of this type is needed.

Pastoral counselling is an opportunity and a challenge in these days. Many of the foreign-born have heavy hearts because of the tragedy of their fatherland and the misunderstanding of their neighbors. Some of the hatreds of Europe may have arisen among national groups in the community. Many young people have personal problems created by the war danger. In many ways the pastor is called to a new responsibility in the cure of souls.

The complexity of international problems, the difficulties of securing adequate information, and the urgency of the world crisis call for intensive study and action. There is need for study conferences on strategy and action techniques for ministers and laymen throughout the country. Those who plan preaching missions and national, state, district, and community conferences, should give major attention to these emphases on the world strategy of Christianity and to very practical techniques for action in the local community. The plans of the United Christian Youth Movement for "workshop" groups for city and rural youth in its area conferences illustrate this practical procedure.

2. PLANNING THE PEACE PROGRAM

If the peace program of the local church is to be effective, the minister's work must be supplemented by lay cooperation. Organization is vital to the development and expression of lay leadership. A valuable form of organization is the representative peace committee to plan and coordinate the peace program. In many churches, no new committee is needed, for its function can be fulfilled by some other church organization: an active missionary society, Bible class, social action or religious education committee. Function is more important than form.

In many situations, the promotion of a community peace council or society is a better starting point than the church committee. In any case, the peace program should be integrated with the other sections of the church program.

A close relationship of preaching and study has been achieved by the Minister-Laymen-Partnership-Plan of the Unitarian Laymen's League. The minister meets with his laymen to discuss subjects from which the topic for a sermon is selected. After the sermon the minister and laymen meet for a discussion of practical ways to carry out the principles laid down in the sermon.

Another valuable method is that of quickening the consciences of church members through "queries of examining conscience," such as those developed by the Society of Friends.

3. GROUP STUDY AND ACTION

The kernel of international peace is group cooperative effort. There are significant existing channels of which the local church should take greater advantage.

(a) The themes of international missionary study for the next several years have significant possibilities for peace education and projects: Shifting Populations, China, Democracy, Christians and World Order, and Latin America. With all denominations and all age groups studying in these areas in the same months the opportunity for extensive cooperative projects should not be overlooked.

(b) The Work Camps and Volunteer Peace Teams such as those of the Society of Friends are extremely challenging to young people and should be promoted widely.

(c) Town Hall and other national radio programs offer unusual opportunities for discussion meetings and forums.

(d) Cooperation with other local churches in the observance of Brotherhood Week, World Day of Prayer, Inter-racial Sunday, Armistice Sunday, Goodwill Sunday and other nationally approved seasons of special worship is recommended. Worship material such as Muriel Lester's devotions for World Day of Prayer should be widely used.

(e) Summer Conferences and Institutes on International Relations and Social Problems offer unusual facilities for leadership training.

The local church and community should, however, originate and develop their own program adapted to the community needs. Some of the things the local church may well undertake are the following:

(a) Peace and world-wide brotherhood education through the usual means of visual education, peace plays, world trade exhibits, selected reading material and study groups, the use of posters and bulletins, and in the wider community peace parades and demonstrations.

(b) Establish inter-denominational, inter-racial, and inter-faith committees to deal with problems of civil rights, economic justice, labor disputes, citizenship and civic progress.

(c) Form a local inter-denominational consultative committee for the selection and distribution of the best peace material.

(d) Use the facilities of local radio stations for well prepared peace programs. The local press should be invited to cooperate on the presentation of pertinent peace events as well as news of peace activities in the church at large.

(e) Especially effective peace programs or projects should be reported to your denominational headquarters so as to be made available to others.

4. POLITICAL ACTION

As Christians, it is important that we become acutely aware of the legislative action of our government. In a democracy we frequently fail to remember that Congress is elected by and is responsible to the people. As a practical means of acquainting Congress with the will of Christian citizens we suggest:

(a) Participation in national peace organizations which do legislative work, and whose programs and policies harmonize with the principles of Christianity; not only that we may cooperate in their activity but also that we may help to promote the development of that unification of spirit and endeavor which has increasingly marked the peace movement.

(b) Promotion of sustained discussion on specific legislation and the background for such legislation: sermons; debates; discussion groups; intimate round table meetings of individuals who may be affected by such governmental action.

(c) Communication with congressmen to discover their position on proposed legislation.

(d) Formation of a legislative committee if one is not already functioning in the community to keep in touch with measures of national and state importance. Subscription to at least one national and if possible one state information service.

(e) All candidates should be visited in an election year for mutual discussion of their position on peace and social issues. The record of those running for re-election should be learned in advance. Reports of interviews should be published through the press, public meetings, and in other ways.

VII. Additional Recommendations[3]

A. TRANSMITTING THE RESULTS OF THE CONFERENCE TO THE CHURCHES

1. The National Study Conference, convened at Philadelphia, Pa., February 27-29, 1940, does hereby express its deep conviction that the insights and results of this Study Conference be without delay mediated and channelled to the denominations and interdenominational groups for continued study and application.

2. We therefore request the Denominations, the Federal Council of the Churches, and the Foreign Missions Conference to give serious consideration to the matter of channelling this information to the local churches and church groups through their state and area organizations, with a view to incorporating the studies of this Conference into the programs of the groups concerned.

3. We believe that the Inter-Council Field Department in cooperation with the Department of International Justice and Goodwill of the Federal Council and the Committee on International Relations of the Foreign Missions Conference offers appropriate facilities for the development of a church-wide strategy whereby the purposes of this Conference can be most effectively brought to the Christian people of America. We therefore recommend that steps be taken to enlist the above named agencies in this endeavor.

B. A UNITED PEACE CAMPAIGN

BE IT RESOLVED *That this Conference* recommend an immediate united peace campaign aimed at keeping America out of war and at stimulating the active participation of America in creating peace.

That this campaign be conducted under the joint auspices of the Department of International Justice and Goodwill of the Federal Council of the Churches of Christ in America and the Committee on International Relations of the Foreign Missions Conference of North America.

That in the development of this united campaign we work in closest possible relationship with Catholic and Jewish bodies to secure the participation of every religious group in America with a view to making a total religious impact.

That each religious body represented in this Conference, and all other interested religious groups, shall appoint representatives to join in this campaign and underwrite it financially.

That the campaign be implemented to the fullest extent by making use of the radio on the national hook-up plan, newspapers, et cetera, to produce a simultaneous crystallization of opinion which will come from every local church and community in America.

---

[1]The Executive Committee of the Federal Council of Churches received with appreciation the Message from the Philadelphia Study Conference, authorized its publication and commended it to the churches for their study and action.

[2]See above, pp. 38-40.

[3]The following resolutions were referred by the Conference to the organizations designated for such action as they might deem appropriate.

Chapter II

AMID ENCIRCLING GLOOM:

"The Churches and the Just and Durable Peace"

Delaware, 1942

INTRODUCTION

Nine months after the Philadelphia Conference and a year before Pearl Harbor, the Federal Council of Churches, at its biennial meeting in December, 1940, created a Commission to Study the Bases of a Just and Durable Peace. John Foster Dulles, Presbyterian layman and international lawyer, was named chairman. The tasks assigned the Commission were "to clarify the mind of our churches regarding the moral, political and economic foundations of an enduring peace," and "to prepare the people of our churches and of our nation for assuming their appropriate responsibility for the establishment of such a peace."

In keeping with its task, the commission proceeded with arrangements for a national study conference on "The Churches and a Just and Durable Peace" to meet at Ohio Wesleyan University, Delaware, Ohio, March 3-5, 1942.

Less than three months before the conference was to convene the Japanese attacked Pearl Harbor, and the United States became involved in war not only in the Far East but in Europe and Africa as well.

On December 30, the Federal Council's executive committee issued "A Message to Our Fellow Christians." Facing the facts of the situation, the message recognized that Christians have "a threefold responsibility: as citizens of a nation which, under God, is dedicated to human freedom; as members of the Church in America, which is called to minister to people under heavy strain; and as members of the world-wide Church, which unites in a common fellowship men of every race and nation who acknowledge Jesus Christ as Lord and Savior." The message in its entirety appears as an appendix to this volume.[1]

In the meantime the Commission to Study the Bases of a Just and Durable Peace went ahead with preparation for the conference. A set of "Guiding Principles" was drafted, and research memoranda and other documents were prepared.

As the delegates made their way to Delaware early in March, the situation looked bleaker even than it had the month after Dunkirk. Newspaper headlines during the week of the conference reported Japan's lightning conquest of Java, the closing of the Burma Road, the sinking of a U. S. destroyer by a German submarine, British paratroop raids on the French coast, R. A. F. attacks upon industrial areas around Paris, and appeals by President Roosevelt for a step-up in war production.

The 377 delegates at Delaware represented almost the same churches and ecumenical bodies as had been present at Philadelphia, including both denominations, allied religious organizations, and city and state councils of churches. Among the delegates were fifteen bishops of five denominations, seven seminary heads, and eight college and university presidents, besides ministers, theologians, denominational executives, and a number of missionaries with wide international experience. In addition there were industrialists, agriculturalists, specialists in economics and political science, and representatives of labor and consumer interests. All in all it was probably the most representative body of churchmen ever to have been drawn together on the North American continent—up to that time—to confront the issues of war and peace.

John Foster Dulles, as chairman of the Commission to Study the Bases of a Just and Durable Peace, shared responsibility of presiding over the sessions with Luther A. Weigle, Dean of Yale University Divinity School and President of the Federal Council.

By arrangement with Ohio Wesleyan University, the Merrick-McDowell Lectures, annually heard at the University, were made an integral part of the conference program and were heard by the student body and faculty of the University, as well as by the delegates. Appearing upon the platform of this lectureship were Francis J. McConnell, Bishop of the Methodist Church; Hu Shih, Chinese Ambassador to the United States; Leo Pasvolsky, Special Assistant to the Secretary of State; William Paton of London, a Secretary of the International Missionary Council and an Associate General Secretary of the World Council of Churches in process of formation; Carl J. Hambro, President of the Norwegian Storting (Parliament) and President of the Assembly of the League of Nations; and John Foster Dulles. The lectures were subsequently published by Abingdon-Cokesbury Press under the title *A Basis for the Peace to Come.*

Bishop G. Bromley Oxnam, as a member of the Federal Council's executive committee, explained at the opening plenary session of the conference that the discussion and findings would be restricted to a consideration of issues relevant to the *post-war* situation. He called attention to the work of special commissions and committees of the Federal Council dealing with the ministry of the churches to men in the armed services, to communities in the proximity of military and naval establishments or defense industries, to conscientious objectors, to aliens and prisoners of war, and to relief needs abroad. Among six such agencies, he told the delegates, the commission sponsoring this conference was the only one primarily responsible for studying problems of the peace.

For purposes of facing up to its task, the conference membership was divided in to four "sections" (in contrast to the six "seminars" at Philadelphia). The first, dealing with "The Relation of the Church to a Just and Durable Peace," was under the chairmanship of Theodore M. Greene, Professor, Princeton University, with John A. Mackay, President, Princeton

Theological Seminary, as reporter. The other three groups and their leaders were: "The Political Aspects of a Just and Durable Peace," Harold W. Dodds, President, Princeton University, and Ben A. Arneson, Professor, Ohio Wesleyan University; "The Economic Aspects of a Just and Durable Peace," Charles J. Turck, President, Macalester College, and Ernest F. Tittle, Pastor, First Methodist Church, Evanston, Illinois; and "The Social Aspects of a Just and Durable Peace," Miss Sue Weddell, Secretary, Foreign Missions Conference, and Leslie B. Moss, Executive Secretary, Committee on Foreign Relief Appeals in the Churches.

Each section met for four two-hour sessions, with editing committees working feverishly at odd moments and late into the night to put into the best form possible the thinking of each group upon the subject at hand. The section reports were then submitted to the conference as a whole in plenary sessions. Some modifications were made as a result of discussion there, but in this conference the pattern begins to emerge that was generally followed in subsequent conferences of making a distinction between the actions of the conference as a whole which were *approved*, and the section reports which were merely *received* by the plenary session and "commended" to the churches "for their favorable consideration and action." In this instance the conference *approved* the Preamble and Guiding Principles and certain general resolutions which appear at the end of the document. The most significant and influential portion of the Delaware Message is probably the statement of guiding principles which comprises Part II.

The significance of the conference was recognized at once by the secular press and journals. *Newsweek* referred to it as "Protestantism's most important meeting so far in this war."[2] *Time* named some of the prominent laymen present—Y. M. C. A. leader John R. Mott, Economist Irving Fisher, and Industrialist Harvey S. Firestone, Jr.—and then went into considerable detail in summarizing the major findings; some of these it termed "sensational."[3]

The conference and its message were received with great respect by Christians of varying points of view on the issues of the war itself and America's foreign policy. This may be seen by noting the reactions of two representative interdenominational periodicals: the *Christian Century*, Protestantism's most influential religious journal, long known for its liberal, pacifist, isolationist leanings, and *Christianity and Crisis*, the neo-orthodox, non-pacifist and internationalist journal, founded in 1941 by Reinhold Niebuhr and others as "a direct protest against the stands of the *Christian Century*."[4]

In their evaluation of the significance of the Delaware Conference, however, these journals were at one. *Christianity and Crisis* declared that the conference personnel was "the most distinguished in a quarter-century of American church assemblies."[5] The *Christian Century* referred to it as "one of the most important gatherings in the history of modern Protestantism."[6] In reference particularly to the Guiding Principles, the latter journal declared that the conference had "laid down certain basic principles which will hereafter govern the church in its approach to this issue and which constitute a firm foundation on which to build."[7]

The Delaware Conference is remembered even today for the solid foundation it laid for a Christian approach to the problems of the post-war world. Again in the words of the *Christian Century*, the American church was now ready, "proceeding from its own theological and moral premises, to launch an independent examination of the whole problem of achieving a just and lasting peace."[8]

While the nation was preoccupied with mobilizing its manpower and economic resources to win a military victory in the war, the Delaware gathering directed its attention to the moral, political, economic, and social requirements for winning the peace.

---

[1]See below, pp. 200 ff.
[2]XVI, No. 11 (March 16, 1942), p. 69.
[3]XXXIX, No. 11 (March 16, 1942), p. 44-48.
[4]J. Milton Yinger, *Religion in the Struggle for Power* (Durham, N. Car.: Duke University Press, 1946), p. 205.
[5]II, No. 5 (April 6, 1942), p. 1.
[6]LIX (March 18, 1942), p. 338.
[7]*Ibid.*, p. 343.
[8]*Ibid.*, p. 342.

A MESSAGE FROM THE NATIONAL
STUDY CONFERENCE ON THE CHURCHES
AND A JUST AND DURABLE PEACE

Delaware, Ohio   **March 3-5, 1942**

I. Preamble

II. Guiding Principles

III. Reports from the Sections

The Church and a Just and Durable Peace
God's Purpose for World-Wide Community; The Churches' Weaknesses and Shortcomings; Their Resources for Healing Wounds of War; The Responsibility of Each Local Church; The Churches' Mission to All Mankind.

Political Bases of a Just and Durable Peace
The Duty of the United States to Cooperate; Responsibilities in the Transitional Period; The Need for an International Authority; Powers Which Must be Delegated; Kinds of International Authorities Needed; International Authority Over Colonies; The Influence of the Churches on Statesmen.

Economic Bases of a Just and Durable Peace
Economic Barriers to Unity and Peace; Inadequacies of the Profit System; The Need for Experiment with Other Systems; International Cooperation Imperative.

Social Bases of a Just and Durable Peace
Brotherhood and Human Rights Basic to Peace; The Task of Relief and Rehabilitation; National Values Within a World Community; Justice for All Racial Groups.

IV. General Resolutions

Presentation of Message to Government Officials; Follow-up of the Conference; Economic Collaboration.

THE CHURCHES AND A JUST AND DURABLE PEACE[1]

I. Preamble[2]

The period through which we are passing is the most revolutionary in world history, when we take into account the vastness of the areas affected. A familiar order of life is hastening to a close and none can predict the shape of things to come. When the present conflict is over, and irrespective of which side wins in the struggle, the world that we know will be radically altered, for better or for worse. That being so, all discussion of a future peace settlement, if it is to be germane to the real human situation, must take full cognizance of the tremendous forces that are operating at the present time.

In consequence of the prophetic tradition of Biblical religion, and in loyalty to the words of Jesus Christ Himself, it is the function of the Church to "discern" the times and the seasons, to "decipher the meaning" of each succeeding era and to bear witness to the word and will of God in each concrete situation. In doing so the Church will issue a call to repentance in which both Church and nation shall acknowledge their separate and corporate guilt before God.

The churches in their purely temporal aspects, and apart from their spiritual functions, are powerful social institutions. As such they must concern themselves at all times in a vital and primary way with social confusion and chaos.

The Church will make plain that peace is much more than the cessation or absence of conflict, following upon the joyous commitment of life to a cause greater than individual or national self-interest. In this respect peace is like freedom, both have their origin not in a release from that which disturbs or curbs, but rather an abandonment to the self-transcending demands of a great devotion. The Church can most adequately meet man's perennial demand for peace and freedom by summoning men to commit themselves to Jesus Christ and to the cause of the Kingdom of God in Him.

II. Guiding Principles[3]

1. WE BELIEVE that moral law, no less than physical law, undergirds our world. There is a moral order which is fundamental and eternal, and which is relevant to the corporate life of men and the ordering of human society. If mankind is to escape chaos and recurrent war, social and political

institutions must be brought into conformity with this moral order.

2. WE BELIEVE that the sickness and suffering which afflict our present society are proof of indifference to, as well as direct violation of, the moral law. All share in responsibility for the present evils. There is none who does not need forgiveness. A mood of genuine penitence is therefore demanded of us—individuals and nations alike.

3. WE BELIEVE that it is contrary to the moral order that nations in their dealings with one another should be motivated by a spirit of revenge and retaliation. Such attitudes will lead, as they always have led, to renewed conflict.

4. WE BELIEVE that the principle of cooperation and mutual concern, implicit in the moral order and essential to a just and durable peace, calls for a true community of nations. The interdependent life of nations must be ordered by agencies having the duty and the power to promote and safeguard the general welfare of all peoples. Only thus can wrongs be righted and justice and security be achieved. A world of irresponsible, competing and unrestrained national sovereignties whether acting alone or in alliance or in coalition, is a world of international anarchy. It must make place for a higher and more inclusive authority.

5. WE BELIEVE that economic security is no less essential than political security to a just and durable peace. Such security nationally and internationally involves among other things the use of material resources and the tools of production to raise the general standard of living. Nations are not economically self-sufficient, and the natural wealth of the world is not evenly distributed. Accordingly the possession of such natural resources should not be looked upon as an opportunity to promote national advantage or to enhance the prosperity of some at the expense of others. Rather such possession is a trust to be discharged in the general interest. This calls for more than an offer to sell to all on equal terms. Such an offer may be futile gesture unless those in need can, through the selling of their own goods and services, acquire the means of buying. The solution of this problem, doubtless involving some international organization, must be accepted as a responsibility by those who possess natural resources needed by others.

6. WE BELIEVE that international machinery is required to facilitate the easing of such economic and political tensions as are inevitably recurrent in a world which is living and therefore changing. Any attempt to freeze an order of society by inflexible treaty specifications is bound, in the long run, to jeopardize the peace of mankind. Nor must it be forgotten that refusal to assent to needed change may be as immoral as the attempt by violent means to force such change.

7. WE BELIEVE that that government which derives its just powers from the consent of the governed is the truest expression of the rights and dignity of man. This requires that we seek autonomy for all subject and colonial peoples. Until that shall be realized, the task of colonial goverment

is no longer one of exclusive national concern. It must be recognized as a common responsibility of mankind, to be carried out in the interests of the colonial peoples by the most appropriate form of organization. This would, in many cases, make colonial government a task of international collaboration for the benefit of colonial peoples who would, themselves, have a voice in their government. As the agencies for the promotion of world-wide political and economic security become effective, the moral, social and material welfare of colonial populations can be more fully realized.

8. WE BELIEVE that military establishments should be internationally controlled and be made subject to law under the community of nations. For one or more nations to be forcibly deprived of their arms while other nations retain the right of maintaining or expanding their military establishments can only produce an uneasy peace for a limited period. Any initial arrangement which falls short of this must therefore be looked upon as temporary and provisional.

9. WE BELIEVE that the right of all men to pursue work of their own choosing and to enjoy security from want and oppression is not limited by race, color or creed. The rights and liberties of racial and religious minorities in all lands should be recognized and safeguarded. Freedom of religious worship, of speech and assembly, of the press, and of scientific inquiry and teaching are fundamental to human development and in keeping with the moral order.

10. WE BELIEVE that, in bringing international relations into conformity with the moral law, a very heavy responsibility devolves upon the United States. For at least a generation we have held preponderant economic power in the world, and with it the capacity to influence decisively the shaping of world events. It should be a matter of shame and humiliation to us that actually the influences shaping the world have largely been irresponsible forces. Our own positive influence has been impaired because of concentration on self and on our short-range material gains. Many of the major preconditions of a just and durable peace require changes of national policy on the part of the United States. Among such may be mentioned: equal access to natural resources, economic collaboration, equitable treatment of racial minorities, international control of tariffs, limitation of armaments, participation in world government. We must be ready to subordinate immediate and particular national interests to the welfare of all. If the future is to be other than a repetition of the past, the United States must accept the responsibility for constructive action commensurate with its power and opportunity.

11. WE BELIEVE that a supreme responsibility rests with the Church. The Church, being a creation of God in Jesus Christ, is called to proclaim to all men everywhere the way of life. Moreover, the Church which is now in reality a world community, may be used of God to develop His spirit of righteousness and love in every race and nation and thus to make possible a just and durable peace. For this service Christians must now

dedicate themselves, seeking forgiveness for their sins and the constant guidance and help of God.

12. WE BELIEVE that, as Christian citizens, we must seek to translate our beliefs into practical realities and to create a public opinion which will insure that the United States shall play its full and essential part in the creation of a moral way of international living. We must strive within the life of our own nation for a change which will result in the more adequate application here of the principles above enumerated as the basis for a just and durable world order.

13. WE BELIEVE that the eternal God revealed in Christ is the Ruler of men and of nations and that His purpose in history will be realized. For us He is the source of moral law and the power to make it effective. Amid the darkness and tragedy of the world of today we are upheld by faith that the kingdoms of this world will become the kingdom of Christ and that He shall reign forever and ever.[4]

III. Reports from the Sections[5]

A. THE RELATION OF THE CHURCH TO A JUST AND DURABLE PEACE

1. We believe it is the purpose of God to create a world-wide community in Jesus Christ, transcending nation, race and class. The Christian Church, accordingly, is responsible not only to proclaim the divine message, but also to contribute by all means in its power, to secure a world-order in which God shall have His rightful place, and the basic needs of mankind shall be satisfied. In the present crisis this responsibility of the Church is made more manifest than ever before. It therefore becomes its inescapable duty to speak both to its own members and to the leaders of our political, economic and cultural life concerning what seems to it to be the will of God for the peaceful ordering of human life.

In order that its witness may be effective in the fullest measure, it is important that the Church reflect in every phase of its own life—congregational, denominational, interdenominational and ecumenical—the reality of the peace, unity and cooperation which it recommends to secular society.

Conscious also of its helplessness apart from God, and of the infinite resources which it has in God for the supply of every need, the Church is called upon to a new ministry of prayer in order that God's saving power may become manifest amid the complexity and tragedy of our life.

2. We are penitently conscious of the many weaknesses and shortcomings of the Church itself in the face of the tremendous responsibilities with which it is confronted. We have not sufficiently borne witness to, nor even adequately recognized for the Church itself, that very unity of mankind,

beyond race and nation, which again and again we have declared in principle.

We call upon our churches, therefore, to enter seriously and immediately upon the task of breaking down the barriers that so easily divide us into opposing groups. We would say to them: If you believe in peace for the world, if you are working for cooperation between nations, governments, races and peoples under the Fatherhood of God, you must set the example for such reconciliation and cooperation. The Christian churches must come to realize as they now do not, that joining the Church of Christ in any of its branches means entering a fellowship world-wide in extent, beyond denomination and race, and should involve responsible participation in the task of making spiritually more real our mystical fellowship in community life and in the world.

We would also call upon our churches to enter upon a new era of inter-denominational cooperation in which the claims of cooperative effort should be placed, so far as possible, before denominational prestige, and that conjoint Christian efforts be not weakened or imperilled by our several denominational allegiances.

3. We declare as the major premise that the Church is a spiritual entity, one and indivisible, which as such is not and cannot be broken by human conflicts. Therefore the Church is in a unique position to heal the wounds of war and bind the world together in a just and durable peace. We recognize the particular rights and responsibilities of the State in connection with the secular order. But we reaffirm the Christian truth that the Church in its essential nature is an ecumenical, supranational body, separate from and independent of all states including our own national state. The spiritual responsibilities of the Church and the spiritual service which it may render derive not from the claims which the State may make but from the freedom and autonomy of the Church itself under the Lord Jesus Christ who is its Living Head.

4. We believe that each local church will do much to create the mood out of which a just and durable peace can grow, and make its own message of Christian brotherhood real to itself and its constituency, if it will give itself to specific acts of service and reconciliation within its own community.

The practice of acts of inter-racial goodwill, aid and friendship for new Americans, assistance to refugees and to bewildered but innocent aliens, a ministry to the victims of war at home and abroad—these and other such immediate acts of helpfulness will be the best educational experience for the church group itself and will build the community attitudes upon which the peace we seek may later come.

In order to prepare and administer an inclusive educational program designed to promote a just and durable peace, we recommend to the Commission:

(a) That integrated and cumulative courses for use in Church schools and study groups be constructed in consultation with the International Council of Religious Education. (These shall include not only bases for discussion but also suggestions for activities and projects.)

(b) That the cooperation of denominational boards of Christian education in adapting and using these courses be secured.

(c) That particular attention be given to further participation and enlarged support by youth through special emphases on youth programs and through the cooperation of existing youth agencies.

(d) That means be sought effectively to counteract hate and vengeance as controlling motives in the present crisis.

(e) That the possibilities of including the study of peace issues in public and private day schools be explored and utilized.

(f) That a synthesis of common elements in the proposals of various peace agencies be made available.

(g) That Christian people be prepared to make sacrifices in the interest of peace.

(h) That the Church should take greater account of (i) the potential power of childhood as bearing on future international relationship; (ii) the importance of Christian education in the home; (iii) the possible motivations for Christian world attitudes encouraged by common response to human needs; and (iv) the results to be obtained by cooperation with service agencies other than the Church.

(i) That all vehicles for the transmission of ideals, including magazines, motion pictures, and radio, be employed.

Moreover, in order effectively to convey to governmental authorities the mind of the Church on principles pertaining to a just and durable peace, we recommend to the Commission on the Bases of a Just and Durable Peace

(a) That studies be undertaken to ascertain: opinions among Church members about social justice and peace; areas where information is lacking; methods of meeting needs thus revealed; best technique of peace education and action by local churches; ways in which ideals of Christian citizens may be brought into relation with the attitudes of legislative authorities.

(b) That the Church be kept informed about legislative proposals and actions, and be aided in rightly understanding their significance.

(c) That full and understanding support be given the efforts of government officials who are promoting farsighted peace proposals.

(d) That churches be informed of the present work of the World Council of Churches, now in process of formation, in steps preliminary to a just peace and that their active cooperation be solicited.

(e) That preparation for a session of the World Council be encouraged in order that through such a session the influence of Christian thought be brought to bear upon the formulation of plans for peace settlement, and that arrangements be made for an adequate Christian representation to meet whenever and wherever any official peace conference or conferences may be held.

5. We believe that if the churches of America are to participate adequately in making peace just and durable, they must develop a more real and vital sense of mission to mankind in the name of Christ, recognizing responsibility for service to humanity in all areas of life, social as well as geographical.

The finest expression of that sense of mission is to be found, we believe, in the missionary enterprises of the Church world-wide. However, the aftermath of war on a world scale will necessitate wide-spread readjustment of program and service to meet the tremendous need of the world. We recommend, therefore:

(a) That the mission boards through cooperative agencies should, at the earliest possible moment, be prepared to interpret to the churches the new opportunities and the necessary adjustments of machinery and study, whatever drastic changes such adjustments may involve.

(b) That a call be issued, if possible through the World Council of Churches, for a more thorough-going participation in the world mission of the Church, urging at the same time close and warmer cooperation among Christians of *all* lands, in working together in Christ's name for our brother-men everywhere.

B. POLITICAL BASES OF A JUST AND DURABLE PEACE

The churches of America face clear responsibilities in seeking to establish a better world when the war has ended. First among post-war duties will be the achievement of a just peace settlement with due regard to the welfare of all nations, the vanquished, the over-run, and the victors alike.

In order that such a settlement may tend toward a better political order, we as citizens of the United States of America, advocate the following principles and measures:

1. That the United States pursue a responsible national policy with concern for the welfare of all peoples and that the United States cooperate fully with all nations and peoples in working towards a world order of justice and peace.

2. That during a transitional period after the fighting has ended, the efforts of the peoples of the world be devoted, in proportion to their ability, to the reestablishment of order, the provision of food, shelter and medical service, and the restoration of stable government and economic activity, especially in the devastated territories. These emergency measures must include policing by joint action for the protection of minorities and disarmed populations, and positive measures of economic and cultural cooperation. They should be carried out under international authorities, representative of all peoples concerned. There should be no punitive reparations, no humiliating decrees of war guilt, and no arbitrary dismemberment of nations. All of these emergency measures should tend toward a growing structure of international order.

3. That among the functions of government that must be performed are the preservation of public order, the maintenance of economic opportunity, the safeguarding of public health and welfare, and the direction of population movements. In large part, these functions must be performed by local and national governments, but in part they can now be effectively carried out only by international authority.

4. That certain powers now exercised by national governments must, therefore, be delegated to international government, organized and acting in accordance with a world system of law. Among the powers so delegated must be the power of final judgment in controversies between nations, the maintenance and use of armed forces except for preservation of domestic order, and the regulation of international trade and population movements among nations.

5. That international authorities competent to perform these functions may be of two sorts. (1) The ultimate requirement is a duly constituted world government of delegated powers: an international legislative body, an international court with adequate jurisdiction, international administrative bodies with necessary powers, and adequate international police forces and provision for worldwide economic sanctions. (2) As steps toward, and potential organs of, such world government, there is need for many sorts of international bodies charged with specific duties, such as the International Labor Organization, and various agencies such as those now acting for the United Nations to coordinate natural resources, shipping, and food distribution. Such bodies must be adapted to the service of world order and government, and must not become a substitute therefor. In the operation of these agencies, and in progressing toward full world government, every

effort should be made to achieve agreement and voluntary cooperation of all concerned.

6. That, utilizing experience with the mandate principle, a system of administration of colonial territories under international authority be developed. In areas now under colonial administration, advance toward self-government should be carried forward in substantial progress. The affairs of peoples deemed not yet capable of self-government should be administered as a common trust, by international authority, in the interest of these peoples as members of a world society.

7. That the influence of the churches shall be employed to keep the foregoing principles before the attention of diplomats and statesmen.

C. THE ECONOMIC BASES OF A JUST AND DURABLE PEACE

1. Our concern with world economics is an obvious consequence of our desire, as Christians, to realize an ever richer spiritual world fellowship. While the strengthening of the spiritual bond may help to prepare for a solution of the economic problems of the world, the spiritual union may itself be gravely impaired or disrupted by conflict arising in the economic realm. We are deeply disturbed by the economic distress of millions of our fellow men and by economic conditions that threaten the extension of the kingdom of God on earth.

2. We view the economic tensions and distresses of our day as symptoms of a general world disorder. In our era production has been carried on primarily with a view to monetary gains. Profit has been the principal incentive relied upon to turn the wheels of industry and to bring forth the fruits of the soil.

This system has in recent years developed grave defects. There have occurred mass unemployment, widespread dispossession from homes and farms, destitution, lack of opportunity for youth and of security for old age. These calamities, which have often been accentuated by short range self-seeking trade policies of various nations, have made for war. There has been a sharp increase in economic nationalism with tariffs being raised, monetary systems adjusted for the benefit of national interests, and a race for colonies on the part of some countries. Out of this economic insecurity has come an atmosphere favorable to the rise of demagogues and dictators. Mass unrest has afforded violent and unscrupulous men the opportunity to seize leadership and has made any rational approach to international disputes impossible.

In this chaotic situation there has arisen in certain countries an alternative way of production which is based on complete management and control of all economic life by government. With this has come a system of compulsion which deprives the individual of freedoms, economic, intellectual and spiritual, necessary to human dignity.

We do not believe that we are limited to a choice between these two alternatives. If this seems the only choice it is largely because the churches have failed generally to inculcate Christian motivation. Willingness to strive and to produce and to render services should not be dependent either wholly upon profit motivation or wholly upon compulsion. We urge upon the churches that they have the great opportunity and responsibility to make possible a generally acceptable solution by bringing people to a different and more Christian motivation.

In the day when revolutionary upheavals have swept away the traditional economic organization in Russia, Italy, and Germany, and now when, by reason of the necessities of war, that economic order is being radically reorganized everywhere, the church has a manifest duty in the economic field, both urban and rural. That duty is not to line up on the side of any economic system and certainly not to prescribe details or advocate panaceas. Its responsibility lies in a deeper moral realm. As Christians we must be vitally concerned for the preservation of human values in any and every system. The Christian doctrine of man as a child of God carries with it the demand that all men, without distinction of race, creed, or class, shall be afforded the economic means of life and growth.

Any economic program which allows the quest for private gain to disregard human welfare, which regiments human beings and denies them freedom of collective bargaining, thus reducing labor to a mere commodity; any program which results in mass unemployment or dire poverty in mine or factory or farm; any program which fails to conserve natural resources and results in soil deterioration and erosion and along with it human erosion and deterioration of rural life in home and school and church, is manifestly wrong. Against such evils the church should arouse the conscience of mankind in every nation. The church must demand economic arrangements measured by human welfare as revealed by secure employment, decent homes and living conditions, opportunity for youth, freedom of occupation and of cultural activities, recognition of the rights of labor, and security in illness and old-age. To secure these arrangements it must appeal to the Christian motive of human service as paramount to personal or governmental coercion.

3. The building of a just and peaceful world involves the building of national and local communites on the basis of justice, freedom and cooperation for the common good.

We believe that a new ordering of economic life is both imminent and imperative, and that it will come either through voluntary cooperation within the framework of democracy or through explosive political revolution. We recognize the need of experimentation with various forms of ownership and control, private, cooperative and public. It is hardly to be supposed that any one system, whether of private, cooperative, or public enterprise is suited to all kinds of production, distribution and service. The production and distribution of goods on the basis of voluntary cooperation is an experiemnt which in many parts of the world is meeting with notable success.

Recommendations:[6]

(a) That every man should have the opportunity to share in the ownership of both personal and productive property, such as a home, a farm and economic enterprises.

(b) That every member and family of the human race have a right to steady employment and to earn an income such as may provide the necessities of life and growth and is in accord with the wealth-producing capacity of their day and the requirements of responsible conservation of natural resources.

(c) That in early years every individual has the right to full-time educational opportunities with reasonable consideration of his talents, interests, and probable vocation; that in later years every individual is entitled to economic security in retirement and the continuation of cultural opportunities; that in the whole span of life every individual is entitled to adequate health service and professional medical care; and that in the productive years there is the universal obligation to work in some socially necessary service.

(d) That every man has the right of employment of a kind that is consistent with human dignity and self-respect, and to such leisure as is essential for cultural and spiritual development; that employers of all kinds should recognize and safeguard these rights.

(e) That citizens, through their governments or other appropriate agencies, have not only the right but the duty

(1) To prevent destructive cyclical trends in business by regulatory measures or, if these prove inadequate, by direct initiative;

(2) To counteract the unemployment resulting from technological change through vocational re-education, through public employment agencies, and, if necessary, through a reorganization of industries and markets.

(f) That industrial democracy is fundamental to successful political democracy, and we therefore recommend that labor be given an increasing responsibility for and participation in industrial management. The principle of democracy in economic relations should be accorded wider expression by the development of stronger *voluntary* producers associations, farm organizations, labor organizations, professional groups, and consumers organizations, and their integration into some form of national economic council, for planning in cooperation with government for maximum production and consumption and the abolition of unemployment. In each industry also, industrial councils should be developed, representative of management, labor and consumers, for democratic direction of industries towards these same ends. The effect of maximum production and consumption in each country would be to decrease the pressure of competition for world markets and thus to mitigate one of the major economic causes of war.

(g) That we cannot find the means of preventing social disorder until we have ended the paradox of poverty in the midst of plenty. We believe that a tax program should be formulated in such a way that the burden be placed in proportion to the ability to pay, to the end that our wealth may be more equitably distributed.

(h) That agriculture has a dual importance, both as a way of making living and as a basis of family and community life. Our economic system must become servant and not master in maintaining the socially significant services of agriculture, such as feeding the world and producing the organic raw materials essential to industry.

(i) In view of the Christian principle that a house divided against itself cannot stand, we urge that the International Labor Organization or its successor organization after the war shall make a special study of all available plans for avoiding or reducing the animosities too often prevailing between Labor and Management and tending to national inefficiency and war.

4. We believe that no nation nor group of nations can solve in a permanent way the economic problems interior to itself without the cooperation in goodwill of the other peoples of the world. The economic prosperity of one nation bears a direct and not an inverse ratio to that of others. It is necessary to abandon injurious forms of economic competition and to avoid entrance upon the disastrous chain of economic counter measures and reprisals which often mark the policy of competing nations. We endorse the principle that "national interdependence now replaces independence and that action by any nation, notably in the economic field, which materially and adversely affects other people, is not purely a matter of domestic policy but is coupled with an international responsibility."

Recommendations:[7]

(a) The progressive elimination of restrictions on world trade, such as tariffs and quotas, under the guidance of an international organization and by other appropriate methods.

(b) "The fullest collaboration between all nations in the economic field with the object of securing *for all* improved labor standards, economic advancement and social security." This is the language of the Atlantic Charter, Article 5. We call attention however to the fact that in Article 4 of this Charter, the obligation "to further the enjoyment by all states, great or small, victor or vanquished, of access on equal terms to the trade and raw materials of the world which are needed for their economic prosperity," is limited by the phrase "with due respect for their existing obligations." We urge that such existing obligations be modified so as to permit the complete achievement of the goal set forth in this same Article. We hold that in all this matter the rights and needs of indigenous populations should be given just consideration.

(c) The establishment of a universal system of money. The money system should be so planned as to prevent inflation and deflation, insofar as this is possible through monetary means.

(d) The establishment of a democratically controlled international bank or banks to make development capital available in all parts of the world without the predatory or imperialistic aftermath so characteristic of large-scale private or governmental loans.

(e) The creation of a world organization to study and make recommendations concerning problems arising from the pressure of population on the means of subsistence. We condemn any attempt upon the part of any nation to solve these problems by measures that discriminate against any people because of race or creed.

We believe that wealthy nations should not only refrain from action that is injurious to their neighbors, but should initiate action that is calculated to benefit their neighbors, as for example, the direction of foreign investments with a view to raising the standard of living of the underprivileged peoples of the earth. No attempt should be made, however, to *impose* an alien culture upon any people.

We recognize that at the close of the war vast populations will be in need of food, shelter, clothing and medical care, and that vast areas will call for physical and economic rehabilitation. We believe that the American people, acting through their government should assume a major share of the responsibility and task of meeting this need.

D. THE SOCIAL BASES OF A JUST AND DURABLE PEACE

1. PRINCIPLES

We are convinced that:

The present struggle of the nations is not just another war in the history of mankind. It is the upheaval of the old order and the birth of a new. The relationships of men will never again be the same, nor should they be the same, for they have not been founded on the eternal truths of God.

Therefore we affirm that whatever peace settlements are presented to the peoples of the world should express the following principles:

(a) Man is a child of God and all men are brothers one of another. The church in its long-established missionary work recognizes its responsibility to bring all men into full relationship as children of God.

(b) Mankind is one in nature and in the sight of God. No group of men is inherently superior or inferior to any other, and none is above any other beloved of God.

(c) The whole earth is given by God and to all men for their common dwelling place, and the resources of the earth should be used as His gifts to the whole human family.

(d) All men should be free to move over the surface of the earth under international agreement, in search of the fullest opportunity for personal development.

(e) Freedom of religious worship, of speech and assembly, of conscience, of the press, of the arts, and of scientific inquiry and teaching should be available to all men everywhere.

2. RELIEF AND REHABILITATION

The present mass suffering of the world requires action on the part of the Church in America far beyond anything yet undertaken. Six million young men in the prison camps of the world; scores of millions of refugees—homeless, helpless, starving; whole regions subjected to slow starvation as a result of the policies of states—these and kindred areas of desperate suffering inflicted upon masses of innocent victims challenge the Church to a demonstration of its basic doctrines of human solidarity and brotherhood in a potential family of God. They provide potent opportunities for creating even now, in the midst of war, responses of goodwill and solid grounds for enduring fellowship.

To rise adequately to a sense of its God-given mission, the Church must:[8]

(a) Make vivid in the consciousness of its entire membership the awful reality of this agony—mass in extent, but personal in intensity.

(b) Provide continual opportunity for material giving on the part of every member, to the point of genuine sacrifice, as a requisite of Christian living.

(c) Recognize cooperating agencies approved by the Committee on Foreign Relief Appeals in the Churches as existing channels for a world-wide ministry of compassion.

(1) War Prisoners' Aid of the World's Committee of the Y.M.C.A.

(2) Central Bureau for Relief of the Evangelical Churches of Europe

(3) Church Committee for China Relief

(4) American Bible Society

(5) American Friends Service Committee

(6) Y.W.C.A. World Emergency Fund

(7) American Committee for Christian Refugees

(8) International Missionary Council

(d) Recognize responsibilities for cooperation with government in areas of rehabilitation which concern the Church but transcend its normal functions. Such areas include the moving of populations, the restoration of the cultural life of peoples, the resettling of refugees, the return and rehabilitation of prisoners of war, and the reintegration into civilian life of men in the armed forces and the civilian public service camps.

The malnutrition and slow starvation of millions of innocent victims of war in conquered countries is heavy upon our Christian consciences. Although we have not reached agreement as to immediate remedial measures to be urged upon governments, we request the Federal Council of Churches to continue its exploration with the governmental authorities with a view to finding practicable means for alleviating these situations.

(e) Prepare now for the tasks of rehabilitation at the end of the war. Such preparation might well include the following:

(1) Relate present war relief giving to the continuing need which the end of the war will not terminate but only more clearly reveal.

(2) Develop courses and emphases in church schools and young people's programs regarding the problems of reconstruction which will prepare our youth for their responsibility. Specialized training should be provided for those people who may be called to serve in reconstruction abroad.

(3) Urge missionary societies to maintain intact, so far as is possible, their field organizations and personnel for large scale and effective reconstruction.

(4) Ask missionary agencies to emphasize a thorough grounding in the technique of relief and rehabilitation for all candidates in training for missionary service.

3. TOWARD A WORLD COMMUNITY

The nations of the world are passing through the crucible of fire and sword. National cultures which have enriched and given meaning to millions of people are in danger of extinction. No nation can escape this crisis. Those nations which, amid the purifying days of suffering, rediscover or preserve their souls from disintegration under the heel of the invader, from the despair of defeat, or from the pride and boastfulness of victory, will be ready to reconstruct their own national life and that of the world upon the ruins of today.

The sovereign power of the nation-state is being modified by economic, political, and military forces which demand a new social order. It will be impossible to return to such extreme practices of national sovereignty as have prevailed during recent decades. We believe that the State is a form of political organization which can and should be modified to meet the needs of the peoples of the world in the emerging situation. At the same time, however, we believe that different peoples have their distinctive places in the divine economy and that any world order must look toward unity in diversity and not to general internationalsim and cosmopolitanism. If we would avoid a superficial solution solution to the world's needs, we must come to recognize the distinction between those cultural values that center around the people, or folk, on the one hand, and the political state and government on the other.

We, the members of the American churches, and a part of the worldwide Christian community believe that the Christian churches in those countries where they are an inherent part of its nation's life, have a task to perform not only in helping to preserve and restore the national spiritual unity of their people but also in relating their people to the larger family of nations.

We believe that no matter what world scheme for political and economic organization may be devised to meet the demands of the modern world, at the heart of such a plan there must be developed an "international ethos" which not only springs from the loyalties of the people to their own nation, but includes their relationship to the welfare of mankind as a whole.

We believe that the Christian Church, because of its universal gospel, its positive world-view and its deep concern for both the individual and the nation stands on the threshold of its greatest opportunity to bear witness to the reality of the world Christian community and to manifest in sacrificial living a spirit through which a suffering broken humanity can be transformed into a world community.

We urge among some of the problems for further study by church people the following statements:[9]

(a) The highest ethical principles which in their operation have hitherto been limited to community and national relationships should now be so extended as to apply in the field of international relations.

(b) The problem confronting the world is how to substitute for the idea of self-preservation of the individual state a concept of world order which will recognize the primary importance of the society of nations, and the principle that the good of the whole takes precedence over the good of the part, since the highest and ultimate good of the part is itself so largely conditioned by the good of the whole.

(c) Whatever may be the political, economic or military form of world organization, for the preservation of a just and durable peace, the rights and duties of peoples to maintain their full cultural freedom must be preserved.

Many of the Christian Churches in the lands of the conquerors and the conquered have during these tragic days remained faithful to the Master. With the central message of the Cross, they have succored the souls of their peoples and have kept them from despair. They have pointed to the God-imposed duty of every people, no matter how small or how large, of whatever race or creed, to go the way of repentance, obedience and complete consecration to His will.

4. RACE RELATIONS AND CULTURES

Among the primary factors in the maintenance of a just and durable peace will be equitable treatment of all racial groups that make up the world's population. Therefore the securing of justice now for racial groups is essential if America is to make its full contribution in securing a just and durable peace.

We acknowledge with profound contrition the sin of racial discrimination in American life and or own share, though we are Christians, in the common guilt. So long as our attitudes and policies deny peoples of other lands the essential position of brothers in the common family of mankind we cannot safely be trusted with the making of a just and durable peace.

In our own country millions of people especially American Negroes are subjected to discrimination and unequal treatment in educational opportunities, in employment, wages and conditions of work, in access to professional and business opportunities, in housing, in transportation, in the administration of justice and even in the right to vote. We condemn all such inequalities and call upon our fellow-Christians and fellow-citizens, to initiate and support measures to establish equality of status and treatment of members of minority racial and cultural groups.

Some local current outrages that have national significance and therefore international effects in the attitudes of other peoples are the recent Missouri lynching and the rioting in Detroit over the Sojourner Truth Housing Project.[10]

We commend the President of the United States for his executive action directed toward the elimination of discrimination in industry and the public services against Negroes and persons of other racial and national origin. We urge that in further pursuit of this policy Negro Americans be given suitable recognition in the Administrative and Judicial Departments of the Government.

We call our fellow-Christians to witness that it is in the nature of the Church that Negro men and women and those belonging to other racial and national minorities should be welcomed into the membership, administrative personnel, and fellowship of our churches, local and national. We urge individual Christians and the corporate body of the Church of Christ to take up the cross of courageous service in action which deals with the problems of race and color in our land.

The modern confusion of culture and race has grown out of the belief that culture is a product of biological heredity and that Anglo-European culture is superior because it has sprung from superior human strains. We believe that all racial groups have contributed outstanding cultural gifts to civilization and the exchange of such gifts has enriched all mankind. A just and durable peace should provide and insist upon a framework that allows more opportunity for creative expression of all groups and for greater exchange of such cultural creations in the field of music, art, medicine, and literature. Assimilation of culture does not mean amalgamation of racial stocks.

We appeal to our fellow citizens to recognize now the crucial importance of justice in race relations in our own country as paving the way for the wider recognition of it which will be essential to world peace. Our attitudes toward other racial groups have all too frequently prevented the operation of justice in the past. We remind our fellow-Christians of the appeal of the Japanese for recognition of racial equality at the time of the Versailles Peace Conference. The refusal of that plea and the imposing of such restrictions on immigration as embodied in the Immigration Act of 1924 are recognized as factors contributing to the breakdown of peace. We would now commit ourselves to the task of protecting the rights of American born citizens of Oriental parentage, who are likely to suffer unnecessarily because of racial prejudice and discrimination of our attitudes towards Asiatics.

We endorse the proposal that the Federal Council of the Churches of Christ in America set up a commission for the study of racial and cultural problems in American life as a necessary measure to support our effort for a just and durable peace among the nations. It is imperative that we put our own house in order so that we can contribute effectively to a sound organization of international life. To that end we need continuous study, interpretation and a device to guide our churches in facing the opportunities and duties of racial and cultural adjustment in the present crisis, both at home and abroad.

Also, when further statements of peace aims are made, we ask our government to clarify in more detail its peace aims toward recognizing racial equality, opportunity and aid for migration, and protection of religious, political, racial, and cultural minorities.

IV. General Resolutions[11]

A. PRESENTATION OF MESSAGE TO GOVERNMENT OFFICIALS

WHEREAS the National Study Conference has noted with deep satisfaction the steps now being taken by the government of the United States to anticipate the needs and problems of the post-war period,

AND WHEREAS this Conference within its competence has been engaged in an effort to make articulate the concern of our churches for a peace that shall be just and durable,

BE IT RESOLVED that this Conference call upon the Commission to Study the Bases of a Just and Durable Peace to lay before the President of the United States and other government officials the findings of this Conference.

B. FOLLOW-UP OF THE CONFERENCE

WHEREAS the National Study Conference recognized the need for a continuous study of the problems with which it has here been concerned, and that this Conference represents the beginning stage in an educational process which must continue through and following the war,

BE IT RESOLVED that the findings of this Conference be transmitted to the several communions, to the city and state councils of churches, to the churches abroad, to the leadership of summer conferences, to secular organizations engaged in similar studies and to the agencies cooperating on the Federal Council's Commission,

BE IT FURTHER RESOLVED that the Conference calls upon the several communions either on their own initiative or in cooperation with the Commission to plan for a series of study conferences in various parts of the country and that they make possible the widest distribution of the reports of this Conference to their own leaders, lay and clerical.

BE IT FURTHER RESOLVED that in view of the imperative need for expanding the work of the Commission the respective communions be urged to give the fullest collaboration and support to the work of the Commission and that each communion be urged to assign for full time service in this work one or more of the ablest leaders who would maintain cooperative relations with the Commission.

C. ECONOMIC COLLABORATION

We note such acts of our government as that reported by Under-Secretary of State Welles at Rio de Janiero on January 15th, 1942, that "It is the policy of the United States to aid in maintaining the economic stability of the other American Republics by recognizing and providing for their essential civilian needs on the basis of equal and proportionate consideration with our own"; also the provisions of article 7 or the Anglo-American Pact of February 26th, 1942, calling the post-war "participation, by all countries of like mind, directed to the expansion, by appropriate international and domestic measures, of production, employment and the exchange and consumption of goods which are the material foundations of the liberty and welfare of all peoples; to the elimination of all forms of discriminatory treatment in international commerce and to the reduction of tariffs and other trade barriers." We instruct the officers of this Conference to communicate to our government our deep satisfaction with such acts. The spirit evidenced thereby is, in our judgment, that which must come to permeate the life of nations if they are to achieve a just and durable peace.

---

[1]The Message was adopted by the Conference. In submitting it to the churches, the officers of the Federal Council noted that the conference, in adopting its Message, spoke only for itself, and assumes full responsibility for the publication of its findings.

[2]This Preamble, while not embodied in the formal findings of the conference, originated in the Section on the Relation of the Church to a Just and Durable Peace and was referred to the Editorial Committee for inclusion in the Message.

[3]In the Fall of 1941 the Commission to Study the Bases of a Just and Durable Peace formulated a tentative draft of a Statement of Guiding Principles. This draft was then revised and submitted to the entire membership of the Commission for final action. The Commission met in Delaware, Ohio, on the evening prior to the convening of the Ohio Wesleyan Conference at which time the Statement of Guiding Principles was put into final form.

The conference received and gave its "general endorsement" to this Statement of Guiding Principles in the following action:

"This Conference, as a representative group of Christian Churches, gives its general endorsement to the Statement of Guiding Principles prepared by the Commission to Study the Bases of a Just and Durable Peace. It accepts the first nine Principles as a formulation of fundamentals of Christian Ethics, and it believes that acceptance of these fundamentals by all peoples and governments is essential to the eventual establishment of a just and durable peace. It recognizes the special responsibilities of the United States as formulated in Principle 10. It emphasizes the unique responsibilities and opportunities of the Christian Church in the present crisis as these are formulated in Principles 11-13.

'The Conference recommends that this Statement of Principles be used as effectively as possible by the Commission and the Federal Council of Churches.

(a) To crystalize public opinion on these basic issues. (The preparation and very wide distribution of a brief summary of these Principles, so simple as to be within the grasp of every American citizen, would greatly promote such crystalization of public opinion.)

(b) To call the attention of specialists in the political, economic and social areas, in their formulation of more concrete proposals, to the preeminent importance of these central spiritual and Christian insights.

(c) To provide our government and other governments with a formulation of the spiritual bases for eventual armistice and peace proposals, and

(d) To provide Christians with criteria for appraising specific armistice and peace terms when these come to be formulated."

[4][Subsequently the thirteen Guiding Principles were reduced to twelve. Point 12 above became point 11. Point 11 became point 12. The major part of point 13 was deleted, except for the concluding phrases which were added to the new point 12 as a conclusion—"upheld by faith that the kingdoms of this world will become the kingdom of Christ and that He will reign forever and ever."]

[5]In acting upon the section reports the Conference proceeded under the following resolution: "That the section reports submitted to this conference be received and approved as to substance, with the understanding that after careful editing and coordination they be commended to our respective constituencies for their favorable consideration and action." But see notes 6 through 10 below.

[6]In conjunction with the foregoing, the conference *approved* the following recommendations and convictions. Insofar as they involve technical applications, they call for special study since, as above stated, the duty of the Church is not to prescribe details. With respect to the recommendations based on Paragraph 3, there was a vote on whether they should be *approved* by the conference or *referred* for further study. *Approval* was voted by a substantial majority. (Italics are the editor's.)

[7]See footnote #6, above.

[8]The following were "adopted" by the conference as a whole.

[9]The statements were also "adopted" by the conference as a whole.

[10]The following statements were also "adopted" by the conference as a whole.

[11]These resolutions represent actions on the conference as a whole.

Chapter III

TOWARD THE DAWNING:

"The Churches and World Order"
Cleveland, 1945

INTRODUCTION

In the months that followed the Delaware Conference the nation and her allies suffered additional military reverses, but eventually the tide turned in their favor. In June, 1944, the Normandy landings were accomplished and Rome was taken. By September the Allied victory in France and Belgium was almost complete.

Anticipating the successful conclusion of the war, representatives of the United States, the Soviet Union, Great Britain and China met in the late summer of 1944 at Dumbarton Oaks in Washington, D.C. where they drew up a proposed plan of world organization to maintain international peace and security. At Yalta the following February the leaders of the first three of these nations called a conference of the United Nations to be held at San Francisco in April, 1945, for the purpose of establishing a permanent world organization.

Meanwhile the churches associated with the Federal Council had been continuing their efforts to guide the thinking of the churches in relation to the war and to prepare them for a constructive role in shaping the post-war world. In December, 1942, the Federal Council commissioned twenty-six of the nation's foremost Christian scholars to study and report on "The Relation of the Church to the War in the Light of the Christian Faith." This commission, under the chairmanship of Robert L Calhoun, Professor, Yale University Divinity School, made its report two years later. This appears as Appendix B to this volume.[1]

During this same period the Commission on a Just and Durable Peace—its name shortened by the omission of the words "to Study the Bases of"—continued its studies and educational activities. In March, 1943, it issued a "Statement of Political Propositions," popularly referred to as "The Six Pillars of Peace."[2] This was an attempt to "spell out," in terms of broad political conclusions, the implications of the "Guiding Principles" approved at Delaware.

In light of the Dumbarton Oaks Proposals and the need for the United States to make up its mind on the matter of world organization—and remembering the nation's failure to support the League of Nations after the first World War—the Commission issued a call to another national study conference to be held at Cleveland, Ohio, January 16-19, 1945. The purpose of the conference was threefold: to study the program of the churches for world order; to study the current international situation in the light of the

Guiding Principles adopted at Delaware and the Six Pillars of Peace; and to adopt such findings and make such recommendations to the churches and the government as might be deemed appropriate.

Two commissions were set up to make preparatory studies for the use of the delegates. The first, under the chairmanship of Walter M. Horton, Professor, Oberlin Graduate School of Theology, prepared a memorandum on "The Program of the Churches for World Order." The second, under the chairmanship of William E. Hocking, Professor, Harvard University, prepared a memorandum on "The Churches and the Current International Situation." A third document, prepared under the direction of both commissions, was entitled, "What Shall the Churches Now Do?"

As delegates converged upon Cleveland in mid-January, 1945, to take up their work, newspaper headlines daily shouted new allied victories: U.S. advances in the Philippines, the sinking by American planes of large numbers of Japanese ships off Indo-China, the rout of German forces from the Bulge, and signal successes of the Soviet offensive in Poland.

Thirty-four denominations were included in the membership of the conference. This was the largest number at any national study conference to that date. Also represented among the 481 delegates were 18 allied religious bodies and 70 city and state councils of churches. Laypersons played a notable role in this conference. Among the participants were members of congress, state department personnel, federal and state court judges, state legislators, college presidents and professors, lawyers, journalists, business men, labor leaders, and workers in the field of social welfare.

The conference opened and closed with services of worship in the Old Stone Church. The address at the opening service was given by John Foster Dulles[3] and that at the closing service by Bishop G. Bromley Oxnam. The conference was noteworthy for the close cooperation of Mr. Dulles and Bishop Oxnam—the former as conference chairman and the latter as chairman of the Message Committee.

For purposes of study and discussion the delegates were divided into three equal groups. Instead of each being responsible for a particular phase of the study, as had been the case in earlier conferences, each group discussed each of the three memoranda drawn up by the preparatory commissions. Thus the attempt was made to confront all participants with all aspects of the problem and to give each a better opportunity to express himself or herself on the whole range of subjects before the conference.

Each group had its own findings committee whose officers were in turn members of the Message Committee. Each section had a different chairman to preside over discussion of each of the three topics before it. Chairs of Group I were Frederick Reissig, Secretary of the Washington, D.C. Federation of Churches; William Scarlett, Bishop of the Episcopal Church; and Miss Georgia Harkness, Professor, Garrett Biblical Seminary. Chairmen of Group II were G. Bromley Oxnam, Bishop of the Methodist Church; E. E. Aubrey, President, Crozier Theological Seminary; and Eugene Barnett,

General Secretary of the National Council of Y.M.C.A. Chairs of Group III were Mrs. Harper Sibley, Rochester, New York; John R. Cunningham, President, Davidson College; and Wilbur LaRoe, Jr., lawyer, Washington, D.C.

Chairman of the Message Committee was Bishop Oxnam; the secretary was O. Frederick Nolde, Dean of the Graduate School, Lutheran Theological Seminary, Philadelphia. This committee, which included members of the three discussion groups, sought to bring together in one document the conclusions of the conference in the three areas surveyed by the preparatory papers. The draft message, presented to the plenary session, was revised in light of discussion there.

Part I of the message deals in general terms with the relation between "Christian Faith and World Order." This comprehensive statement, theologically based, makes an appropriate introduction to later documents which deal with more concrete issues.

Part II deals with "Christian Standards and Current International Developments." The heart of this section is the recommendation "that the churches support the Dumbarton Oaks Proposals as an important step in the direction of world cooperation." Coupled with this, however, are nine suggestions for the improvement of the Proposals, and further important statements on political and economic collaboration for peace, human rights, dependent peoples, and the peace settlements in Europe and Asia.

Part III deals with concrete "Recommendations for Action." Appended to the message are a brief "Conclusion" and "A Message to Christians of All Lands."

The conference message was widely reported both in the daily press and in secular and religious periodicals. Most attention, naturally, went to the approval of the Dumbarton Oaks Proposals and the recommendations for their strengthening and improvement. *Time* magazine, in its extensive coverage of the conference and message, referred to the hope of the Commission on a Just and Durable Peace that the conference would set forth "a vigorous point of view on international affairs which would be compatible both with the highest Christian ethics and with the ugly facts of human life in a sinful world."[4] Judging from the tone of its report, one gathers that the editors of *Time* felt that the conference had done just that.

The *Christian Century* commented editorially on the representative character of the gathering and "the spirit in which the delegates came together. There was no pressure to desert or muffle deeply held convictions, but there was a pervasive intent to pursue the conference's purpose until a common program had been framed."[5] In the judgment of the *Christian Century* the three most important actions were those dealing with the Dumbarton Oaks Proposals, those in reference to dependent peoples, and those relating to the post-war treatment of Germany. *Christianity and Crisis* made no editorial comment, but it reprinted Mr. Dulles' address in full (except for the opening paragraphs) and gave a detailed summary of the conference message in its news columns.

A significant footnote to this Cleveland Conference is the testimony of many to the influence it had both in marshalling popular support for United States adherence to the United Nations Organization, and the influence many of the suggested amendments had upon developments at San Francisco the following June.

Some months later Henry R. Luce, editor of *Time* and *Life*, speaking of the improvements of the San Francisco charter over the Dumbarton Oaks Proposals, declared: "In my observation, the greatest single influence at work in bringing about this salutary transformation was the Federal Council of Churches' Commission on a Just and Durable Peace."[7]

John Foster Dulles resigned as chairman of the Commission on a Just and Durable Peace to accept appointment as a member of the United States Delegation to the San Francisco Conference on World Organization at which the United Nations was formally established. Ten years later the San Francisco Council of Churches held a "Festival of Faith" in celebration of the founding of the United Nations. Speaking on this occasion, John Foster Dulles paid tribute to the work of "the religious people" who "organized and campaigned widely to develop a public opinion favorable to world organization." To this, he said, "the political leaders quickly responded on a bipartisan basis." Out of his own first-hand experience and knowledge, Mr. Dulles declared further:

> Our religious people also exerted a profound influence upon the form and character which the world organization would take. As originally projected at Dumbarton Oaks, the organization was primarily a political device whereby the so-called great powers were to rule the world....
>
> It was the religious people who took the lead in seeking that the organization should be dedicated not merely to a peaceful but to a just order. It was they who sought that reliance should be placed upon moral forces which could be reflected in the General Assembly, the Social and Economic Council, and the Trusteeship Council, rather than upon the power of a few militarily strong nations operating in the Security Council without commitment to any standards of law and justice.
>
> The great debates of the San Francisco Conference of 1945 centered on these issues.[6]

Members of the Cleveland Conference, and of the Christian Churches in America, could take some satisfaction that their studies, moral judgments, and exhortations were of practical significance in helping to shape the structure of the United Nations. In addition, they helped to create a climate of opinion which undoubtedly helped temper the peace that was made with our war-time enemies following their surrender.

Another significant outcome of the Cleveland Conference—and those which had gone before—was the launching of a similar and parallel series on the church and economic life. Inasmuch as "a just and durable peace is conditioned by the ability of our own nation to achieve economic stability and interracial justice in its domestic affairs," the conference recommended that the Federal Council initiate conferences, "similar to this Conference on a Just and Durable Peace," in these two areas.[8] The first national study conference on "The Church and Economic Life" was held in Pittsburgh, February 18-20, 1947. Other conferences in this series was held at Detroit in February, 1950, at Buffalo in February, 1952, and at Pittsburgh in April, 1956 and again in November, 1962.

---

[1]See below, pp. 255 ff.

[2]See below, p. 96, footnote #2.

[3]*Christianity and Crisis*, IV, No. 24, (Jan. 22, 1945), 2-6.

[4]XLV (Jan. 29, 1945), 22-23.

[5]LXII, (Jan. 31,1945), 136-137.

[6]John Foster Dulles, "The Moral Foundations of the United Nations," U.S. Department of State, Public Services Division, released June 19, 1955.

[7]Address at Duke University, Feb. 12, 1946, cited in John C. Bennett, *Christian Ethics and Social Policy*, (New York: Scribner, 1946), p. 114.

[8]See below, p. 95.

A MESSAGE TO THE CHURCHES FROM THE NATIONAL STUDY CONFERENCE ON THE CHURCHES AND A JUST AND DURABLE PEACE

Cleveland, Ohio   January 16–19, 1945

I. Christian Faith and World Order

> The Christian Faith; The Churches' Mission; Principle and Action; American Attitudes and World Peace; Domestic Order and World Order.

II. Christian Standards and Current International Developments

> The Dumbarton Oaks Proposals; Political Conduct Required to Promote Further Collaboration; Economic Cooperation; Human Rights; The Peace Settlement in Europe; The Peace Settlement in Asia; Dependent Peoples.

III. Recommendations for Action

> The Churches and Federal Unity; Youth and the World Order; Study and Action for American Participation in International Cooperation; Relief and Reconstruction; Race Relations; Proposal for Other Study Conferences; Recommendations with Regard to Specific Immediate Action.

IV. Conclusion

THE CHURCHES AND WORLD ORDER[1]

I. Christian Faith and World Order

1. THE CHRISTIAN FAITH

We are living in a uniquely dangerous and promising time. It is dangerous because we are faced with widespread evidence of religious and moral disintegration as well as with effects of war in increasing suspicion, fear and hatred. It is promising because a new spiritual vitality is manifesting itself under the Providence of God and witnessing to that quality of the Christian faith which demonstrates its strength in adversity. In our effort to make decisions and to take action which shall help to guide the world from anarchy and chaos forward to a just and creative peace, we are called to reaffirm our faith.

It is the Christian faith that God's righteous rule is over all men and nations; that in Christ He confronts us all alike in judgment and mercy; that men, though sinful, are made in His image and are not only the concern of His saving work but His agents as well, each of value in His sight without distinction of class, race or condition; that the Church, the body of Christ and the fellowship of Christ's followers, is the creation of His spirit, and the steward of His purpose; that His Kingdom on earth is an unconquerable Kingdom of justice and mercy and truth in which it is our responsibility to bring human laws and human institutions into increasing accord with His holy will.

In this Christian faith, the purposes which we seek to realize are fashioned. As we affirm the worth of man in God's sight, so we must act by the Christian principle of reverence for human personality. God sees His children united in one family whose individual and corporate life is the goal of redemption: we must be joined in the common effort to make effective in individual relations and in corporate acts, the Christian principles which we affirm. God's way is the way of justice, love and mercy; justice, love and mercy must rule our life with our fellows. While compulsion and control are needed for the restraint of evil in a world of imperfection, the ultimate victory over evil must be by way of redemptive good will, by which alone, can good be created. God's way with men is the way of freedom and responsibility; man's true life as a man is achieved only when that way is freely chosen and freely wrought out. As we need humility and penitence in standing before God, so do we need humility and penitence in our dealings with men. Whenever human practice goes counter to these principles which root in our faith, the Christian must raise his voice in protest.

It is in this Christian faith that our confidence is grounded. For our confidence is in God, the establisher of the order within which men and nations work, and in the forces of the spirit which God employs. We believe in the might of truth as against falsehood and deceit and in the power of right to command the conscience and to overcome oppression and wrong. We believe in the power of good will as greater than selfishness and force; in the value of mutual trust as against distrust and suspicion; and in the might of faith as greater than cynicism, doubt and despair. God's grace, made manifest in Christ, rescues men from despair, has power to remake them when they turn to Him for healing and forgiveness, and redeems all their life. We see this power even now at work in the world in lives made new, in sins forgiven and conquered, in hopes rekindled.

We rejoice in the Church of Christ as a world fellowship which today unites men in faith and love transcending nation, race and class. We rejoice that a growing number of men of good will outside the Church, in recognition of the moral law, seek with us the creation of "one world" of justice and security for all men. Let the Church purge itself of inner division, unite with all who work for these high ends, and so live out its principles of justice and love in the face of all dictates of selfishness and counsels of expediency as to create new faith, new conscience and new hope.

2. THE CHURCH'S MISSION

Out of the continuous creative vitality of the Christian faith has grown the Church of which we are a part. The Church as bearer and sharer of the revelation of God in Christ, stands under a divine compulsion to serve the world, with equal responsibility for all people. The misery, want and sin of the world today bring to us a new sense of the urgency of the commission "Go ye into all the world."

"Home Missions" and "Foreign Missions" are aspects of the one world mission to which the Church is called. Both are significant in the Church's contribution to world order. The most effective assurance for justice in an abiding world order is in the expansion of allegiance by men and nations to the Christian faith. This is as greatly needed within America as elsewhere. The reconstruction of devastated lands, the rebirth of hope and the expression of that hope are central in the Church's mission.

The world mission of the Church has helped to create among our people concern about international affairs and has opened channels for the efforts of the churches toward a just and durable peace. Through missionary agencies relief is and can be administered, reconstruction can be furthered in many areas, and the long range objectives of world order promoted. The immediate and practical necessities of mission work as well as the impulse to unite in Christ have promoted widespread interdenominational coopera-tion. This, in turn, has given impetus to that ecumenical movement which now brings promise that the energies of the churches will be utilized to face their overwhelming opportunities. This cooperation must be further developed. What is called for is a united Protestant missionary movement. The churches are therefore urged immediately to strengthen and unify their missionary enterprise both at home and abroad so that their unique contribution to world order may be equal to these opportunities.

3. PRINCIPLE AND ACTION

Christians must act in situations as they exist and must decide what God's will demands of them there. At all times they must keep the ultimate goals clearly in view but they have equal responsibility to mark out attainable steps toward those goals, and support them. An idealism which does not accept the discipline of the achievable may lose its power for good and ultimately lend aid to forces with whose purpose it can not agree.

If we accept, provisionally, situations which fall short of our ultimate objective, we cannot be morally bound to sustain and perpetuate them. That would be stultifying. It is the possibility of change which is the bridge from the immediate situation to the Christian ideal. That possibility is an imperative for Christians, who must constantly maintain tension with any secular order.

The churches through their leaders have the task of assisting people in situations of this kind. Specifically, in the realm of world order, the churches must declare their understanding of the will of God for life among the peoples of the world. They must do this while proposals are being framed. They must continue to do it after governments have made their decisions. When a concrete proposal for world organization is presented, Christian leaders must help the people to decide whether it marks a presently obtainable step in the right direction and, if so, urge them to give it their support.

4. AMERICAN ATTITUDES AND WORLD PEACE

Whether America will be a help or a hindrance in building a peaceable world depends upon the attitudes of individuals and groups in our nation. We call attention to the dangers which lurk in complacency towards existing injustices; the frequent contradictions we tolerate between our ultimate beliefs and our conscious aims; the false sense of national security which —in spite of the lessons of two tragic wars—holds that the United States can live apart from the rest of the world and its problems; intolerance and discrimination; selfishness which refuses to recognize that we are members one of another and is unwilling to run risks for the sake of the world community; blind devotion to national sovereignty; the cynicism which believes there always must be wars and puts its reliance upon force alone; and the spirit of hatred and vengeance toward other peoples. It is our concern that such attitudes should not prevail, but rather that in us and in our fellow citizens those attitudes should be developed which support the growth of world community.

5. DOMESTIC ORDER AND WORLD ORDER

Over a century and a half ago it was given to the American people to determine by struggle and experiment whether government by the people could be established and maintained on the earth. Upon the success of this adventure rested a great hope of mankind. In the intervening years the growth of the United States as a home for human freedom has been a notable fact and influence. It must now be demonstrated that human freedom is compatible with economic security. A new challenge is offered to the people of America to establish along with political democracy an opportunity through productive employment to earn an income sufficient for the basic needs of food, clothing, shelter, health, recreation and cultural pursuits, and assurance to every individual of whatever race of an equal and unsegregated opportunity for worship, protection in time of unemployment, illness or need, and full political and civil rights.

The economic system which proved adequate in an earlier period has in our day, revealed grave defects and inadequacies under the strain of modern industrial conditions. All elements in the economic system—consumer, employee, management, capital, and government—should move from the strife and restrictions of our present situation to a full and free cooperation with the objective of greatly increased production and distribution. We recognize the need of experimentation with various forms of ownership and control, private, cooperative and public.

A challenging effort in the United States in the solution of our domestic economic problem will be followed by favorable repercussions in the economic and spiritual life of the world, thus contributing to the establishment of a just and durable peace.

The right of private property is not an absolute right but a right qualified by the public interest. Likewise freedom of enterprise does not imply absolute freedom but operation of enterprise consonant with the interest of the public and the welfare of the nation. In the use of property and in the operation of enterprise, therefore, the welfare of society should be given primary consideration; and it is the duty of the state to prescribe such regulation of industry and of the conditions under which it is carried on as will result in wholesome conditions of employment and fair treatment to those who are engaged in it and to the public at large.

The Church must therefore condemn any failure of our economic system to meet the basic needs which have been indicated. We must ask our people to recognize that in order to supply these needs for all, many changes may be necessary in our economic practices. These changes will probably lie in the direction of a larger measure of social planning and control than characterized our pre-war system. They should be brought about by democratic processes and should be consistent with Christian principles with respect to the worth of personality and the value of freedom. We should not allow our devotion to any single system or method to deny to anyone the basic requirements for "the good life." Nor should we allow our preference for our economic or political system to prevent us from collaborating, for the achievement of world order and world peace, with peoples who have a different system.

In order to maintain our democracy at a high level it must continually be adjusted to meet the necessities of history and the demands of justice. Only if our domestic order is born again with fresh vision and determination to meet the needs of men can America fulfill her new mission and bring hope and encouragement to a broken world.

II. Christian Standards and Current International Developments

The decisions and actions of governments in the present international situation will have direct bearing upon the extent to which nations will collaborate in the postwar period. Tentative proposals for an international organization were agreed upon at Dumbarton Oaks by delegations of the United Kingdom, the Soviet Union, China and the United States. They have been offered to the public for discussion.

In the light of the Guiding Principles and the Six Pillars of Peace,[2] we offer our appraisal of the Dumbarton Oaks Proposals and we call attention to certain related matters which we believe must be considered in connection with any international organization for world order and security.

1. THE DUMBARTON OAKS PROPOSALS

We commend these Proposals to the consideration of the churches.

The Proposals are the only plan which governments have thus far evolved and therefore are the only available index to the extent of agreement which is now possible.

They set forth certain purposes and principles essential to world order and peace.

They provide for continuing collaboration of the United Nations, and in due course of other nations.

They provide through an Assembly for the periodic consultation of all member nations and for promoting cooperation in the interest of the general welfare.

They provide an Economic and Social Council for facilitating solutions of international economic, social and humanitarian problems and for coordinating international policies and agencies in this field.

They provide, through a Security Council, for continuing consultation of representatives of the greater powers and of selected lesser powers with a view to a peaceful settlement of disputes and the restraint of aggression.

The Proposals now stand at a formative stage and the way has been opened for recommendations for improvement which will make them more acceptable to the Christian conscience.

Accordingly, we recommend that the churches support the Dumbarton Oaks Proposals as an important step in the direction of world cooperation but because we do not approve of them in their entirety as they now stand, we urge the following measures for their improvement:

(1) *Preamble::* A Preamble should affirm those present and long range purposes of justice and human welfare which are set forth in the Atlantic Charter and which reflect the aspirations of peoples everywhere.

(2) *Development of International Law:* The Charter of the Organization should clearly anticipate its operation under international law and should provide for the development and codification of international law, to the end that there shall be a progressive subordination of force to law.

(3) *Voting Power:* A nation, while having the right to discuss its own case, should not be permitted to vote when its case is being judged in accordance with predetermined international law.

(4) *Colonial and Dependent Areas:* A special Commission should be established wherein the progress of colonial and dependent peoples to autonomy, and the interim problems related thereto, will become an international responsibility.

(5) *Human Rights and Fundamental Freedoms:* A special Commission on Human Rights and Fundamental Freedoms should be established.

(6)*Eventual Universal Membership:* The Charter should specify that all nations willing to accept the obligations of membership shall thereupon be made members of the Organization.

(7) *Limitations of Armaments:* More specific provision should be made for promptly initiating the limitation and reduction of national armaments.

(8) *Smaller Nations:* There should be provisions designed more clearly to protect and defend the smaller nations from possible subjection to the arbitrary power of the great.

(9) *Amendment*: In order to permit such changes in the Charter of the Organization as may from time to time become necessary, the provision for amendments should be liberalized so as not to require concurrence by all the permanent members of the Security Council.

2. POLITICAL CONDUCT REQUIRED TO PROMOTE FURTHER COLLABORATION

There are four principles of conduct which are needed to bring collaboration out of the realm of theory and into that of reality.

(1) We believe our government should adopt and publicly proclaim its long range goals. These should stem from our Christian tradition and be such as to inspire and unify us. Without such defined goals we will lack enthusiasm and sense of direction; we will not be able to measure our progress.

(2) We believe our government should not merely talk about its ideals. It must get down into the arena and fearlessly and skillfully battle for them. It must do so, not merely sporadically, but steadily. It must do so even under conditions such that partial and temporary defeat is inevitable.

(3) We believe our government must, however, battle for its ideals under conditions such that no particular setback need be accepted as definitive. It must be made clear that collaboration implies not merely a spirit of compromise but equally a right, on the part of every nation, to persist in efforts to realize its ideals.

(4) We believe our electorate, demanding the foregoing of its government, must judge its government accordingly. It should not judge it merely by the immediate results attained. It must rather judge it by its announced long term objectives, by whether it works competently to achieve them and by whether it brings into actual functioning procedures of peaceful change so that the world may evolve away from present harsh necessities. If our government will meet these tests, the electorate should applaud such conduct irrespective of dissatisfaction with immediate results.

3. ECONOMIC COOPERATION

The economic aspect of human life concerns the Church in two ways: through the widespread fact of poverty and through those maladjustments which, never the sole causes of war, may predispose populations to war.

Poverty concerns the Christian conscience not alone because men hunger but also because their spirits tend to be stunted by it and their freedom limited. Low standards of living over large areas diminish the possibilities of trade and also of cultural intercourse. Morality and self-interest combine to show that in a world tending toward unity by communication, the standard of living of men anywhere is a concern of men everywhere.

Poverty is not to be dealt with primarily by charity but by aiding undernourished populations to use their own resources, to develop agricultural techniques and industries suitable to their region, and to participate in world trade.

In order to prevent recurrent depression the goal of full employment of labor and of economic resources on a world scale should be continuously pursued.

Because of the growing interdependence of peoples, the development of backward regions has become a common task of mankind, in which regard for one's neighbor joins a long range self-interest. The immensity of the task, which is equally economic and educational, requires cooperative investment and effort on a world scale. Here some form of world organization, such as the Economic and Social Council proposed at Dumbarton Oaks, must be sought as a supplement to private undertaking. The International Labor Organization and the organized labor movement are also to be recognized as having an important role in raising the standards of living of the peoples of the world.

Economically advanced nations constitute among themselves a community in which no one can prosper through the disadvantage of others. Their policies can no longer intelligently follow the line of economic nationalism. Barriers to world trade, whether in the nature of tariffs or of cartels, have become doubtful props of national welfare; and all of those acts, economic and political, in which one people affects the fortunes of another become subject both to the judgment of self-interest and of morality. A world point of view must be developed in economics, and the appropriate institutions developed. In such institutions our own nation must actively participate both for its own welfare and for the common good.

Such intelligent supervision of world agriculture, resources, markets, currencies, and communications, and of world trade, may not imply in each case an authoritative regulating agency; but it does require an active self-regulation with a sense of responsibility and of stewardship for the just and constructive use of economic power.

The right of property is based, not upon man's animal need, but upon his personal nature as man. Private property is an essential aid to the maturing of human personality. It has been customary to set communism and capitalism over against each other on this point, the one denying private property, the other holding private property an absolute claim over against the state. Neither of these positions is now held in this extreme form; in both types of economy property is recognized as important for human character and is therefore the proper subject of public interest; so all economies today are mixed economies, showing a degree of private and a degree of common property. Neither is a fixed system, and to some extent in practice they tend to converge. To the extent that the sacredness of the human person, his liberty and responsibility to God, is acknowledged by both systems their cooperation in building a peaceable international order is facilitated. But in any case they can and must cooperate.

4. HUMAN RIGHTS

We have recommended that, in connection with the World Organization proposed at Dumbarton Oaks, there be established a special Commission on Human Rights and Fundamental Freedoms. We believe that religious liberty is basic to all human rights and that it should be accompanied by equal and unsegregated opportunity for all races. The Commission we have recommended should seek an international agreement on the rights and freedoms to be secured to all people; it should further formulate the procedures for their realization by action of the World Organization and of the separate states. This is in harmony with our sixth pillar of peace which declares, "that the peace must establish in principle, and seek to achieve in practice, the right of individuals everywhere to religious and intellectual liberty." It also follows a purpose set forth in the Dumbarton Oaks Proposals, "to promote respect for human rights and fundamental freedoms."

5. THE PEACE SETTLEMENT IN EUROPE WITH SPECIAL REFERENCE TO GERMANY

In respect to the peace settlement in Europe, we share the following convictions:

The settlement following the war should be inspired by the desire to secure the maximum of collaboration among the peoples of Europe and encourage the economic development of Europe as a whole including Germany. The unilateral determination of boundaries would impair such collaboration. The settlement should insure to the smaller and weaker nations the fullest measure of autonomy consistent with European unity and world organization for peace.

The settlement should make possible the reconciliation of victors and vanquished. That implies that it should remove the power as well as the will of aggressive elements within Germany to make war. However, the necessary discipline of Germany because of the crimes committed in her name should not be vindictive. The partition of Germany into separate states should not be imposed upon the German people. The treatment of Germany should be committed to liberal civil policies and to international cooperation.

Among the constructive forces upon which a new Germany and a new European concord can be based, the churches are of primary importance. As they have been centers of resistance to tyranny and injustice within Germany and within the occupied countries so they may become a medium through which reconciliation may be accomplished, and through which the process of the re-education and reconstruction of Germany may be carried out in the only way that gives any promise of success—voluntarily from within. The World Council of Churches will greatly aid in the process of reconciliation and reconstruction as the churches of the defeated, the liberated and the victorious nations are brought together into conference and collaboration.

6. THE PEACE SETTLEMENT IN ASIA WITH SPECIAL REFERENCE TO JAPAN

We are convinced that a just and durable peace in the Ear East is possible only in the framework of world organization, supplemented by regional cooperation for security and welfare.

China desperately requires unrestrained opportunity for internal development. It is of urgent importance that China's voice in international affairs be given special heed, in order to cement new relationships between oriental and western peoples.

As in the case of Germany, so with Japan, the power and will to make war must be removed. However, Japan's basic economic problems, aggravated by the war and by the expected loss of her colonial possessions must be met by "access, on equal terms, to the trade and raw materials of the world" as pledged by the Atlantic Charter "to all States, great or small, victor or vanquished." Treatment of Japan by the United Nations should be favorable to constructive forces within Japanese society, and should aim to bring Japan at an early date into normal relations with the world community.

We can enter into right relations with the vast and significant populations of China, Japan and Southeast Asia, none of them white, only upon the basis of the equality of races in justice and law. Indeed, a Christian outlook upon the Far East discerns that a world order is impossible if color discrimination is maintained. The churches recognize a special responsibility for reconciliation in such ways as may be possible after the war,

ADDENDUM TO 5 AND 6. THE PEACE SETTLEMENT WITH SPECIAL REFERENCE TO GERMANY AND JAPAN

We urge that the time is at hand when the governments of the allied nations should make a more explicit statement as to the status of both Germany and Japan following the war. We believe such a statement is needed in order to satisfy Christian concern and to prevent needless sacrifice of life upon the battlefield.

7. DEPENDENT PEOPLES

Long and intimate relationships with the dependent peoples of Africa, Southeast Asia, and other parts of the world, place on the Christian churches a responsibility to champion their right to freedom and to develop their capacity for self-government.

We therefore call upon our government and others:

(1) to proclaim self-government as the goal for all dependent peoples;

(2) where dependent peoples are ready for self-government, to give it now;

(3) otherwise, to initiate progressive steps suitable for each area for achieving that goal; and

(4) in the interim to provide that all such areas shall be administered under the supervision of world organization.

We cannot in good conscience be a party to the dismantling of Japanese colonial possessions without at the same time insisting that the imperialism of the white man shall be brought to the speediest possible end. We cannot have a sound or stable world community so long as there is enforced submission of one people to the will of another whether in Korea, in India, in the Congo, in Puerto Rico or anywhere else.

III. Recommendations for Action

The task now before us is to channel the spiritual power generated in this Conference into deeds. Solemn pronouncements are not enough. Upon the minds and consciences of our people must be laid the duty and opportunity of using the world-wide resources of the Church to bring about a world organized for justice and peace.

1. THE CHURCHES AND FEDERAL UNITY

The present structure of denominational Protestantism is not adequate to deal with the issues of our time. The problems of war, of labor, of the chaplaincy or the returning veteran, of the world-wide mission of the Church, of our relations with the Christian churches of Europe and Asia and with other faiths, are all too vast and difficult for solution by our separate denominational units. While we are asking for cooperation and unity in the political and economic field, Protestants themselves must take seriously to heart the duty of achieving a far higher degree of unity. We have already come far on the road of cooperation. But we must achieve a more vital and visible federal unity than we now have—a unity that will preserve the freedom of various denominational groups, and at the same time release the undeveloped and uncoordinated resources of Protestantism and focus them on the solution of these pressing problems. We, therefore, urge the denominations to consider earnestly the possibilities in ways not now envisaged of realizing more fully the ecumenical fellowship by implementing the principles of federal unity on local, state and national levels.

2. YOUTH AND THE WORLD ORDER

If our purposes are to be achieved the new leadership of the churches must be world-minded and trained in the techniques of building a Christian world community. In these efforts, youth itself must lead and the youth agencies be strengthened to provide more challenging programs resulting in life dedicated to Christ. Increased representation of youth in all the agencies of the churches should be speedily provided.

The churches are urged, in their total educational process, but especially through the church-related colleges, the student Christian movements and the theological seminaries to expand and adjust their programs in order to enlist and train world-minding churchmen who will take their place in the ecumenical movement.

3. CHILDREN AND WORLD PEACE

Parents and teachers in the home and in the churches are called upon to teach children the conditions of world peace. Particularly, they should be helped to develop constructive attitudes, devoid of hate toward other peoples. Christian education for children must include study dealing with missions, race relations, and community life. Adults must help children develop attitudes and ways of behaving essential for Christian world citizenship.

4. STUDY AND ACTION FOR AMERICAN PARTICIPATION IN INTERNATIONAL COOPERATION

The Protestant churches must use all their facilities, denominational and interdenominational, to secure American participation in international cooperation. New methods of education and all legitimate means by which public opinion is formed must be utilized in this effort. We urge a concerted program of intensive study of the Message of this Conference, with the appropriate social and political action as an integral part. This program should include youth in churches and colleges, men and women in our military and civilian services, church members, and all men and women of good will in the community.

5. RELIEF AND RECONSTRUCTION

Assistance given to those in special need will be conducive to the mutual sympathy and trust which are essential to international cooperation. War-ravaged peoples in many lands will require help in their struggle to re-establish civic order. Basic welfare relief will need to be supplemented by assistance to the churches to reconstitute their services within their local communities in order to become effective centers of vital life and hope. The churches of America are urged to support to the fullest their agencies of relief and reconstruction already in operation in order to assist the churches of other lands in this period of reconstruction. The World Council of Churches and the national Christian councils in Asia will afford channels of immediate services thus undergirding stable world order.

6. RACE RELATIONS

Race prejudice is a primary obstacle to world brotherhood. It is strongly urged upon churches and church members that they wage a continuing campaign against race prejudice in all its forms. The churches should not only support all efforts to wipe out discriminations against minority groups, but they should also deliberately arrange cooperative programs in which racial barriers are broken down. We recommend active support by the churches of legislation: providing for a permanent Federal Fair Employment Practices Commission; providing for the repeal of poll tax and other discriminatory laws; providing for housing projects without discriminatory practices; and other measures designed to advance the well being and constitutional rights of Negroes and other underprivileged groups.

The Church must counteract hate in all its forms and expressions. Anti-Semitism represents a rising threat to brotherhood and must be wiped out. The Oriental Exclusion Act should be repealed and all Orientals be placed on the quota system. The Churches should uphold the civil rights of Japanese Americans as they return from relocation camps and wherever they may be.

7. PROPOSAL FOR OTHER STUDY CONFERENCES

A just and durable peace is conditioned by the ability of our own nation to achieve economic stability and interracial justice in its domestic affairs. Therefore, it is recommended that national study conferences (1) on industrial relations and rural economics, and (2) on race relations, similar to this Conference on a Just and Durable Peace, be held under the auspices of the Federal Council.

8. RECOMMENDATIONS WITH REGARD TO SPECIFIC IMMEDIATE ACTION

1. We urge a meeting of the United Nations, at the earliest possible moment, to consider the Dumbarton Oaks Proposals.

2. We concur in the resolutions of the Federal Council of Churches and many other religious and educational bodies urging that Congressional action on Peacetime Military Conscription be deferred until after the war.

IV. Conclusion

The unique contribution of the Church is to bring to all these tasks the maximum of Christian faith and the full development of its power, its motivation and its resources. Before we can do Christ's work, we must appropriate more of His life. Basic to all else are greater depth of Christian faith, greater endurance in Christian fortitude and courage, more whole-hearted devotion to Him and a more universal experience of His forgiving and creative grace.

As the Christian Church faces its duties and the dangers of this hour, it must undergird its own life and the life of its people with prayer through which is made available to men the infinite resources of God. Without Him we can do nothing. With Him we can advance toward His Kingdom of righteousness and brotherhood.

V. A Message to Christians of all Lands

We have met to rededicate ourselves to the fulfillment of our responsibility toward establishing a just and durable peace, and to consider what that task requires of us. We have been constantly aware of our comradeship with you within the Church of Christ.

We thank God that through these years of separation His grace has sustained those who have been faithful to His will. Many of you have withstood the violence of destruction, the outrages of persecution and the sorrow of loss in degrees far beyond our experience or our full comprehension. We have been humbled and inspired by such faith and valiant loyalty to our common Lord.

We look forward to the day when we may again meet with you in more direct fellowship, laboring together to reconcile the estranged peoples of the world and to lead them to the paths of righteousness and peace.

Even now we assure you that you are near to us in prayer and that we live in confidence that God is leading His Church to new power in the world.

"Now unto him that is able to do exceeding abundantly above all that we ask or think, according to the power that worketh in us, unto him be glory in the church by Christ Jesus throughout all ages, world without end, Amen."

[1]In transmitting the Message of the Cleveland Conference to the Churches for their study and action, the Commission on a Just and Durable Peace of the Federal Council of Churches pointed out that the Conference, in adopting its Message, spoke only for itself, and not for the churches of the Federal Council, to which the message had not been submitted before printing.

[2]The Guiding Principles were adopted at the Delaware Conference in March, 1942, (See above, p. 54) and later by the Executive Committee of the Federal Council

of Churches. The statement of Political Propositions (the Six Pillars of Peace) was developed by the Commission on a Just and Durable Peace and made public in March, 1943. [The latter document "embraces certain broad political conclusions which seem to flow from the Guiding Principles." The "Six Pillars" follow:

"1. The peace must provide the political framework for a continuing collaboration of the United Nations and, in due course, of neutral and enemy nations.

"2. The peace must make provision for bringing within the scope of international agreement those economic and financial acts of national governments which have widespread international repercussions.

"3. The peace must make provision for an organization to adapt the treaty structure of the world to changing underlying conditions.

"4. The peace must proclaim the goal of autonomy for subject peoples, and it must establish international organization to assure and to supervise the realization of that end.

"5. The peace must establish procedures for controlling military establishments everywhere.

"6. The peace must establish in principle, and seek to achieve in practice, the right of individuals everywhere to religious and intellectual liberty."]

Chapter IV

THE DISILLUSIONMENTS
OF VICTORY:

"The Moral Use of American Power"
Cleveland, 1949

INTRODUCTION

The horizon was bright with the promise of peace during the spring and summer following the Cleveland Conference of 1945. Germany and Italy laid down their arms in May, the United Nations was established in June, and the Japanese surrender followed in August.

But peace was fleeting. Four years later the "one world" of San Francisco had fallen apart into two worlds. The Soviet Union and the United States, mutually suspicious and fearful, were making threatening sounds and building up alliances each against the other.

The realities of the international situation and the mood of church people at the time can be sensed from these lines in the *Christian Century* of March 2, 1949. Said the editors:

> The problem of securing a just and lasting peace grows more baffling, more difficult with every passing week.... American churchmen feel a tremendous weight of responsibility because of the power now wielded by their government. But they are of a hundred different minds as to how their government should be discharging the obligations of power...

> Next week's Cleveland Conference will face a tougher assignment than confronted the delegates at Delaware or at the earlier Cleveland gathering.

> ...These representatives of the churches will meet at a time when reason and the liberal spirit are at a heavy discount. Nations are not speaking to nations these days in such terms; instead, they are employing the argument of naked power. The "one world" hope which flamed high four years ago has all but vanished in the presence of a two-world reality.[1]

The second Cleveland Conference was held March 8-11, 1949. It met under the auspices of the Federal Council's Department of International Justice and Goodwill, whose chairman, Bishop William Scarlett of the Episcopal Church, presided over the sessions.

The conference theme was "The Moral Use of American Power." Attention was focused on such specific issues as the proposed North Atlantic treaty, Soviet-American relations, United States policy in the Far East, and the United Nations. The purpose was to evaluate these and related issues in the light of Christian principles.

Study committees were set up several months in advance. In collaboration with the staff of the Department of International Justice and Goodwill, these committees prepared background papers which were then circulated among the delegates for study.

Newspaper headlines on the eve of and during the conference reflected the gravity and tenseness of the world situation, plagued as it was by the Cold War. Foreign capitals weighed the meaning of Vishinsky's appointment to replace Molotov as head of the Soviet Foreign Office. The Soviets announced their refusal to recognize the West German state being founded with the support of the United States, Great Britain, and France. The Security Council's approval of the admission of Israel to the United Nations stirred up strong Arab reaction. Portions of the Chinese press attacked Chiang Kai-shek and suggested that he "go abroad," while Chinese Premier Sun Fo and his cabinet resigned as the threat of civil war in that country became more apparent. Meanwhile the North Atlantic Security Pact was in the headlines daily as additional nations weighed the possibility of adhering to it, rumors appeared as to what the pact involved, and it was announced that the draft text would soon be released to the public— "probably next week."

The 450 participants in the conference represented 34 denominations, 15 allied religious bodies, and 51 city and state councils of churches. They came from 38 states and Canada.

The sessions opened with a service of worship at Old Stone Church with Hazen G. Werner, Bishop of the Methodist Church for the Ohio area, presenting the sermon. Two major addresses were delivered before plenary sessions of the conference. John Foster Dulles, chairman of the American delegation to the United Nations General Assembly, gave the keynote address,[2] while Reinhold Niebuhr, of Union Theological Seminary, discussed "The Christian Approach to American Power in the World Community."

The five background papers prepared by the study committees were formally presented to the conference in plenary session by Walter M. Horton, Professor, Oberlin Graduate School of Theology, Francis B. Sayre, United States representative to the United Nations Trusteeship Council, G. Bromley Oxnam, Bishop of the Methodist Church, Mrs. Leslie E. Swain, President of the Women's American Baptist Foreign Missions Society, and Howard Y. McClusky, Professor, University of Michigan.

The discussion procedure at this conference combined the two major strategies used in previous conferences. The membership was divided into three groups. At one stage each of the three sections discussed "Guiding Principles of the Churches for World Order." Chairs for the discussion of this topic were Justin Wroe Nixon, Professor, Colgate-Rochester Seminary, Mrs. J. D. Bragg, and Sidney E. Sweet, Dean of Christ Church Cathedral,

St. Louis. At another stage each of the three sections considered "The Church's Strategy for World Order Education and Action." Chairs for these discussions were Mrs. Paul Gebhart, Hubert C. Noble, and Paul C. Payne, General Secretary of the Board of Christian Education, Presbyterian Church in the U.S.A.

At still a third stage, each section was given a special assignment for which it alone was responsible. Section I considered "The Churches and the United Nations"; O. Frederick Nolde, Dean of the Graduate School, Lutheran Theological Seminary, Philadelphia, chaired the discussion. Section II dealt with "The Churches and American Policy in Europe," under the chairmanship of Bishop Oxnam. Section III dealt with "The Churches and American Policy in the Far East," with Eugene Barnett, General Secretary of the National Council of the Y.M.C.A., as chairman.

Findings of the sections on the two common topics were brought together in one pair of documents. These, with the section reports on individually assigned topics, were discussed in the plenary sessions, amended slightly, and commended to the churches for their study and action. They represent in a general way the consensus of the delegates but are not *official* declarations of the conference as such.

At the same time a Message Committee, under the chairmanship of John Foster Dulles, prepared a more general and comprehensive statement on "Moral Responsibility and United States Power." This was debated more extensively and edited more carefully so as to state more precisely the thinking of the total membership. It was adopted unanimously as the conference's official "Message to the Churches." Two other formal actions of the conference as a whole were "A Message to Christians in All Lands" and "A Statement on Religious Freedom."

The statement of "Guiding Principles of the Churches for World Order" grew out of the section discussions of the first topic. Firmly based on the 13 Guiding Principles laid down at Delaware, this seven-point statement focused more particularly on the question of the use of power. It was designed to give the major conclusions of the conference in brief compass for those who might not have the patience to go through the longer documents.

More perhaps than any of the study conferences that had preceded it, that of Cleveland, 1949, was frustrating and seemingly inconclusive. The diversity of judgment as to America's duty in the face of the current situation was painfully evident. Many delegates resented what they felt was the effort of the conference officers to "sell them a bill of goods," namely the proposed North Atlantic Security Pact. Indeed many felt they were being sold "a pig in a poke," since the government had not yet released sufficient information about the proposed pact to permit a sound judgment regarding it. There was also widespread feeling against the time allotted to State Department representatives to "explain" the Atlantic Pact.

In reference to the Atlantic Pact, *Time* magazine reported that the conference "wrestled with a troublous subject." But, it went on, "they had an expert coach" (sic) in John Foster Dulles, who in his opening address had "done his best to prepare them" to accept it. From the discussion on the floor, *Time* declared, it appeared that half the delegates were "dead set against it." Consequently, the conference "side-stepped the issue [and] called upon the Senate to postpone final action on it until the nation had an opportunity for full discussion of all its provisions and implications."[3]

The most heated controversy came over the "Statement on Religious Freedom." Prompted, doubtless, by the imprisonments in Hungary of Lutheran Bishop Lajos Ordass and Joseph Cardinal Mindszenty, the statement called for "Protestants and Roman Catholics at the highest level of leadership" to join forces against such anti-clerical tactics of the communists. More specifically the resolution called upon World Council of Churches leaders to negotiate with the Vatican on "issues of religious liberty and related human rights...in order that clear understanding be reached as to what each means by religious liberty for all men...and as to the methods whereby the fullest observances should be sought." When this matter came before the conference in its closing minutes, an amendment was proposed which declared that "the ecclesiastical organization and policies of the Roman Catholic Church do not accord with the preservation and extension of religious freedom." The debate became so heated that it was necessary to refer the matter to the Federal Council's executive committee for further consideration.

Time was quite correct in noting that at Cleveland, 1949, there were "none of the ringing affirmations that distinguished the conference's meetings of 1942, when it called for a post war world organization, or of 1945, when it called for the Christian concepts of justice, law and human rights in the U.N. charter."[4]

Christianity and Crisis paid no attention to the findings of the Conference. The *Christian Century* titled its editorial assessment "Cleveland Strikes Out." Three weeks after it had referred to the conference in prospect as "the most important interdenominational conference to be held in this country since the close of the war,"[5] this influential journal asserted in retrospect that the conference "capped the efforts of the churches in this field with a resounding anticlimax!... If this is the best the churches can do, it is to be hoped that the third national study conference will be the last." The *Christian Century* reported that the majority of the leaders "were disillusioned by the course of political events, resentful of the pressures which they felt government was applying to their meeting and yet incapable of producing any clear lead for the churches on their own account."[6]

The *Christian Century* reflected quite accurately the feelings with which many left Cleveland. Perhaps the feeling of frustration was inevitable— given the disillusioning events since the previous conference, and the difficult choices that had to be made. The churches had learned to face and deal with war. They could envision and prescribe for peace. But cold war like that of 1949 called for choices between the lesser of evils—and these churchmen generally find it difficult to make.

Yet a reading today of the opening "Message to the Churches" makes it clear that the conference was not by any means a total loss. While it may not have been able to speak out with any clear voice regarding the more controversial issues before the public, it did issue a statement of fundamental convictions on the subject of "Moral Responsibility and United States Power," which, in the main, is still valid and has provided a solid foundation upon which later conferences were able to build. There also were other timely and constructive results, among them the emphasis upon the essential role of the United Nations and the need for church members to support it, and the temperate and realistic words about the necessity of coexistence between the Soviet Union and the United States under the heading of "The Churches and American Policy in Europe."

---

[1]LXVI (March 2, 1949), 263-264.
[2]For a good summary of the address see *Time*, LIII, No. 11 (March 14, 1949), pp. 65-66.
[3]LIII, No. 12 (March 21, 1949), pp. 67-68.
[4]*Ibid.*
[5]LXVI (March 2, 1949), 263.
[6]*Ibid.*, (March 23, 1949), p. 359.

MESSAGE AND FINDINGS OF THE
THIRD NATIONAL STUDY CONFERENCE ON THE
CHURCHES AND WORLD ORDER

Cleveland, Ohio   March 8–11, 1949

I. Moral Responsibility and United States Power: A Message to the Churches

II. Reports from the Sections

> Guiding Principles of the Churches for World Order; The Churches and the United Nations; The Churches and American Policy in Europe; The Churches and American Policy in the Far East; The Churches' Strategy for World Order Education and Action.

III. Other Actions

> A Message to Christians in All Lands.

> A Statement on Religious Freedom.

THE MORAL USE OF AMERICAN POWER

I. Moral Responsibility and United States Power: A Message to the Churches[1]

In this National Study Conference on the Churches and World Order we have concentrated our attention on the moral use of United States power. We have done so because an outstanding fact of recent history is the sudden emergence of our nation as materially the most powerful on earth. The possession of such power involves great moral hazards and fateful consequences for the world. To use our power rightly requires the moral and spiritual insight which is derived from the Christian faith. It is especially appropriate, therefore, that the churches should address themselves at this time to the question of our nation's power. The kingdoms of this world must become the kingdom of our Lord and of His Christ.

A. CHRISTIAN UNDERSTANDING OF OUR WORLDLY POWER

As Christians we believe that this nation holds its power under the providence of God, to whom all nations are subject. We reject all interpretations of our destiny which would ascribe it merely to historical accidents without moral or religious meaning. We equally reject all interpretations which would regard this power as chiefly the fruit of virtue. We seek that our nation shall resist both the temptation to use its power irresponsibly and the temptation to flee the responsibilities of its power.

B. RESPONSIBILITY IN THE USE OF POWER

The corollary of all power is responsibility. Power can corrupt. So, too, it can be made to serve worthy ends. Power can be used as an instrument of aggression. So, too, can it be used as an instrument of law and order. Power can be used exclusively for purposes of national self-interest. So, too, can it be used for the development and preservation of world community. Power is a trust for which we are accountable to God. The nation that ignores this truth courts disaster.

We have, in the past, glimpsed our national responsibility, but today we see that its magnitude far exceeds our earlier imaginings. Our nation now has an economic productivity almost equal to that of all the rest of the world combined. It has immense military power. It has the confidence of many in other lands who belive that our people have no lust for conquest and genuinely desire a just and lasting peace in a free world. Freedom-loving peoples look to us for leadership, and without that leadership there would be demoralization in the world. Still it remains to be seen whether, as a people, we have the spiritual power which fits us for such leadership. This question should be a paramount concern of Christians.

C. DANGERS OF WORLDLY POWER

Human pride, as we know from Scripture, is a primal human sin; and those who are prosperous and powerful are prone to it. A nation as fortunate as ours must resist the temptation to vulgar boasting and conceit.

We have been vaulted with incredible speed into our present position of responsibility. Inexperience in the use of power exposes our nation to further danger of using that power awkwardly and thus, even without intent, aggressively. This danger would be aggravated should we succumb to arrogance. Many fear that this may happen.

There is danger also that we may lose sight of human values in our pursuit of technical supremacy. We are working intensively to make atom bombs and jet bombers, super flat-tops and Snorkel submarines. We are devising machines to calculate flights of missiles that are beyond human calculation. We are performing miracles of production through the use of ever more efficient tools. What is the purpose of all this? Presumably it is to save mankind from falling under the sway of a materialistic rule that holds that man's chief end is to glorify the state and to serve it forever. But we shall not accomplish that great and worthy purpose if we are deaf to the cry of the people for deliverance from the death, the misery, and the starvation of body and soul visited upon them by economic disorder and recurrent war. We must be compassionate in our exercise of power.

D. POSITIVE USES OF POWER

Our people have demonstrated their willingness to use a substantial portion of our economic wealth for the benefit of others. Through UNRRA, the European Recovery Plan, and other economic aid, we have given away, since fighting stopped, about thirty billion dollars' worth of goods and thereby provided, for many nations, the economic margin for the survival of their people.

But more—much more—remains to be done. In the competition of ideologies and systems for the allegiance of man, communist leadership is astute in aiming its assaults against positions that are indefensible, morally or practically. Unhappily, there are many such positions, political, economic, and social.

The whole East is restless. Century-old patterns of government, education, industry, religion, and family relations have broken down. New desires have been awakened. In the Far East there is a continuing struggle for independence and for improved living conditions. Confidence in the system of Western democracy has been shaken. Two world wars and a great economic depression have seemed to indicate the inability of the West to control either national rivalries or the mechanisms of production and distribution. Unjust discriminations and segregation based on race and color still persist in America and weaken her moral influence throughout Asia and Africa.

There was a time when the Western democracies had great prestige because of their dynamic pursuit of liberty, equality, and fraternity; their great experiments in political freedom; and their industrial revolution which multiplied the productivity of human effort. It is time to undertake some new experiments with promise of benefit to others. In this connection we welcome President Truman's proposal for a pooling of technological resources for the advancement of under-developed areas.

There is no policy so barren, so certain to fail, as that of merely maintaining the *status quo.* If our nation's leadership is to be worthy, it must develop constructive and creative programs that will capture the imagination and enlist the support of the multitudes whose interest in battling political, economic, and racial injustice is greater than their interest in defending such injustice merely because communism attacks it.

We need not commend or seek to stabilize whatever or whomever communism attacks. Our material support should principally serve to sustain, fortify, and enlarge human freedom and healthy economic and social conditions. Otherwise we become over-extended materially and discredited morally.

1. SOVIET-AMERICAN RELATIONS

In relation to Soviet Russia, the use of our nation's political power presents a problem of extreme difficulty and delicacy. Soviet communists believe in and practice methods of violence and terrorism to extend the area of their control. There exist as yet no international law and international police force to protect those who are unable to defend themselves against these methods. The power of the United States provides today the chief material force which can induce restraints to protect human rights and fundamental freedoms where they still exist.

There is, however, great danger that such use of power may in fact lead to war. This could come about either because of over-zeal or corruption of motive on the part of those in our nation who determine the direction of our power or because of the misunderstanding or willful misinterpretation of our purposes by the leaders of Soviet Russia. That danger can easily be progressive as tension grows, public opinion becomes inflamed and war is increasingly assumed to be inevitable.

We reaffirm our calm conviction that war with the Soviet Union is not inevitable, and we believe that it is improbable, given proper use by the United States of its powerful influence. This assumes that the United States will seek to keep open all available channels of negotiation and reconciliation. Contradictory ideologies can co-exist without armed conflict if propagated by methods of tolerance. There is accumulating evidence that Soviet leaders are coming more and more to realize that under present conditions their methods of intolerance are ineffectual against a good society. Therefore a preventive war would be folly as well as sin. The just society is impregnable to Communism, which, although it may lift some burdens, fastens upon the common people other burdens greater and more grievous to be borne. Our major attention should, accordingly, be directed to establishing justice within the condition of freedom throughout the earth.

2. THE UNITED NATIONS

Power that concerns many should so far as practicable be exercised in consultation with the representatives of those who are affected. The United Nations is the international organization through which this can best be done. It was established, among other reasons, as a center for harmonizing the actions of its members and for coordinating their resources for the common good.

We call upon the American people to give the United Nations their loyal support and to make apparent their desire that their government use to the full the possibilities of the United Nations. The power and authority of the United Nations are as yet inadequate and ought to be enlarged as rapidly as can be done without jeopardizing its present universality. In this connection, however, it must also be borne in mind that law and order cannot be achieved on a world-wide scale without adequate acceptance of the moral principles upon which that law and order are based. This means that development of the United Nations will increase as a sufficient number of men all over the world have an increased understanding of the spiritual nature of man and a more nearly common standard of right and wrong. Such conditions will promote mutual trust and the development of laws by which relations in an international society can be governed.

It is precisely at this point that Christianity can make one of its greatest contributions. In proclaiming the Gospel to the uttermost parts of the world, the Christian Church will be faithful to its primary mission of bringing men to God in Jesus Christ and will contribute substantially to a moral climate in which a world of independent nations can grow into a unity of justice, order, and brotherhood.

3. REGIONAL PACTS

Since the foundation for a universal structure of law and order is still inadequate, the United States can properly join its political power with that of other nations in such regional pacts as are authorized and encouraged by the United Nations Charter. Regional pacts can add to the total of

common security if they are genuinely within the universal framework of the United Nations; if they are based upon a natural community of interest and are in fact designed and operated to preserve and to promote the general welfare of participating nations. Such pacts can on the other hand add to insecurity if their words conceal what is essentially a military alliance which might validly appear to others to be aggressive.

The United States is already a member of the hemispheric pact of the Americas. An Atlantic pact is now in the process of negotiation. We do not take a position with regard to that proposed pact because its final text is not now available to us and because there is no opportunity for this Conference to study its principles and consider its implications. We do call upon the United States Senate not to take final action on this pact until the American people have had opportunity to gain full understanding of its meaning.

4. REDUCTION AND LIMITATION OF ARMAMENTS

The Charter of the United Nations contemplates a general limitation of armaments. Thus far, efforts to achieve that end have proved futile. We call upon the government of the United States to look upon present obstacles as offering a reason, not to abandon its efforts, but rather to intensify its efforts to surmount these obstacles. The end sought is imperative—not only in terms of economic welfare, but also in terms of ending peacefully an armament race that otherwise may end in disaster. The goal of multilateral and balanced reduction of armaments, subject to adequate international inspection and control, should be kept at the forefront of our national policy.

5. LIQUIDATION OF WESTERN POLITICAL SUPREMACY

We need in all our foreign relations to be aware of the changing relationship between the West and other areas. There is in process a most spectacular transformation, as nearly half of the human race are liberated from political shackles that were formerly imposed and are assuming the full stature of self-governing peoples. Most of Asia has acquired a new political freedom. As symbolic of the trend toward independence in Africa, three territories are moving toward self-government under United Nations trusteeship. In this hemisphere the status of the United States has changed from that of hegemony to one of equal fellowship. We rejoice in these developments. Our people should be constantly aware of the rightness of this transformation and should assist those entering upon their political freedom as with inexperience they face difficult political problems under conditions of acute economic strain.

E. CONTROL AND COORDINATION OF POWER

The new power that the United States now possesses in the world calls for new measures for its control to keep it in appropriate place under American tradition. We have never before had such power in peace to use for peace. Our present power came into being only during the late world war when the military might and productive capacity of the United States were immensely increased and when all the other so called "Great Powers" were grievously weakened. Since our power was a war factor, it fell under the direction of military strategy and it still remains largely under that direction, especially that of the National Security Council, the Joint Chiefs of Staff, and the War Department. It is not unnatural that this should be so, because victory has not brought formal peace and there is apparent risk of new war.

If, however, our national power is to serve the ends of peace, our basic national strategy should be made by persons who have faith in the achievability of peace and who are qualified by experience and training to use and to evaluate the great possibilities for peace that reside in moral and economic forces, in organizations like the United Nations and the World Court and in the resources of diplomacy and conciliation. We do not reflect upon the patriotism or the sincere desire for peace of the leadership of our armed forces. Their professional training, however, does not qualify them to lay down the strategy for peace and to calculate the risks that always have to be taken for peace if we are to win it, just as risks have to be taken in war for victory.

Once our nation's basic strategy for peace is defined, there should be coordination sufficient to ensure that all forms of official activity, whether military or civilian, fit into that strategy to ensure its success. Today unrelated acts in Germany or Japan, or the independent exploits of military or civilians, while well meant and perhaps intrinsically sound, may cumulatively jeopardize the success of any overall national strategy for peace. There is required far greater coordination than exists today.

Such power as our nation now possesses is a truly frightening responsibility. We are confident that it can be used to assure peace. But this assumes the use of that power in scrupulous accord with the dictates of enlightened statesmanship. Misuse, however inadvertent, can spell disaster. Our citizens and all those in authority should concern themselves urgently with the task of controlling and coordinating all elements of our power.

F. SPECIAL TASK OF THE CHURCHES

During recent years the churches have helped to make clear what Christian principles mean in terms of the actual problems Christians face as citizens. Today the moral climate in the United States is more favorable to international cooperation. As a people, we have abandoned political

isolation. We have shared in establishing a world organization and are supporting it. We have abandoned economic isolation. We are employing a larger measure of our material resources to help those who are weak. We have resisted the assumption that war is inevitable. In all this the churches have had a creative part.

Today more than ever it is an urgent and continuing mission of our churches to sharpen the sense of moral obligation, to mitigate national pride and pretension, to urge our people to a steadfast exercise of our enlarged responsibilities.

As we encounter those who would make national interests the end of our action, we shall preach the Majesty of God under whose sovereignty we are called upon to build a more inclusive community of mankind.

In opposition to those who would seek to solve our problems merely by increasing our military power or by resting our security upon a monopoly of atomic weapons, we shall insist that our security rests in a more perfect mutual support of all freedom-loving peoples and in healing the breach between the two worlds.

As against all who increase the tensions of our world by hysteria and hatred, induced by vain conceptions of our own virtues, we shall seek to preserve a sense of humility, remembering that in God's sight we are all in need of His mercy.

If America's leadership is to deserve the confidence of the world, it must be characterized by a righteous and dynamic faith. No people is ever great, even in worldly terms, without a faith, and nothing would be more dangerous than to have the present material power of our nation employed carelessly, detached from the guiding direction of a policy based upon righteous faith.

By both word and deed we must cultivate a faith which provides a serene courage amidst the insecurities of our day. There is no simple resolution of our complex responsibilities. Our generation is destined to live in the midst of uncertainty and turmoil. In such a world we declare that God rules. We are not doomed to chaos. We are laborers together with God, and with Him all things are possible.

II. Reports from the Sections[2]

A. GUIDING PRINCIPLES OF THE CHURCHES FOR WORLD ORDER

We recognize that this is a period in which ideologies supported by powerful nations contend for mastery over the minds of men. It is a time of struggle between great powers and a time in which new nation states are claiming a place in history. It is a time of tension in which even the powerful nations feel insecure. The insecurity which marks the present is likely to continue for many years. The tensions of today will not be easily resolved. For the fear and suffering in our world we acknowledge our share of responsibility. Therefore we should repent; and our penitence should express itself in creative action for world order and justice.

We believe that the 13 Guiding Principles for a just and durable peace, approved by the Delaware Conference in 1942, still must be supported vigorously. These are vital principles; bringing social and political institutions into conformity with the moral law; penitence for the sickness of our time due to violation of moral law; rejection of the spirit of revenge; support for replacing international anarchy by a higher authority, for building greater economic security, for developing international machinery for peaceful change, for autonomy for subject peoples, for making national military establishments subject to law under the community of nations, for promotion of human rights and freedoms without regard to race, color, or creed; recognition of the responsibilities of the United States, of the Church and of Christian citizens; trust in God, the Ruler of the Universe.

In the present situation we stress the following as guiding principles on the use of power:

1. *We believe that the most needed power is spiritual power that comes from God.* The greatest power and the power most needed now in our world is the power which comes from communion with God. This is the power that enables men to forgive even their enemies and to seek their welfare, to endure misunderstanding and persecution, to do the right as God gives them to see the right, and to act with penitence and humility. With faith in God's power men can live without despair and without false hopes.

2. *We believe that power is a trust.* All power is a trust for which men are accountable to God. When a nation ignores this truth it courts disaster.

3. *We believe that our country's power should be used for righteousness and peace.* War is not inevitable. A preventive war would be a crime against humanity and a sin against God. The power which our country possesses at this time should be used under God to establish a just and humane world order.

4. *We believe that the power of our nation involves special responsibilities in the manner of its use.* The use of our country's power should be subject to

the higher law of the common interest of mankind. It is a power which should be used in cooperation with other nations. Our country should be willing to take risks for peace as it has taken risks for freedom. It should seek opportunities for settling problems by negotiation. It should develop fully the enormous possibilities for peace available in moral forces and economic measures, and in the United Nations.

5. *We believe that military power should be subordinated to civil authority.* The greater the military power the greater the need for civilian control. Military considerations cannot be disregarded; but primary reliance should not be put on military power. Civilians trained in the art of peace are best qualified for the task of making peace.

6. *We believe that compassion is especially needed by the powerful.* Without compassion and human sympathy power cannot be used for great and worthy purposes. Power can be used for good or evil. The possession of material power tends to corruption, pride, and the hardening of the hearts of men. Therefore the compassion which is of God is especially needed by those who have material power entrusted to them in order that they may not lose sight of human needs everywhere and serve those needs as brothers.

7. *We believe that Christians should face calmly the dangers of our situation.* There can be no assurance that even our best efforts to use our power aright can guarantee peace. Our generation seems destined to live in the midst of uncertainty and turmoil. Nevertheless we share the confidence of the Apostle Paul, "Neither death, nor life, nor angels, nor principalities, nor powers, nor things present, nor things to come, nor height nor depth, nor any other creature, shall be able to separate us from the love of God which is in Jesus Christ our Lord."

B. THE CHURCHES AND THE UNITED NATIONS

As the fourth anniversary of the adoption of the Charter of the United Nations draws near, it is well that the churches and church people of America take stock of the progress made, the successes and failures in international cooperation, and the possibilities that lie immediately ahead in the field of international relations.

We reaffirm our faith in the United Nations, and pledge ourselves anew to support this hopeful venture, trusting that the very trials through which the nations have passed in these years when open hostilities have ceased, but when peace has proved elusive, may strengthen the growing organization and confirm the wisdom of its founders. We do this in full knowledge that the United Nations has not succeeded in eliminating the causes of conflict among the nations, especially in the realms where rival ideologies clash. We are aware that many who hailed the birth of the United Nations have felt disappointed and disillusioned. But we are confident that there is ample cause for satisfaction with the progress made in many areas.

There is ground for hope that even greater progress will be made in other areas, as experience tempers the bonds drawing nations together in a mutual interdependence that must be ever closer in a world where the barriers of distance have been all but annihilated.

The American churches, acting through the Federal Council of the Churches of Christ in America, have been closely related to the conception, birth, and early growth of the United Nations. In December, 1940, the Federal Council instituted the Commission to Study the Bases of a Just and Durable Peace. In a National Study Conference at Delaware, Ohio, in March, 1942, there was outlined a Statement of Guiding Principles, followed in 1943 by a Statement of Political Propositions. The first of these Propositions stated that "the peace must provide the framework for a continuing collaboration of the United Nations and, in due course, of neutral and enemy nations." A long step was taken toward this when, in the fall of 1944, an international conference at Dumbarton Oaks, near Washington, D.C., drafted a Charter for a permanent United Nations Organization.

A second National Study Conference at Cleveland, Ohio, in 1945, carefully considered the Dumbarton Oaks draft, and recommended certain far-reaching changes in the proposed Charter to bring it into harmony with the Christian ideals set forth in the Delaware Conference statements. Many of these changes were incorporated in the Charter of the United Nations, which was adopted at San Francisco in the spring of 1945.

Now we are met in a third National Study Conference, to take stock of this international organization with the foundation of which we were so vitally concerned. In so doing, we find causes both for rejoicing and for concern. We are aware that the situation of the world is grave, perhaps more so than in 1945. Yet we do not feel that there is justifiable cause for despair nor for abandonment of our confidence in the United Nations.

1. THE UNITED NATIONS AFTER FOUR YEARS

We have become increasingly aware that we must be willing to take some risks for peace, and to move forward boldly along channels that cannot always be fully charted in advance. We are certain that, despite the tensions of the relationships between the nations of the West and those of the Soviet orbit, which are the most conspicuous feature of contemporary international relations, the achievements of the United Nations are of a kind to warrant the continuing support of the churches and the whole-hearted cooperation of our people. These achievements have been impressive.

The United Nations provides a meeting place where the representatives of 58 sovereign governments assemble to discuss international problems of common concern. Through this process the danger spots of the world are kept in bright illumination. In providing a platform to which statesmen are summoned to make an accounting of the actions of their respective governments, the United Nations has performed and is performing a service of vast significance to the cause of peace.

The United Nations, in certain instances, has been instrumental in modifying the conduct of member states in the interest of world order. For example, Russian troops maintained in Iran contrary to treaty obligations were withdrawn from that country under the influence of the Security Council. Similarly British and French troops were withdrawn from Syria and Lebanon. Because of Assembly action, the United States reversed its position with respect to continuing discussion on control of atomic energy.

Through its Committee of Good Offices the United Nations, while unable to prevent bloodshed in Indonesia, has contributed substantially to the progressive steps thus far taken toward Indonesian independence.

The Security Council was instrumental in securing a cooling-off period in the dispute between India and Pakistan respecting Kashmir, during which a truce was effected and arrangements made for a plebiscite peacefully to determine the ultimate disposition of this disputed territory.

Under the watchful eye of the General Assembly's Special Commission on Korea an election was held in Southern Korea and a democratic government established.

Persuasive efforts at the U.N. General Assembly created an atmosphere which opened the way to an armistice between the Israeli and Egyptian governments.

Various agencies of the United Nations have amply proved their value. Among many instances, we cite especially the following:

Through the Trusteeship Council, the United Nations is supervising the administration of nine trust territories. Under the aegis of the Trusteeship Council a mission was sent to Western Samoa and the resulting recommendations in favor of greater self-government were put into effect by New Zealand, the administering power. Through reports submitted to it, the United Nations keeps under constant review the progress being achieved by the peoples of trust areas toward political, economic, and social advancement.

Through its fact-finding functions the Economic and Social Council is collecting the necessary data for informed international cooperation.

The International Children's Emergency Fund is currently engaged in providing food and medical aid to several million children in Europe on both sides of the "Iron Curtain," and in the Near and Far East.

The General Assembly on December 10, 1948, approved a Universal Declaration of Human Rights which had been drafted, following prolonged negotiation, by the Human Rights Commission.

The General Assembly has approved a Convention on the Prevention and Punishment of the Crime of Genocide and this Convention is now before the Senate of the United States for ratification.

Three conventions covering freedom of information have been formulated: one on freedom of press and information, one on the gathering and transmission of news across national boundaries, one on rights of official correction in case of false reporting. These will be under consideration by the General Assembly when it convenes in April.

Through its Commission on Narcotic Drugs, the United Nations has taken steps to control the traffic in narcotics.

Through its specialized agencies, the United Nations is fostering cooperation in many social, cultural, economic, educational, and health fields. The Food and Agricultural Organization has sent missions of experts to certain countries to the end that food production may be increased, initiated irrigation and swamp-drainage projects, and made recommendations concerning allocations of exportable food supplies. The International Bank and Monetary Fund is assisting in reconstruction projects in many nations. The United Nations Educational, Scientific and Cultural Organization is engaged in the reconstruction of educational facilities in war-devastated countries and is sponsoring conferences and seminars on the cultural standards of under-developed areas. The World Health Organization mobilized the world's cholera-fighting equipment and through its swift action brought to a speedy end a cholera epidemic in Egypt. The International Refugee Organization is seeking a permanent solution to the refugee problem and is providing emergency help to upwards of a million refugees and displaced persons. An International Trade Organization is in the process of formation through which it is hoped discriminatory trade practices can be ended and trade barriers reduced. The Charter of the International Trade Organization is now before the Senate of the United States for ratification.

Regional economic commissions have proved strong agencies for international recovery and rehabilitation. Three of these are in existence, for Europe, Latin America, and Asia; and one for the Middle East is in process of formation.

While hailing these achievements, the churches should be mindful of the limitations, failures, and shortcomings of the United Nations. It is only by an honest appraisal and evaluation of such facts and factors that an intelligent program of support and improvement can be projected.

The threat of war still persists despite the fact that the United Nations was established to remove that threat.

It is a matter of grave peril to our own and other nations that no agreement has yet been reached on international control of atomic energy or conventional armaments. As a consequence there is under way today a wide open race in armaments, a race made more ominous than at any time in history by reason of the atomic bomb and experimentation in bacteriological weapons of war.

The practice of some states to boycott certain of the agencies established by the General Assembly has raised many questions regarding the ability of the United Nations to advance the cause of peace in such troubled areas as Greece and Korea. Despite the efforts of the United Nations, guerilla warfare continues in Greece. Despite the establishment of a democratic government in Southern Korea under the direction of the United Nations, that country remains divided by an ideological conflict which has thus far prevented Korea from achieving the national statehood to which it is entitled.

The non-participation of certain states in the work of specialized agencies related to the United Nations hampers the processes of peaceful change which these bodies were meant to facilitate. Even those states that hold membership in the specialized agencies have been so preoccupied with pressing political problems that they have given insufficient attention to the curative and creative efforts of these organizations.

The frequent use of the veto has obstructed the work of the Security Council and rendered that body incapable of performing many of the duties assigned to it under the Charter.

No agreement has been reached respecting the principles governing the organization of the armed forces and facilities to be placed at the disposition of the Security Council for enforcement purposes.

It is with no thought of minimizing these and other failures and shortcomings that we point to the difficulties confronting the United Nations occasioned by the fact that the war-time unity of the Great Powers has disappeared. In place of unity there is disunity and the ideological clash between Russia and the West has divided the one world envisaged by the United Nations into two worlds. Also, certain of the failures of the United Nations are to be attributed to the fact that the two major peace settlements are yet to be negotiated. When due consideration is given to the difficulties encountered by the United Nations since its inception, the wonder is that the United Nations has been able to accomplish so much. All things considered, the achievements of the United Nations have more than balanced its failures. In it there is ground for hope.

2. OBSTACLES TO FULL EFFECTIVENESS

The fact that international tension persists to a threatening degree and that the United Nations has been unable to accomplish its purposes by rapid or direct measures prompts an inquiry into the possible handicaps under which it works. Are these primarily or solely matters of structure? Are they susceptible of elimination and, if so, by what methods? These are vital questions.

To understand what the United Nations can or cannot do, the following should be taken into account.

As to structure, the United Nations is in no sense a world government. It was founded at San Francisco upon the principle of "sovereign equality." The charter specifically asserts that the United Nations cannot intervene in a matter within the "domestic jurisdiction of any state" and there is no authority whereby domestic jurisdiction can be defined. The court has no unqualified compulsory jurisdiction over legal questions, though 35 states have submitted to such jurisdiction in accepting the "Optional Clause."

It should be noted, however, that even with respect to these retentions of sovereignty and limitations of action it is entirely possible, through the processes of evolution and affirmative interpretation, to move in quite the opposite direction. For example, the references in the Charter to human rights presumptively connote that a matter hitherto reserved for national jurisdiction is now invested with international concern. The scope of the International Court of Justice may readily be widened by common consent. Thus the United Nations could be strengthened and even modified in character without altering its structure.

It should be clearly noted furthermore that the United Nations by its Charter has more power than it has seen fit or has been able to use. For example, the Security Council is authorized to

> decide what measures not involving the use of armed force are to be employed to give effect to its decisions, and may call upon the Members of the United Nations to apply such measures. These may include complete or partial interruption of economic relations and of rail, sea, air, postal, telegraph, radio, and other means of communications, and the severance of diplomatic relations. (Art. 41)

Beyond this,

> Should the Security Council consider that measures provided for in Article 41 would be inadequate or have proved to be inadequate, it may take such action by air, sea, or land forces as may be necessary to maintain or restore international peace and security. Such action may include demonstrations, blockade, and other operations by air, sea, or land forces of Members of the United Nations. (Art. 42)

Why has the United Nations not used the authority here given? When this question is raised, the answer is usually two-fold. First, the major nations cannot agree when their interests are involved and therefore have recourse to the veto. Second, the United Nations has not been able to devise an acceptable plan for an international "police force" and it has not been able to establish a system for the regulation of national armaments.

The answers are correct as far as they go, but they do not go to the root of the problem. Four further factors must be considered:

First, there is no adequate common basis for standards of morality and justice. Where these do not exist, universal law for determining right and wrong cannot be developed and codified. Laws must reflect the opinion of the community to which they apply so that they will be voluntarily accepted by the great majority. Otherwise, they will be enforceable only by what is in fact war.

Second, if the United Nations were to use existing coercive powers, it would encounter serious risk of war. The Charter gives the Security Council power to take certain decisions and back them with sanctions that would be very effective against peoples or states which have no veto power. But where the United Nations has attempted to get results by the process of issuing orders, rather than by persuasion, it has largely failed because there were not behind the orders a sufficient weight of public opinion and sufficient voluntary acceptance, and the use of sanctions would have risked war.

Third, nations are divided by mutual suspicion and distrust. Any proposal advanced by one nation is received on the assumption that it cloaks ulterior, selfish motives. Until mutual confidence is developed, concerted action by international force, consequent upon limitation of national armaments, is unattainable.

Fourth, there is no agreement as to the meaning and function of government. Some nations, like our own, are dedicated to the proposition that all men are created free and equal, and that government should be of the people, by the people, and for the people. Others hold that government is a machine in the hands of the ruling class for suppressing the resistance of its class enemies and that man achieves his highest goal in serving the State.

3. LINES OF DEVELOPMENT

It must be demonstrated whether the United Nations, by its slower processes of debate, forming world judgment, recommending remedies, and persuasion, can remove the threat of war. There are many who claim that it will not be able to do so. In face of the reasons here cited for the inability of the United Nations to work at a maximum of effectiveness, what steps should we advocate in order that it may become a more effective instrument?

The Federal Council of Churches (1946) in a statement entitled "The Churches and World Order" declared that "the nations must make full use of the provisions of the United Nations Charter and develop as rapidly as possible a spirit of world community which will be reflected in world government."

We reaffirm that goal of world government, a goal which can be achieved just as rapidly as fundamental requirements are met. We should seek this end, but we must not close our eyes to realities in the present situation. The United Nations is the only political organ which holds together, even in tenuous fashion, an otherwise divided world. Any effort to establish a world government which would at the same time impair or endanger the United Nations would be disastrous. This means that patience and wisdom must be exercised in progressing from a union of sovereign states to some form of world government. To press for changes more rapidly than the nations are prepared to accept might conceivably destroy the only organ which now provides regular channels for international negotiation and decision.

Maximum use of the facilities and resources which are now available in the United Nations to solve immediate problems and to prevent their recurrence will be the surest way to move in the direction of a stronger organization. By working together to serve the best interests of all parties concerned and by doing that honestly, nations and peoples can develop facility in cooperation and tend to overcome distrust. While common standards, whether of morality or government, cannot be expected to emerge suddenly, a better understanding of differing points of view can be developed. If on no basis other than expedience, nations may learn that, even though differing in ideology and governmental form, they can and must exist together and compete peacefully with each other. The best way to strengthen the United Nations is to use if faithfully for the solution of the problems within its competence.

The processes of using and strengthening the United Nations must be made concrete. There are lines of action which must be insistently pursued. Some will yield quite promptly to intelligent efforts. Others will require greater diligence and persistence. The moral stature of the United States would be increased if the Congress were to make it clear that, at this critical time when the fate of humanity hangs in the balance, our great nation is ready to take the lead in surrendering its sovereignty to the extent necessary to establish peace through the ordering of just law. Among the immediate possibilities are these particularly:

(1) Rapid development and expansion of the United Nations functional agencies working to promote human welfare and understanding, including regional economic commissions.

(2) Regional agreements designed to promote cooperation in the interest of welfare and peace. These should observe the following safeguards:

(a) preserve the over-arching responsibilities of the United Nations.
(b) avoid return to "balance of power" and military alliances.
(c) be open to all nations that are reasonably entitled to membership and that do not exclude themselves because of an unwillingness to accept its provisions.
(d) should be submitted to the General Assembly for approval.

(3) Expansion and greater use of mediation and conciliation by the United Nations.

(4) Direct United Nations control and administration over certain troubled or disputed areas.

(5) The regulation, limitation, and reduction of national armaments, under the supervision of the United Nations.

(a) The establishment of an armed guard force under the Secretary General to assist officials of the United Nations in the performance of their function.
(b) The early voluntary contribution by member states of armed forces for use by the Security Council in accordance with Article 43.

(6) Adequate financial contributions, and development of direct sources of revenue, so that the United Nations can accomplish its work.

(7) Continued effort to eliminate those factors responsible for the presence of the veto and to secure agreement for elimination of use of the veto in the pacific settlement of international disputes under Chapter VI of the Charter and as regards admission of new members.

(8) More widespread acceptance, without reservations, of the Optional Clause of the Statute of the International Court of Justice. This would establish compulsory jurisdiction of the court over a wide area of legal disputes between and among nations without necessity of amending the Charter.

(9) Widening the categories of justifiable disputes among nations.

(10) Development of international procedures for encouraging and enforcing respect for the human rights which members agree upon in accordance with their pledge under Article 56 of the Charter, including recognition of the responsibility of individuals.

4. SOME NEXT STEPS IN THE AREAS OF CHRISTIAN ACTION

Christian people share in the obligation of creating world-wide conditions under which constructive tasks can be more effectively pursued. The General Assembly has recommended a program of education on the purposes and activities of the United Nations. To this endeavor the churches can contribute the stimulation and direction of Christian ideals and Christian motives. Through a positive and widespread educational program reaching into local communities, they can help to dispel ignorance or misunderstanding and replace skepticism with realistic confidence. The work of education does not, however, in any sense exhaust the responsibility of the churches. Christian judgments, formed through careful study and by democratic processes, must provide direction for our government in shaping and carrying out its foreign policy. Therefore, we recommend the following:

(1) We believe our government should conform foreign policy to its commitments under the Charter of the United Nations. The moral use of American power requires that there be no by-passing of the United Nations by our government.

(2) We believe our government should persist in its efforts to reach agreement on the international control of atomic energy and of conventional armaments.

(3) We believe the proclamation of principles embodied in the Universal Declaration of Human Rights, as approved by the General Assembly, should as rapidly as possible be translated into legally binding covenants. We believe the behavior of the Christian community in the United States should be brought into harmony with the principles defined in this Declaration. So, too, must the behavior of our government be made consistent with these principles. As an earnest of its purpose to act in accordance with these principles we believe the Congress of the United States should promptly enact such legislation as will safeguard the civil, political and economic rights of our entire citizenry without discrimination as to race, creed, and color.

(4) We believe the Senate of the United States should promptly ratify the Convention on the Prevention and Punishment of the Crime of Genocide.

(5) We believe our government should take vigorous steps promptly to secure the negotiation of the peace settlements as an aid in strengthening the processes of the United Nations.

(6) We believe that our government should take steps immediately for full participation in and support of the International Trade Organization.

(7) We believe that our government should give greater financial support to the specialized agencies related to the United Nations, and to the International Children's Emergency Fund.

(8) The Displaced Persons Act should be liberalized so that the United States will expedite the admission and facilitate the settlement of its fair share of displaced persons.

(9) We believe that our government should pursue a legislative policy in relation to matters affecting international cooperation that will be consistent with and will support our commitments within the United Nations and its specialized agencies.

If the United Nations is to continue its service to the world and progressively become a more adequate instrument, the nations must join their resources in ordered relationship. The United States is here called upon to assume a position of leadership. More than any other nation, our people have the capacity to influence decisively the shaping of world events. If the future is to be other than a repetition of the past, the United States must consistently meet a responsibility for constructive action commensurate with its power and opportunity.

We have stressed particularly the part which the United Nations can play in promoting just and peaceful relations among the nations of the world, and the support which its activities merit. That support, we are convinced, requires a better informed public opinion. Thus we have set forth our analysis to assist in judgment and decision. However, our Christian people would be under great delusion if they thought that such measures, important as they are, could in themselves accomplish the ends of world order and justice.

In order that mankind may escape chaos and recurrent war, social and political institutions must be brought into conformity with moral order. That will be possible only when a sufficient number of men all over the world have a common understanding of the spiritual nature of man and a common standard of right and wrong. Such conditions will be favorable to a community of mutual trust and to the development of laws by which relations in an international society can be governed.

It is precisely in this area that Christianity has its greatest contribution to make. In proclaiming the Gospel to the uttermost parts of the world, the Christian Church will be faithful to its primary mission of bringing men to God in Jesus Christ and will contribute substantially to a moral climate in which a world of independent nations can grow into an interrelated society of justice, order, and brotherhood.

C. THE CHURCHES AND AMERICAN POLICY IN EUROPE

1. SOVIET-AMERICAN RELATIONS

The churches must reaffirm the principle of stewardship when considering the issue of power. Power is a trust. The American people are trustees of the power that lies in economic resources and military might, and are responsible for the use of that power to the end that a true community of nations may be established on the earth.

Soviet-American tensions raise anew the whole question of the use of power and summon the churches to reaffirm the moral principles upon which Christian conduct is based. "There is a moral order which is fundamental and eternal, and which is relevant to the corporate life of men and the order of human society." Indifference to or the violation of these principles results in the sickness and suffering of society and contributes to the contemporary crisis.

All share in responsibility for present evils. There is none who does not need forgiveness. A mood of genuine penitence is therefore demanded of us—individuals and nations alike. "A true community of nations" is dependent upon the practice of cooperation and mutual concern. Believing as we do that "that government which derives its just powers from the consent of the governed is the truest expression of the rights and dignity of man," we believe ourselves obligated to cooperate with other freedom-loving peoples to resist the destruction by force of such governments and the further extension by force of totalitarian regimes that through the tyranny of dictatorship repudiate this principle.

A self-righteous separation from the responsibilities placed upon us by the possession of power, upon the ground that our power is the product of our virtue, is to reject the obligations of stewardship, and by refusal to meet our responsibilities is a contribution to the tyranny suffered by others as well as an accentuation of tensions.

Every phase of American foreign policy should be consistent with our commitments under the Charter of the United Nations. The people of the United States have a responsibility to help in preventing the extension by force and intimidation of Soviet communist power, but there should be no attempt by our government or any non-communist government to destroy communist institutions in the Soviet Union or to interfere with the right to any nation to choose freely its own form of political and economic organization.

Economic recovery and security are requisite to peoples who seek to maintain freedom. We favor continued hearty support and adequate financial assurance for the European Recovery Program. Economic aid should be administered under the principles enunciated by Secretary of State Marshall when the recovery plan was proposed, but should not be used to buttress undemocratic or fascist regimes. Mr. Marshall said, "Our policy is directed, not against any country or doctrine, but against hunger, poverty, desperation, and chaos." Such aid should not be used to force American institutions or practices upon other people nor should it be used to dictate to free people the kind of economic order they must maintain.

We must direct our efforts toward the abolition of poverty and the creation of abundant life for the common man. The democratic principle must be extended to the economic order so that within the conditions of freedom, justice may be established. Christian brotherhood and democratic principle demand the end of racial segregation. A man's opportunity to earn his living should be based on his character and capacity, not determined by his race, creed, or color. Men who have experienced liberty and are convinced that progress is being made toward equality and fraternity are immune to communism. Communist bacteria find a congenial host in the empty stomach, the diseased body, the frustrated mind, and the starved soul. The just society is impregnable, the unjust society is vulnerable no matter how great the armed force at its disposal. Thus our major attention should be directed to establishing the conditions of justice throughout the earth.

Communist concern for the underprivileged and communist proposals to abolish the exploitation of man by man and to establish a classless society constitute an effective appeal to the masses. Contemporary facts, however, lead to the conclusion that, though communism may lift some burdens, it fastens upon the backs of the common people others greater and more grievous to be borne. It has outlawed some discriminations only to establish others. The extension of Soviet communism has been accompanied by the threat and use of force; thus, instead of becoming the deliverer of the poor, it has become the jailer in a regime of terror and tyranny. As Christians, we would unhesitatingly condemn such policies if practiced in our nation. We condemn their practice in Soviet Russia and her satellites.

We are aware of the fact that tens of millions of our fellow-Christians live within the Soviet Union and that our Christian love must transcend all boundaries of nation, race, color, and class. We believe that war with the Soviet Union is not inevitable. Contradictory ideologies can co-exist without armed conflict, if propagated by the methods of tolerance. We must maintain sufficient strength to convince Soviet Russia that attempts to impose an ideology by force cannot succeed.[3] We must demonstrate that a non-aggressive Soviet Russia has nothing to fear from a democratic America.

Policies developed in an atmosphere of hysteria and of hatred are not likely to be wise, and the suspicion that flows from hysteria divides the nation at the moment unity is essential. The government has full right, in fact the duty, to eliminate from positions of responsibility involving national security those persons whose loyalty, after proper investigation and public hearing by due process of law in accordance with the traditions of a free people, has been proved untrustworthy. To date the number of such persons has been shown to be very small. While recognizing the values that lie in Congressional investigations, some of the methods of the former Un-American Activities Committees, and the practice of many private agencies that sell their services by feeding the fears of their subscribers, should be condemned and discontinued, particularly the practice of smearing innocent victims through the use of the principle of "guilt by association." The churches should do all in their power to end hysteria and remove hatred from the hearts of our people.

The avenues of formal negotiations between the governments of the United States of America and Soviet Russia must be kept open, and a way should be cleared for informal conferences between unofficial religious, educational, business, labor, and cultural groups of both nations. The American people covet conference as a basis for understanding. We believe that the method of tolerance that is basic to conference will enable each to learn from the other, and give opportunity for the extension of this method upon which peace in a world of contradictory ideologies depends.

2. THE NORTH ATLANTIC SECURITY PACT

We do not pass upon the proposed Atlantic Pact because (a) the final text is not available and (b) time is not available for adequate study of its implications.

We call upon the Senate of the United States to postpone final action on this pact until the nation has had opportunity for full discussion of all its provisions and implications.

For the consideration of our government and people in the coming discussions we offer the following suggestions:

(1) No defensive alliance should be entered into which might validly appear as aggressive to Russia as a Russian alliance with Latin America would undoubtedly appear to us.

(2) Regional pacts may make for common security and welfare provided (*a*) that they stay within the framework of the United Nations; (*b*) that they are based upon a natural community of interest; and (*c*) that they pursue this interest in ways that do not jeopardize world community.

(3) Regional military alliances are, of course, no substitute for the relief of human distress, the meeting of human needs, and continuing aid to economic recovery and stability within the area; and they must not be allowed to take primacy, financial or otherwise, over such constructive programs.

History indicates that the most that can be achieved by military alliances is a temporary balance of power, while they easily give rise to menacing armament races ending in war. The tragedy of our times calls for heroic efforts in new directions. We must increase our efforts for the universal reduction and control of armaments, and, more, we must launch "bold new programs" looking to the general elevation of living standards throughout the world, and the assurance of a fair chance in life to all men regardless of race, color, creed, or nationality.

D. THE CHURCHES AND AMERICAN POLICY IN THE FAR EAST

In the providence of God forces have been released among the peoples of Asia which cause present upheavals, but hold hope and possibility for higher levels of life.

The whole East has been shaken by the impact of Western culture. Century-old patterns of government, education, industry, religion, and family relations have been broken. New desires have been awakened, which have aroused discontent with the present state of affairs, even though it may represent advances over the old conditions. The flood-tide of Western imperialism reached its highest point early in this century, since which time the ebb-tide has been running more and more swiftly. This process has been accelerated by two world wars and a great financial depression which alike have shown that Christians have not sufficiently influenced the countries of the West to control either the forces of national rivalry or the factors of production and distribution within its own economy.

It has been demonstrated that political liberty in itself does not necessarily result in social or economic justice or guarantee the general welfare. It has also become evident that the patterns of democracy which the West has developed cannot be transferred, by fiat or simple legislation, to other peoples, especially those whose historical experience and moral development have been diverse from our own, and whose education and experience in self-government under modern conditions have been more limited than our own.

Throughout the Far East there is a continuing struggle for national independence, for government by and for the people, and for improved living conditions. There is a widespread upsurge of revolt against exploitation and inefficient government, whether by outsiders or by their own rulers.

The peoples have come to question the disinterestedness and good faith of those who bring proposals for their welfare. Nevertheless, they still crave fellowship and recognition of their proper place in the family of mankind. They are open-minded, but still uncertain in what direction they should turn for the fulfillment of their aspirations.

It must be recognized that the conditions resulting in the present upheavals have been long in the making and decades or even generations will be needed for their final correction. It is our conviction that the revolutionary desires of the Far East can be ultimately satisfied only by the faith, program, and discipline to be found in Christianity.

In the face of this situation, these peoples see in America the most powerful nation in the world. We must make clear that our power at its best derives not only from our economic and military strength, but also from our experiment in democracy and our spiritual heritage. Let us not fail the hopes of these people by undue preoccupation with the attempted containment of Russian expansion or by the subordination of their welfare to American security measures or our own economic advantage. We must not try to impose upon others our own pattern of doing things. Wherever possible, we must use our power not unilaterally but in fullest cooperation in goodwill with all nations and peoples. We must endeavor to use this power in the interests of all the people rather than of particular parties or groups. We must not make our aid contingent upon conformity to our own economic and political patterns.

Rather, so powerful a country as ours must try to understand what goes on in the minds and hearts of the people of other countries whose cultural and economic background is so different from our own. We must endeavor to share our resources in ways that will enable these peoples to develop their insights and capacities to the full under their own leadership.

Our present power is terrifying and humbling. We must use it as trustees conscious of the great responsibility which great power begets.

1. TO THE CHURCHES

In our message to the churches in America, we would re-emphasize the genius of our American Protestant fellowship in carrying out its world mission. It continues to be our purpose to proclaim the Gospel of Christ to all men, to assist in the establishment of self-governing, self-propagating, and self-supporting churches in all lands, the selection and training of indigenous leadership within these churches, and the development of a program of education and service which will bring Christ's Gospel of redemption to bear upon all areas of individual and social life.

We give thanks to God for the present reality of the church in the Far East. It has stood the test of fire and has achieved an increasing sense of mission and responsibility for the evangelization of the people in these countries. We rejoice in the increasing measure of unity in faith and practice which is being demonstrated. We count it a privilege to cooperate with these churches and their leaders. Our common fellowship in the Ecumenical Church is enriched and strengthened by the fidelity of their witnesses and ministry during these critical times.

(1) We challenge our churches to match in devotion and sacrifice these sister churches in their day of dangerous opportunity. Cooperating with these churches and strengthening them is a high priority for Christian people in America. Whatever happens, we must do everything possible to help the churches maintain their witness and ministry. We pledge our continuing prayers and financial support to these churches and the missionaries working with them as they continue their labors in places of special difficulty and danger.

(2) The churches in these areas may have to adjust themselves to new conditions and new limitations which will require complete restudy of our own missionary techniques and strategy. We affirm our confidence that Christianity has a word of judgment and guidance for the social and economic life of every nation including our own. Such a word calls

for an understanding not only of Christian principles but also of the technical problems involved in their application. The new conditions may require radical departures from the customary patterns of missionary work and courageous pioneering in new forms of witness by deed even where the spoken word is forbidden.

(3) American Protestantism in making its contribution to the processes of reconstruction should support Christian workers overseas in their use of such techniques of Christian evangelism and service as the comprehensive Christian rural program, Christian service in the labor movements, guidance to students, the development and distribution of Christian literature, and the use of modern media of mass communication on a scale commensurate with the opportunities offered.

(4) American Protestantism should undertake a vigorous campaign of enlistment for added missionary personnel firmly grounded in the Christian faith, with winsome Christian character, understanding of the new ideologies, specialized technical training, mastery of the language, and a desire under all sorts of conditions to identify themselves with the people among whom they work.

(5) We commend to American Protestants the world missionary program in which the churches are engaged. We particularly commend the integrated program of advance, "One World in Christ," projected by the foreign mission boards through the Foreign Missions Conference of North America. Through this program the people of our churches by their loyal support of their own church agencies may work together to fulfill their God-given task of building a better future.

(6) Through their individual agencies and corporately through Church World Service, American Protestant churches have helped to ease the suffering growing out of the war in other lands. The wounds of war have not yet been healed. The continuing emergency calls for a present sacrificial outpouring of funds so that we may continue our ministry of compassion and expand greatly our program of relief and rehabilitation.

(7) The present situation in these lands requires that American Protestants should examine their present practices of Christian stewardship and drastically raise their standards of giving on behalf of the world mission of the church. At a time when vast expenditures are being made upon national security and personal indulgence, we call upon the people of our churches for an advance in giving commensurate with the present disorder, suffering, and urgent opportunity.

2. TO THE GOVERNMENT

In addressing ourselves to the government of the United States we recognize our responsibility as citizens to participate in the formulation of our national policies in this time of world crisis. We declare our deep conviction that our American democracy has demonstrated its ability to meet both national and international problems effectively, when motivated and controlled by high ethical principles. We would reaffirm our faith in the ability of government of the people, by the people, and for the people to survive and function not only in this land but in every land.

While reaffirming our belief in the separation of church and state, we believe also that the Christian Church has an inescapable duty to focus attention upon the moral responsibilities of government in its conduct of affairs at home and abroad. Therefore, in view of the present critical situation in the Far East we would declare that:

(1) Our government must not relax its efforts to provide a treaty structure for the Far East that will (*a*) reflect due regard for the moral and material welfare of the peoples directly concerned; (*b*) safeguard the fundamental rights of the human person; (*c*) contribute to and be an integral part of a world settlement; (*d*) provide for that mutuality of interest and creative effort which can increase international understanding and fellowship; (*e*) encourage nations to share their scientific and technical resources with one another.

(2) Our government should enact immigration and naturalization laws, fully within the quota system, based upon the principle of equality for all peoples without any discrimination whatsoever on grounds of color or nationality. We urge Congress speedily to adopt legislation in accordance with this principle.

(3) Our government should maintain a policy in keeping with the sympathy of the American people with the movements for political independence that are now under way in many of the areas of the Far East. The United States must be prepared for patient cooperation with these peoples as they assume their responsibilities in full self-government. Justice as well as consistency would require us to grant political equality to all our own citizens.

(4) Our government should proceed promptly to implement the "bold new program" as announced by President Truman in his Inaugural Address "for making the benefits of our scientific advances and industrial progress available for the improvement and growth of undeveloped areas." The aim of this program "should be to help the free peoples of the world, through their own efforts, to produce more food,

more clothing, more materials for housing, and more mechanical power to lighten their burdens."

We further subscribe wholeheartedly to the view of President Truman that "This (program) should be a cooperative enterprise in which all nations work together through the United Nations and its specialized agencies wherever practicable." All aid, both technical and material, should be offered to the Far Eastern peoples, under such conditions as will safeguard the freedom of the people and promote genuine and adequate economic development. Such aid should be offered to all countries, irrespective of regime, which will meet the conditions and cooperate in the program under satisfactory guarantees.

(5) Our government should complete its present program of assistance to the Chinese people through the Economic Cooperation Administration and provide for its extension. Such assistance should be designed to contribute to the welfare, freedom, and livelihood of the Chinese people. Our government should respect the right of the Chinese people without outside pressure to determine by their own free choice the form of government under which they live. We sincerely approve the decision of the Department of State to retain its diplomatic and consular officers at their posts in all parts of China and to recognize the desirability of other American civilians remaining, thus keeping open a door for the free exchange of information, contact with the Western world trade, education, and Christian ministry.

(6) Our government should review its occupation policy in *Japan*, in the light of the decision of the Far Eastern Commission approved June 19, 1947, which decision was designed (a) to ensure that Japan will not again become a menace to the peace and security of the world; and (b) to bring about the earliest possible establishment of a democratic and peaceful government which will carry out its international responsibilities, respect the rights of other states, and support the objectives of the United Nations. We urge the earliest possible conclusion of a peace treaty with Japan. If the general international situation makes the negotiation of a treaty with all the powers concerned impracticable, we should seek an interim agreement providing for these things. The steps already taken to give Japan access to raw materials and trade opportunities should be extended having due regard to the welfare of neighboring peoples.

(7) Our government should be supported in its long-range policies for Korea enunciated by the Department of State: (a) to establish a self-governing, sovereign Korea as soon as possible, independent of foreign

control and eligible for membership in the United Nations; (*b*) to insure that the national government so established shall be fully representative of the freely expressed will of the Korean people; (*c*) to assist the Koreans in establishing a sound economy and an adequate educational system as essential bases of an independent, democratic state. We support such measures as our government can take, through the United Nations, to give practical effect to these objectives. Since a duly elected and responsible government of the Republic of Korea is now functioning in Southern Korea and since provision has been made for inclusion of representatives of the North Korean prefectures if and when they are permitted to cooperate, we request our government to continue to support the application of the Republic of Korea for membership in the United Nations.

(8) Our government should cooperate with the policies of the Republic of the Philippines in preserving its natural resources with a view to ensuring the continuing material prosperity and general welfare of its people, and should review the "Parity Bill" in the Philippine Trade Act passed in 1946 by the Congress of the United States and the military agreements now existing between the two governments, for the purpose of safeguarding in every possible way the sovereignty of the Republic.

(9) Our government is to be commended for its support of the resolution approved by the Security Council of the United Nations (January 28, 1949) which called upon the Government of the Netherlands to ensure the immediate discontinuance of all military operations in *Indonesia*; to release immediately and unconditionally all political prisoners; to undertake negotiations with representatives of the Government of the Republic of Indonesia with a view to carrying out the expressed objectives and desires of both parties to establish a federal, independent and sovereign United States of Indonesia at the earliest possible date. We commend the further provision in the resolution which specified that the transfer of sovereignty over Indonesia by the Government of the Netherlands to the United States of Indonesia should take place at the earliest possible date and in any case not later than July 1, 1950.

We ask our government to seek through the Security Council of the United Nations, in all possible ways, including the imposition of economic sanctions if necessary, to secure consent of the Government of the Netherlands to abide by the decisions of the United Nations in respect to the Indonesian situation.

E. THE CHURCHES' STRATEGY FOR WORLD ORDER EDUCATION AND ACTION

Following are suggestions designed to translate the findings of this Conference into effective Christian action.

1. SUGGESTIONS FOR PERSONAL ACTION

(1) *Examine our own personal views.* Too often our personal life and relations to our fellowmen in work and social life produce attitudes which if incorporated in wide-scale social action would menace the welfare of the world.

(2) *Pray.* Make the concern for world order a regular part of our devotional life.

(3) *Be informed.* Study carefully the church papers, the publications of the Federal Council of Churches and of the World Council of Churches, together with the related materials produced under denominational and other auspices, as a supplement to and possible corrective of newspaper and radio information. We have a moral duty to secure more and better information in order to be able to disregard what is unreliable.

(4) *Think.* Make up our own minds—bring our own prayerful judgment to bear on the issues of the day.

(5) *Talk.* In the family circle and with our friends. Test our ideas and explore issues of world order:

> (a) With persons who are in a position to take action; talking with the right people at the right time, with the right points, can produce positive change;

> (b) With members of other cultural groups to further intercultural understanding.

(6) *Write* to government leaders and legislators; to the public opinion columns in the press; to radio stations, commenting on programs.

(7) *Get into politics.* In addition to voting, be active in political organizations, starting in the precinct and ward. National policies and leadership are frequently determined in these spots where church members are conspicuously absent.

(8) *Share* with suffering people in other lands through denominational missionary and world relief funds, in their coordinated program of Church World Service, and through other accredited agencies such as CROP, CARE, etc. Through personal correspondence, share yourself. "The gift without the giver is bare."

2. SUGGESTIONS FOR LOCAL CHURCH AND COMMUNITY

(1) *Assign responsibility* for world order concern to the appropriate unit (committee, board, etc.) of the local church. This responsibility includes infiltration of the entire program of the church with education and action for world order through such operations as: sponsorship of special world order days, setting up church night programs, and organizing study courses and activities of men's, women's, and young people's groups.

(2) *Preach.* World order should be dealt with in sermons on special days. In addition, issues bearing on world order should be brought before the congregation in the normal preaching schedule.

(3) *Relate*:

(a) The world order concern of one church to that of other churches, either through the machinery of the local council of churches, or, where a local council is lacking, through a special inter-church committee set up for collaborative effort.

(b) The educational program of world order to the missionary enter-prise of the church. This is one of the most effective methods of producing a climate in which world order will thrive, and a world leadership with common standards of right and wrong.

(4) *Interrelate the church's work for world order with the community*

(a) Through the presence of church men and women in the membership of non-church organizations and/or

(b) Through those responsible for the world order emphasis of non-church groups or combinations of groups.

3. SUGGESTIONS FOR DENOMINATIONS AND INTERDENOMINATIONAL AGENCIES

(1) *Cooperate for united action.* Churches that are calling for nations to yield sovereignty must themselves yield some sovereignty in the interest of long-range joint planning between denominations and interdenominational agencies in the protection of major emphases, programs, and campaigns.

(2) *Support the area conferences.* to be projected by the Federal Council of Churches in cooperation with denominational agencies and state and city councils of churches.

(3) *Take world order to the people via mass media.* Specifically, we urge:

(a) That the Protestant Radio Commission give priority to world order issues in its expanding program. This may be done by strengthening the program *Religion in the News,* and by providing for other programs giving the Christian interpretation of world news. There is a tragic need for informed, honest, and dispassionate commentary on the news, of which we have been deprived in recent years by the loss of some of our ablest commentators.

(b) That the Associated Church Press, the social action agencies of the churches, and the Federal Council of Churches confer on plans for the dissemination of world order information.

(c) That national interdenominational agencies and state and local councils of churches take active measures to secure in the non-church press more adequate coverage of Protestant concerns in world news.

(d) That these agencies encourage more factual reporting and less news distortion on the part of the press, radio and motion pictures.

(4) *Train leaders:*

(a) Seminaries should assume responsibility for training the clergy to take positions of leadership in promoting world order.

(b) Plans should be designed by all churches for training clergy and lay leaders in public affairs and techniques through such programs as Washington and United Nations seminars, summer training schools, work shops, and institutes.

(c) Church and publication boards should make it possible for editors and representatives of the church press and radio to gain experience and understanding of international processes through carefully prepared seminars and work shops at meetings of the United Nations here and abroad, and in the State Department in Washington. The Department of International Justice and Goodwill is urged to arrange for such seminars and workshops.

(5) *Help youth serve:*

(a) Encourage and cooperate with youth and student organizations in their programs for world order.

(b) Endeavor to secure active youth participation in the planning and programs of local world order conferences.

(c) Give financial aid and other encouragement to hemisphere and world conferences of Christian Youth.

(d) Encourage experimentation in sending youth service missions to other parts of the world, particularly to the Far East and Middle East.

(e) Encourage the wider development of two-way student exchange programs through European Cooperation Administration counterpart funds and other governmental and private resources.

(f)Make use of the rich backgrounds of the thousands of foreign students now in this country by enlisting them in our world order program. There is great need also to help these future leaders to get a balanced picture of American community life by inviting them into the homes of church people on week-ends and during vacation periods.

(g) Help bring together American youth of diverse cultural background with a view toward promoting cultural democracy in America.

(h) Seek immediate aid for the 2,500 Chinese students now stranded in the United States because of the unsettled conditions in China.

(i) Encourage and assist youth and children to study and participate actively in the missionary programs of the church.

4. COOPERATION WITH CHURCHES IN OTHER LANDS

It is of crucial importance that wherever and whenever possible our American churches cooperate with the churches of other lands in the quest for world order. The Commission of the Churches on International Affairs, established by the World Council of Churches and the International Missionary Council, is an agency through which such cooperation may be carried forward.

In line with the expressed aims of this commission the attention of the churches should be called:

(a) To problems that should be the concern of the Christian conscience at any particular time, and to suggest ways in which Christians may act effectively upon these problems in their respective countries and internationally.

(b) To the formation of agencies through which the consciences of Christians may be stirred and educated as to their responsibilities in the world of nations.

(c) To the development of understanding by the exchange of clergy and lay leaders across national boundaries and to explore the possibilities that funds for such exchange may be secured through peace foundations.

We would add to these aims:

(a) Exploring the possibility through the World Council of Churches of expanding the present American observance of World Order Sunday on an international basis.

(b) Encouraging the Churches of other nations to set up conferences on world order similar to the present Cleveland Conference.

The outcome of this struggle, from the human perspective, is uncertain. But the obligations of Christians, despite the perils and uncertainties, are clear. To turn aside from the quest for peace because of the difficulties, or to falter because of discouragement, is not the course of the Christian. "It is required of us that we be faithful and obedient. The event is with God."

III. Other Actions[4]

A. A MESSAGE TO CHRISTIANS IN ALL LANDS

To: Our Fellow Christians
      In All Lands,
      Grace to you and peace from
      God the Father and the Lord Jesus Christ

We are 450 delegates from American churches assembled in a national study conference to consider questions of world order and peace. It comforts us to know that in the midst of chaotic world conditions the world community of believers of which Christ is the head remains unbroken. We draw courage from the fact of growing Christian unity and we pray and labor for world unity and peace.

We rejoice with our fellow-Christians in lands that are experiencing a new-birth of freedom and hope. We grieve with our fellow-Christians in lands devastated by war, wracked with civil dissensions, or oppressed by tyranny. We are deeply moved by the witness borne by Christians in such lands, often in the face of threat and persecution. This encourages us to proclaim that Christian witness can be borne under all conditions and that this witness has power.

We note with humble rejoicing that missionaries of our churches, sometimes in posts of great danger, are demonstrating the reality of a fellowship in Christ that transcends all barriers. We beseech for them the comfort of God's presence, the guidance of His word, and the communion of His Holy Spirit.

We are sustained by the knowledge that Christians in all lands are upholding in their respective nations the same standards of divine justice and pressing on toward the same goal of a world order worthy of the name of our common Lord. Above all, we are sustained by the knowledge that the gracious God revealed in Christ is at work in human history, turning even the greatest evils into good, and that His will of mercy cannot finally be defeated.

B. A STATEMENT ON RELIGIOUS FREEDOM

The Conference endorses the recent statement of the Executive Committee of the World Council of Churches on the matter of religious freedom and commends it to the most earnest attention of the churches. The statement says in part—

> In numerous countries of Europe and Asia, governments which claim to guarantee freedom of conscience and religion are in fact denying it. The freedom of the Church to preach the Word of God to all men in all realms of life is restricted. Religious instruction of young people is hindered. Christian youth movements are prohibited. There is interference with the training of the clergy and the appointment of church leaders. Obstacles are put in the way of public evangelism and missionary work. Officers and members of the Churches have been arrested and imprisoned on an ever-increasing scale. In some areas, the Churches face the possibility of the complete disruption of their life as Churches and communities. We see in these measures a deliberate attempt to undermine the witness of the Churches by forcing them either to withdraw completely from public life, or to become the tools of a secular policy.
>
> In some countries where the tradition of freedom is apparently maintained, increasing government control over the action and thought of people, domination of public policy by military and strategic considerations, and the infringement of the rights of religious minorities constitute an accumulating menace of which Christians seem to be as yet largely unaware.

"God alone is Lord of the conscience." When threatened by autocratic or tyrannical power, Protestants will therefore take their stand according to the dictates of conscience, and will protest against any earthly coercion, political or ecclesiastical, that assumes the prerogatives of God and attempts to proscribe the individual conscience.

We thank God for all brothers of the faith everywhere who by their supreme loyalty to God and in His strength are bearing witness against totalitarianism, reminding the nations of the world of the divine basis of all human rights and freedoms and the ground of all sound world order and peace.

[1]This Message to the Churches was adopted by the conference. It was subsequently approved by the Executive Committee of the Federal Council, March 15, 1949. In transmitting the other findings and actions of the conference, the Executive Committee made it clear that in these actions the conference spoke only for itself, and not for the churches or for the Federal Council.

[2]Section reports were not "approved" by the conference as a whole but were "received and transmitted to the churches for their study and appropriate action."

[3]Some members of the conference feel under obligation to record their conviction that any war or any resort to military measures would be morally evil and practically self-defeating. They hold that the attempt temporarily to maintain the huge military force adequate to balance Russian military power and to force "moderation" of Soviet policy provides only the illusion of security. It means the continuance of the cold war and the armaments race, not the certain prevention of war.

[4]Like the "Message to the Churches," these two concluding actions were "approved" by the conference as a whole.

Chapter V

AFTER KOREA:

"Christian Faith and International Responsibility"
Cleveland, 1953

INTRODUCTION

Immediately following the 1949 conference, world attention was focused largely on the Far East. Events moved rapidly in China. The People's Republic was proclaimed in September, and Communist forces rapidly expanded their hold on mainland China by pushing the Nationalist armies relentlessly toward the sea. Chiang Kai-shek was forced to move his base of operations to the island of Formosa in December. Six months later, in June, 1950, fighting broke out in Korea. The United States, along with other members of the United Nations, became involved almost immediately in what was euphemistically known as a "police action." The People's Republic of China put 200,000 troops into the conflict in November. After a costly and relatively inconclusive war, an armistice was signed on July 27, 1953.

As the Korean stalemate continued, feelings of frustration and resentment became widespread in the United States. These were expressed in mounting attacks upon the United Nations and growing opposition both to continuing the war in Korea and to all forms of economic and technical assistance abroad. In this situation another national study conference was called to convene in Cleveland, October 27-30, 1953.by the National Council of Churches, formed in 1950 by the merger of the Federal Council and twelve other interdenominational organizations.

"Our country has become the most powerful nation in the free world," and "this power carries with it great responsibility," said Bishop William C. Martin, President of the council, in his "Call," issued in February, 1953.

> In a world threatened by tyranny, by rising nationalism, and by unrest in the less developed areas, the power of a great nation like ours must be exercised with restraint and humility to avoid appeasement on one side and total war on the other....

> It is precisely in these difficult and anxious times that the churches of Christ in the United States must speak and speak clearly.... What can the churches say to the people? What insights can the churches give to those who make decisions that affect millions of persons throughout the world?

Between the issuance of the call and the convening of the conference, significant events transpired on the world scene: the death of Stalin; the signing of the Korean armistice; the official Soviet announcement of their first A-bomb explosion; and the German election returning Konrad Adenauer to power. Certain of these events gave those who came to Cleveland some grounds for hope, but others increased their forebodings for the future.

In the days just before and during the conference, dispatches from Panmunjom reported a deadlock in talks on the exchange of prisoners-of-war, and those from Washington and the United Nations told of an impasse over Communist insistence that neutral powers be permitted to participate in the forthcoming Korean peace talks. Other top news stories dealt with the further build-up of NATO forces, the five power conference on Trieste, and United Nations wrestling with the perennial Israeli-Arab problem.

The thirty member communions of the National Council and several others were invited to send voting delegates to Cleveland. State and local councils of churches with professional leadership, certain units of the National Council, the National YMCA, the National YWCA, and the United Student Christian Council were also invited to send delegates. Members of the National Council's Department of International Justice and Goodwill, participants in the five preparatory study commissions, and staff from certain units of the National Council were invited to take part as nonvoting consultants.

Participating in the deliberations at Cleveland were 380 delegates and 50 consultants. There were 51 registered observers, including six Germans. The delegates and consultants came from 26 communions, including 11 consultants from the United Church of Canada. There were 67 delegates appointed by 12 state councils of churches and 28 local councils, representing a total of 18 states. Delegates and consultants came from 36 states and Washington, D.C.

Of the 430 participants 243 (56.5 percent) were ordained and 187 (43.5 per cent) were laypersons. Vocationally there were 121 church executives (including 17 from the National Council), 109 pastors, 43 from college and seminary faculties, 23 church editors and writers, and 20 executives from other nonprofit agencies. There were also 54 housewives, 29 business executives, 9 lawyers, 11 students, and 11 from other vocations. Ninety-five (22 per cent) of the delegates and consultants were women.

At the invitation of the conference committee the State Department sent three resource persons and the Foreign Operations Administration sent one. These were the only government officials present at the conference with the exception of Assistant Secretary of State Thruston B. Morton who gave an address at the public meeting on the evening of October 27. John Foster Dulles, who had assumed the cabinet post of Secretary of State under the Eisenhower administration, was not present.

The presiding officer of the conference was Mrs. Douglas Horton, chair of the Department of International Justice and Goodwill and former President, Wellesley College. Angus Dun, Bishop of the Washington, (D.C.) area diocese of the Episcopal Church, gave the keynote address on the conference theme, "Christian Faith and International Responsibility." Herman F. Reissig, Secretary of the Congregational-Christian Council for Social Action, also addressed a plenary session. Along with Thruston B. Morton, Eleanor Roosevelt spoke at the public meeting on the opening night of the conference.

For purposes of study, discussion, and formulation of reports, participants were divided into four sections. Each of these groups met for nine hours on its specially assigned topic. A Message Committee met parallel to the other groups as Section I. Each of the other sections sent two persons to represent the interests and concerns of their groups.

Five study commissions had been set up to prepare background papers for the use of the sections. Commission I, "Christian Faith and International Responsibility," was chaired by Bishop Dun. The paper prepared by this commission was used as the basis of discussion by the Message Committee under the chairmanship of Mrs. Horton. In the case of the other sections the discussion was chaired by the chairman of the commission which had produced the preparatory document on the same theme. Section II, "The United States and the United Nations," was chaired by Mrs. Edith Sampson; Section III, "The United States and Foreign Economic Policy," by Willard L. Thorp, Professor, Amherst College and former Deputy Assistant Secretary of State; Section IV, "The United States and the Less Developed Areas," by Emory Ross, Secretary of the Foreign Mission Conference of North America; and Section V, "The United States and Collective Security," by Frank P. Graham, United Nations mediator, who previously served as United States Senator from North Carolina and President of the University of North Carolina.

Sections differed in the way in which they formulated their reports. Some used the preparatory papers as the basis of their findings, revising them more or less drastically. Others took these papers as a starting point for discussion, but finally discarded them and started out afresh to draw up their own findings.

The message, adopted by the conference, noted that two massive realities dominated the world at that moment: revolutionary upheavals in major world areas, and conflict between the Soviet world and the free world. It urged America to meet these issues by encouraging the creative possibilities of the ferments in technically less developed areas, and by supporting efforts to resist expansion of communist totalitarianism. The message, which is titled "Christian Faith and International Responsibility," summarizes the main points of the section reports and provides a good over-all view of the major concerns and emphases of the conference.

Reports of the sections dealt in considerably more detail with various areas of the United States' involvement in the world scene: its relation to the United Nations, its foreign economic policy, its relation to the less-developed areas, and the subject of collective security.

It was in connection with this last section report that the most highly controversial issues were introduced. In the plenary session motions were made to delete the paragraph which begins, "We support, during this interim period of historical evolution...our present collective defense system," and also the next item, "We support the United Nations collective action against aggression in Korea..." After extended debate both motions lost by a vote of approximately 2 to 1. These paragraphs were retained by three votes more than two-thirds of those present and voting. The basis for the dissenting opinion was included as "A Minority Statement" appended to the section report.[1]

Apart from this, the judgments of the conference seem to have been quite unanimous, and members were able to agree on an even dozen resolutions on such concrete issues as negotiations with the Soviet Union, technical assistance, racial discrimination, and the Immigration and Nationality Act of 1952. These resolutions were also made part of the conference report.

Neither *Time* nor *Newsweek* gave any attention to the conference, although the daily press accorded it good coverage.

Pleased by the "realistic" attitude on the issues of collective security and the Korean action, *Christianity and Crisis* referred to the conference's message as "an eloquent and mature analysis of America's position in the world, and of the responsibilities which are the concomitants of our power."[2]

Not happy with these particular actions, the *Christian Century* remarked that "the conference registered the effect another four years of cold war has had on the thinking of church leaders." It also commented on the lack of time to deal adequately with such a comprehensive agenda. Still it commended the fairness of the conference leadership and reported that "the general spirit...was one of restraint, of trying honestly to confront issues, but at the same time to keep the church sufficiently detached so that it can stand off from politics and render Christian judgments and act in a Christian way."[3]

It may be appropriate to note the evaluation not only of this particular conference but of the trend in previous conferences by one who was among the minority voting against support of collective security and the "police action" in Korea. A. J. Muste, of the International Fellowship of Reconciliation, said that from Delaware to Cleveland, 1953,

> The general trend has been toward less "controversy," more "unanimity." Cleveland, 1953, went farthest in this direction. Is this really a good sign or simply an indication that the general trend toward conformity and the avoidance of "dangerous" themes is affecting the psychological climate of church circles? The impact of all these conferences has been to put the American churches back of the Administration of the moment and of the internationalist elements in the major parties, to give sanction in effect to World War II and the Korean war, to avoid revolutionary analysis and proposals, to play down the

prophetic and to hew out a "responsible," practical middle-of-the-road line.[4]

While there were doubtless others who shared some of Dr. Muste's feelings and misgivings, it is significant that another member of the minority put a different interpretation on the events—at least at Cleveland, 1953. Prof. Georgia Harkness, of the Pacific School of Religion, admitted that the recent conference

> did not say all that either Dr. Muste or I would have liked it to say. However, it said so much that is right, true and *Christian* that I came away rejoicing. Its spirit, its method and its findings were a major contribution to Christian thinking.
>
> It does not seem to me accurate to say that "the object was to come out with a program which would strengthen the hands of Mr. Eisenhower or Mr. Dulles." Rather, its object was to find, as far as the limits of human wisdom and four days of time would permit, a corporate Christian answer to the problems created by existing conditions in the Orient, in Europe and in the United States. Naturally its conclusions could not satisfy everyone, but the high degree of unanimity achieved was not the result of compromise or avoiding issues.[5]

Granting with Ms. Harkness that this conference said many things that were "right and true and *Christian*," one nevertheless has the feeling that there are elements of truth in Mr. Muste's indictment. The conference did at certain critical points seem to pay undue deference to the views and policies of the State Department now presided over by John Foster Dulles. Not that there were overt pressures upon delegates in 1953 as there had been in 1949. "If there was pressure on the delegates from the Department of State or any other source outside the churches, they were unaware of it,"[6] said the *Christian Century* concerning the 1953 conference. Yet the conference leaders and a majority of the delegates did accept their nation's foreign policy rather uncritically as the votes on the two amendments on collective security and Korea make clear.

One is tempted to speak of the conferences of both 1949 and 1953 as the period of the Babylonish Captivity of the national study conferences.[7] The 1958 conference was to show much more independence of judgment and greater freedom by calling into question certain basic concepts of American foreign policy. Cleveland, 1958, was to reflect much more of the independent, prophetic spirit of Delaware, 1942, and Cleveland, 1945.

---

[1]See below, p. 190.

[2]XII, No. 20 (Nov. 30, 1953), 153.

[3]LXX (Nov. 11, 1953) 1286, 1288.

[4]"A Footnote to Cleveland," *ibid.* (Dec. 9, 1953), p. 1421.

[5]"Another Footnote," *ibid.*, LXXI (Jan. 13, 1954), 49.

[6]LXX (Nov. 11, 1953), 1286.

[7]While the 1949 conference did not "buy" the Atlantic Pact, failure to do so was due largely to the fact that the text was not yet available and to resentment against such overt State Department pressures. By 1953 church leadership had taken NATO for granted, along with the other implementations of the concept of collective security.

CHRISTIAN FAITH AND INTERNATIONAL RESPONSIBILITY: REPORT OF THE FOURTH NATIONAL STUDY CONFERENCE ON THE CHURCHES AND WORLD ORDER

Cleveland, Ohio   October 27–30, 1953

I. Christian Faith and International Responsibility: The Conference Message

II. Reports from the Sections

The United States and the United Nations; The United States and Foreign Economic Policy; The United States and the Less Developed Areas; The United States and Collective Security.

III. Conference Resolutions

Negotiations with The Soviet Union; Treaties and Executive Agreements; Technical Assistance; International Financial Assistance; Surplus Foods in the United States; Dependent Peoples; Racial Discrimination and Foreign Policy; Universal Disarmament; Refugees; The Immigration and Nationality Act of 1952; Communist China and the United Nations; Palestine.

IV. A Closing Statement

I. Christian Faith and International Responsibility: A Message to the Churches[1]

1. WE BELONG TO A WORLD-WIDE COMMUNITY

As Christians, we belong to a community of faith, knit together by the grace of our Lord Jesus Christ and our common loyalty to him. That community joins in one world-wide fellowship those who in ages past, today, and in ages yet to come call upon the name of the Lord and seek to serve his righteous will. We are also members of the community of mankind, created in God's image and all held within the embrace of his loving purpose. Despite the sins and shortcomings of Christians everywhere which obscure the unity and universality of the Church, we yet know that it is one and universal and that it claims the whole-hearted loyalty of each of us. We believe it to be the will of God to bring all men into that perfect communion with himself and with each other in which Christ's commandment is fulfilled that we love God with all our heart, mind, soul, and strength, and our neighbors as ourselves.

We acknowledge that as members of Christ's one church, we are members of one another with all our fellow Christians across the world. All of us together are inescapably involved in the conflicts of national power, of race, of dominion, of social systems which ravage our world. The ties which bind us to our brothers in Christ and to all men everywhere require of us a concern for all that burdens and distorts their lives and our relations with them. This concern goes beyond that which arises from the fact that our own lives are burdened and threatened by the political and economic disorders of our world.

2. WE SPEAK AS CHRISTIANS AND AS U. S. CITIZENS

While we necessarily speak out of a background of our Christian heritage, we are nevertheless aware of the significant and valid contributions which people of other religious and cultural traditions have made and are making to the solutions of the problems confronting us. We eagerly seek their contribution and welcome the light which they bring to the solution of our mutual problems.

Along with our Christian brothers in other nations we accept, as part of our Christian duty, responsibility toward the civil society in which we live. As American Christians, citizens of a nation with great wealth and power, we feel with special urgency the need to affirm our common bond with Christians and with the people of all other nations. Yet at the same time we must speak of the world crisis as Christians who are also citizens of the United States.

We will seek, therefore, to speak as Christians and as American citizens to American citizens about American responsibilities in the world community. In this task we greatly need the insights and concerns of Christians in other lands to correct our limitations and prejudices as citizens of one nation.

Central in the faith which unites the Christian community is the conviction that God who is revealed in Christ is the Lord of history, the Ruler of men and nations. He wills justice, peace, freedom, and brotherhood. One of the Church's tasks is to challenge in His name the pride and the pretensions of men and nations, and in the light of God's law and reconciling love to prompt them into courses of action which are in harmony with his purposes. The Church also has the responsibility of providing an example of true community in its own life and fellowship.

Yet faith and hope and love need to be implemented with conscientious and continuing study of existing conditions and of historical trends in order to provide guidance for a responsible foreign policy.

3. OUR DECISIONS STAND UNDER THE JUDGMENT OF GOD

Our Christian faith requires that man acknowledge his responsibility to God. As a nation and as individuals our responsibility to him rises above all other claims and responsibilities. We can find peace and order only as our ways are conformed to his ways. We stand under his judgment and, in the light of that judgment, must make our decisions in international relations with humility and contrition. Our faith in God and love for him and for our neighbors help us to make decisions and to act in the face of all our failures and perplexities. Our faith culminates in an indestructible hope that at the last God will fully manifest the sovereignty of his love in Christ and gather all that he finds acceptable in history into the fulfillment of his kingdom. In that hope we can live and act in quietness and in confidence amid the darkness and insecurities of our time.

The Christian faith does not provide us with clear-cut blueprints or easy answers for the tragic problems of the world's disorder. We must guard ourselves and others from the illusion that there is any simple or permanent solution of them. It is difficult for nations to develop and maintain the will to pursue a responsible policy. As American Christians we need to resist the temptation to believe that a nation which publicly professes Christian ideals is thereby assured of divine approval of its policies. And we must especially avoid the assumption that a solution lies in making the rest of the world over as nearly as possible into the pattern of the United States.

4. REVOLUTIONARY UPHEAVAL IN VAST AREAS

Two massive realities dominate the world situation. One is the revolutionary upheaval in vast areas of the world. The other is the conflict between the Soviet world and the free world. These two major realities are distinct yet interrelated. Each needs to be seen and understood in its own character, yet any dealing with one is complicated by and bound up with our dealings with the other.

One of the chief facts of our time is the ferment among the peoples in technically less developed areas. This ferment is complex. It includes a passionate nationalism in rebellion against colonialism and domination in every form. It is a revolt against hunger and misery associated with feudal patterns and foreign or domestic exploitation. It is pervaded by resentment against racial arrogance and discriminatory practices of the dominant peoples of the West.

This ferment is in part induced by progressive elements in the indigenous cultures, and in part by influences from Western societies. High standards of living, democratic ideals and practices and, not least, the impact of the missionary movement have helped to convert resignation to age-old evils into revolt against them. Of central importance has been the emphasis upon the worth and dignity of persons.

As the Western societies face the new and changing situation in the technically less developed areas, there are many factors on both sides which make understanding and the establishment of equitable and stable relations difficult to achieve. Inexperience, extremism, and persistent suspicions on the part of peoples in the technically underdeveloped areas; complacency, fear, and attachment of privilege on the part of technically more advanced nations combine to trouble relationships.

As Christians, we have a special obligation to see both the creative and the destructive possibilities in this new ferment, which the preaching of the Gospel has helped to create. The ending of ancient injustices, the movements toward national self-respect and self-government or political independence, the coming into their own of the darker-skinned peoples of the world, the struggle for economic development and social equality—all these carry with them creative possibilities. On the other hand, the tendencies to excess and to rabid and self-enclosed nationalism, the uprooting of traditional loyalties and disciplines without accepted substitutes, the clear danger of a new tyranny for these peoples in process of emancipation—these have grave portents for the future.

5. SOVIET COMMUNISM VS. THE NON-SOVIET WORLD

The other major issue is the conflict between an aggressive Soviet Communism and the non-Soviet world. To meet this explosive situation responsibly, American policy must meet two immediate requirements. One is to resist the extension of Communist totalitarianism. The other is to avoid a third world war. The need to overcome the threat of both tyranny and war will in all likelihood be with us for a long period and to it the United States must be prepared to commit its power and resources. We cannot succeed in this negative task unless we persistently and constructively seek to establish the positive conditions for peace and justice.

Soviet Communist power combines faith in a system of ideas, emphasis upon technological and social programs, propaganda which exploits human hopes and resentments, ruthless suppression of every form of dissent, a world-wide conspiracy, all backed by great political and economic power and a mighty army. The Western societies must meet all aspects of this threat, but with methods consistent with political and spiritual freedom. Military strength seems to most of us to be essential, but political and economic health, social and spiritual vision are more basic.

Beyond the immediate challenges of the Soviet-free world conflict, Christians must insist upon continuing analysis of the possibilities and limitations of co-existence between the Soviet and the free societies. The differences are so fundamental and the lack of confidence on both sides is so deep and stubborn that anything worthy of the name of reconciliation appears impossible at present. Since it is our Christian faith that God can bring about changes that seem beyond human power, we refuse to believe that such reconciliation is finally impossible. Meanwhile, the free societies must make every effort to negotiate workable agreements with the Soviet world without compromise of basic convictions. In the face of atomic death which menaces all mankind, every possible advance toward adequate control of armaments and toward the mutual trust essential to this end must be seen as an urgent necessity.

6. CO-EXISTENCE WITH THE SOVIET POWER SYSTEM

The minimal basis for co-existence is the recognition on both sides that peace is better than armed conflict, especially when war threatens mutual annihilation. In the light of our faith in the creative sovereignty of God over history we cannot accept another global war as inevitable or close the door to the possibility of a genuine relaxation of the present tensions. Indeed, every opportunity to develop even a temporary easing of tensions should be seized by the United States, and we should give no grounds for accusations of intransigence or of closing the door to negotiations. Co-existence with the Soviet power system does not mean acquiescence in its tyrannous cruelty nor indifference to the fate of peoples living under its rule. For these peoples we must continue to cherish freedom from external control of their own destiny, and conditions more favorable for the development of political and spiritual freedom. By example and persuasion, by humanitarian measures, and by actions in accord with the purposes of the United Nations, America must do all within its power to assist peoples under Soviet Communist rule to cling to the goals of a free and responsible society, in the hope that there may be changes in the Soviet system and policy conducive to freedom and peace.

These peoples in Communist countries, human beings like ourselves, must not be identified with the cruelty and tyranny of Soviet power. Many are Christians, all are persons beloved of God. Our churches have a responsibility for making clear the distinction between these peoples and the Soviet power system.

The two massive realities we have analyzed are distinct yet interrelated. We must be on our guard against over-simplifying the situation by viewing one of these facts as only an expression of the other. Indeed, they involve basic contradictions. There is a tendency in some quarters to see every revolutionary movement in the world and every evidence of resentment or hostility as the direct result of Soviet machinations. But we shall deceive ourselves if we believe that the removal of Communist power would eliminate all the problems arising out of the ferment among the peoples in the technically less developed areas or elsewhere. In other quarters, there is a tendency to see communism as simply the result of economic deprivations and social injustices. But, again, it is too simple to imagine that the improvement of the economic and political health of the non-Communist world would alone insure a genuine transformation of Kremlin policy or a radical modification of the Soviet empire.

If these two major realities confronting us have independent roots, they are also interrelated and must be dealt with as such. Soviet communism moves into every area of ferment and resentment, offering promises of immediate and far-reaching solutions. Sometimes natural sympathy with movements for national freedom must take account of the danger of leaving a young country open to Soviet domination. In seeking both to resist Soviet aggression and to further the conditions of freedom and justice throughout the world, the United States and other free societies are faced with grave decisions, which can be rightly made only with a humble sense of our human limitations. The situation in which we as a people are called to act responsibly is not only economically burdensome and politically dangerous, but also morally complex and difficult.

7. U. S. NEEDS THE RESTRAINT OF INTERNATIONAL CO-OPERATION

The power of the United States has increased so rapidly in recent decades that it is difficult for our people to be aware of its proportions and of the responsibility it carries with it. As Christians we believe this power is a trust from God; neither a historical accident, nor the fruit of special virtue. The churches are called to help our nation measure up to its responsibility and to avoid alike the temptation to use its power recklessly or to evade the burdens it brings.

Because of the magnitude of our world responsibilities, we Americans should welcome the counsel and criticism which naturally result from international co-operation. By so doing we may be enabled to use our great power and to express our generosity and our national idealism with greater effectiveness. It is easy to lose patience with the complex ways of international diplomacy. We find it hard to understand why other nations may regard our wealth and our power with a mixture of respect, fear, envy, and misgivings. It is difficult for us to be sufficiently sensitive to the feelings of friends and partners with fewer advantages. As a people we must learn to accept other nations not only as partners but also as instruments of judgment on our national action. It is for us to remember that no nation is good enough, wise enough, or strong enough to go its way without a decent respect for the opinions of mankind.

Against this background we American Christians should evaluate United States foreign policy, especially the role of our country in the United Nations and in the various regional security arrangements to which it is a party. Our Christian recognition of the self-centeredness and finiteness of men should guard us against expecting more from these associations than they can offer even while our faith keeps us sensitive to the claims of our neighbors upon us.

8. THE UNITED NATIONS: ACHIEVEMENTS AND LIMITATIONS

The United Nations came into being as an instrument for peace and cooperative action among nations. Its achievements have been great although the obstacles in the world situation have been serious. The United Nations has provided a world forum for discussing explosive issues and a means of settlement in a considerable number of situations which otherwise might have led to war. It has been a constant force for collective security; has brought into new focus the oneness of mankind; has given to the world its first comprehensive Declaration of Human Rights; has channeled large sums into the rehabilitation of war-ravaged countries; has set up an extensive program of technical co-operation; and has initiated a variety of specialized services for men, women, and children.

We would face realistically the existing limitations in the organization and operations of the United Nations. Some of these grow out of the continuing fact of human selfishness and fallibility; others are inherent in any structure in which sovereign nations endeavor to work together. The divisions of our contemporary world cannot be overcome by mere structural changes in the international organization. For example, the goal of universality is qualified in theory by the willingness and ability of prospective members to fulfill the commitments of the Charter, and in practice by various considerations of political expediency. Such abuses as that being made of the veto power may be lessened by revisions of the structure but will be eliminated only by winning nations to a new purpose and spirit of co-operation.

As Christians and citizens of the United States we have an inescapable obligation to support the United Nations as a body essential to the freedom of nations and the peace of the world. Likewise, we have responsibility for its growth and improvement. This we can discharge only by honest concern, by criticism of weaknesses and recognition of strength, by contributing to an improved international climate, by urging the United Nations itself to effect further specific advances within the framework of the present Charter, and by encouraging such revisions as may strengthen the Charter and the organization.

We look forward to the further development of the United Nations into a far more effective instrument of collective security, replacing war with the rule of law, freedom, and justice.

9. THE PERIL OF WITHDRAWAL AND ISOLATION

We call upon our nation to rise above partisanship, to deal with issues upon their merits, to endeavor to work understandingly with nations whose policies differ from ours as well as with those of similar policies, and to remain steadfast in loyalty to our Charter obligations.

Within the United States there are powerful factors moving us toward co-operation, and other forces which would lead us to withdrawal and isolation. Recognition that even enlightened self-interest requires responsiveness to the world's needs has been shown in the employment of American skill and wealth in rebuilding war-ravaged economies through the Marshall Plan and in upbuilding technically less developed areas through the Point IV Program. Over against such acts of statesmanship examples of irresponsibility toward the world community can be cited, such as pressure for restrictive tariff policies, discriminatory sections in the Immigration Act of 1952, and wholesale resistance to continuing foreign aid without offering a constructive alternative. Christian faith teaches us that we are placed by God in an order of material and spiritual interdependence, and that we go against the grain of his order when we fail to recognize that interdependence or to play our full part in the processes of mutual co-operation which it demands.

10. TECHNICAL CO-OPERATION AND FOREIGN INVESTMENT

The idea of technical assistance is one of the great ideas of our time. Indifference to existing contrasts between plenty for the few and want for the many cannot be reconciled with the law of love. Moreover the way in which America shares its skills and resources with peoples endeavoring to improve their conditions of living is of paramount importance. Americans should rejoice in the revolt of these peoples against immemorial misery and stand ready to associate themselves with this struggle for a better future. We should urge upon our government patient and persistent participation, through its own agencies and through the United Nations, in constructive programs of technical co-operation. These programs will be more effective if kept free from subordination to military considerations. Governmental and intergovernmental action may be essential for a long time; so likewise will discerning and responsible action by business and industry, private philanthropy, Christian missions and other non-governmental agencies. This enterprise in all its aspects should engage the service of persons who possess not only the requisite skills but also a humble sense of vocation and of genuine identification with those among whom they work. To raise up among its sons and daughters such servants of the common good is a major responsibility of the Christian Church.

We believe there should be an expansion of private long-term investment abroad. Through private investment there is opportunity to contribute to the economic development of other countries to our mutual advantage. However, in the light of unstable conditions and considering the kind of investment in large-scale noncommercial projects needed in many countries, it appears necessary that for some time at least a substantial part of investment abroad may have to be accomplished through public investment on either a single national or an international co-operative basis. We should increase our support for the development of the underdeveloped countries, recognizing the particular services which the United Nations can contribute to this high purpose.

11. U. S. PRODUCTIVITY AND INTERNATIONAL TRADE

The tremendous influence throughout the world of U. S. economic strength and policies makes it imperative for us to judge major policy alternatives in the light of what we believe to be the moral responsibility of our country. We should support those policies which lead at home to greater productivity, economic stability and high employment, and in the rest of the world foster economic development and stability and higher living standards. The economic well-being of our country is in part dependent upon what happens in other countries. It is likewise true that the maintenance of our domestic prosperity and productivity is one of the major contributions to world economic stability which our nation can make.

In light of these principles, we believe that Christian citizens should work for the growth of world trade and the gradual reduction or elimination of artificial barriers to trade. Accordingly, it is our conviction that the United States should reduce or eliminate import tariffs and trade quotas principally through a more than temporary continuance of the Reciprocal Trade Agreements program and participation in the General Agreement on Tariff and Trade (GATT) on a multilateral as well as bilateral basis. Also, continued efforts to simplify tariff and customs classifications, valuations and procedures are desirable.

We believe that a willingness on the part of the U.S. to accept more imports is not only economically and morally the logical resultant of our creditor position but also is beneficial both to the world economy and to our own. By increasing our imports we can reduce the necessity for foreign economic aid.

12. THE UNITED STATES AND COLLECTIVE SECURITY

The United States has a moral obligation to protect her own security. This obligation extends not only to her own security; it involves the effort to realize through many channels the values of freedom, justice and peace for other nations and eventually for the entire world community. Actually this is the best, and it is increasingly becoming the only, adequate method to protect our nation. This method is called collective security which is a far more inclusive term than military defense.

This country is committed to the pursuit of collective security through the UN. We believe that the UN furnishes the basic framework through which our nation should seek its security. Until there has been developed a trustworthy system of collective security under the UN it has been deemed necessary for our government to join with friends and allies in pacts, such as NATO, for mutual defense in accord with the provisions of the UN charter.

But we now live in the age of the hydrogen bomb. Therefore, we must explore every possible means of ensuring collective security, apart from the use of military power.

We urge our government, therefore, to press for the largest practicable degree of disarmament through the UN, as we seek the goal of universal enforceable disarmament. We urge also that the functions of the UN in developing moral judgment as to conditions causing tensions and threatening war be magnified. We ask our own government to take the lead in emphasizing all those activities of the UN which aim at the substitution of good offices, mediation, conciliation, arbitration and the counsel of the world community for armed force as a means of settling disputes. Without the development of peaceful alternatives, collective military effort may win a temporary victory, only to plunge the victors into new conflict.

13. NATIONAL SECURITY AND CIVIL RIGHTS

In the face of the critical and morally perplexing decisions our country must make, the internal health and strength of America are of crucial importance. An informed and courageous public opinion provides the essential support for our policymakers and is a major factor in the meaning of the United States for other peoples. Yet there is a serious danger that in an anxious quest for security in an insecure world, our people shall fail to distinguish between a legitimate *security from espionage* and a bogus *security from dissent*. The threats of subversion from within and the much larger threats of aggression from without are real and ugly facts. But security purchased at the price of free discussion is a false security. The demagoguery which, in the name of "Americanism," seeks to exploit fears, foment suspicion, by-pass due process of law, and stifle differences of opinion, is a most grievous type of un-Americanism. Through such behavior the strength of America's policy in the world is sapped at its source.

Peoples abroad are made to wonder what American freedom now means. Our young people at home are confused by the way the safeguards of freedom are set aside. Genuine security depends on freedom—including the right to dissent from the majority. This is the genius of our democratic inheritance and an unfailing source of our strength. Only by guarding this freedom can America have an informed and courageous public opinion. Only by guarding it can our nation offer leadership to peoples struggling for freedom against powers which brutally suppress all dissent.

Another source of America's strength in world affairs is the variety of racial and national groups within our borders. The cry for justice has quickened the national conscience, which finds expression in the progress of racial and cultural relations. Yet this progress moves too slowly to satisfy either the demands of conscience or the needs of world freedom. Every evidence at home of discrimination because of race weakens the influence of America for justice and peace abroad. If our condemnation of racial injustice overseas, such as policies of "apartheid" in South Africa, is to carry conviction, it must be grounded on a greater measure of racial justice at home. On this issue the need for a courageous Christian witness and action, in obedience to God's will for righteousness, is clear and compelling. Our churches can make no effective witness here save as we press forward persistently toward making every house of God a place where men of every race and tongue may enter freely to make their peace with God and overcome their estrangement from one another.

14. FEAR NOT THE BOMB, BUT MAN

One task of the churches is to leaven public opinion in our nation by a living testimony to the moral law with which God undergirds his world. A nation that considers only its own self-interest will inevitably conceive it too narrowly. As Christians we are called upon to remind the nation of God's truth that "he who loseth his life shall find it." Only by going beyond self-interest shall we serve even this interest fully. The service of the welfare of the whole human community is not a violation of our national interest, but rather is essential to our well-being as a nation. Men and nations are dependent upon one another. We need the strength which flows from generous co-operation and mutual criticism. Our national interest must be defined in terms broad enough to include the rights, needs, and interests of other nations and peoples, including those we now count as hostile. Christians, as members of a world-wide brotherhood, are in a special way the guardians and bearers of this witness.

Human organizations are in the hands of fallible men. World catastrophe may now result from the use of power by men without moral restraint. The thing to fear is not the bomb but man. Here the witness of the Church speaks to the need of our time. We must urgently preach the Gospel. God makes men new creatures in Jesus Christ.

II. Reports from the Sections[2]

A. THE UNITED STATES AND THE UNITED NATIONS; REPORT OF SECTION II.

In the providence of God, the United Nations was created in response to the longing of peoples for a just and durable peace. Its work is in many respects directed toward goals which Christians believe to be in accordance with God's will for justice among his children. Christians, therefore, have a duty to study the issues before the United Nations, and to pray and work for a better fulfillment of the purposes set forth in its Charter. In the early years of its history, its achievements have been significant in face of the distressing obstacles which are part of the world situation.

1. POLITICAL SETTLEMENTS MADE THROUGH THE UNITED NATIONS

The United States of Indonesia came into being when the United Nations successfully shifted operations from the battlefield to the round table conference at the Hague. As a result of its good offices respecting Greece, a threatening situation in the Balkans was stabilized, full-scale war prevented, and the return of some of the kidnapped Greek children facilitated. While perplexing issues remain to be resolved in Palestine and Kashmir, the UN provides facilities for their settlement by peaceful means. In the corridors of the UN informal conversations between Western Powers and the Soviet Union led to the lifting of the Berlin Blockade. When the Great Powers were unable to reach a settlement on former Italian colonies, the UN laid the foundation for an independent Libya, and constructive action has also been taken to safeguard the political integrity of Eritrea and Somaliland.

By an overwhelming majority, the United Nations voted to recommend collective action when its commission in Korea reported that aggression had been perpetrated. In spite of tragedy and error, the UN has demonstrated its power to resist and to stop aggression. It now remains to be seen whether peace can be established and the objective of an independent and unified Korea achieved by peaceful means.

2. EFFORTS TO EXTEND HUMAN RIGHTS

In the area of human rights and fundamental freedoms the UN has advanced on many fronts. For the first time in history there has been given to the peoples of the world a Universal Declaration of Human Rights. While this Declaration does not have the status of law it does set forth a definition of the minimum rights and freedoms to which men everywhere are entitled. The Declaration has been translated into 36 different languages and the moral impact of its affirmations can be seen in the constitutions and laws of a number of states.

Steady progress has been achieved in the drafting of Covenants of Human Rights. Many difficulties stand in the way of the completion of this task. It is reassuring, however, that the UN is determined to persist in its efforts to establish under law the rights and freedoms of people everywhere. For the first time in history, there has been negotiated an International Convention for the Prevention and Punishment of the Crime of Genocide which places the mass murder of defenseless minorities, political, cultural, or racial, under the ban of international law. A Convention on Political Rights of Women has been approved and submitted to the member states of the UN for ratification.

3. ECONOMIC AND SOCIAL ACTIVITIES

In the area of its economic activities the UN has initiated and carried forward a program of technical assistance. If an enduring peace with justice is to be achieved there must be gradual improvement of the living standards of those peoples who now suffer from grinding poverty and many other forms of economic and social deprivation. To this end the UN is pooling the technical resources of the world community in an adventure of goodwill that corresponds at many points with the Christian thesis that those who are strong shall bear the burdens of the weak. Some 1,500 specialists recruited and trained by the UN are presently engaged in such tasks as increasing the productivity of agriculture, improving health standards, and training personnel in fields of social welfare and public administration.

Through the UN efforts are being made to facilitate world trade, to encourage the promulgation of policies of land reform and to meet the complex problems related to population pressures.

Through the UN the world community has assumed responsibility for a ministry of relief to refugees and displaced persons. It is presently caring for the needs of some 874,000 Arab refugees and for the millions of persons displaced by the hostilities in Korea.

The well-being of subject and dependent peoples is a concern of the United Nations made manifest in a wide variety of constructive measures designed to ensure their political, economic, social, and educational advancement. Through its Specialized Agencies the UN is rendering a service of genuine benefit to mankind.

Over and beyond its more specific achievements it has brought into focus the essential oneness of mankind and provided an opportunity for the fuller expression of universal brotherhood. It has permitted the exercise of moral judgments and thus has forced governments to take into greater account common interests of nations. In many instances the work which the United Nations has done has provided an alternative to war as a method of settling international disputes and harmonizing the interests of nations. Through its arrangements for formal and informal consultation by nongovernmental organizations it has opened the way for the voices of the people to be heard directly in its deliberations. Considering the formidable issues confronting this young organization in the first eight years of its life, it is astounding that it has accomplished so much.

4. THE VALUE OF CONSTRUCTIVE CRITICISM

We do not overlook certain limitations inherent in the structure of the UN as now constituted, nor do we deny the wholesome value of construc- tive criticism in regard to its operations. Any hope of progressive devel- opment toward greater effectiveness depends in large measure upon the continuation of a realistic appraisal, which is both intelligent and objective.

At the same time, it would be folly to ignore clear evidence that there are in the United States organized campaigns of deliberate misrepresenta- tion and vicious attacks upon the UN are being widely pressed. Such unfounded criticism by the use of falsehood, half-truths and distortions could undermine the steady progress being made to improve the UN. Churchmen and church agencies must be vigilant to offset this threat by a ministry of truth.

5. THE UN IS AN ASSOCIATION OF SOVEREIGN STATES

A fundamental limitation is based upon the fact—which some tend to overlook—that the UN is not an international government, but rather an association of *sovereign* states. Its degree of effectiveness in areas where national interests clash depends upon the voluntary decisions of independ- ent member governments. Whenever these member governments, because of misunderstandings, fears, or unilateral interests, are unwilling or unable to cooperate toward the achievement of desired goals, the authority of the UN cannot go beyond that of moral pressure. The frustrations resulting from such situations in UN procedures merely reflect the disorders of a divided although interdependent world. The fault lies in the nations themselves and in the tensions among them, as well as in certain inherent limitations of the UN.

6. STRENGTHENING THE UNITED NATIONS

In order to meet the changing needs of an even more interdependent world community, the United Nations must grow. This growth can take place along at least three complementary lines.

(1) The UN can be strengthened by better, more responsible use of the instrumentalities provided by the Charter. The member states have failed at many points to live up to their commitments under the Charter. Issues too often are considered, not on their merits, but on the basis of short-range

interests and domestic political considerations. Debates are frequently used as a form of political warfare rather than as a means for concerting the actions of states for common and constructive ends. The resources required for the carrying out of agreed policies are insufficiently supplied. The UN is too often bypassed through unilateral action.

(2) The United Nations can grow through the evolution of powers inherent in the Charter or delegated to it by common consent. The Charter is flexible enough to permit the development of UN potentialities in many directions. Examples of such natural growth are seen in the recognition of the "abstention" as a useful procedural device, and in the establishment of new procedures for the General Assembly, through the Uniting for Peace Resolution, to cope with Security Council deadlocks on threats to the peace.

(3) Further, there is the question of Charter revision, scheduled for debate by the UN General Assembly in 1955. While major, formal changes in the Charter require the concurrence of the permanent members, and thus face in intensified form the obstacles which hamper the present operation of the UN, it is important that discussion of Charter revisions should go forward within and outside the United Nations.

Christians and other men of goodwill should be alert to opportunities for improving the United Nations through Charter revision. At the same time, it is important to be equally alert to the dangers of premature efforts at Charter revision for which the essential pre-conditions of mutual confidence and common interest have not been established. The present charter was created out of the sufferings and hopes of a world engulfed in global war while the major victors were still bound by common urgencies. The development of the "cold war" and of other conflicts provides a much less favorable climate today, but every possible improvement should be urgently sought. There are important forces which would attempt to use Charter revision to weaken or destroy the United Nations. Thus Christians must also guard against moves to undermine the organization or to kill it through extreme and unrealistic demands.

Some revisions of the Charter would seem to carry relatively little risk and could, in fact, strengthen the United Nations. The rule of unanimity among the major powers (veto) could be limited so that it will not apply to the admission of new members nor to decisions on the peaceful settlement of disputes. The Disarmament Commission which was set up by the General Assembly could be made a permanent organ and given a status comparable with that of the major UN councils. We support such Charter revision as is necessary to give the UN the authority to carry out an effective plan of universal and enforceable disarmament.

Other revisions would appear more difficult to effect and carry the danger that weaker provisions may result. The changes in voting procedure in the General Assembly, the complete abolition of the veto, increased international responsibility for dependent territories in their progress toward self-government, and increased powers of the General Assembly should be explored with clear understanding of the risks involved.

We believe that our government, well in advance of the 1955 UN General Assembly, should present to the American people and the governments of the other member states proposals for revising the Charter.

7. RECOMMENDATIONS ON SPECIFIC ISSUES

The extent of growth and effectiveness of the UN will depend in a large measure on the decisions taken on many specific issues. We submit recommendations on six of these issues, [one of which follows].[3]

Human Rights: We recognize that world tensions must be eased in order to provide a climate in which adequate texts of the international covenants and measures of implementation may be completed, and their adoption by the UN and ratification by member governments secured. We are seriously concerned that the government of the U.S has given advance notice that it does not intend to ratify the covenants. We strongly oppose any tendency to reject in principle the device of an international covenant as one form of international action to promote the observance of human rights. We deplore the failure of Congress to ratify the Conventions on Genocide and the Political Rights of Women. At the same time, we welcome the initiative of our government in proposing an action program on human rights whereby the UN will enlist the co-operation of member governments and we express the hope that with necessary modifications it may be given effect.

8. HOW THE UNITED STATES CAN WORK MORE EFFECTIVELY IN THE UN

The great economic and political power which the U.S. has and the role of leadership it exercises in the world today require that it participate as a responsible member of the United Nations. This means that the U.S. should use the UN as a major instrument of its foreign policy and accept the moral restraint imposed by genuine co-operation in the community of nations. With due appreciation of the part which our government seeks to play, we call attention to certain ways in which its contribution can become more effective.

(1) In fulfilling its obligation of membership in the UN, we believe that the U.S. should appoint delegates whose public records reflect a regard for democratic principles and who are equipped for the specific tasks which representation imposes.

(2) The UN provides for its member states a forum and an atmosphere congenial to the settlement of their disputes. Our government should always keep the door open to negotiations and should refrain from

rigid political prejudgments that may become barriers to agreement when conditions become more favorable.

(3) The U.S. is called upon not only to appropriate its full share of the UN annual budget, but also to support the various activities operated by the UN.

(4) The American tradition of devotion to freedom and self-government for dependent peoples must not be obscured by our support of metropolitan countries when disputes with their dependencies are brought before the UN. Without ignoring legitimate claims of our allies upon us, we must press as rapidly as the best interests of dependent peoples warrant for their independence or self-government.

(5) We believe that purely party interests should be subordinated to the achievement of a clear U.S. policy of full participation in and support for the UN. In order to avoid confusion and to promote effectiveness, there is need for greater co-ordination of U.S. agencies responsible for the formation and interpretation of our foreign policy.

(6) We commend our government for its policy of consultation with the representatives of United States nongovernmental organizations and express the hope that facilities therefore will continue to be provided. We favor the continuance by the Department of State of its conferences for NGO representatives and its program of information and interpretation to the public. These arrangements, supplementing the normal democratic procedures, help to bring the considered judgments of the American people to bear upon foreign policy decisions.

The churches exercise a major role in forming U.S. public opinion. They should accept the responsibility of dealing fairly with the UN, neither claiming too much for it so raising false hopes, nor dismissing it as irrelevant in the world of nations today. There is need for study of the UN as an important instrument of the nations through which God's will for community, justice, and freedom on earth may be furthered.

B. THE UNITED STATES AND FOREIGN ECONOMIC POLICY; REPORT OF SECTION III.

1. OUR ECONOMICALLY INTERDEPENDENT WORLD

As Christians we believe that our country is responsible to God and to the world community for the effects that its economic practices have on people wherever they may be. As Christian citizens we have a clear duty to work for those national policies which lead to a healthy and expanding economy and greater equality of opportunity in the United States and to economic development and improved living standards in the rest of the world. We believe that economic welfare is of the community of justice and freedom which God wills for all men, a community in which all persons accept their responsibility to their neighbor and acknowledge God as their Father.

We recognize and affirm the economic interdependence between our country and other nations and peoples. We have a common interest in each other's economic advancement. We see in this mutual dependence the essential unity of mankind under one God. National policies which fail to recognize the mutual dependence and mutual responsibilities of all peoples fall short of the ethical demands of the Christian faith.

We acknowledge the complexity of economic issues and the need for technical understanding. But we have a right and duty to consider the overall policy alternatives facing our country in the light of our Christian faith, to express our convictions about the goals of U.S. foreign policy, and to work for their realization.

As Christians we recognize the ever-present dangers of seeking our own economic advancement at the expense of others and of forgetting that God is the source of all things. We should seek the guidance and forgiveness of God in carrying out our economic responsibilities to the world.

Economic policy must take into account political and military considerations as well as strictly "economic" factors, particularly in a world confronted with the threat of Soviet aggression. Often our national "economic" goals are in conflict with other goals and difficult decisions must be made. Christian insight should help us arrive at a priority of goals in a particular situation.

The policy-makers of a democracy must take seriously the values and goals of the people in whose name they act. Public opinion to be effective must be openly expressed, and directed to the executive branch, to the Congress, and through the channels of influence provided by the major political parties. Careful study of Christians should result in a truer understanding of issues, convictions as to the directions policy should take, and in some cases specific conclusions.

2. FIVE FOREIGN ECONOMIC GOALS

In the light of U.S. responsibility to the world community and to the American people, we believe that Christian citizens should work for the following interrelated national economic policy objectives:

(1) The maintenance of high level income and employment in the U.S.

(2) The fostering of world trade and the reduction or elimination of trade barriers.

(3) The expansion of long-term American investment abroad.

(4) The continuance of foreign economic aid and technical assistance to meet clearly established needs.

(5) Co-operation with other nations in constructive programs for the promotion of world economic health.

The issues involved in U.S. foreign policy today cannot be understood without recognizing the extent to which the economic well-being of our country is dependent upon what happens in other parts of the world and also the tremendous influence which the U.S. has on the world through the sheer weight of its economic power. In our present interdependent world both political and economic isolation are impossible.

The influence of the United States in the economic field on the rest of the world is exerted mainly through policies in connection with (*a*) our domestic level of employment and income, (*b*) our commercial and international monetary policies, and (*c*) our foreign investment and aid programs.

3. U.S. PROSPERITY AND THE WORLD ECONOMY

The maintenance of prosperity and increasing productivity in the United States is one of the greatest contributions to world economic stability and development that our nation can make. Our country is the world's greatest single market for exports from other lands. The prosperity of many countries depends to a large extent upon their ability to sell in the American market and on our willingness and ability to buy. Political stability and social development in other countries are often dependent upon domestic prosperity and all three suffer if we cut down on imports.

A decline in economic activity here is quickly passed on to other countries by a cut in the imports we buy from them, thus reducing their badly needed dollar earnings. When, on the other hand, prices of raw materials, manufactured goods, and foodstuffs go up here, countries which import these items must pay more for them, which tends to induce inflation both in their economies and in the world market. In short, the ups and downs in the level of income and employment in the United States, with their impact on the volume and the prices of imports and exports, constitute perhaps the greatest single influence by this country on the prosperity and stability of the rest of the world.

While the U.S. has been slow to recognize the international effects of its domestic economic fluctuations, the Employment Act of 1946 does represent a national commitment on the part of the American people to use available economic knowledge and known policy tools in an effort to maintain a high level of income and employment within the framework of democratic procedures and a modified free enterprise system. Since, however, even minor economic fluctuations have serious consequences abroad, we must be willing to consider means of offsetting their adverse effects. As Christian citizens we have a moral duty to work for a stable, productive, and full employment economy without which our nation will be unable to fulfill its responsibility to its own people and to the world community.

4. THE EFFECT OF U.S. TRADE POLICIES

Although U.S. exports amount to only about five per cent of our total output of goods and services each year, these exports vitally affect our whole economy because they absorb sizeable percentages of the production of our agriculture and mass production industries. A substantial loss of foreign markets will fall hardest on particular sectors of agriculture and industry and on particular sections of the country and will certainly mean unemployment for many workers and lower profits in the farms and enterprises directly affected.

A healthy U.S. economy requires imports as well as exports. Although our country is rich in resources, our high level of industrial and consumer demand requires many products which we do not produce at all or which we have only in short supply. Our need for imports is likely to increase as we further deplete some of our irreplaceable resources.

Imports are important also because the dollars we pay for them are used to buy goods and services from us. We cannot go on selling without buying unless we are willing to make up the balance through grants or some other form of economic assistance. For some years, world economic conditions, including U.S. policies, have not made it possible for most other countries to obtain sufficient dollars to permit their citizens to buy U.S. goods without restriction. The two elements which today largely bring international supply and demand into balance—restriction by foreign governments of demand and the provision of foreign aid by the U.S.—provide temporary solutions only. In the long run, it is clearly desirable to free international trade from unnecessary barriers so that human and natural resources may be used in the most efficient way and each country may benefit from the specialization of others.

5. U.S. TARIFFS HURT THE WORLD ECONOMY AND U.S. ECONOMY

Our national trade policies affect the level of exports and imports. A restrictive or high tariff policy in the U.S. leads other countries to set up various controls aimed at reducing imports from the U.S. It makes it difficult for us to provide leadership towards the removal of barriers. The resulting network of trade and exchange restrictions holds back economic expansion throughout the world. We believe that a willingness to accept more imports in the U.S. will benefit not only the world economy but our own as well. By increasing our imports we can facilitate the payment of debts, reduce the necessity for foreign economic aid, and provide a sounder market for our exports. A parallel responsibility, of course, rests on other countries to produce the high quality and competitively-priced goods that foreign markets will want to absorb.

One of the unhappy aspects of the cold war has been the reduction of East-West trade. Although such commerce has modest significance for the U.S., it has larger significance for many other nations. Now, when we are exerting pressure on friendly nations to curtail their trade in strategic products with the Soviet bloc, we have a special obligation to help them find alternative markets. Some expansion of East-West trade in non-strategic items can perform a useful service in breaking down barriers and establishing contact.

Protectionism is rooted deep in American history. Protectionists sometimes argue that imports constitute "unfair" competition because foreign workers are paid less than American workers and also that imports will create domestic unemployment. The important question, however, is not what imports do to a particular industry but what they do to the economy as a whole. A greater volume of imports will necessitate adjustments within certain industries but these are likely to be insignificant compared to the benefit our economy and the rest of the world will receive.

The principal barrier to imports is the tariff, but there are also quotas, embargoes, processing taxes, and other restrictions, as well as a bewildering maze of complex customs regulations and procedures. "Buy American" legislation, passed in 1933, requires federal and state governments to buy domestic rather than foreign products unless this is "inconsistent with the public interest." Furthermore, duties on foreign products are sometimes regarded as less restrictive than the uncertainty of the regulations importers must observe. Under the "escape" clause in the Reciprocal Trade Agreement Act a domestic producer may claim undue injury by imports and petition the Tariff Commission for an increase in a duty previously reduced in a trade agreement. The "peril points" amendment requires the Tariff Commission to place limits on tariff reductions which cannot be exceeded by the President without an explanation to Congress.

The protectionist controls built up over the years cannot be abolished overnight. In working for their progressive reduction, however, the following four principles might be observed: (*a*) tariff reductions should be gradual, not abrupt; (*b*) tariff reductions should be selective; (*c*) tariff policy should be designed to reduce uncertainty; (*d*) means might be devised for relieving serious hardship to domestic industries and communities resulting from tariff reduction. Observance of these principles would tend to maximize the benefits to be derived from tariff reduction while minimizing the problems created.

6. RECOMMENDATIONS FOR INCREASING IMPORTS

In the light of this analysis, we recommend for consideration the following suggestions for increasing imports and for making U.S. foreign economic policy more responsible to the world situation.

(1) Continuation of the Reciprocal Trade Agreement program on a permanent basis with elimination of the "escape" and the "peril points" clauses.

(2) New legislation permitting the United States to lead the way toward trade liberalization by means of unilateral tariff reductions.

(3) Consolidation of our various import controls and enactment of further legislation simplifying import procedures.

(4) Repeal of "Buy American" legislation.

(5) Detailed study of agricultural protectionism, particularly the quotas and embargoes, and an attempt to resolve the conflicts between our foreign trade interests and the desire of farmers for greater economic security.

(6) Encouragement of foreign travel by our citizens as a major source of dollar earnings to other countries.

(7) Reconsideration of the requirements that a minimum of 50 per cent of foreign aid cargoes be carried on American-owned ships in the light of the major purpose of the foreign aid program, which is to assist other countries.

The United States also influences the world economy through its international monetary policies—exchange rates, exchange controls, and gold movements. The position taken by the U.S. on gold purchases, exchange rate policy and international currency arrangements has a significant effect, helping or hindering world trade. Christian citizens should study these technical matters and should support those policies which seem most likely to promote expanding multilateral world trade and investment.

7. THE EXPANSION OF LONG-TERM AMERICAN INVESTMENT ABROAD

The United States is the chief source of capital in the world today. Poorer countries are limited in developing economically by the fact that their national income does not make substantial saving and investment possible. We support the expansion of long-term American investment abroad because of its potential contribution both to the world economy and to the

U.S. economy. American investors abroad have been increasingly concerned with the needs and rights of the people in the communities where their operations are located. We commend and would encourage this recognition of social responsibility.

The political, social, and economic climate of the world today is not conducive to private foreign investments. The world is torn by ideological conflict, burning nationalistic sentiments, social upheaval, and civil and military strife. The potential American investor usually feels the risk is too great and the return too small. The areas that need development capital most (Asia, the Middle East, etc.) often are the ones with the least attractive climate for investors. There will probably be no substantial expansion of private investment until there is greater peace and stability in the world.

Most evidence indicates that a larger proportion of foreign investment in the near future will be provided by governments directly or through international agencies, especially since capital is needed largely for purposes such as irrigation, roadbuilding, and power. Activities of the Export-Import Bank as the main U.S. government agency for making loans to other nations should not be curtailed; if anything, they should be expanded. The most ambitious attempt to revive international investment, however, has been the establishment of the International Bank for Reconstruction and Development, known as the World Bank, which started operations in 1947. The purpose of and conditions surrounding each loan are carefully investigated by the Bank and the exploitation of less-developed economies is thus prevented and economically sound and socially beneficial investment promoted. This institution is worthy of full U.S. support.

8. U.S. PROGRAMS OF FOREIGN AID AND TECHNICAL ASSISTANCE

The U.S. is currently carrying on various types of foreign assistance programs, including military, economic, relief, and technical. Military assistance has been given primarily, though not exclusively, to our Western European partners in NATO. Economic and relief aid have been distributed more widely and have sought to aid refugees, reconstruct shattered economies, and deal with balance of payments problems. Most Americans have regarded this as emergency aid and acknowledge that it has been usefully spent. After Korea and the decision of the free world to embark on a program of partial mobilization, a new economic crisis arose among U.S. allies necessitating a continuation and expansion of foreign aid. Considering the issues at stake and what the high cost of *not* giving aid might have been, it would appear that the economic and political accomplishments have been eminently worthwhile.

Technical assistance to the economically less developed areas of the world is by far the least costly of our aid programs but its significance cannot be measured by its size. Its objective is to wage war on poverty, ignorance, and disease by making available specialists and technical knowledge, from more developed countries. Our country has its Point IV Program and also contributes to the technical assistance program of the UN. The United States should increase both its technical and financial aid to economically underdeveloped areas and should provide this aid as far as possible through the medium of the United Nations. The plan to establish a Special United Nations Fund on Economic Development (SUNFED) merits study.

The U.S. is a member of all the specialized agencies of the United Nations and also of many other international organizations promoting political, economic, and cultural co-operation. The UN was never designed to "solve" social, economic, or political problems. It was established to promote co-operative action among sovereign states in facing all such problems. The accomplishments through the UN in the field of economic and social policy have been substantial. We support the full participation of the U.S. in those UN and other international agencies which are working for economic stability and development in the world.

C. THE UNITED STATES AND THE LESS-DEVELOPED AREAS; REPORT OF SECTION IV.

1. PLENTY FOR THE FEW, POVERTY FOR THE MANY

Our present world presents a contrast between plenty for a minority of its people and a severe shortage of the basic necessities of life for the majority. In North America, Western Europe, Australia, New Zealand, and a few other areas the majority of men and women have access to education, competent medical care, and at least minimum requirements of food, clothing, and shelter. But in Africa, the Near East, Asia, and Latin America most people still do not have the basic necessities of life. Hunger, disease, and illiteracy exist on such a scale as to shock the moral conscience and threaten all hopes for genuine community: local, national or world-wide. Despite the ravages of war and gaping inequalities, Western people and particularly North Americans must confess that they live on a plateau of plenty, so high above the plains where live the majority of the world's people that those on the plateau can scarcely comprehend the misery in which most of their fellow men exist.

In Asia, Africa, the Middle East and Latin America there is a many-sided and growing revolt. It is a revolt against poverty, against domination by politically and technologically more advanced nations, against the doctrine and practices of "white supremacy," against colonialism, against their own feudalistic systems, often against inefficient or corrupt domestic government. There is a swelling demand for food, education, health, freedom, equality, and self-respect.

Misery is no longer to be accepted as the unalterable fate of great masses of men. Modern technological development has made a better living standard for all people a practicable aim.

Another aspect of the same struggle is that for centuries, and reaching a climax in the early years of this century, a large proportion of the people in Asia, Africa, and the Near East lived in a state of political and economic subservience to Western nations. In self-governing countries of Latin America and elsewhere stratified social systems and single-product economies condemn large masses of people to conditions of subjection, ignorance, or want.

2. THE DEMAND FOR SELF-GOVERNMENT

More than 140 millions are still in nonself-governing territories. The colonial order had beneficent aspects, but in the minds of dependent people, and with much justification, it meant primarily outside control without consent, local resources used chiefly for the enrichment of foreigners, and attitudes of superiority whose expression ranged from polite condescension to brutal disregard of human dignity.

Few now defend the old colonial system. Almost all give a least lip-service to the goal of self-determination and freedom. But the suspicions and resentments created over many years cannot quickly be dissipated. Most Americans do not appreciate the sweep and fervor of feeling on this issue. The fact is, the colonial powers of yesterday and today are generally not trusted by the people in the underdeveloped areas. And because the United States is involved in the colonial system and is closely associated with the nations that have been or are great colonial powers, this distrust is directed also toward our country.

Any tendency on the part of the more powerful nations to deal with questions involving Asia or Africa without consulting the responsible leaders in those areas is quickly resented and denounced.

3. TECHNICAL CO-OPERATION WITH LESS-DEVELOPED AREAS

Today the United States government directly and through the United Nations is giving technical assistance to certain economically less developed countries which request such aid. Church groups, foundations, corporations and other nongovernmental agencies are also engaged in technical assistance programs.

The purpose of these programs of technical co-operation is to raise the standard of living in the host country by improving public health, raising educational standards, and increasing economic productivity generally. Experts from more developed countries are invited to less-developed areas where, working shoulder to shoulder with local people, they seek to raise more food, control disease, improve sanitation and health services, teach people how to read, improve roads and start new industries. Technical aid helps people to help themselves.

The U.S. bilateral program of technical assistance (Point IV) is carried on through the Foreign Operations Administration. It was formerly administered by a separate agency of the State Department. FOA is responsible also for economic and military aid formerly administered by the Mutual Security Agency. The 1953-54 appropriation for technical aid is $118,234,500. This is $22,000,000 less than the President requested.

In addition to its own program the U.S. has contributed 60 per cent of the budget for the technical assistance program of the UN. Congress appropriated $9,500,000 for this year's program, $13,750,000 less than the President requested.

Church and other voluntary agencies with experience in technical assistance abroad have advised and assisted the UN and U.S. programs.Technical aid is no panacea. It does not meet all human needs. Even if pursued with utmost energy, it could not alone in a few years refashion the material basis of great and ancient societies. Feudalism, landlordism, political corruption, tradition, superstition, and other barriers cannot easily be overcome.

4. THE POINT IV IDEA IS PROFOUNDLY RIGHT

Despite some failures and justifiable criticism Point IV assistance has been favorably received. The fundamental idea is profoundly right and a good beginning has been made. Some 1,400 Americans were recently at work in 35 countries. More than 850 nationals from less developed areas are in the U.S. for special training. U.S. and UN teams have succeeded in reducing the incidence of malaria, raising agricultural productivity, improving sanitation, and a hundred other things. When held to its central purpose—helping people to help themselves—and administered in the spirit of mutual sharing the technical assistance program can be an instrument of great good. Plenty for the few and want for the many cannot be reconciled with the Christian law of love.

5. THE IMPACT OF DEMOCRACY AND CHRISTIANITY

Some of the unrest in the less developed areas may be the result of Communist propaganda. But much more important have been the example of high living standards in the West, the democratic ideals and practices, and, not the least, the impact of the Christian missionary movement.

There has been some deliberate misrepresentation of America in these areas. Movies and tourists have often given a distorted picture of our life and values. Nevertheless, there are genuine weaknesses in our culture which are barriers to full co-operation with the peoples in less developed areas. The most vulnerable aspect of our national life is our racial segregation and discrimination. Significant gains in improving the situation have not succeeded in erasing the impression in some quarters that the U.S.S.R. is a greater champion of human rights than the U.S.

6. RECOMMENDATIONS FOR ACTION

In the light of the above analysis, we make the following recommendations to the churches:

(1) Christians should share more boldly than ever before the resources of their faith, which in the midst of social upheaval give ultimate meaning and direction to human life. The missionary witness must take full account of the actual social situations and needs of men and make clear the relevance of the Christian faith to the problems of community and national life.

(2) In addition to maintaining the spiritual witness through overseas missions, American Christians should increase greatly their support of reconstruction agencies and mission boards in their programs of helping people to help themselves.

(3) Both public and private bodies with overseas programs should choose dedicated representatives who are not only technically competent but who embrace humility and other spiritual qualities which will enrich their work and their incidental contacts.

(4) Our churches should lift up, along with opportunities in Christian missions, the need for Christian service abroad in government, private industry, and voluntary agencies.

(5) Christians should continue to press for the progressive elimination of economic and political colonialism. Definite timetables for the assumption of self-government should be established as rapidly as possible and the training of capable national leaders should be intensified. Our churches should be especially concerned with those areas for which the U.S. is directly responsible, the trust territories of the Pacific and the Ryukyu Islands. We also urge the churches to give intelligent support to the work of the UN Trusteeship Council and to promote full U.S. participation in it.

(6) (The recommendation on racial discrimination submitted by this Section was adopted by the Conference as a Resolution. See page 193.)

(7) Technical co-operation should be an expression of goodwill, divorced from military aid and security objectives. These programs should be conducted always to conserve and promote human dignity and the freedom of individuals and nations. They should be based on a pooling of available experts and financial resources.

(8) The U.S. should fully support the UN Expanded Program of Technical Assistance by increasing its financial contribution.[4]

(9) The U.S. should conduct its bilateral Point IV program so it will supplement and strengthen rather than compete with the UN program.

(10) The U.S. program and the U.S. contribution to the UN for technical aid should be regarded as a long-term commitment, so that participating countries can be assured of U.S. aid.

D. THE UNITED STATES AND COLLECTIVE SECURITY; REPORT OF SECTION V

The God who is at work in the world is the Redeeming Lord of all men and nations and the Source and Judge of all power. All nations, therefore, are ultimately responsible to God for the ordering of their affairs and for the exercise of the power which they have. Apart from this responsibility there is no adequate foundation for the security and freedom, the justice and peace, which many nations so earnestly seek.

1. NATIONAL SECURITY IS A CHRISTIAN CONCERN

The United States has a responsibility commensurate with her power. It is a responsibility both for national security and for the larger values of freedom, justice and peace throughout the world.

As Christians we are deeply conscious that the justification for this defense of the security of the United States, by methods which will preserve and enhance the freedom and other values which this nation represents, depends upon the quality and kind of national life thus defended. A responsible defense of United States security recognizes (*a*) our own failure adequately to fulfill our democratic and religious heritage, (*b*) our own limited power and resources, (*c*) the necessity for allies and friends joined together in regional and collective self-defense arrangements under the United Nations charter and (*d*) the need for steady co-operation with them.

2. THE NEED FOR COLLECTIVE SECURITY

In the mid-twentieth century world, the nation-state by itself alone can neither defend its own values nor establish a general freedom and justice; only in co-operation with other nation-states can it adequately meet either responsibility. While we defend our own security we must at the same time try to realize to the fullest possible extent the values of freedom, justice and peace, for other nations as well as our own, and eventually for the entire world community. Actually this is the best and possibly the only way to defend our national security. Moreover, according to the Christian gospel, nations as well as men that are concerned solely with security and self-defense lose even these. When we seek simply to have security we get into a vicious circle, we never have enough. The United States today may be too exclusively concerned with the problems of defense. Security is a necessary national goal, but it cannot be achieved by making it the supreme national goal. We are morally obligated to seek the fullest measure of freedom, justice and peace for the international community which the tragic limitations of a sinful world permit.

Here, too, U.S. responsibility necessarily involves co-operative action with other nations. The UN represents the primary commitment we have made to such co-operation.

The clear duty of the Christian in the United States as elsewhere is to have and to preach a humble awareness of the temptations of national pride and the actuality of national limitation and sin.

To fulfill our responsibility, both to ourselves and to others, for security and for larger values, the United States must participate today in collective security arrangements.

It is tragically difficult to respond to God's justice and love in specific political decisions. Moral dangers are inherent even in the better choices. This is illustrated in the search for security. Each nation tends to seek its own national security which is good, but at the expense of its obligations to the world community, which is bad. Yet the desire for national security, in the present world, almost inevitably draws nations together in mutual obligations and assistance.

The Christian has a clear judgment here. God's justice and love commit us to work for political arrangements which connect national security with the good of the world community. Spiritual advance and danger are both found at each level of joint action by nations.

3. COLLECTIVE DEFENSE ARRANGEMENTS

The North Atlantic Treaty Organization (NATO), for example, contains concrete obligations which go beyond a narrow view of national security. Properly used, it may develop mutual understanding and community, and be a valuable step in the painstaking work of building world-wide security. We must not, in our desire for more ideal arrangements, fail to take such effective action as we can take through such real and existing instruments.

But such groupings also have the danger of a narrow interpretation of security, ignoring the world-wide nature of God's love and justice.

We want to develop a strong joint defense against Soviet imperialism, but as we do so we must not fall prey to a tribal religion. God is Lord of East and West, judging and working for the redemption of both. Though we must resist the gross evil in the Soviet totalitarian system, we must not in doing so assume that the U.S.S.R. has a monopoly of evil or the United States of good.

To conceive of Soviet imperialism as the only, and total, evil leads to the ugliest kinds of nationalist and absolutist pride and injustice. It may also be an un-Christian attempt to deny our own guilt by loading it all on others. We must, therefore, work not only to oppose Soviet imperialism but to make the free world more truly free.

4. COLLECTIVE SECURITY DIRECTLY UNDER THE UNITED NATIONS

As a member state in the United Nations, the United States has a direct obligation to support the inclusive collective security system of the UN, and a further implied obligation to make every effort to strengthen that system.

We believe that United Nations Collective Security System is a step forward from conditions where each nation relies for security entirely on its own armed forces and military alliances with other armed nations. Therefore, the United Nations collective security system should be supported. It would be a backward step for the United Nations to withdraw from the security field leaving world's military power in complete anarchy.

We believe, however, that United Nations collective security, depending on the general promises of armed nations to prevent or check aggression is not, ideally, a satisfactory solution.

The United Nations should move as rapidly as possible to a system of collective security which prevents preparation for aggression through world disarmament.

5. A MORE EFFECTIVE COLLECTIVE SECURITY SYSTEM IN THE UN

Even in a more effective collective security system which may emerge in the UN, dangers and difficulties would exist. No ultimate realization of God's justice and love can come at any level of collective arrangement.

Any such collective system may become an instrument for the defense of the status quo in the face of just protests against it. A collective organization of nations, formed on the basis of an existing set of power relations, will tend to represent the interests of the major powers which formed it. It will tend to justify its defense of the status quo in the name of the defense of peace, saying that anyone who revolts is upsetting the peace. Therefore it may tend to perpetuate the injustice in a static situation. A collective security system must not leave the group which protests, in the name of what it believes to be justice, no recourse but violence. Justice is not always on the side of the keepers of the peace. There must be means for peaceful change and the peaceful adjustment of claims must be made still more effective. It has been well said that peace to endure must be endurable.

6. VALUES AND DANGERS OF COLLECTIVE SECURITY

The most serious long-range problem of the development of the collective instruments now emerging is that of change. The willingness of nations to admit that they stand under a universal God and a universal justice is a necessary condition of any "just" and "durable" peace. This means that there must be flexibility and willingness to use diplomatic means of adjustment in every nation's policy. The development of the political means by which change may be peacefully brought about is a crucial, long-range practical problem, as well as an immediate problem which must be met as best it can with the means presently at hand.

These dangers and difficulties must not keep Christians from working for effective collective security. The gravest moral danger of all is not one of those we list above, but the danger that we will shirk our responsibility to co-operate with other nations in maintaining the values we hold in common, and at the same time in making a concerted effort to strengthen the collective will, especially through the United Nations.

The Christian faith impels us to insist upon our obligations to others. We can never "go it alone"; we can never have a "free hand," for we are bound together in mutual responsibility with all others whom God made and loves.

As instruments in fulfilling our universal responsibility, collective arrangements have the distinct moral advantage, other things being equal, of providing a concrete restraint on the egoism and pride of each nation. All nations are limited and sinful and all nations should remain open to, and even welcome the restraint which other nations provide.

Collective arrangements also can increase the mutual awareness of problems and points of view. Most important of all, collective arrangements increase the possibility of attaining security, freedom, justice, and peace.

The Christian is warranted by his faith in accepting the possibility that God will use even the difficulties and dangers in the road to real collective security as instruments in the achievement of his purposes.

These dangers and difficulties arise because in our sin and ignorance we tend to overestimate our own security needs and to underestimate our responsibility to the world community. In this time of excessive concern for security, Christians must emphasize the larger understanding of security in which there is that daring and willingness to take risks which express faith in God and his justice.

7. RECOMMENDATIONS FOR MORE EFFECTIVE COLLECTIVE SECURITY

In light of the foregoing analysis of the issues confronting the United States in the area of collective security, the following recommendations are made:

(1) We urge continued and vigorous support of the United Nations. This does not mean that we endorse all the actions of that body without qualifications; we could not do this, for it is a human institution. But the United Nations is at present our best hope through the organization of nations for

the attainment of the collective security of all nations and peoples. It provides the framework for the functioning of a system of collective self-defense, and at the same time furnishes the most favorable atmosphere for the patient and determined building of a more universal and effective system of collective security.

(a) We recommend that the United States encourage the UN to give the Peace Observation Commission and the Collective Measures Committee larger responsibilities.

(b) We recommend that the United States urge the creation of a United Nations liaison committee to give guidance in political matters when a collective security action is being carried out.

(c) We recommend that studies be set in motion by churches, by other voluntary organizations, and by government agencies, concerning the review and possible revision of the Charter as provided for in Chapter 18 of the Charter, in the light of the constitutional development of the UN in action and in the light of the further needs for the strengthening of the purposes and procedures of the United Nations for more effective collective security.

(2) We recommend to further the development of a collective security system, that increased efforts be made to find effective methods for the just and peaceful settlement of disputes and for the establishment of social, economic, and spiritual conditions in which tensions leading to violence are diminished. In keeping with the mission of the Christian Church for preventing war and advancing peace, is the work of the United Nations for the reconciliation of nations and people through negotiations, good offices, mediation, conciliation, arbitration, and commission reports. We strongly recommend the development of these procedures in as many fields of international tensions as possible.

(3) We recommend that the United Nations move as rapidly as possible to a system of collective security which prevents preparation for aggression through universal disarmament with adequate safeguards.[5]

(4) We support the proposal of the President of the United States and leaders of both parties that the immense savings from disarmament be used not only for the strengthening of the economic and social base of a free America, but that a large part of such savings be devoted for the recovery, reconstruction and well-being of all the people of the earth for our sake and their sake in the development of the collective security of freedom and peace in the world.[6]

(5) We support, during this interim period of historical evolution to a more adequate organization for world security our present collective defense system under Article 51 of the United Nations Charter, and

continue to do so wherever and to the extent that we are convinced of the relative justice of its cause. NATO, the Rio and the Pacific pacts represent collective self-defense arrangements which are crucially important in our joint opposition to Soviet totalitarian tyranny and all other forms of imperialism. They are necessary to preserve both our own national security and that of other free nations, and promote freedom, justice and peace, as well as security, but they must never be allowed to obscure our vision or obstruct our progress toward the ultimate goal.

In supporting collective defense arrangements we urge the strengthening of the nonmilitary, political, economic, social and cultural aspects of these arrangements. In connection with our support of NATO we urge that the United States take the lead in the formation of a Consultative Assembly composed of representatives of legislative bodies of the NATO nations, meeting regularly to discuss problems of mutual interest and making recommendations to the Council of NATO.[7]

(6) We support the United Nations collective action against aggression in Korea although we are keenly aware that military action is a tragic compromise of the Christian ideal. The UN action is not only a collective defense of the freedom and other values this country represents, but is also a hopeful step in the direction of a broader collective security system. From the Korean experience we can learn much about the difficulties and possibilities inherent in such action. We urge the U.S. to increase its already substantial help for the relief of this tragically devastated country.

(7) We urge upon our own nation the patience and vision and intelligence to choose policies in this time with restraint and moral insight. We in the churches help to mold the moral climate in which the delicate and agonizing task of collective security is worked out. We must confess our failure to build an understanding of the problem of policy and the moral courage to make the hard decisions they require. We suggest to ourselves, in the churches, that we acknowledge our own impatience and lack of vision, and work to correct it as we try to increase the patience and vision of the people of our land.

The way is hard, as the moral requirements of life are always hard in a sinful world in which war has long had a part. Collective security requires patience, sharing and give-and-take with each other, a steady and disciplined moral purpose and the willingness to make sacrifices. We are bound together with our friends in all nations to make our way with all moral fortitude through these hard days of trial. We move forward toward a world order in which war will be eliminated.

We pray to Almighty God, revealed in Jesus Christ as the Father of all, for the brotherhood of all. May we with Christian faith and hope take courage for patient work in these difficult times of the long human pilgrimage toward the kingdom of God.

A MINORITY STATEMENT

A motion to delete the two paragraphs under point five on pages 188f were lost by a vote of 149 to 69. The entire report of Section 5 was received by the Conference for transmission to the churches. There were 14 negative votes. The minority statement prepared by a group of delegates who favored the deletion of point five follows:

Recognizing the force of the reasons which have prompted the formation of regional military alliances, we nonetheless desire to record our convictions:

(1) That the adoption of point five seems to throw the weight of approval on rearmament rather than on disarmament, thus contradicting the admirable statements made elsewhere in the report.

(2) That the system of military alliances will tend to lead to war rather than to peace in the future as in the past.

(3) That the support of such alliances will effectively curtail the pursuance of the nonmilitary objectives of the United Nations.

(4) That the extension of the regional defense principle will heighten existing international tensions, deepen rather than reconcile present cleavages and may eventually imperil the continuance of the UN.

(5) That the mission of the church is to help our country make historic decisions in a spirit of world-wide rather than regional concern.

(6) That the church should be the church, and mindful of the experience of the church in other lands, we hold the conviction that our conference should refrain from aligning itself in support of military policies based on existing political cleavages and rival military systems among the nations.

III. The Conference Resolutions[8]

A. NEGOTIATIONS WITH THE SOVIET UNION

We believe that the United States should persist in negotiations as the method of settling international disputes in spite of all the frustrations that have been experienced.

Our country should give no ground for the accusation of intransigence or of unwillingness to make a new approach when new possibilities of action arise.

The differences between the Soviet sector of the world and the sector of the world that is free from Communist control are so fundamental and the lack of confidence on both sides is so deep and determined that a trustworthy general settlement will be most difficult to achieve. Meanwhile the nations opposed to communism should make the most of any present opportunity to ease tensions, even temporarily, and should seek to negotiate agreement without compromising basic convictions. We believe that our government should be open to such negotiations on all levels though it is beyond our competence to say in what order negotiations on various levels should proceed.

B. TREATIES AND EXECUTIVE AGREEMENTS

The principle of co-operation and mutual concern implicit in the moral order and essential to a just and durable peace, calls for a true community of nations. The United States can best insure its own peace and security by strengthening, and not weakening, the processes by which our nation exercises its rightful influence within the family of nations.

The power of our government to negotiate treaties and to make executive agreements should be so maintained as to ensure (*a*) that the United States will not be hampered in taking expeditious and effective action in fulfilling our responsibility as a member of the world community of nations and (*b*) that the United States should be in a position to make its full contribution to the continuing development of international law and to bring international relations into greater harmony with the moral law. Convinced that adequate safeguards respecting the making of treaties and executive agreements are already provided, we express our opposition to any Constitutional amendment which would hamper our government in carrying forward and making effective a responsible foreign policy.

C. TECHNICAL ASSISTANCE

Recognizing the critical importance of increasing the social, economic and moral strength of the less developed areas through greater use of technical co-operation and related economic assistance and development programs, we urge:

(a) That these programs be recognized as of prime and long-term importance in United States foreign policy.

(b) That the United States provide sustained and increasing financial support for the United Nations expanded program of technical assistance.

(c) That financial support of the United States technical co-operation program be substantially increased.

(d) That separate United States programs be conducted in such a way as to strengthen the United Nations programs of technical assistance.

(e) That United States technical co-operation be directed to the service of broad human need and be free from subordination to United States military and strategic requirements.

(f) That both public and private agencies make every effort to select representatives who are not only technically competent but also possess with humility high moral and spiritual qualities as well as a devotion to the welfare of the people of the host country and a sympathetic understanding of their culture and traditions.

D. INTERNATIONAL FINANCIAL ASSISTANCE

We recognize the need for international financial assistance to supplement technical assistance efforts. We urge that the United States give serious and sympathetic consideration to the need for international financial assistance for economic and social development, particularly when its aim is to help establish conditions in less developed regions which will enlist expanding capital investment, both private and public, both domestic and foreign.

We deem the proposed Special United Nations Fund for Economic Development worthy of study and possible endorsement by the churches.

Further, we urge that additional United States action on such financial assistance in no way be made dependent or contingent on disarmament.

E. SURPLUS FOODS IN THE UNITED STATES

In a world where a large proportion of the population is still hungry and malnourished, the United States has a continuing responsibility to see that its surpluses of food are used at home and abroad. Through the Food and Agriculture Organization and other agencies, the United States should continue to strive for ways to assure adequate production and distribution of food to meet the world's need. We commend the steps taken by Congress in 1953 to appropriate money for the disposal of surplus food now on hand, but we call attention to the fact that the steps taken thus far are inadequate to move the present surpluses to people in need.

F. DEPENDENT PEOPLES

The United States should support clearly and consistently the principles of the United Nations charter designed to promote the "well-being of dependent peoples including their advance toward self-government and the development of their free political institutions." The United States should be prepared to offer technical and financial assistance, and with special attention to training for national leaders to facilitate the rapid and peaceful achievement of these objectives for people still dependent and to enable countries which have recently achieved their independence to build the necessary economic, social, and political foundations for playing their full part within the interdependent world community.

Since governmental and intergovernmental agencies are restricted in their action in this field, we call upon church, business and voluntary agencies to explore opportunities to render assistance in these areas, and especially for direct aid to responsible persons and/or groups seeking technical and financial aid for sound and constructive development projects.

G. RACIAL DISCRIMINATION AND FOREIGN POLICY

Racial discrimination and segregation in the West, and particularly in the United States, has become a powerful factor in world affairs. Segregation and discrimination in churches, in employment, in housing, in the right to express one's political views and in public service undercut our moral position among the darker-skinned peoples of Asia and Africa. As American Christians we must do everything in our power to eliminate discrimination, both in our churches and in society at large. We also urge agencies of the United States government, of philanthropy and of religion to make their staffs racially inclusive both at home and abroad. While significant progress has been made in eliminating segregation in the United States and in the employment of minority groups in operations abroad, we have a long way to go before even the minimum requirements of our democratic heritage are fulfilled.

H. UNIVERSAL DISARMAMENT

We support the principle expressed in the bipartisan House Concurrent Resolution 132, now before the House Foreign Affairs Committee, which states that "it continues to be the declared purpose of the United States to obtain, within the United Nations, agreements by all nations for enforceable universal disarmament" under the United Nations inspection and control. We urge development of plans for the transfer of resources now being used for arms to constructive ends at home and abroad in fulfillment of such hopes as those voiced in the proposals of the late Senator Brian McMahon and by President Eisenhower.

I. REFUGEES

We note with satisfaction that the United Nations Office of the High Commissioner for Refugees has been extended for a period of five years. We urge the United States government to continue full co-operation with this Office and to contribute to the UN Refugee Emergency Fund. It is highly important, on all problems of statelessness and migration, that the policies of our nation should be determined in close co-operation in the appropriate UN and other international agencies. With respect to refugees who do not now fall within the responsibility of the High Commissioner—as in the case of Palestine, Korea, and other lands—we believe the United

States should, to the fullest extent possible, work through and support generously the UN organs and other intergovernmental agencies. In addition we should receive within our own borders our fair share of refugees.

J. THE IMMIGRATION AND NATIONALITY ACT OF 1952

We observe that the Immigration and Nationality Act of 1952 continues certain negative and restrictive aspects of the immigration laws it has superseded. We believe that the United States needs in this period of world tension a more enlightened immigration policy imbued with the spirit of justice and fair play. While acknowledging the complexity of the problem we believe that the allocation of quotas embodied in this legislation is arbitrary, unrealistic, and indirectly discriminatory in character and that a more equitable basis of allocation should be sought. We believe that the provisions of this legislation respecting the civil rights of immigrants are not in harmony with basic American principles. In view of the foregoing, we believe the Immigration and Nationality Act of 1952 should be amended. We urge the members of our churches to give careful study to this problem and to communicate their recommendations to Congress.

K. COMMUNIST CHINA AND THE UNITED NATIONS

The United Nations has formally designated the Peoples Government of the Republic of China as a party to aggression in Korea. So long as this indictment stands, the problem of recognition and acceptance of representatives at the UN is not a matter for immediate decision. We do hope that changed circumstances may make possible a revision of policy and urge that the changes regarded as necessary be carefully studied and clearly stated.

We, therefore, recommend that the Department of International Justice and Goodwill be requested to initiate a study of the problems here involved in order to identify any moral principles that may be relevant to provide Christians with information on which sound decisions can be based.

We strongly urge the United States government to adopt a flexible policy and, by resisting pressure to decide now what its policy shall be at some future time, to maintain such freedom as will permit wise action on the basis of conditions as they may progressively develop.

L. PALESTINE

We record our concern about recent border incidents in Palestine which reflect a deep-rooted conflict and which taken together imperil the peace of the Middle East as well as of the world. We view with appreciation recent measures of our government designed to put a stop to the violation of border agreements. We believe:

(a) That the United Nations, firmly supported by the United States, should find ways to end tensions and move from the present stalemate to permanent peace.

(b) That every effort must be continued to find agreement by negotiation whether under the UN or by direct consultation of the governments immediately concerned.

(c) That, pending the settlement of differences by negotiation, the UN should make available an accurate and objective analysis of the causes underlying these tensions.

(d) That, since the solution of the Arab refugee problem is dependent upon economic and political settlements, the United States and the UN should seek fresh and creative approaches which will be just and impartial both for the Arab countries and for Israel.

IV. A Closing Statement[9]

Our task has been to think together of God and of our country; especially of our country in its relations with other countries. We have tried to think of them together that we may help, if only a little, to bring them together. We have sought to see our country as God sees it and to see other peoples and our relations with them as God sees them. Since for us God is the overruling Power and the just and loving Will served by Christ and coming among us in Christ, we have sought to think of our country and of Christ together. And when we do this we cannot think of our country alone. He constrains us to look with him and to move with him out towards our brethren everywhere, even towards our enemies.

1. WE LOVE OUR COUNTRY

We love our country. We love that part of the good earth which is ours. We love home and kindred. We are proud of its memories, its heroes, its inventive genius, its tradition of freedom, its tolerance of differences, its generosity. But we cannot forget that other men love their countries, too.

Within those patterns of common life which we call *peoples* and *nations* our personal lives are set from birth to death. Largely according to where we were born, we share the blessing or the curse, the burdens or the opportunities of our people or nation. For the Christian the place in which he finds himself is the place where he is called to honor God and serve his neighbor.

We Americans find ourselves in a pleasant land. We are rich, as the world goes; rich in natural resources and in human skills. We are strong in productive capacity, in the health of our people, in the position we occupy. We are disquietingly strong in the weapons we possess.

When we think of our nation and of God together, there is much for which we can give thanks, with humility. So much that is ours is more a gift than an achievement, or an achievement made possible only by a gift. With the gift comes responsibility to the Giver.

2. OUR PART IN THE STRUGGLE FOR FULL HUMAN DIGNITY

In vast areas there are peoples who know hunger as we have never known it, people who have not achieved the mastery over nature that we enjoy, peoples who have been subject to foreign rule and have felt themselves looked down upon by white people like most of us. These peoples stir with hopes and resentment. They seek liberation and nationhood and full human dignity.

Because we have the memory of a struggle for independence we sympathize with those who struggle for independence. But until our pride is broken by God we are inclined to feel superior to those peoples, because they are foreigners and darker skinned. In some cases we are fearful—and with reason—that if they gained their freedom they will be so weak that hostile powers will occupy and violate their land and increase the threat to us. Naturally we try to tell ourselves that we are thinking of their good as much as our own. But that is not quite clear. A worldly wisdom tells us that we need friends in a dangerous world. A higher Wisdom asks us whether without guile we are sharing good gifts with brother men in need—how to sow better seed, how to harness rivers, how to guard against disease, all that we call technical assistance.

Far more disturbing than the ferment among the peoples of the technically less developed areas of the world is the hostility towards us and all that we value, of the other strongest power in our world, Soviet Russia. In that vast land a revolutionary movement has gained control. It carries within it a fanatical faith in its power to create an earthly paradise by violence. It is godless and openly materialistic. It has shown a frightening capacity to master technical skills for the purposes of war and conquest. It has infiltrated and overwhelmed neighboring peoples. It has gained control of China and other countries.

Even in the face of this threat we are called to think of God and our country and our relations with other peoples together. We shall not find wisdom in fear. We shall not gain strength from hate.

3. WE MUST RESIST THE EXTENSION OF TYRANNY

We are called to be strong, strong to resist the extension of this tyranny, and to accept the burdens of remaining strong. And even in our strength we are called to look ceaselessly for every way to reduce by agreement the strength that destroys and to build the strength that brings life and healing and reconciliation. We are called to be patient, patient to outwait and to outlive this tyranny, if that is granted us, and not to take upon ourselves before God the responsibility of loosing upon his world the horrors of global war. And while we gather and hold our strength, we are called to set forward in every way open to us the positive conditions for justice and peace which are his will for us.

The terrible responsibility which God has laid upon us reaches into every area of our national life and our relations with other peoples.

In our relations with the peoples we most fear, every opportunity to develop even a temporary easing of tensions must be seized by the United States. No grounds must be given for accusations of intransigence or of closing the door to negotiations.

4. WE MUST CO-OPERATE WITH OTHER NATIONS

Just because our power is so great we must learn to accept other nations not only as partners in the struggle for collective security but also as enlargers of our limited vision and as checks upon our too ready assumption that our self-interest coincides with the world's interest.

Because God has placed us in an order of material and moral interdependence, we have an urgent obligation to support the United Nations as the instrument which now most fully expresses and channels that interdependence. We must accept its limitations which are part of our human limitations even as we seek the ways of strengthening it.

Americans should rejoice in the revolt of long depressed peoples against immemorial misery. We must share our skills with these peoples in the fullest measure that our economy will permit.

In the economic sphere, we should support those policies which lead at home to greater productivity, economic stability and high development and stability and higher living standards.

The internal health and strength of our country can be maintained only by guarding our freedom, including the freedom of dissent from the majority. And only by guarding it can our nation offer leadership to peoples struggling for freedom against powers which brutally suppress all dissent.

Every evidence at home of unjust discrimination because of race or religion weakens the influence of America for justice and peace abroad.

We cannot foresee or control what the future holds for us or for our children. We are not responsible for the unforeseen or unforeseeable consequences of our own actions. We are responsible for doing all within our power to bring the wealth and strength of our country into the service of God's will for his children in the confidence that in that service alone our nation can find its freedom and its peace.

---

[1]Adopted by the conference as a whole.

[2]Reports from these four Sections were "received" by the conference and "commended to the churches for their study and appropriate action."

[3]Five of the six recommendations from Section II were adopted by the conference as resolutions. They are: Treaties and Executive Agreements, Technical Assistance, Refugees, Communist China, and Palestine. These resolutions are found on pp. 191-192, 193-194, 194-195. The sixth recommendation is this on Human Rights.

[4]The recommendation concerning economic development is treated more fully in the Report of Section III.

[5]This resolution has been abbreviated because the substance of it is found in the Conference Resolution on Universal Disarmament, p. 193.

[6]See note 5 above.

[7]The Conference voted to permit a statement of a minority view, opposing the inclusion of the two paragraphs under recommendation 5, to appear as a footnote at the end of this Section report. See p. 190 .

[8]In addition to adopting the Conference Message and receiving the reports from the four Study Sections for transmission to the churches, the Conference adopted twelve resolutions on current United States foreign policy issues. These resolutions voice the judgment of the Conference and were commended to the Department of International Justice and Goodwill for its guidance in the preparation of study materials and in the formulation of policy statements for subsequent submission to the General Board of the National Council of Churches.

[9]This statement, written by the Rt. Rev. Angus Dun at the request of the Conference Message Committee, was approved by the closing plenary session. Bishop Dun was chairman of Preparatory Commission No. 1 which wrote the background paper, "Christian Faith and International Responsibility." This paper served as the basis of discussion in the Message Committee.

Chapter VI

FACING THE NUCLEAR-SPACE AGE:

"Christian Responsibility on a Changing Planet"

Cleveland, 1958

INTRODUCTION

Among major developments on the world scene following the 1953 conference were continued frustration of efforts between the West and the Soviet Union to reach a rapprochement, increased build-up of military alliances and forces on both sides, and Russian successes in orbiting the first man-made satellite around the earth and developing the first intercontinental ballistic missiles. 1954 was the year of the French withdrawal from Indo-China, failure of efforts at German unification, signing of the Southeast Asia Defense Treaty, and reaction against the United States for its hydrogen bomb blasts in the Pacific which seared and took the lives of Japanese fishermen. 1955 saw the failure of the Geneva Summit Conference, convening of the Asian-African Conference at Bandung, beginnings of German rearmament, signing of the Warsaw Pact, and launching of the Atoms-for-Peace program. 1956 was the year of the Suez crisis, mobilizing of the first international police force under the United Nations, the revolt of the Poznan workers and the Hungarian massacre, coupled (curiously) with Krushchev's reversal of the tough Stalinist policies of the U.S.S.R. 1957 saw the launching of the first Russian Sputnik and ICBM, the birth of Ghana and Tunisia as republics, of the Federation of Malaya as a constitutional monarchy, and the West Indies as an autonomous unit within the British Commonwealth. It was the year also of the Eisenhower Doctrine committing the United States to military aid to Middle East nations menaced by international communism.

In light of these rapidly moving developments, the General Board of the National Council of Churches in May 1957 authorized its Department of International Affairs to convene another National Study Conference on the theme "Christian Responsibility on a Changing Planet." Pursuant to this action President Eugene Carson Blake issued a call to the constituent bodies for a conference to be held in Cleveland November 18-21, 1958.

> Our faith and world revolution constantly challenge us as Christians and as churches to new action in international affairs. Dynamic changes thrust themselves upon us in nuclear developments, space penetration, rapid social shifts, rising nationalism, anti-colonialism, the birth of nations and new alliances....
>
> We see a rising popular interest in Christianity and a resurgence of other religions, but we discern as yet only little evidence of increased

moral responsibility in human relations, as in international affairs. On the other hand, questions are being raised by some as to whether international affairs are at all related to religion and morality. It is imperative that we now re-examine our Christian responsibility in this changing world in light of the theological and moral aspects of our faith.

As the member denominations and related state and local councils proceeded to select their delegates and the Department of International Affairs set up study commissions to begin preparations for the conference, the United States narrowed the "missile gap" by successfully firing its first Atlas missile in December and launched four space satellites between January 31 and July 26.

As delegates converged upon Cleveland in mid-November, headlines in the daily press reflected increasing Soviet pressure on the Western powers to get out of Berlin, renewed shelling of Quemoy and Matsu by China, impending collapse of efforts to work out a nuclear test ban agreement at Geneva, new rebel offensives in Cuba with heavy fighting in Oriente Province, Eisenhower's plea to the Colombo Plan conference for a crusade against world hunger, and debates within the nation as to the soundness of United States policies in regard to nuclear testing and foreign relations generally.

The 515 delegates at the Conference came from 37 states and the District of Columbia. Two-thirds were lay delegates, and one-fifth of the total were women. Delegates appointed by 27 denominations constituent to the National Council numbered 302, and 10 persons were appointed by other communions eligible for Council membership. State and local councils of churches and units of the National Council appointed 146 delegates; the YMCA and YWCA sent 16; the United Church of Canada sent 10. The other 31 participants came as members of the preparatory commissions, or as consultants from government and from overseas, or as guests from other faiths. The delegates represented people from all areas of service within the churches, and the Conference was fully representative of age groups, denominations, political philosophies, and theology.

As they began their deliberations delegates had the benefit of a dozen background papers which were put into their hands before they set out for the conference or on their arrival in Cleveland. These had been prepared by experts in various fields who had served on study commissions which had been at work on the subject of the conference for nearly a year. The scope of the subjects covered in these papers and the competence and varied experience of the authors are clear from the following list:

John C. Bennett, "Theological and Moral Considerations in International Affairs"

John C. Bennett, "Some Presuppositions of the Cold War"

Alford Carleton, "Missions, and Service, and International Relations"

Richard M. Fagley, "International Institutions and Peaceful Change"

D. F. Fleming, "Can the Cold War Be Ended?"

Ray Gibbons, "The Changing Dimensions of Human Rights"

David Owen, "Responsibilities in the International Community for Development in New Member States"

George W. Rathjens, Jr., "On Some Conflicts in Military Policy"

Harold E. Stassen, "The Power Struggle and Security in a Nuclear-Space Age"

Wolfgang F. Stopler, "Christian Responsibility Toward Economic Development in Areas of Rapid Social Change"

Kenneth W. Thompson, "National Security and the Moral Problem"

Willard L. Thorp, "Economic Development and the Christian Point of View"

The conference was under the chairmanship of the Honorable Ernest A. Gross, Chairman of the National Council's Department of International Affairs, former U.S. Ambassador to the United Nations, and former Assistant Secretary of State. The keynote address was given by Methodist Bishop G. Bromley Oxnam, veteran of many previous conferences. Two public meetings were addressed by the Honorable John Foster Dulles, Secretary of State, the Hon. Thomas K. Finletter, former Secretary of the Air Force, and Dr. Ralph W. Sockman, Minister of New York's Christ Church, Methodist.

The work of the conference was accomplished in the four sections to one of which each delegate was assigned. Working for approximately ten hours on its particular topic, each section prepared a draft statement for presentation to the plenary sessions. Here the documents were discussed and debated by the conference as a whole. The sections were numbered II, III, IV, and V to correspond with the preparatory commissions which had worked on the same topics.

Papers from these four preparatory commissions were referred to the appropriate conference sections. The papers prepared by Commissions I and VI were considered of concern to all four working sections and were thus referred to all for their consideration.

Preparatory Commission I, under the chairmanship of Methodist Bishop Gerald H. Kennedy, with Union Seminary Dean John C. Bennett as rapporteur, had dealt with "Theological and Moral Considerations in International Affairs." Preparatory Commission VI had considered "Missions, and Service, and International Relations," under the chairmanship of Dr. Hugh Borton, President, Haverford College, with Alford Carleton, Executive Vice President, American Board of Commissioners for Foreign Missions, as rapporteur.

Working Section II dealt with "The Power Struggle and Security in a Nuclear-Space Age," under the chairmanship of Paul H. Nitze, Special Consultant to the Defense Department, and former Co-ordinator, Inter-American Affairs, and Director of the Policy Planning Staff, Department of State. Co-chairman was Kenneth W. Thompson, Associate Director for the Social Sciences, Rockefeller Foundation. Rapporteurs were Harold E. Stassen, former Special Assistant to the President of the United States on Disarmament, President of the University of Pennsylvania, and Governor of Minnesota; Raymond E. Wilson Editor, *Washington Newsletter*, Friends Committee on National Legislation; and George W. Rathjens, Jr.

Section III on "Overseas Areas of Rapid Social Change" was chaired by Wesley F. Rennie, Chairman, U.S. Commission for World Council of Churches Study of Areas of Rapid Social Change, and former executive Director, Committee for Economic Development, and Associate General Secretary, World's Alliance, Y.M.C.A. Co-chairman was George Carpenter, Executive Secretary, International Missionary Council. Rapporteurs were Wolfgang F. Stolper, Professor of Economics, University of Michigan, and Graduate Research Fellow at Center for International Studies, Massachusetts Institute of Technology; Clifford J. Earle, Secretary, Department of Social Education and Action, United Presbyterian Church in the U.S.A.; and Margaret E. Kuhn, Associate General Secretary, Office of Social Education and Action, United Presbyterian Church, U.S.A.

Section IV dealt with "The Changing Dimensions of Human Rights." Its chairman was Frank P. Graham, United Nations Representative in India and Pakistan, former President, University of North Carolina, and United States Senator; and its co-chairman was Ernest S. Griffith. Rapporteurs were Ray Gibbons, Director, Council for Social Action, United Church of Christ; and Mrs. Clifford A. Bender, Associate Secretary, Christian Social Relations, Woman's Division of Christian Service, Methodist Church.

Section V dealt with "International Institutions and Peaceful Change" under the chairmanship of Clarence E. Pickett, Nobel Peace Prize Recipient, and Secretary Emeritus, American Friends Service Committee. Co-chairman was John W. Nason, President, Foreign Policy Association. Rapporteurs were Richard M. Fagley, Executive Secretary, Commission of the Churches on International Affairs; and Murray S. Stedman, Director, Office of Information, United Presbyterian Church of the U.S.A.

Soon after the sections began work upon their assigned areas, a message committee of thirty-two persons was drawn out of the working sections. Members were selected by leaders of the various denominational delegations. This committee was under the chairmanship of Professor John C. Bennett, with Theodore A. Gill, Managing Editor, *The Christian Century*, as rapporteur. The message committee kept in frequent communication with the sections and endeavored to draft a message that would gather up the major concerns of all the sections and at the same time represent a consensus upon which the conference as a whole might agree.

On the afternoon of the third day the conference in plenary sessions began to discuss reports of the sections which were distributed and read to the delegates. The section reports were not intended to be official statements of the whole Conference, but rather the judgments of those who had given detailed consideration to the particular topics. Some differences of opinion were expressed on portions of the reports of Sections II and IV, but all four section reports were finally "received by the Conference and referred to the churches for study and appropriate action." Besides considering and "receiving" the section reports, the Conference in plenary session discussed and adopted resolutions from the Sections on a number related topics. These were understood to represent the views of the conference as a whole.

The Message to the Churches was discussed, amended, and adopted at the closing plenary session. While there were differences of opinion among delegates as to portions of this statement, the final vote on the Message was unanimous.

The most highly controversial issues arose out of the discussions and report of Section II, many of which were subsequently incorporated into the Conference Message. The Section and Conference questioned the validity—in the light of the new dimensions of nuclear warfare—of such popular concepts as "deterrence," "limited war," "massive retaliation," and "the power to win a war." They also agreed on the great urgency of disarmament ("Disarmament conferences...must not be permitted to fail.") and the necessity for "co-existence." Some difference of opinion, however, greeted the report of the Section which declared "Since we as Christians could not ourselves press the buttons for such destruction, we must now declare our conviction that we cannot support the concept of nuclear retaliation or preventive war." In Resolution A on "Nuclear Retaliation, Preventive War, and Elimination of War" the Conference as such dissociated itself from this extreme statement. Also questioned in plenary sessions was Section II's recommendation that the United States government "reconsider" its policy in regard to the People's Republic of China. The plenary session went along with this recommendation after some discussion, and after the statement of the Conference Chairman on the subject, which statement was incorporated into the report of the conference, (cf. footnote #2 to the Conference Message, below).

Not particularly controversial as far as delegates were concerned, but still not in harmony with general public attitudes, were the warnings against our self-righteous stance in regard to the communist countries ("We should...cease the practice of continual moral lectures to them by our leaders.") and an extreme anti-communism at home which would "inhibit the self-criticism which is essential to the health of a democracy." The Message also urged a rejection of the "posture of general hostility" toward the communist countries and to the government's effort to drive every nation into one bloc or the other, characterizing this "as mistaken as it has been unsuccessful."

Less startling but no less important considerations were brought up in the other section reports and in other parts of the Message. These include our responsibilities to areas of rapid social change, the quality of our own life as a nation, and the strategic role of the United Nations and other international institutions in facilitating peaceful settlement of international problems.

It will be obvious from the hints given above—and from the reading of the message and section reports—that the conference was at certain points openly critical of policies and attitudes of the Department of State and its respected Secretary John Foster Dulles. Mr. Dulles' appearance before the conference the evening of the opening day was in many ways a moving experience—especially for veterans of past conferences. He was greeted with a standing ovation by the delegates who admired and respected him personally and held him in highest esteem for his key role in launching and developing the national study conference approach to the problems of the churches and world order. Yet from the keynote address that afternoon by his friend Bishop Oxnam to the the final action of the conference in approving the Message to the Churches, the conference applauded expressions and took actions highly critical of basic concepts and key policies in the Secretary's foreign policy. Cleveland, 1958, was a far cry from the conference of 1949 when *Time* magazine could truthfully speak of Mr. Dulles' role as that of a "coach." In 1958 the conference was on its own. The players were not unappreciative of the fundamentals they had learned from their old "coach." But now they had matured to the point where they looked to captains on the field as together they planned their strategy and picked their plays.

This is not to say that a "bunch of preachers" in high but naive idealism turned their backs on the more mature counsel of a practical man of affairs. The fact is that the leadership of the conference—especially in the person of the chairman and much of the key personnel in the sections (notably Section II which dealt with the most controversial issues)—was itself heavily loaded with persons with considerable experience in important policy roles in the United States government and the United Nations.

Secular periodicals reporting the Conference commented on the independent spirit of the delegates and then focussed immediately upon the most highly controversial issue—that of "recognizing Red China." *Time* magazine began its story:"Sharply disagreeing with official U.S. policy, the leaders of U.S. ecumenical Protestantism committed themselves last week to 1) friendlier relations and cooperation with Communist countries and 2) U.S. recognition of Communist China and its admission to the United Nations."[1] *Newsweek* reported that "the delegates heard a speech on foreign policy by John Foster Dulles...then, after four days discussion, came up with some foreign policy of their own." "The delegates unanimously endorsed disarmament conferences, disapproved of 'limited' wars, and urged recognition of Red China and its admission to the U.N."[2]

The editor of the *Christian Century*, writing from Cleveland before the conference closed, declared that the conference had already "showed more Christian independence in its views on national policy than did any of its predecessors except the first." Referring to the applause with which the delegates greeted John Foster Dulles, the editor declared,

> The Conferees gratefully recognized the influence of his churchly conviction that the churches must speak out in world affairs, and had not forgotten that in all the earlier conferences Mr. Dulles had been active and that in most of them he had been dominant.

> But the fifth conference wasted no time in telling the world that it was riding nobody's coattails, certainly not those of the secretary of state.... Its resolutions revealed a mood of sharp criticism of many aspects of our overseas program, most notably our China policy.[3]

Christianity and Crisis, which has traditionally been critical of study conference actions which seemed to give insufficient weight to the power factors in international affairs, commented on

> at least four important respects [in which the Conference] proved worthy of its responsibility. First, impressive leadership emerged to fill the roles formerly played by men like the present Secretary of State [mentioned were John C. Bennett and Paul H. Nitze]....

> Second, the delegates tackled many new and unsolved problems in contemporary foreign policy with vigor and imagination [the Red China issue was singled out for mention]....

> Third, faithful attention to the real issues by scores of ordinary delegates underlined a sense of urgency often called for by American leaders but not always apparent in public response....

> Fourth, statements and opinions were expressed with remarkable candor.

At the same time the author of the editorial appraisal, Kenneth W. Thompson, was concerned by certain tendencies which to him were not reassuring. To him "the conference demonstrated that many honest, sensitive and troubled people have returned to essentially uncritical pacifist thinking"—as seen in the "enthusiasm for far-reaching disarmament solutions" which made them "impatient with any more limited contributions."[4]

A newcomer to the field of religious journalism since the previous national study conference was *Christianity Today*, whose editor Carl F. H. Henry gave extensive coverage to the conference. Henry opened his editorial report with the statement, "By sharp criticism of American foreign policy and demand for softer approaches to Russia and Red China, the Fifth World Order Study Conference virtually repudiated major facets of Free World strategy shaped by Secretary of State John Foster Dulles, one of the National Council of Churches' own elder statesmen."[5] The editor noted that

> From the outset...the social strategy of Union Theological Seminary's Professor John C. Bennett ("the absolutizing of 'compromise,'" one delegate called it) shadowed the sessions. Conference initiative...lay with the so-called "realists" who stressed the sinfulness of man and history, shied away from revealed principles, urged reliance upon temporary axioms, and proclaimed the inevitability of sinful choices.[6]

In a subsequent issue, *Christianity Today* focused particularly on the "Red China" issue and urged its readers to participate in a "survey of Protestant opinion" by recording themselves, on a form provided, for or against "U.S. recognition of Red China" and "U.N. admission of Red China.[7]

Public discussion of the Cleveland Conference was largely limited to the issue of "recognizing Red China." In addition to *Christianity Today*, many other groups and religious leaders came to the defense of the government's policy of non-recognition and the generally "hard" line in foreign policy personified by John Foster Dulles. Among these were the National Association of Evangelicals, Carl McIntire and his American Council of Christian Churches, Dr. Daniel Poling, and Dr. Norman Vincent Peale. Lay groups like the Circuit Riders and leaders of the far right who combined religious fundamentalism with super-patriotism made common cause in attacking the National Council for, as they alleged, coming out in favor of recognizing the communist government of China.

In an attempt to set the record straight and to show the rationale for Christian concern for issues of public life, the General Board of the National Council of Churches, at its meeting December 3-4, 1958, commented as follows:

> 1. The recent World Order Study Conference, speaking for itself and not for the Council nor for its member churches, has put into public discussion issues of high moral and spiritual, as well as political,

significance. The members of the conference, two-thirds of whom were lay persons, were a highly representative cross-section of the member churches of the National Council. More than this, they were in their own persons broadly representative of the interest and competence of the national Protestant community in foreign affairs. They spoke for no one but themselves, but they spoke with a mighty voice.

2. What has often been said must be said again. The Christian churches of the United States and their councils not only have the right but also the duty to study and comment upon issues, no matter how controversial, in the realm of politics, economics, and social affairs, in view of their common faith in Jesus Christ as both Lord and Savior. For all matters of concern for human beings are matters of concern to the churches and to the Churches' Lord. The Study Conference at Cleveland has performed a valuable function in helping the churches and their members carry forward the process of the American people's development of their foreign policy.

3. If and when in this process it appears that specific pronouncements in any area of international affairs should be made by the National Council of Churches, such pronouncement will be developed by the responsible departments and divisions of the Council for adoption by the General Board.

4. We call upon our constituency and all American citizens to study carefully the full text of the message of the Cleveland Conference, and later, when available, its full report, to the end that reasoned progress may be made by the people of the United States and their government toward solving the serious problems faced by our nation in its foreign relations.

The attacks upon the "Red China" section of the Conference Message unfortunately drew public attention away from other and perhaps more vital aspects of the message. The Message and Section Reports still speak relevantly to many of the most crucial issues before Christians of the United States.

---

[1]LXXII, No. 22 (Dec. 1, 1958), 38.
[2]LII, No. 22 (Dec. 1, 1958), 82.
[3]LXXV (Dec. 3, 1958, 1387.
[4]XVIII, No. 21 (Dec. 8, 1958), 170f.
[5]III, No. 5, (Dec. 8, 1958), 25.
[6]*Ibid.*, p.26.
[7]*Ibid.*, No. 6 (Dec. 22, 1958), p. 23.

CHRISTIAN RESPONSIBILITY ON A CHANGING PLANET
REPORT OF THE FIFTH WORLD ORDER
STUDY CONFERENCE

Cleveland, Ohio   **November 18–21, 1958**

I. Christian Responsibility on a Changing Planet: The Conference
Message

II. Reports from the Sections

The Power Struggle and Security in a Nuclear-Space Age; Overseas
Areas of Rapid Social Change; Changing Dimensions of Human
Rights; International Institutions and Peaceful Change

III. Conference Resolutions

Nuclear Retaliation, Preventive War, and the Elimination of War;
The Middle East; Population and World Economic Development;
Human Rights in the United States; Local Action by the Churches;
Genocide; Human Rights Conventions; The Right of the Press to
Travel Abroad; Religious Freedom; Oppressed Peoples; Fraternal
Support.

I. Christian Responsibility on a Changing Planet The Message to the Churches[1]

From churchmen assembled in Cleveland at the Fifth World Order Conference of the National Council of Churches; to the Churches of Christ in the United States of America. The peace of God be with you, and His grace be with all who study the peace of His world.

1. BACKGROUND OF FAITH AND ETHICS

We have been moved to this meeting by that faith in the redeeming love of God revealed in Jesus Christ which requires us and enables us as Christians and citizens to live in the world as it is. We have come to Cleveland in the conviction that such faith mandates and strengthens us to make hard choices between real alternatives without self-deception or despair. We have dared the hard choices in the confidence that as receivers of divine mercy we can bear the burden of evil involved even in the best that we can do. And we have not delayed this address to the churches because in the knowledge of God's mandate and in the strength of His promise we all must deal *now* with suddenly pressing problems, filled with unprecedented possibilities of good and evil in the life of our nation. Our troubled concern is for more than our nation. Because of the power of the United States, what happens here may bless or torment all the nations of the world. And our Christian concern is for every people.

We believe in God, Creator of heaven and earth, Sovereign over time, history, nations and peoples. He has made of one blood every nation of men, and wills that men should live together in an order of freedom and justice, and at peace with one another.

We believe in Jesus Christ, the Son of God, through whose life and teaching, death and resurrection, God gave reality and power to the life of reconciliation. In the Lordship of Jesus Christ in and over the world, God is at work bringing all nations and peoples under His sovereignty, calling men to loyalty and obedience as instruments of His purposes.

We believe in the Holy Spirit through whom God in Christ transforms the hopes and fears, the motives and capacities, the lives and destinies of men and nations into conformity with His redemptive purposes for the world and for all men.

We believe that Christians are members of the worldwide community of the church, and as such must strive to provide within their own fellowship as well as in their common life as citizens, the kind of community God wills for the world.

Ever and again in the course of human history, evil intrudes itself on men in new magnitudes of urgency and terror. The ultimate question is not whether man can destroy himself with the freedom which he has been given by God, or whether God would allow such destruction. The ultimate question is whether, in confidence in the triumph of God's righteousness, men will live in faithful obedience to God.

2. OLD TENSIONS AND NEW ISSUES WITH PERIL AND PROMISE

All the old tensions still tear at the peace of the world. They stem from such primordial deeps as the pride and egotism of nations, from such continuing disappointments as anarchy among the nations, from such standard conditions as the struggle for more tolerable existence (sometimes for existence itself) that is fought wherever resources are scarce.

But what has peaked history so dangerously today is the whole range of new terrors, exasperations and divisions now superimposed on the old issues. The five years since the last such conference on international relations, for instance, have brought no noticeable adjustment of the moral and ideological conflict between communist and noncommunist nations, no noticeable abatement of the suspicions that set them still at such dangerous odds. Instead, more and more frightening scientific discoveries—ever vaster destruction guaranteed ever swifter delivery—are still advanced as military reassurance. Inventive probing in "outer space" bewilders us with both its military and non-military potentialities. Revolutionary forces have created new nations featuring a passionate and fractious nationalism; strong and all too justified resentments against the western world—resentments now compounded by the deterioration in race relations in our own country; and often, unstable governments now increasingly suspending even the form of parliamentary and constitutional government.

Meanwhile, threatening even such tentative adjustments and satisfactions as are attempted, is the inundation of a vastly swelling world population.

New perils must not be allowed to obscure new promise, of course. Nuclear science continues its developments in the fields of creative power and medicine. Productivity increases in foods and goods—not just in population. The International Geophysical Year has demonstrated the possibility of a new kind of cooperation between nations. The United Nations reaches for new effectiveness. The churches become more practiced in their participation in the determinations and decisions of public life.

But it will not do to rehearse the promises, cross fingers, and hope for the best. Christians are not fools. They know that the capacity for destruction possible in war today exceeds the most ominous forebodings of yesterday. Should either the United States or the Soviet Union commit its full power to all-out international war, mutual destruction would ensue. Great cities would lie in ruins; whole populations would be annihilated; a radio-active plague would settle on the earth; the well-being, perhaps even the existence, of future generations would be placed in grave jeopardy.

Therefore, the immediate task of every Christian is to seize the initiative in the prevention of war and the achievement of peace in a world of inter-continental ballistics, thermonuclear weapons, and platforms in outer space for missile launching sites. We cannot sit complacently and hopefully behind the moral subterfuge which divides the world into "good" and "bad" peoples, waiting for the "bad" ones to be converted to our position. To do this is to insure the inevitability of war. The processes of peace are more than the problem of the citizen of the United States; they are the concern of every Christian who is dedicated to "the sovereignty of love" in human affairs.

3. WEAPONS WITH NEW DIMENSIONS OF DESTRUCTIVENESS

Lulled by well-worn policy phrases of "deterrence," "limited war," "massive retaliation" and "the power to win a war," the people of the United States may still not realize the magnitude of the destructive weapons at the instant command of Washington and Moscow. While such conceptions may have served a significant purpose in an earlier stage, the development of modern weapons places grave doubt on their meaning and usefulness today. "The power to win a war" has lost its significance when used in connection with such weapons. With bombers and missile bases under constant alert, there is little possibility of conclusive advantage from surprise attack and every reason to expect the immediate administration of blows of irreparable damage to both sides. Thus we find ourselves always on the brink of annihilation. In case of a real or imagined attack, the decisions that may lead to ultimate war will have to be made in a few moments. There is real danger that error in judgment, born of panic, may precipitate the war no one wants and no one can hope to survive. Under these perilous conditions the policy of deterrence, however necessary it may be considered, may cease to deter, thus posing the threat not alone of military defeat for the aggressor, but of mutual suicide as well.

Limited wars have in the past been conducted with the expectation that they could be contained in time, space and violence by the will of the powers involved. While such wars may continue until means for prevention, including more reliable methods for the peaceful settlement of disputes, have been effectively developed, the advent of nuclear weapons and their increasing availability for all forms of conflict pose a danger of utmost gravity. The expectation that man shall be able to deal with local conflicts in this way must not be separated from the new dimension of terror now implicit in their close proximity to an all-out holocaust. The new weapons now in being and the even more fateful ones now in prospect both on this planet and in outer space raise moral problems of new dimensions for Christians which we must not seek to evade, and underscore the imperative need of concentration on the prevention rather than the limitation of war.

4. PROBLEMS AND POSSIBILITIES OF DISARMAMENT

Progress toward universal disarmament is of major importance: 1) in the achievement of world order; 2) in reducing the threat of war; 3) in lessening the tensions between nations; 4) in curbing the spreading influence of military establishments on the entire life of nations; 5) in lifting the staggering cost of armaments from peoples everywhere, thus freeing them for constructive purposes.

Disarmament is a process involving spirit and will as well as conferences and treaties. We urge Christians to exhort their government to continued willingness to meet and discuss the means of disarmament by multilateral agreement involving satisfactory inspection and control of nuclear weapons as well as the progressive reduction of conventional arms. It is highly important that the United States, which gave initial impetus to international action for the peaceful uses of atomic energy, should fully and faithfully support the International Atomic Energy Agency. The suspension of nuclear tests under appropriate control and inspection is a first step toward halting the manufacture and stockpiling of nuclear weapons. We renew the plea made by the National Council of Churches for the abolition of Universal Military Training.

Disarmament conferences are a most important phase of the total process and they must not be permitted to fail. They are an essential part of the continuing process of building world law and order. The alternative confronted in the breakdown of any given conference is not a renewal of the arms race, but a renewal of negotiations. The patience to persist must be equal to the urgency of the need. The process of disarmament can begin as a result of a mutual interest in reducing the dangers of war. Yet every agreement that is reached, no matter how small, can lead to confidence only as there is growth in good faith. Disarmament also must begin in our spirits and minds. We deplore the tendency to discredit the motives and proposals for disarmament when made by anyone but ourselves. Vigilance and realistic precautions are necessary, but cynicism about the good faith of each other on all counts is a poisonous atmosphere in which to try to conduct negotiations.

We call upon the churches to take the lead in urging, promoting and engaging in the process of disarmament as an essential phase of the prevention of war. We must reaffirm our historic purpose to seek peace and pursue it with all diligence. It is not enough to deplore war and call for its abolition; we must engage and urge our country to engage without reservation in the things that make for peace.

5. THE UNITED NATIONS AND PEACEFUL CHANGE

The procedures available through the United Nations provide the main new resource for peaceful settlement and peaceful change. The record of the UN to date, even though it necessarily reflects the weakness of a divided world, proves that it lives and grows in this time of troubles. As a world forum, as a means to peaceful settlement, as a method of harmonizing the actions of nations for human welfare, the UN has made important headway. Chiefly in the field of security has the original plan envisaged in the Charter broken down. Yet even here, the existence of the UN has made a difference.

It is gratifying to see the vitality exhibited by certain organs and activities of the UN in relation to peaceful settlement and change. The General Assembly has made important contributions in this field. The programs to further economic and social development, to promote the advancement and emancipation of non-self-governing peoples, and to help care for those uprooted by war and tyranny, stand in the front rank of efforts for peaceful change. We would particularly congratulate the Secretary General cn the initiative he has shown in helping to bring about the peaceful settlement of disputes through the exercise of "quiet diplomacy" and the powers inherent in his office.

Christians are cautioned against the drastic criticism of the UN heard on one side from unimaginative nationalists who cannot see what the world would have been had there been no UN for the last ten years, and heard on the other side from disengaged idealists who cannot see the world in which the UN has done well to play even its limited role for the last ten years. Christians are counselled to support the UN in every way now open, and then to seek new ways to defend, sustain and enhance the institution as a diligent, presently active servant of the world's welfare and as the most ready, best flexed instrument of reconciliation now available to the nations.

6. NEW ASSUMPTIONS IN THE COLD WAR

Churchmen in this country need to reassess their attitudes to relationships with countries having Communist parties in control of government. In such a review the Christian proceeds from boundless faith in the overwhelming power of God's love and the ultimate triumph of His righteousness. The Marxists hold that Communism will inevitably prevail.

The "cold war" of today is a result of the tensions which spring both from ideological differences and from conflicting national aspirations. It had its roots in the Russian Bolshevik Revolution of 1917, and its intensity has grown with the extension of communist domination. In Russia and China communist philosophy has endeavored to assimilate the deep traditional sense of national destiny. The struggle has thus assumed realistic geographical dimensions with roots as well as objectives in national economy, culture and social organization. However, this process of assimilation of ancient religiously imbued cultures into a Godless culture is not complete; in fact, there is evidence that God continues to live in the hearts of millions in countries where the Communist party has achieved control.

Factors entering into the cold war are highly complicated. There is a moral challenge to conviction and principle, to which we cannot yield. There is also a threat to our national security, heightened by the almost limitless destructiveness of modern weapons. To reduce the total tensions to moral terms is unjustifiable. Where Communism is strong in its power of attraction, military power on our side may be quite irrelevant and much brandishing of it on our part may weaken our cause. Though military power in the non-communist world remains a necessity, its limits should be more clearly recognized, and far more of our attention and of our resources should go into the task of helping nations find their own way to solutions of their social and economic problems.

We believe that recent events, far from reducing the reality and role of Christian faith, emphasize both its meaning and its necessity. Men and nations are reacting variously, in fear and hope, frustration and boasting, apathy and frenzy. For us as Christians, our faith and the fellowship of the Church press us to see life steadily and whole, to respond neither with complacency nor panic, but with confidence and appropriate action (Statement of Policy adopted by the General Assembly of the National Council of Churches, December 1957).

Stronger efforts should be made to break through the present stalemate and to find ways of living with the communist nations. Sometimes this is called "co-existence," but we are concerned with something more than the minimum meaning of the word. Our relationship with the communist nations should combine competition between ways of life with cooperation for limited objectives; our resistance to communist expansion goes with recognition of the fact that communist nations as nations, have their own legitimate interests and their own reasonable fears. We should avoid the posture of general hostility to them and cease the practice of continual moral lectures to them by our leaders.

In the cold war we allow ourselves to drift into a defensive position in which we hesitate to admit any imperfections in our society, lest it confirm the communist indictment; thus we inhibit the self-criticism which is essential to the health of a democracy. We tend to make opposition to communism the touch-stone for policy both in domestic life and international relations.

There is real hope that new generations within the communist countries will be less fanatical in their ideological convictions and that they will be more preoccupied with peace, with economic well-being and with tentative experiments in cultural freedom than with the attempt to dominate other nations. It is not to be expected that they will formally renounce what we consider to be their errors. It is enough for the kind of living together described above if their emphasis and priorities change. The establishment of good relations will require tireless negotiations with them and imaginative programs of communication, cultural exchange and personal contacts.

We should welcome the fact that the world is not divided into two solid political blocs. Our own government's pressure on nations, forcing them to choose between two blocs, has been as mistaken as it has been unsuccessful. It has demonstrated a frightening insensitivity to international realities. The frightened, resentful, have not become friends.

With reference to China, Christians should urge reconsideration by our government of its policy in regard to the People's Republic of China.[2] While the rights of the people of Taiwan and of Korea should be safeguarded, steps should be taken toward the inclusion of the People's Republic of China in the United Nations and for its recognition by our government. Such recognition does not imply approval. These diplomatic relations should constitute a part of a much wider relationship between our peoples. The exclusion of the effective government on the mainland of China, currently the People's Republic of China, from the international community is in many ways a disadvantage to that community. It helps to preserve a false image of the United States and of other nations in the minds of the Chinese people. It keeps our people in ignorance of what is taking place in China. It hampers negotiations for disarmament. It limits the functioning of international organizations. We have a strong hope that the resumption of relationships between the peoples of China and of the United States may make possible also a restoration of relationships between their churches and ours.[3]

7. OVERSEAS AREAS OF RAPID SOCIAL CHANGE

During recent years our planet has undergone astounding and far reaching changes, not least of which are advances in technological knowledge. The churches must be concerned with the cultural and social changes which have occurred at home and abroad. We must give particular attention to overseas areas of rapid social, cultural and political changes. During the last fifteen years more than twenty nations have achieved political independence. Significant economic changes have come about in parts of Africa, Asia and Latin America, especially in the villages in which the vast bulk of the people dwell. Agricultural reform in respect of land tenure and methods of cultivation have taken place. The impact of Western civilization has brought about increased industrialization and urbanization in many lands. Vast increases in population have taken place. In some places broad and far-reaching government plans for the development of higher standards of living for many peoples have been launched. The traditional subsistence economy has been thrown out of balance, family patterns and community relationships disrupted.

All these economic changes have brought in their train radical social and cultural changes. Some are good; others are not so good; still others evil. Christians everywhere must be sensitive to the changes and to their mixed consequences. More than one hundred fifty years of the Christian mission have been at least partly responsible for some of the present turmoil. The Gospel of Christ gives new status to every individual. Christian schools, colleges, hospitals, clinics, agricultural stations and health programs have shown millions how unimaginably better life could be for them and for their children.

8. RESPONSIBILITIES OF CHRISTIANS IN THE U.S. IN AN INTERDEPENDENT WORLD

Christians in the United States will be most sensitive of all, though, because United States development of its economy of abundance—in a world where millions still are needy and illiterate—has given substance to hungry dreams and undeniable force to human demands. Our responsibility is heavy under these circumstances. Who has raised hopes must be ready to help. To whom much is given, of him shall much be required.

Our churches and our nation are, therefore, urged again to get under the world's needs. We must discover the real needs of others: not what we want to give, but what they must have for economic and social development. Aid from outside cannot be thrust upon any country. Such aid must be mutually agreed upon by the recipient and by the giver—in the interest of helping the recipient help himself and without compromising his political independence or his self-respect. In many cases this mutuality will be in the interest of the donor, as well as of the recipient.

For mutuality is the new fact of life in a shrunken world. The weal or woe of each nation has everything to do with every nation. What at one level has always been the hope of the Christian is now at another level the historical fact for every man. We have everything to do with each other. It will not do just to subsidize other countries for our defense. Rancors fostered so contribute finally to no defense. But our support of far peoples' reach for economic fulfillment, spiritual freedom, national justice—this is defense indeed for us all.

The arsenal for this defense of life and hope—and finally of peace, freedom, order, justice—is full. Government aid has been advanced by the United States, sometimes bi-laterally, sometimes multi-laterally. A relatively small enlargement of the tiny part of our Gross National Product given to such aid would aggregate all the governmental and private aid which could now be effectively absorbed by the underdeveloped countries. Christians are urged to undertake themselves, and to exhort their government, to more liberal, imaginative aid.

Non-governmental agencies, too, must be supported in their contributions to the health of new nations on whose well-being the healing of the world depends. Foundations spend vast sums abroad for health and education. Voluntary agencies—including the churches' denominational and ecumenical bodies—conduct world-wide programs of technical assistance and emergency relief and distribute governments' and citizens' surplus commodities where they are most needed. Private capital is invested by Americans in other countries. Most benefit accrues both to the United States and to the other countries when American investors risking their capital are not given reason to be nervous about expropriation and when countries invested in are not given reason to worry about being bled.

Beyond all the monetary earnests of our concern, there are the persons— United States citizens who can and should move in the world as pledges of our goodwill and understanding, as symbols of the nations' mutuality. 100,000 Americans live and work abroad today: business men, consular officials, exchange students, missionaries. Tourists by the millions see, and are seen. Christians among them will affirm other peoples as they are, for themselves, thanking God for the abounding variety in His creation, and out of gratitude acting at home and away from home to reconcile the nations.

9. THE QUALITY OF OUR LIFE

We cannot separate the policies of our country from the quality of our life as a people. Often what we do within our own borders contradicts our professed convictions concerning justice and freedom for all men. We have made great progress in overcoming poverty and in securing economic opportunities for our people as a whole. We have also come a long distance from the atmosphere of fear and intimidation in relation to the expression of opinions which prevailed a few years ago. But we face a grave crisis in relation to the civil rights of Negro citizens and other racial minorities.

We reaffirm the declarations of the National Council of Churches and of many denominational bodies which express strong support for the implementation of the decisions of the Supreme Court concerning school integration. We are aware of the delicate problems in many communities but we call upon the Churches to give strong support for policies in each state which provide for positive steps toward the integration of schools and the overcoming of all interference with political rights and of all other disabilities from which any racial group now suffers. The Churches must begin with themselves. There is a great gulf between what they say on a national or denominational level and what they do or encourage or permit in many communities. The Churches should call upon the Federal Government, both the President and the Congress, to give strong leadership in favor of policies of desegregation.

(1) We ask our fellow churchmen to give careful consideration to the selection of political leaders who will challenge the forces of massive resistance and other forms of defiance of the Court's decision.

(2) We also call upon our fellow churchmen to work to overcome segregation in all areas beginning with their own congregation and

including housing, public services and economic or occupational opportunities.

(3) Also we believe that Churches should support the ratification of the genocide convention and be prepared to support the ratification of adequate covenants relative to human rights.

10. IN CONCLUSION

The Church is called to mediate the love and the judgment of God to this threatened world. Our response to His love, which is expressed in our love for our neighbors should sensitize us to the needs, the aspirations, the fears and the sensibilities of all peoples affected by the policy of our nation. Many of the moral failures of policy are failures of empathy; they come from an inability to see the world as it appears to nations whose traditions and conditions of life are different from our own.

We must be far more open than we have been to the needs and aspirations and fears of other nations. We must continuously, ruthlessly, re-examine the hardness of mind and heart that comes from our too little noted national self-justification. We must face new realities and problems with the freshness of mind that is the fruit of repentance. We must press the Church to the education and invigoration of its members in relating their faith as Christian citizens to their decisions as citizen Christians.

II. Reports from the Sections[4]

A. THE POWER STRUGGLE AND SECURITY IN A NUCLEAR-SPACE AGE: REPORT OF SECTION II[5]

1. THREATS TO SECURITY

We remind ourselves, in considering this subject, that we are thinking and speaking, not only as citizens but more particularly as Christians. Ours must be a sustained effort to relate the love of God as revealed in Jesus Christ to the complex problems of our time. Two temptations must be resisted: on the one hand, the temptation to be so impressed with complexities and difficulties that we fail to say clear words on issues that require moral judgment; and on the other hand, the equally strong temptation to overleap concrete problems in the enunciation of general principles.

Christians have a loyalty which transcends the nation. The security they seek cannot be limited to any nation or group of nations. Their obligation is to God-given life. All of it! But this, again, does not mean that Christians should be indifferent to the survival of the nation. For the survival of a nation may be important to the defense of human personality, as the Christian faith understands it.

In the contemporary world situation, the question for Christians in the United States is not simply whether the nation is righteous but also whether our national existence is valuable, both to the people of this country and to the life of mankind. Some aspects of life in the United States could, without loss, perish, just as some characteristics of life in nations opposing us are worthy of survival. Nor should Americans claim that this nation, taken as a whole, is better for human life than any other nation. We can, however, say that the present and potential character of our country makes it possible for the United States to be of continued service to human welfare. Not to try to preserve the security of our nation *could* be moral dereliction to mankind. Although the Christian's national loyalty is always qualified, it may, nevertheless, be a part of his loyalty to mankind. This does not exclude recognition of the possibility that mankind may be served and enriched by a wide variety of social forms and cultures.

It is implicit in what we have said that security should not be thought of primarily in national terms. The Christian obligation to mankind and the technical developments of our time now combine to make a purely national concept of security wrong from every point of view. Freedom, justice, social welfare and security are indivisible. And the nationalistic approach to these goods is both morally and practically obsolete.

What today threatens our security? The manifold aspects of the revolution of our time constitute both a profound challenge and a threat to the basic security of the U.S. and others of the older nations. The continuing security problem comes from the age-old problem of nations struggling for strategic advantage and competing in national armaments, in a situation lacking order and often approaching anarchy. The growth of Russian and Chinese military power controlled by and coupled with the communist movement and ideology constitute the present focus of this struggle.

The Marxist-Leninist view of man and society, coupled with a national and personal urge to world-wide power, make the contemporary struggle profoundly serious. The communist powers are resolved to win the world-wide struggle. They expect to win. They will acquiesce in a genuine "coexistence" only when their own continued existence clearly demands it, or when, with the passing of time, some of their basic convictions have been eroded.

That the intransigeance and aggressive tactics of the communist powers are caused, in part, by fear for their own security is not to be denied. The tragic experience of the Russian people in two world wars and the history of Western imperialism must be taken into account if we are to understand contemporary communist attitudes. American nuclear stockpiles and widely scattered military bases, some of them near the borders of the Soviet Union, arouse apprehension. Accordingly we, on our part, must try, more earnestly than we have done, so to conduct ourselves that communist nations will have less cause to fear our intentions. But their fear also arises out of a legitimate Western response to their aggression. The aggressive aims of the Communists are a real and formidable factor in world tensions and a responsible national policy must take this into account.

From some such appraisal of the threat to security, all considerations of the most effective methods of dealing with the threat should start. It should be added that our response to Communism should always include the recognition that the whole Western world, and particularly the Christian Church in pre-revolutionary Russia, carries heavy responsibility for the movement's emergence, because of an inadequate emphasis on social justice and human welfare. Communism is, in part, a judgment upon our sins of omission and commission. Humility and repentance are incumbent upon us. But to underrate the threat is no service to human well-being or to world peace.

2. THE SECURITY ROLE OF THE UNITED NATIONS

Neither the United States nor any other nation can insure its security in the years ahead through the unilateral development of military or other power. It is our firm conviction that the best hope for the creation of a system of world order lies in an increase in the power of the United Nations to assume wider responsibilities. Very frequently it may appear that actions taken by that body, in the resolution of disputes, will not be, from the short term point of view, to the best interests of the United States. We hold, however, that there must be an increased recognition that U.S. interests can find their long term satisfaction only within a far wider structure of interests that includes those of the rest of mankind. The United States should show a greater willingness than has heretofore been demonstrated to resolve disputes through the organs of the United Nations including the World Court.

We are agreed that if military force is to be used it should be sanctioned by, and under the control of the United Nations.

The United Nations is deterring aggression and in resolving disputes relies upon the authority and moral force of its recommendations backed by the support of those nations committed to the principles of the Charter.

Much more emphasis must be placed upon the development of economic and political stability, efforts to settle disputes as early as possible, and the amelioration of situations before they break down into armed conflict or result in situations that invite aggression.

Our basic goal would be a system of international disarmament and security to supersede continued reliance upon military pacts and alliances such as SEATO and the Baghdad Pact.

3. TOWARD CONTROL, REDUCTION AND ABOLITION OF
ARMAMENTS

Progress toward the goal of universal disarmament is of major importance in the achievement of world order, in reducing the threat of war, and
in lessening the tensions of the power struggle. It is urgent that greater
emphasis and multiplied efforts be made by the United States and other
nations to reach disarmament agreements because of the rapidly increasing
destructiveness of nuclear weapons and intercontinental missiles; because
of the growing difficulty of bringing these weapons under adequate inspection and control; and because of the large sums now being spent on
armaments compared to aid and technical assistance, in a world characterized by widespread hunger, disease and illiteracy.

It is not possible at a Conference such as this to spell out the process
of arms reduction and control in detail, but the following are suggestions
for continued efforts. In its efforts toward world disarmament, the United
States should:

(1) Assume greater initiative toward bringing national armaments
under international inspection and control in a process directed toward
their consequent limitation, reduction and eventual abolition.

Toward this end, we should follow up on the progress of the United
Nations negotiations and the successful Geneva scientific talks and
keep pressing for an early agreement to stop nuclear weapons tests and
to install a United Nations inspection system to verify the fulfillment
of the agreement, along the lines recommended by the conference of
scientists at Geneva. We believe the United States Government should
continue its present suspension of tests, unilaterally if necessary, for a
sufficient period of time to permit full exploration of the possibilities
of arriving at a definitive international agreement.

(2) Follow up this significant first step of inspection and limitation by
additional steps of international control and reduction.

(3) Continue to seek an international agreement setting up a UN agency
for the peaceful exploration of outer space, and a control system to
assure the use of outer space for peaceful purposes.

(4) Cooperate in establishing the proposed inspection system of the
International Atomic Energy Agency in the hope that this may help
furnish the pattern necessary for supervising worldwide cessation of
production of nuclear weapons.

(5) Continue negotiations with the U.S.S.R. for a mutual aerial and ground inspection system to guard against surprise attack and thus seek to aid in creating a climate where more far-reaching disarmament negotiations may be undertaken.

(6) Recognize the close relationship between political settlements and disarmament and be more willing to broaden the framework of disarmament negotiations. These discussions might include the possibility of mutual withdrawal of nuclear forces from points of closest proximity, and disengagement in areas such as the Middle East or Central Europe.

(7) Work to reopen, as soon as possible, disarmament discussions within the UN for the purpose of prohibiting production of nuclear weapons and other weapons of mass destruction, to transfer nuclear weapons stockpiles to peaceful purposes, and to begin the process of reducing arms and armed forces.

(8) Press for the creation of a permanent UN police force for border patrol, inspection, and the various functions of a genuine international police system.

Within its governmental system, the United States should:

(1) Enlarge the staffs and strengthen the programs of the Executive Branch for studying the problems of world disarmament and formulating workable plans for its accomplishment. The proposal of a carefully worked out, safeguarded, comprehensive disarmament plan by the United States would serve as a focus for specific negotiations and for rallying world opinion.

(2) Expand and make permanent the important work of the Special Subcommittee on Disarmament of the Senate Foreign Relations Committee.

(3) Undertake a coordinated program among government agencies to work in cooperation with management and labor for making the transition in as orderly a manner as possible, to an economy less dependent on military expenditures, and to remove the fears that disarmament steps will result in a depression.

(4) Offer to devote a substantial percentage of the savings from armaments to allocations for development of underdeveloped countries, using the United Nations as far as feasible.

(5) Abolish the system of military conscription and allow the authority of the Selective Service System to draft men to lapse on its expiration next June. The government should consider ways of encouraging recruitment to meet those of its manpower requirements as would result from following the interim military policy suggested in the next section of this report.

4. INTERIM MILITARY POLICY

Until substantial progress has been made toward disarmament, we must use all our influence to see that wisdom and imagination are used in limiting and controlling military force.

As citizens we have a natural concern for the security of our nation. As Christians we have a wider concern for the security of mankind. We cannot therefore, view with equanimity preparations for nuclear war which might result in the genetic distortion of the human race as well as widespread destruction of civilized life. Since we as Christians could not ourselves press the buttons for such destruction, we must now declare our conviction that we cannot support the concept of nuclear retaliation or preventive war.[6]

During the interim period prior to a strengthened system of world order, law and disarmament:

(1) We urge our government to consider all methods for contributing to world security other than reliance upon nuclear weapons.

(2) If the government continues to rely in any way upon nuclear defenses, we urge that it be only for the deterrent effect that their possession by us may have on their possible use by anyone else.

(3) If any such weapons are to remain in United States possession, we urge that the United States government shift the character of the nuclear weapons it is developing away from systems implying very rapid and inadequately considered decision in the event nuclear warfare is believed to have, or has been initiated by others. Weapons systems more nearly invulnerable to surprise attack would permit time for political consideration, for negotiation, for the exercise of third party judgment, and for the force of the moral opinion of mankind to be brought to bear before a decision would have to be made as to the appropriate reaction in such a crisis. Such a shift in weapon systems would materially reduce the danger of nuclear war arising from misunderstanding or error.

With respect to providing military aid to other nations, the United States should give due regard to the character and objectives of the recipient governments, the effects of the aid on their economic and political systems, and the effects on neighboring states.

5. PEACEFUL COMPETITION AND INTERNATIONAL COOPERATION

The nuclear stalemate prompts both U.S.S.R. and ourselves to shift competition to nonmilitary fields. Presumably, American leaders ought to welcome peaceful competition in ideas, institutions and opposing conceptions of the good life. Yet, up to the present, national initiative has not been equal to the task. Why have American policies been unsuccessful in this sphere?

Five reasons are advanced for these failures. First, American attitudes have been too one sided in seeing the cold war in simple, military terms. The power of Communism rests in part in its offering opportunities for rapid economic development to technologically underdeveloped nations. In the next decade, the results of Chinese and Indian experiments will be watched for the object lessons they carry for other new nations.

Second, we have hesitated to accept the fact of living with two major communist nations for an indefinite period and of recognizing that hostile grimaces and provocative acts will be of no avail.

Third, we have not seized every opportunity to react creatively to more hopeful developments within the communist world, particularly within the so-called satellite nations.

Fourth, Americans are disposed to see the present struggle as a conflict between good and evil. A simple black and white moralistic approach may impair the effectiveness of our policies toward satellite countries or those whose political goals are not immediately our own.

Fifth, many assume that the world is and must be divided into two ideological blocs. In fact, an important part of the world's peoples are not aligned with either side. More understanding and effective policies must be evolved for cooperation with this part of mankind.

The United States should:

(1) Seek continuation over a five year period of the International Geophysical Year.

(2) Extend trade and travel with mainland China, Eastern Europe and the Soviet Union.

(3) Encourage association and fellowship of various professions and groups across the Iron Curtain; for example, exchange of farmers, students and religious groups.

(4) Explore more effective use of its surplus food for distribution in communist countries and in underdeveloped nations.

(5) Evolve more seminars and conferences for social scientists and scientists from the Soviet bloc and the West. We commend the Department of State for persisting in negotiating an agreement for expanded exchange of persons with the Soviet Union and urge the lifting of restrictions on the travel of Soviet visitors in the United States.

(6) Implement programs for common attacks on basic human problems of disease, such as malaria, and threats to crops, such as wheat rust, that may be carried across national boundaries.

(7) Invite wider participation by the U.S.S.R. in UN technical assistance programs.

(8) Encourage private investments in underdeveloped areas with appropriate safeguards both for the private investor and for the host nation.

(9) Encourage the religious and philosophic dialogue above the level of present political struggles. In particular, we urge that all opportunities be utilized, through the World Council of Churches and other channels, for meetings of churchmen from the Soviet nations and the West.

6. POINTS OF POLICY WITH RESPECT TO SPECIFIC AREAS

Several of the areas of the world pose particular challenges to American foreign policy at this time.

With respect to China, United States policy has not been responsive to the realities. While we cannot condone many of the things for which Communism stands, it is the part of wisdom to admit that we see no reasonable alternative open to us other than to recognize that Communist China is a nation of tremendous and growing importance with whom we must live. To continue to treat this great power as an outcast can serve only to deepen existing tensions and to further developments in China which we must deplore. Moreover, continuation of such a policy by the United States is indefensible. We feel that the stiffness of our attitude has already cost us dearly in world opinion, and has made the resolution of our difficulties with China more difficult than might have been the case had there been official channels of communication from the beginning.

The Section would urge a more flexible approach to the Far Eastern problem in the interest of a more adequate representation of American purposes and objectives. In the interest of greater stability in the Far East, Washington should encourage the Chinese Nationalist Government to evacuate exposed positions that may be militarily unsound and politically detrimental, and submit to the UN the question of securing peace and security in the area of Formosa. The people on Formosa should be protected in their right freely to determine their own future.

At minimum, the Western world should not be prevented from liberalizing trade relations with any Far Eastern country. The United States should liberalize its policies with respect to travel of Chinese nationals in the U.S. and of U.S. citizens within Communist China. At the same time, our policy should move in the direction of an acceptable solution of the problems of participation by the People's Republic of China in the counsels of the United Nations and the establishment of diplomatic relations with that government by the United States.

We feel that, with respect to peaceful competition with Communism, one of the most crucial contests is that being waged in India. Inevitably, all of the underdeveloped nations of the world will compare progress in India with that in China; it will be tragic if the comparison is unfavorable. We, therefore, urge that special consideration be given to providing India with sufficient economic and technical assistance to insure the success of her development program. The fact that India has been unwilling to identify itself with us in our military policy should not deter us in this. Rather, we should welcome the fact that free, uncommitted nations can exist in the world today, and that they may facilitate settlement of disputes in which any of the great powers is involved.

At the heart of any settlement of European problems is the question of the two Germanys. Moreover, the continued isolation of West Berlin is clearly a source of great vulnerability to the West. We see no means of materially reducing tensions in this part of the world while remaining faithful to our obligations to the people of West Germany, and of Berlin particularly, other than in unification, We, therefore, urge that our government continue to support the unification of Germany.

We are deeply concerned that Christians better understand the involved and explosive situation in the Middle East. With humility and penitence we confess that our own lack of understanding and sympathy, both in our reluctance to resettle in Christian countries the oppressed Jews of Europe, and in our disregard of Arab rights, has contributed to the tragedy of Palestine. We believe that Christians must join with Muslims, Jews and others in a continuing search for just and durable peace in the area. We urge that every effort be continued to find agreement by negotiation whether under the UN or by direct consultation among the governments immediately concerned. Particularly we call for the implementation of the UN resolutions providing for the return, where possible, of the Arab refugees to their homes; and, where not possible, for adequate compensation for their loss. We believe the Christian community should stand ready to assist in the repatriation or resettlement of the Arab refugees.

We call on our government to support the legitimate aspirations of the Arabs for unity; and of Israel to survive in peace.

We firmly record our support of the UN recommendation providing for the internationalization of Jerusalem and its environs.

In general, we feel that our attitudes toward the whole Middle East should be conditioned less by our fear of Soviet expansion into the area and become more responsive to the needs of the peoples of the region. We must recognize the aspirations of the people in the area for independence and economic development. The United States should generously support a widespread program for economic development of that region. We feel that the Baghdad Pact and the Eisenhower Doctrine are not responsive to the major problems of the area, and that the former in particular, may have hindered the development of peaceful solutions to Middle East Problems.

7. CALL TO THE CHURCHES

We call upon the members of the Christian churches:

To dedicate themselves to the task of working in a spirit of Christian love for the healing of the nations;

To pray for a spirit of penitence for the selfishness of our affluent society in a world of hunger and need;

To make common cause with the disadvantaged and dispossessed for the realization of their hopes and freedoms;

To transfer the conflict of ideas and ideologies from the battlefield to the realm of peaceful competition and the rule of law;

To translate into reality the old Russian proverb, "Mountains may never come together but men can";

To multiply their efforts toward beating swords into plowshares and achieving a warless world.

B. OVERSEAS AREAS OF RAPID SOCIAL CHANGE: REPORT OF SECTION III[7]

Christian responsibility toward the areas of rapid social change comes from the beliefs, common to all Christians, that all men are children of God with the same right of food, health, and the pursuit of happiness; that all the goods of the earth are free gifts of God, given to us in stewardship and to be used for the benefit of mankind; that Christ died for all men everywhere; that the love of God impels us to love our fellowman, wherever he may be; that we cannot love God unless we love our fellowman; that indeed what we do toward the least of our brothers we do to Him; and that the richness of God's grace in our hearts naturally overflows into deeds of love for the benefit of others.

As Christian citizens we recognize that all nations, including our own, stand under the judgment of God. While we must take account of the national interest, we cannot disregard the whole human family which God has made. Policies based on selfish and narrow conceptions of national interest will in the end be self-defeating. The great resources committed to us, we hold under God, not as owners but as stewards. We have no right to use them to exercise domination or control over other peoples, but we must seek in mutuality and brotherhood to promote the common good of all mankind. Association with people from many lands in the ecumenical Christian fellowship has deepened our sense of responsibility and extended our understanding of the needs of other nations and the most effective ways of working with them.

1. DIMENSIONS OF THE PROBLEM

We are in a period of profound revolution. Previously static societies are on the move. The needs of these societies are enormous and aggravated by population explosions to which the societies find it difficult to adjust. These are challenges to us as much as to the societies themselves. The very fact that the societies are changing creates continually new problems which the societies have to learn to handle. There are no simple or cheap solutions. Together with the peoples in the areas of rapid social change we must face the fact that, even under the best of circumstances, it will take years to meet their just aspirations. Citizens in the United States must be prepared to share with their overseas brothers the burden of constant frustrations and long-continued effort.

2. OUR RESPONSIBILITY AS CHURCHMEN

In one person there are many dimensions: at the same time we are church-members, citizens, professional people, workers, investors, etc. We cannot in our actions separate political, ethical, economic, and other aspects even if we want to. No matter what we do, we cannot escape the consequences of our actions. And even if we do nothing, we shall have to face the consequences.

It is natural that we think of our Christian responsibility first in connection with the work of the churches. Missionaries and other Christian workers have pioneered in the areas of health, education and development. True to their tradition, they will continue to seek new ways of serving the peoples and of satisfying their needs. They will, as before, cheerfully cooperate with anyone, private or governmental, church or secular, to achieve the will of God. Christians should, to the best of their ability, support their missionary activities, their coordinated effort in Church World Service and the Division of Interchurch Aid and Service to Refugees of the World Council of Churches, their denominational programs and a multiplicity of services designed to meet a variety of needs. This support involves giving money, goods, and the service of persons. It should also involve the obligation of each Christian to be informed, and of the churches to enable their members to acquire information and understanding.

3. OUR RESPONSIBILITY AS CITIZENS

Many problems, however, cannot be solved by the Church or by other private groups alone. Christians are also citizens. They must influence the policy-making of their government. This includes participation in selecting the best representatives they can find. We have the responsibility to share in making proper laws and in formulating proper goals. We are charged with making sacrifices as taxpayers.

We believe that substantially larger sums of money should be made available through the government as well as individual and voluntary groups for economic development in the areas of rapid social change, for the purpose of helping the countries in those areas establish sound economies. We strongly believe that military and economic aid should be separated. At the present time only a minor fraction of so-called foreign aid goes for economic and technical assistance proper. We note with approval the growing recognition of the importance of such assistance on the part of the Federal government and the increased support being given. Yet the problem is of such great dimensions as to call for a much more substantial program. We could increase our support at least four times and still be allocating for this purpose less than 1 per cent of our Gross National Product.

Money should be made available for economic development through as many channels as can be usefully employed, both bilateral and increasingly multilateral: U.S. and UN technical aid programs, the new U.S. Development Loan Fund, the UN Special Fund, increase in the capital of and contributions to the International Bank for Reconstruction and Development (World Bank) and the International Monetary Fund, continued support of the International Finance Corporation, support of the proposed International Development Authority, etc. Even though some time will elapse before such larger sums could be usefully and efficiently employed, we feel that they should be provided to make long-range programing and flexibility possible. These resources should be in addition to, and not in place of, private aid and private capital because of the vast needs for schools, hospitals, roads, dams, and other basic facilities which are prerequisite for subsequent development but do not have an immediate payoff.

These resources must be used wisely and effectively. We do not believe it is wise to attach political and military strings to economic aid. But the scarcity of resources imposes the need for standards of efficient use. Waste of resources is a sin.

We are concerned that decision-making be mutual. It is neither our task nor our right to impose on others what we think they ought to want. The scarcity of physical resources and of experienced manpower compared to the need makes it imperative, however, to develop some order of priorities.

We realize that we have our own problems, such as urban renewal, more adequate care of the old and sick, the need for schools; problems which are as legitimate as the needs of our brothers abroad. We are aware of the magnitude of these problems. We urge fellow-Christians to be ready to make the necessary sacrifices to meet these goals of our conscience, to be ready to pay more taxes and to reduce temporarily our own consumption standards if necessary. To the extent to which our own production increases or to which it becomes possible to reduce armaments, the required sacrifices become smaller.

We are aware that many of our domestic policies will have relevance to our desire to help. Christians should be aware of the need to pursue domestic policies which will raise our own efficiency so that we may use our resources more effectively for all urgent needs. Unemployment is not only a personal tragedy, but a waste of resources. We urge Christians to support the reciprocal trade program, the proposed Organization for Trade Cooperation, and the increased use of our surplus commodities under such arrangements as will further economic development as well as alleviate immediate suffering.

Although we talk about economics, we are interested in the total well being of people. Yet, as long as the average life expectancy in large parts of the world is less than 30 years, as long as there are periodic famines and thousands of people become homeless through disasters that could be averted, it is necessary first to establish the minimum basis for a decent life.

4. RESPONSIBILITIES IN THE FIELD OF BUSINESS AND INDUSTRY

We urge that American enterprises operating abroad make greater efforts to carry over into less developed areas the human and social gains which are the fruits of a century and a half of business and labor leadership in the Western world, of social awakening, of education and of legislation. The many human costs which a generation ago were outside the scope of "profit and loss" reckoning are now increasingly recognized as legitimate and necessary charges. Many business operations overseas in which American capital and management are involved now make provision for these costs; but others still participate in socially destructive practices such as restrictions based on race, forms of migratory labor which preclude normal family life, and submarginal remuneration. The establishment of minimum standards in this field should be the joint concern of ownership, management and trade-unionism. Many American Christians participate in one or another of these categories, and have the special responsibility of their basic ethical concern for other people. It is recommended that the Department of the Church and Economic Life give continuing attention to the Christian implications of American involvement in overseas investment and industrial development, in consultation with the appropriate ecumenical Christian agencies.

5. CHRISTIAN CONCERN WITH PERSONS

We can never forget that our central concern is with persons. This concern permeates everything we do. It has been noted that Christian churches and missions have worked for decades in the area of technical assistance, having pioneered in the fields of health, medicine, education, agriculture, and social work.

The human factor plays the crucial role in all programs. Trained, competent and devoted leadership is essential to all development programs. Higher education and technical training must have high priority. International visits and exchanges are important factors in promoting mutual understanding and in furthering development.

The fellowship which Christians have together has produced a succession of devoted men and women over the years who, learning languages and cultures of other countries, have identified themselves with their peoples and have been able to make outstanding contributions. They have opened up channels of fellowship and understanding, of interpretation and service, which overleap the barriers that governments too often face.

Thus, they make it possible for our good intentions to become effective through the love of our fellowmen and the ecumenical Christian fellowship. In addition to missionaries, many thousands of American Christians are now serving overseas in a great variety of secular capacities. Their potential influence is incalculable.

We recommend that facilities be made available under interdenominational auspices for Christian orientation, training, and guidance of American personnel entering upon service overseas; that links of mutual helpfulness be formed wherever possible between such persons and the church bodies in the areas where they serve; and that consideration be given to the formation of a fellowship of committed, witnessing Christians engaged in professional service overseas.

We recommend also that provision be made under suitable auspices for the establishment of an Ecumenical Placement Service whereby qualified Christian personnel from many countries could more readily be found for professional and technical service with agencies of development.

C. THE CHANGING DIMENSIONS OF HUMAN RIGHTS: REPORT OF SECTION IV[8]

A star of major magnitude has risen upon the horizon of international affairs within our lifetime—the rising expectations of people in every nation throughout the world for the fulfillment of human rights and fundamental freedoms. In the lands which have won their freedom from colonial control, in countries where the people are oppressed by dictatorial rule, in nations where human rights have not been enjoyed by minority groups, as well as in those which have long enjoyed a large measure of civil and political rights, there is insistent, inescapable demand for human dignity embracing social, economic, moral and religious values. We, as Christians, welcome this stirring of hope, this noble aspiration in the souls of men. We believe it promises a new day a-dawning, in which there will be the breaking of ancient bonds, the freeing of demeaned persons, and the liberation of the human spirit.

We rejoice not only in the deepening demand for human rights but also in the widening scope of the concept itself. Goals and rights that have been considered desirable but impossible are now deemed to be attainable. Where formerly human rights were limited mainly to those political rights which governments have protected, they now extend their orbit to include a whole galaxy of social and economic goals in the attainment of which people look to their democratic, representative governments as instruments.

The Universal Declaration of Human Rights, which in these brief ten years has had such influence upon the constitutions of governments, the treaties of nations, and the deliberations of the United Nations, embraces such goals as equality before the law without discrimination, freedom of travel from one's own country and return thereto, freedom of religion, the right to marry and found a family, the right to work and to protect one's interest through trade unions, the right to a standard of living adequate for the health and well-being of one's self and family, and the right of everyone to a free public education for at least the elementary and fundamental stages. These rights defined in the Universal Declaration of Human Rights enlarge the range of our expectations. We believe they are necessary and attainable for all persons in the United States and for all peoples everywhere.

In addition to the recognition of national responsibility for human rights, we note the increasing recognition of international responsibility for these rights and the growing awareness that the denial of rights to people in any nation becomes a threat to the peace of the world and is a proper concern of international relations and the organs and agencies of the United Nations. National decisions as to what constitutes the human rights of any people are becoming increasingly a subject of concern to the international community.

We look with and hope to this heightening expectation for the fulfillment of human rights because the God revealed in Jesus Christ has given us His own image as the assurance of our human dignity. We recognize that all men are created by Him and promised sonship by His complete identification with man in the Incarnation. Above all, He sent His own Son to redeem mankind. His life, teachings, crucifixion and resurrection reveal and reestablish man's worth as a son of God, and brother of all people. From this spiritual core spring our human rights and fundamental freedoms.

Our Christian faith constrains us to confess our creaturehood, our tendency to error, our evil, and our sin. Before Him we are equal not only in our essential dignity but in our dependence and our need. We stand together under the judgment of God, for we have not attained the nobility He would give us, nor have we achieved it for others. We recognize that God is the Lord of history and that our human rights are the gift of God, and therefore should not be withheld by human beings. We acknowledge our responsibility not only for our own use of the rights bestowed upon us, but also for the attainment of our neighbor's rights, even though he may not appear to desire them, and some may wrongly think he does not deserve them.

Another basis for human rights rests in the sovereign rule of God as observed in the laws of nature. The Declaration of Independence of the U.S.A. speaks of "certain unalienable rights among which are life, liberty, and the pursuit of happiness." The Declaration states that men are endowed by their Creator with these natural human rights.

A further expression of man's basic natural rights is to be found in the Universal Declaration of Human Rights which recognizes "the inherent dignity and . . . the equal and inalienable rights of all members of the human family." This dignity inheres in man as man, whether rich or poor, citizen or alien, a member of the majority or minority. It resides in man regardless of his race, color, nationality, religion, social or class origin, language, citizenship, or any outward circumstance. Human rights, as recognized in the Western world, derive from the endowments of God as observed in His natural law.

The people of some nations find another ground for human rights in the consent or agreement of peoples. This often gives us a basis of cooperation with non-Christian and non-Western nations for the attainment of human rights.

In totalitarian states, whether communist or fascist, it is held that the state confers or withdraws such rights, not that these rights derive from divine sanction, natural law, or democratic consent. We oppose this view. Human rights belong to persons because of what in God's grace they are, not because of the political power of the state.

As Christians we hold that rights and duties are as inseparable as two sides of the same shield. Every right implies a corresponding duty. No one can claim a right at the expense of a more important right for others. We cannot act lawlessly and expect freedom, or refuse to work and expect a high standard of living as a matter of right. We also have the very important duty to seek the fulfillment of human rights within the experience of each person, and to encourage their attainment by our neighbor, whatever he may be, and whatever be his condition. We acknowledge our responsibility, as Christians, to seek by peaceful means the attainment of human rights for every human being, and we humbly confess our frustrations and failures to achieve such rights for ourselves, our fellow-countrymen, and our neighbors in other lands. We do not believe that our failure to realize these rights in our own country diminishes our responsibility to work with men of good will for their attainment everywhere. This we do because we are bidden to love our neighbors as ourselves, and because all men are children of Him who so loved us that He sent His only Son to save us.

We further recognize that we have fallen short of His expectations and the just aspirations of human beings in the attainment of what belongs to man by right. In many lands, including our own, serious obstacles prevent the attainment of essential rights. Among these are the economic, racial, and regional limitations of education, economic opportunity, and democratic experience; and the moral and religious foundations which support and strengthen human rights. We regret that many now living will probably not enjoy the full spectrum of human rights and fundamental freedoms. These goals are yet-to-be-attained. We must work continuously and resolutely for their realization at the earliest possible moment and in the fullest possible degree. Human rights, for all people, are attainable and must be furthered with all deliberate speed.

In conclusion, while recognizing the importance of actions on the part of churches, governments and the United Nations, we are very mindful of our individual and personal responsibility for the attainment of human rights. All our human relationships affect human rights; and we realize that our daily actions either contribute to or detract from the realization of human rights.

God's Holy Word speaks to our present condition. "And what does the Lord require of you but to do justice, and to love kindness, and to walk humbly with your God?" "Whoever would be great among you must be your servant, and whoever would be first among you must be slave of all!" "I came that they may have life and have it abundantly." "God made from one every nation of men to live on all the face of the earth." In the light of these truths we rededicate ourselves and our churches to the furtherance of human rights for all people.

D. INTERNATIONAL INSTITUTIONS AND PEACEFUL CHANGE: REPORT OF SECTION V

As the world becomes increasingly knit together and interdependent, we must recognize that more and more areas of life become affected with an international interest. As national decisions and activities, such as trade and monetary policies or immigration legislation, impinge on the lives and livelihoods of other peoples, the traditional definitions of domestic jurisdiction are seen to be too sweeping. Failure, through lack of consideration or consultation, to take this expanding international interest into account spells tensions and trouble. Thus there is new urgency for developing reliable methods of peaceful settlement and peaceful change.

The need is magnified by the revolutionary pace at which international life is changing. In an atomic age, moreover, the dangers involved in failure to achieve peaceful adjustment of relations to changing conditions are of a new order of magnitude. Therefore, the task of developing new and revitalized procedures of peaceful settlement and change, to harmonize the policies of nations, to reduce injustice, and to ease conflicts arising from discordant interests, presses a primary claim to attention. To be effective, such procedures must be readily available, dependable, and objective.

Attention is here directed to the better utilization and improvement of available procedures. However, new international methods and institutions for the pursuit of justice and reasonable compromise, which are consonant with the United Nations Charter, seem clearly needed and merit greater international attention. It is recognized, moreover, that many of the issues which divide the nations can be "solved" in the long run only through the extension of community whether on a narrow or broader front, whereby clashes of interest can be transcended in the establishment of a common interest. This process can also be described as a pooling of sovereignty, whether in a limited or specialized sphere or along more inclusive lines. The principle of being "members one of another" has application to nations as well as to persons.

As churchmen, it is not our function to spell out technical answers to the question of peaceful settlement and peaceful change. Rather it is our duty to remind our people and government of the heightened importance this question has assumed, to press for responsible measures, and to help create the attitudes which will sustain them. Beginning at the parish level, it is necessary to cultivate a new understanding of, and sensitivity to, the international implications of national actions, and a new willingness to delegate sovereignty in specified areas to international authority. The accelerated tempo of interdependence must be matched by the quickened acceptance of its obligations.

1. DIPLOMACY

In the world now emerging, with its multiplied international contacts and conflicts, diplomatic relations acquire an enhanced significance. The new channels provided by media of public information offer potentially useful supplements to diplomacy, but not a substitute. We need to appreciate more fully the important role which a well trained and responsible diplomatic service can play both in the day-to-day adjustment of differences between nations, and in reinforcing the available multilateral procedures. Competent young people should be helped to find a Christian vocation in this field.

In line with this perspective, we believe that the traditional concept of diplomatic recognition as a means for talking with a government in power is more relevant to today's needs than the newer idea of recognition as a sign of moral or political approbation. The latter notion, if applied consistently, would greatly reduce diplomatic contacts which the times require.

2. THE UNITED NATIONS

The procedures available through the United Nations provide the main new resource for peaceful settlement and peaceful change. The record of the UN to date, even though it necessarily reflects the weaknesses of a divided world, proves that it lives and grows in this time of troubles. As a world forum, as a means to peaceful settlement, as a method of harmonizing the activities of nations for human welfare, the UN has made important headway. Chiefly in the field of security has the original plan envisaged in the Charter broken down. Yet even here, the existence of the UN has made a difference.

The principle of universality of membership, as urged by the National Study Conference of 1945, seems to us a sound principle: that all nations willing to accept the obligations of the Charter be admitted. While many members, including the United States, have not lived up fully to their Charter obligations, and some have been gravely disloyal, member states have undoubtedly acted in ways more consonant with the principles of the Charter, being under the disciplines of membership, than would have been the case had they been outside. Membership provides the international community with opportunity for affecting the attitudes of States and consequently with leverage for modifying their policies. Important issues like disarmament require an inclusive approach for effective solutions. For such reasons, we urge the government to pursue, and our people to support, a course designed to complete the membership of the UN. This would mean inclusion of mainland China without exclusion of Taiwan, and some interim arrangement regarding Germany, Korea, and Vietnam, pending reunification.[9]

While the United Nations must continue to grow if it is to live, we do not find revision of the Charter to be a live option at this time. The lines of division are too strong and the common foundations too weak. There are, however, important possibilities for growth in the better utilization of existing instruments, in the development of powers inherent in the Charter, and in the creation of new powers by common consent without formal change in the Charter.

It is gratifying to see the vitality exhibited by certain organs and activities of the UN in relation to peaceful settlement and change. The General Assembly has made important contributions in this field. The programs to further economic and social development, to promote the advancement and emancipation of dependent peoples, and to help care for those uprooted by war and tyranny, stand in the front rank of efforts for peaceful change. We would particularly congratulate the Secretary General on the initiative he has shown in helping to bring about the peaceful settlement of disputes through the exercise of what he has called "quiet diplomacy" and of the powers inherent in his office.

The availability of various instruments for peaceful settlement and change, however, does not mean that these are adequate. Reinforcement is needed along various lines. We believe that the United States and other governments which have gravely limited the operation of the International Court of Justice through domestic jurisdiction reservations, should remove these obstacles to judicial handling of justifiable disputes. By these reservations the nations involved have retained for themselves the decision as to whether an issue is domestic or international in character. To this extent, said countries act as judges in their own cause. In practice, the reservations have had a crippling effect on the work of the Court. The Court, rather than a party to a dispute, should decide whether the dispute is international in character.

Likewise the procedures of the Peace Observation Commission and kindred means for peaceful settlement need to be made more dependable, and more automatic in operation. Delegation of authority for initiating such procedures to international rather than national decision could help to this end. Thus, the decision to send POC teams or representatives of the Secretary General into an area of tension might well rest with the POC, the Secretary General or some other UN body, rather than depend upon the initiative of a nation caught in a crisis. This shift in responsibility could be helpful even if the countries concerned retained the right to determine whether or not to receive the team or representative. A constructive action complementary to that suggested above would be for nations to join in an advance commitment to receive UN observers when sent by such an international decision.

If it is not practical or desirable to establish at this time a permanent UN peace force, we would urge that the UN give further thought to the ways and means of bringing an emergency force into being on the shortest possible notice.

In regard to anticipatory consideration of situations likely to generate a threat to the peace, resort might be had to special UN commissions of inquiry acceptable to both sides. The ground rules for such commissions would need to be worked out carefully, lest their work aggravate tensions rather than prove remedial and curative. Our main point is that more attention needs to be paid to wise anticipatory action, before tensions generate crises. It seems clear that better procedures for the pursuit of international justice are required to reduce the perils of this atomic age.

3. REGIONAL INSTITUTIONS

We believe that churchmen and the people of the United States generally should pay much more attention to the wide variety of regional associations in which the United States participates. These bodies, insofar as they are congruent with the purposes of the United Nations and subordinate to its jurisdiction, can supplement the peacemaking functions of the UN in highly important ways. Where such associations are based on the common loyalties and interests of a regional community, they can reduce the issues which press upon the world organization, and pioneer in the development of international procedures for which the latter is not yet ready. We believe that the curative functions of regional bodies should be emphasized and undergirded, i.e., their work for economic and social advancement and for the development of international law.[10]

In this Section it was urged that Africa provides an ideal opportunity for constructive regional action. This underdeveloped continent continues to exhibit far too much of what has been injurious in the system of colonial power. The pace of advance, though helpfully and hopefully manifest here and there, is far too slow to meet the urgent needs of the native peoples, and by far too slow in the presence of the scientific and technical resources and organizing genius which Western Christians possess. We owe it to God and to the whole of humanity to put forth whatever cooperative and sustained effort is necessary to demonstrate our common concern to develop and sustain the political, economic and social institutions of human freedom and dignity on this as on other continents.

It is our considered judgment that the newly emerged and emerging nations—economically underdeveloped, insufficiently possessed of scientific, technical and organizational personnel, inadequate in educational resources—need far greater help from us than they are receiving. In the name of our common God and Father we call upon our nation and upon our brothers among the Western European powers to provide the needed help. Let us overcome, once for all, the measurement of our responsibilities in this field by the scales of benevolent parsimony. Let us hasten ourselves to that measure of effort and sharing which the steady advancement of economic adequacy and human freedom require of us.

Reference should also be made to functional international organizations, such as the UN specialized agencies and lesser bodies which unite nations around common problems or common interests. By building a sense of community in limited fields, such as agriculture or communications or navigation, these specialized groups can develop habits of cooperation which are helpful in easing conflicts in other areas. Also they can make essential contributions to the furtherance of peaceful change.

4. THE CHURCHES AND OTHER VOLUNTARY ORGANIZATIONS

The churches, their missionary and service agencies, their organizational and interdenominational departments, make important contributions to better understanding and to the peaceful settlement of problems. So may business and labor organizations and many non-governmental organizations focusing on international affairs.

The Christian belief in the Fatherhood of God and the brotherhood of all men places a moral mandate on all church members to inform themselves on world affairs, to support their own church and religious agencies, and to witness to their Christian convictions in civic and other organizations. As citizens, Christians have a major responsibility to bring constructive influences, grounded in the principles of their faith, to bear upon the formulation and conduct of foreign policy. Peace depends on the hearts and minds of men, and the Christian has a vocation to contribute to the peace of his world through his efforts as an individual and as a member of a church and its agencies.

Through contacts between churches across international boundaries, as well as through the broader relations of the ecumenical and missionary movements, Christians can help to build mutual understanding and creative efforts for peaceful change. Through such channels, Christians can help to fashion a favorable climate of opinion both for peaceful settlement and peaceful change. It is particularly important that the American churches seek to develop contacts with churches across the divisions of the major conflicts of our time.

In pursuance of these contacts, we urge our government to demonstrate its support of the principle of an open society by promoting the exchange of persons and ideas across the iron and other curtains or barriers. We further urge the abolition of travel and exchange restrictions both for private citizens and for diplomatic personnel.

The section on "Political Bases of a Just and Durable Peace" of the 1942 National Study Conference (Delaware) advocated: "That certain powers now exercised by national governments must . . . be delegated to international government, organized and acting in accordance with a world system of law. Among the powers so delegated must be . . . the maintenance and use of armed forces except for preservation of domestic order. . . ." Unfortunately, these requirements for peace have not yet been achieved. Massive national armaments, under no world control, reflect world anarchy, not world order.

We recognize the urgent necessity of creating a world system which will help to exclude war from human affairs. This means that the world must move rapidly toward a new system of security based on just law and disarmament of nations, peace fully inspected and enforced; for example, through a United Nations arms control commission, police and courts.

This also means building world community through much larger use of the United Nations in all constructive fields, especially in meeting the needs of peoples for self-government, food, health care, education, and economic development. The United Nations thus would assume much larger functions, moving toward real world community and world order. Recognizing the immense difficulties in achieving this goal, we believe that its attainment is in harmony with God's will, and is worthy of dedicated Christian effort.

III. THE CONFERENCE RESOLUTIONS[11]

A. NUCLEAR RETALIATION, PREVENTIVE WAR, AND THE ELIMINATION OF WAR[12]

The Conference, in receiving the report of Section II and commending it to the churches for study and appropriate action, wishes to record that there were differences of views in the Conference on certain statements in that report, specifically, regarding the fourth sentence of Part 4[13] of the Section Report.

Members of the Conference agree in categorically rejecting the concept of preventive war.

There are many of us who emphatically do not agree with the inference that deterrence through the capability for nuclear retaliation is to be bracketed with preventive war.

Such peace as there is today, precarious as it may be, rests to some measure upon the capability for nuclear retaliation. The world's hope of achieving international agreements leading toward universal disarmament may similarly rest in part upon that capability.

In expressing these views, it was made clear that this is not to be taken as approval by the Conference of the moral acceptability of all-out nuclear retaliation, or as modification of the view of the Conference that the elimination of nuclear warfare and of war itself is a Christian imperative. The problem of whether or not a Christian can support nuclear warfare in any form must be squarely and prayerfully faced by the churches.

The Conference directs that this resolution be recorded in the appropriate place with the published version of Section II's report.

B. THE MIDDLE EAST

We are deeply concerned that Christians understand better the involved and explosive situation in the Middle East. With humility and penitence we confess that our own lack of understanding and sympathy, both in our reluctance to resettle the oppressed Jews of Europe in Christian countries, and in our disregard of Arab rights, has contributed to the tragedy of Palestine. We believe that Christians must join with Muslims, Jews and others in a continuing search for just and durable peace in the area. We urge that every effort be continued to find agreement by negotiation whether under the United Nations or by direct consultation of the governments immediately concerned. Particularly we call for the implementation of United Nations resolutions providing for the return, where possible, of the Arab refugees to their homes; and where not possible, for adequate compensation for their loss. We believe the Christian community should stand ready to assist in the repatriation or resettlement of the Arab refugees, and in the meantime should urge less grudging and more generous support of the United Nations Relief and Works Agency for Palestine Refugees in the Near East.

We firmly record our support of the United Nations recommendation providing for the internationalization of Jerusalem and its environs.

The United States should support the legitimate aspirations of the Arabs for unity, of Israel for survival in peace, and of both for political and economic progress. In particular, our country should continue its search for plans satisfactory to both the Arab States and Israel for the development, to their mutual benefit, of water and other resources.

C. POPULATION AND WORLD ECONOMIC DEVELOPMENT

The Conference calls attention to the serious threat to human well-being posed by the rapid rise of population; commends the efforts of the Commission of the Churches on International Affairs and other bodies to direct attention to this problem; and urges the churches to seek an agreed Christian basis of understanding and action with respect to population control and family life.

D. HUMAN RIGHTS IN THE UNITED STATES

For many years there has been developing a growing goodwill among the races in the United States. Some of this goodwill was unfortunately associated with certain assumptions of inherent racial inequality. This we repudiate as unworthy of followers of Christ. Goodwill was also based upon the more fundamental respect for the dignity of human beings as equal in the sight of God.

In parts of the country we now witness a tragic worsening of the situation in human relations provoked by propagators of fear, prejudice and hate, resulting even in bombings of schools, homes, synagogues and churches. As Christians concerned with human brotherhood, with human rights, with the dignity of the individual, and especially with the full flowering of the possibilities of childhood and youth, we believe the time has come for our governmental leaders at the national and state level to give vigorous leadership to the enforcement of the law, and for a conference of local, state and national leadership to be called immediately by the President. Such a conference would be designed to give focus, encouragement and support to the healing and law-abiding forces throughout our nation, our states and our localities. We believe that such leadership could develop a program whereby, in all parts of our country, steps could be taken faithfully to comply with the Supreme Court decisions, with due recognition of local difficulties and of the need for cooperative and continuous progress.

E. LOCAL ACTION BY THE CHURCHES

Whereas the national and regional church bodies have strongly supported the decisions of the Supreme Court, and have otherwise concerned themselves with human rights in the field of race relations, we call upon the churches and their members to carry out the provisions of these resolutions in the local churches and communities. We recommend that as soon as possible state and local councils of churches and/or ministerial unions call for this purpose meetings of ministers and lay members across racial lines. We further recommend that at these meetings a detailed plan be developed for implementation of the church bodies' resolutions in the local churches. We believe that such gatherings would give strength to the local churches, the social action groups and the ministers, and would help them fulfill the teachings of our religion and the provisions of resolutions already adopted by the churches. We recommend that the Department of International Affairs, in cooperation with the Department of Racial and Cultural Relations, seek funds from the churches, foundations, business institutions and unions to further this purpose.

F. GENOCIDE

We strongly urge the Department of State to present to the United States Senate, with strong support, the Genocide Convention adopted by the General Assembly of the United Nations and ratified by fifty-eight sovereign states. This convention to prevent the persecution and extermination of minorities was initiated by an American citizen and supported by our delegates in the United Nations. For various reasons, the convention never reached the floor of the United States Senate for its consideration and action. We believe this convention should now be considered and ratified by the Senate so that this nation, in company with other free and sovereign states, may stand as a champion of the weak, oppressed, and persecuted.

G. HUMAN RIGHTS CONVENTIONS

We further urge our government to consider, on their individual merits, the other conventions drafted by the United Nations for the enforcement of human rights. We respectfully request the administration to present such conventions to the United States Senate for its consideration.

H. THE RIGHT OF THE PRESS TO TRAVEL ABROAD

We support the right of representatives of the press to travel in other lands, there to collect materials and information, to the end that such information may be freely and widely disseminated.

I. RELIGIOUS FREEDOM[14]

As Christians we are under obligation to seek for other faiths the same religious freedoms we ask for ourselves. In view of reports coming out of the Soviet Union concerning efforts steadily to undermine the Muslim faith in its beliefs and practices, especially in those parts of Central Asia less exposed to foreign visitors, and to eradicate the Jewish religion, culture, schools, synagogues, publications and Scriptures; as well as to deny the right of Jewish people to leave the country; we request the Department of International Affairs and the Department of Religious Liberty of the National Council of the Churches of Christ in the U.S.A., in consultation with the Commission of the Churches on International Affairs, to conduct an inquiry into reported moves to destroy the human rights of Muslims, Jews and any other minority groups in the Soviet Union and its captive and associated nations, and if warranted, to make a strong representation to the United Nations through appropriate governmental channels to prevent any anti-Semitic or any renewed anti-religious movement such as those by which our civilization has been, in the past, too often betrayed. We ask a similar investigation of the reported moves in Spain to deny the rights of religious minorities in that land.

J. OPPRESSED PEOPLES

In view of further reports of oppression of peoples in many parts of the world, we call upon the United States government to give positive support by all peaceful means: to the attainment of responsible self-determination of peoples; to the maintenance, protection and development of the distinctive cultures of racial, ethnic, and linguistic groups and the protection of the right of minorities against extinction or forced assimilation; and to the achievement of human rights by people to whom they have been denied. We also call upon our government to safeguard financial assistance to countries where oppressed people live so that these funds may be used for the welfare of all the people rather than to support leadership which is in conflict with the rightful ambitions of the people. We believe that such positive support of oppressed people is more consistent with the heritage of the United States and more fully expresses the spirit and genius of our people than does our abstention from instruments designed to protect and support the attainment of human rights.

K. FRATERNAL SUPPORT

Resolved, that this conference commends and expresses fraternal support of those persons in government and private life who are working creatively to hasten implementation of desegregation in churches, education, employment, recreation, social services, and housing in this country.

---

[1]Adopted by the Conference as a whole.

[2]In accordance with a recommendation of the Steering Committee, the chairman read at a plenary session the text of a statement he had prepared on Sino-American Relations. It was agreed without objection that it be incorporated in this Report. The statement of Hon. Ernest A. Gross was as follows:

"Five years ago, the Conference on the Churches and World Order declared that in the light of the indictment by the United Nations of the People's Government of the Republic of China as a party to the aggression in Korea, the problem of recognition and acceptance of their representatives at the U.N. was not a matter for immediate decision. It was accordingly recommended that the Department of International Affairs initiate a study of the problems here involved in order to identify any moral principles relevant to provide Christians with information on which sound decisions can be based.

"The Conference urged the United States Government 'to adopt a flexible policy' and to resist pressure to prejudice future policy so that freedom would be maintained to permit wise action to be taken 'on the basis of conditions as they may progressively develop.'

"During the past five years, the problem of American relations with the People's Republic of China has been of continuing concern to the Department of International Affairs of the National Council and we have given the matter anxious consideration prior to this Fifth World Order Study Conference.

"It is the view of many members of the Department and of this Conference, that the United States Government has not adopted a sufficiently flexible policy and that it has not adequately resisted pressures to prejudge its future policies, and is in danger of losing its freedom to act in accordance with the imperatives of progressive developments. The views expressed herein are those of the Chairman, and reflect the fact that in a democratic society the duty of each citizen is to seek to reach morally valid judgments on matters of national concern.

"Neither the Government nor the American public have, in my view, faced with sufficient candor or courage the dilemma posed by the requirements of a sound China policy.

"On the one hand, it is obvious that the aggressive policy of the Chinese communist regime fails to accord with standards of international conduct. Our people remain well aware of the significance of this fact, without the stimulus of demagogic appeals or of official statements which, sometimes in the name of recording public sentiment, tend rather to inflame it. For the United States to grant judicial recognition to the Chinese communist regime so long as it pursues its present course appears to many of us to confer upon that government a benefit to which it is not entitled.

"The other horn of the dilemma, however, has not been the subject of equally forthright public analysis.

"The assertion that lawless behavior on the part of a nation is a ground for excluding it from the organized society of nations ignores the rudimentary requirements of world order. Considerations of Christian morality and of United States national interest both lead to the conclusion that the People's Republic of China should be brought within the rule of the code of conduct of the United Nations Charter and subject to its processes.

"That government is a major party to an international dispute concerning the future of the Island and the Straits of Taiwan. It is a dispute which must ultimately be resolved in accordance with the principles of United Nations Charter and with due regard to the judgment of world community as expressed in the UN. No major party to the dispute, including the government of the Republic of China now located in Taiwan, can be expected to acquiesce willingly in judgment of a society of nations from which it is excluded as a member in equal standing with others.

"Moreover, it has now become inescapably clear—if there ever had been reason for doubt—that the cooperation and participation of the People's Republic of China is essential to the effective operation of major programs of disarmament, suspension of nuclear tests and warnings against surprise attack. The atmosphere above the nations of the earth and the space above the earth are now pathways of destruction, of both slow radio-active poison and of sudden nuclear devastation. There are no ideological frontiers in planetary space.

"Accordingly, we are morally obligated to ourselves and to each other to face with candor the dilemma with which we are confronted. We do ourselves a great national disservice when we permit the notion to become prevalent that if the People's Republic of China were ultimately to be seated in the United Nations—a decision over which, in any event, we have no unilateral power of control—that the United Nations would thereby lose moral stature or that our relationship with the organization would be modified or impaired."

[3]Two proposals to amend the Message with respect to its views on China were voted down with less than 25% in their favor. The final vote on the Message as a whole, however, was unanimous.

[4]These reports were "received by the Conference and referred to the churches for study and appropriate action."

[5]Resolutions A and B below, pp. 242-3 , relate to the subject of this report.

[6]Resolution A below, p. 242 , reflects the dissatisfaction of the Conference as a whole with this particular statement.

[7]Resolution C below relates to the subject of this report.

[8]Resolutions D through J below relate to the subject of this report.

[9]The delegates of the Eastern Orthodox Faith strongly feel that before this Conference can support approval of any moves to accept a country into the United Nations, there be an examination of all circumstances to determine whether in fact United Nations requirements for membership have been met. In particular, they hold that there must be fair evidence of religious freedom in that country, coupled with guarantees which preclude any discrimination because of the exercise of the right to worship in accordance with one's own conscience; and that there be evidence that the country involved, opposing aggression, intends to live peaceably with its neighbors, without political or imperialistic designs at the expense of rights of self-determination of peoples or groups, or the integrity of territorial boundaries.

[10]It was agreed to append on behalf of a minority, a statement which reads as follows:

> "Looking at the whole problem of peace, we believe that military alliances, especially alliances extending American military power into Asia, on balance injure the cause of peace. We believe that our nation should move toward liquidation of its present military alliances, and put our resources into developing economic and cultural ties with the people of these areas."

[11]In addition to *adopting* the Conference Message and *receiving* the reports from the four Study Sections for transmission to the churches, the Conference *adopted* eleven resolutions on current issues before the American people.

[12]There was some dissent to this Resolution on the part of those who preferred the statement in the Report of Section II, Part 4.

[13]This sentence reads: "Since we as Christians could not ourselves press the buttons for such destruction, we must now declare our conviction that we cannot support the concept of nuclear retaliation or preventive war."

[14]This resolution was adopted by the Conference with some dissent. Considerable opposition was due to the formulation of the resolution, not to its substance. Some dissenters wanted the resolution to include reference to our Christian brethren in the Soviet Union. Others wanted the statement to refer to all countries where religious liberty is suppressed, without singling out any particular faith or nation. The last sentence of the resolution, referring to Spain, was added as an amendment from the floor. One person opposed the resolution as being based on reports which might have been distorted. The decision of the majority to avoid specific reference to Christians in the statement was based on the fact that reports from the Soviet Union deal with increasingly unfavorable treatment of Muslims and Jews but not of Christians.

APPENDICES

The following pages contain five statements or reports issued by committees, commissions and boards of the Federal Council of Churches and the National Council of Churches of Christ in the USA on issues of war and peace related to the statements issued by the churches in the main body of this book.

REFERENCES

APPENDIX A

CHRISTIAN DUTY IN TIME OF WAR:
"A Message to Our Fellow Christians"*

Federal Council Executive Committee, 1941

The war which oppresses our world today marks a deepening crisis in civilization. The calculated treachery of recent aggressions has evoked instant condemnation. It is a manifestation of a great flood of evil that has overwhelmed nation after nation, destroying human rights and leaving men the victims of irresponsible force. We do not disclaim our own share in the events, economic, political and moral which made it possible for these evil forces to be released. But these forces have now brought war to our shores, and our nation has joined in the world's struggle that it may preserve the ideals and institutions of free men.

Yet we must realize that the war is but the most shocking sign of the demoralization of modern life and international conduct. The laws of God have not been honored. Now the awful consequences are laid bare. Conscious of our participation in the world's sin, we would be humble and penitent before God.

But we do not despair. Our trust is in God, in whose Hand is the destiny of men and nations. They have wandered through long dark nights; but God has not forsaken them. We today must turn from proud and frantic worldliness to God. Then we may be chastened and strengthened even by calamities and become His instruments for fashioning a free, just and neighborly world. The issue of all our striving is with Him.

We have a three-fold responsibility: as citizens of a nation which, under God, is dedicated to human freedom; as members of the Church in America, which is called to minister to people under heavy strain; and as members of the world-wide Church, which unites in a common fellowship

*The attack on Pearl Harbor took place on December 7, 1941. On December 30, the executive committee of the Federal Council of Churches issued this message.

men of every race and nation who acknowledge Jesus Christ as Lord and Savior.

As citizens we gratefully acknowledge a priceless national heritage of freedom and democratic ideals for which earlier generations struggled and sacrificed. We cherish this heritage more deeply when we see it attacked by a totalitarian threat. We are resolved to defend it from the menace of rival systems from without and from the degradation of abuse or neglect from within. It is our high obligation to bequeath our heritage unimpaired and strengthened to those who follow us. We rededicate ourselves to the highest purposes of this nation and to its unfinished task of building a more truly free and democratic society.

As members of the Church in America we have responsibilities which only the Church can discharge. The Church must ceaselessly bring to judgment those individual and social sins, at home and abroad, which are the cause of such disaster. The Church must minister in every Christ-like way to men in the midst of war. More than ever, in such an hour, people need its ministry. They cannot withstand the tensions of wartime without moral and spiritual resource. The Church must maintain its distinctive service, but now with all the greater devotion and skill. It must inspire men, in the armed forces and at home, with faith and hope and courage. It must bring guidance to the perplexed, and comfort to the distressed—God's strength for our struggle and His peace for our pain.

The host of young men who in this hour of crisis answer their country's call are a special concern of the Church. It encompasses with gratitude and prayer all now summoned to render sacrificial service, whether in the armed forces or in other work of national importance. It honors the sincere conscience of every man. It sends many of its ministers to serve as chaplains and seeks to create a wholesome environment in every camp community.

In days of trial, the Church cleaves to a steady faith. When bitterness and hatred may easily overwhelm us, the Church is still the stronghold of goodwill. It counts dear all basic human rights. It befriends loyal minorities, including those of alien birth or those descended from peoples with whose governments our country is now at war. The Church cannot abrogate its Gospel of Eternal Love.

The Church should minister in mercy to those on whom the cruelty of war most heavily falls. To the full measure of its ability it should care for refugees and prisoners of war and all others caught in the appalling suffering of our world.

The Church must be in the vanguard of preparation for a just and durable peace. The great sacrifice of treasure and of life must not be in vain. We must build now the spiritual foundations for a better order of the world. This task is immediate and cannot be delayed.

As members of the world-wide Church, which transcends all differences of race and nation, we have oblitations which reach beyond our own country. We must preserve at all costs the world-wide Christian fellowship, without which no free world order of justice and peace can be achieved. In times of war Christians in different nations are still members of the one Body of Christ. They must pray, not merely for their own national interest, but that God's will may be done in and through all nations. They must remember that in every warring nation there are men and women who, in spite of different political allegiances, are one with us in the ecumenical Church and who also pray for its fuller realization and the coming of God's Kingdom in the world. As this universal Church strengthens and extends its fellowship and deepens its loyalty to one Lord and Master it will be the greatest of all forces binding a broken world together.

We therefore call upon our fellow-Christians—to bow in penitence before the judgments of God, who is the Ruler of nations and the Father of mankind; to devote themselves to preserving and strengthening the ideals of freedom and democracy; to withstand any propaganda of hatred or revenge and to refuse it the sanction of religion; to manifest Christian goodwill toward those among us whose origin was in nations with which our country is now at war; to succor with generosity all who suffer from the ravages of war; to minister to the deeper needs of men in the nation's service; to pray constantly that our national leaders may be guided and strengthened by the Spirit of God and that after this tragic conflict there shall come a new world of righteousness, justice and peace for all nations; to strive for national policies in conformity with the will of God, rather than to seek the divine sanction for a human purpose; to work actively and persistently for justice and goodwill among all racial groups both in our own country and throughout the world; to maintain unbroken the fellowship of prayer with Christians everywhere; to be steadfastly loyal to the Holy Catholic Church (holy—sanctified to the redemptive purpose of God; catholic—of all believers and in all ages); to pray without ceasing that God's name may be hallowed and His will be done in earth as it is in Heaven; to maintain confident faith in God as the refuge and strength of His people even in the darkest night, and to trust in the triumph of His will.

"Now unto Him that is able to do exceeding abundantly above all that we ask or think, according to the power that worketh in us, unto Him be glory in the Church by Christ Jesus throughout all ages, world without end."

THE THEOLOGY AND ETHICS OF WAR:
"The Relation of the Church to the War in the Light of the Christian Faith"*

A Commission of Theologians, 1944

This report is not a pronouncement in the name of the Christian Church, but a word spoken, we trust, in the faith of the Church, to our fellow Christians, and to all our fellow men. It is a statement of what we have found to be some of our common convictions about the concerns of the Church in a time of global war: its gospel, its relations to individual Christians, Christian groups, the various national communities, and the changing world society, and its consequent duties and opportunities of our day.

The ecumenical judgment of the Protestant and Orthodox Churches concerning modern war was pronounced at Oxford in 1937. It has been reaffirmed innumerable times and we affirm it again as our own. But the theological grounds and implications of that judgment need to be worked out more explicitly than Oxford or any other conference has worked them out. If it be true that war is "a defiance of the righteousness of God as revealed in Jesus Christ and Him crucified," that fact involves most urgent problems of life and thought for the whole body of Christian citizens. For war is no longer a contest between sovereign princes and professional

---

*At the biennial meeting of the Federal Council of Churches in December 1942, it was voted to appoint a group of Christian scholars to a commission to study and report on "the relation of the Church to the War in the light of the Christian faith." It was agreed that the commission should think of itself not as formulating policies for the council but as engaged in a long-range examination of the nature of Christianity and of what this means for the Church in a war situation. The report which follows was submitted two years later. A list of the members of the commission can be found at the end of the report.

armies. Wherever modern democratic government has come into being, a decision to engage in war is made in the name of a whole people; and in the conduct of modern war, no matter what the form of the belligerent governments, civilians as well as members of the armed forces are participants. Willingly or unwillingly, every one is somehow involved. What, then, has the Christian faith to say to the church and its members when war develops, since uncritical participation in war does violence to a Christian judgment solemnly and repeatedly avowed, while complete detachment is no longer possible?

That is the problem with which this report is concerned. It goes without saying that the answer proposed here is neither complete nor undebatable. We who have worked on it, individually and together, know best of all the limitations of time, knowledge, wisdom, and faith which it reflects. We know, too, the fearful urgency, magnitude, and obscurity of the human plight with which it deals, and the likelihood that words that have come to have agreed meanings for us during prolonged discussion may have other meanings or none for many to whom the report is addressed. On the other hand, we are not conscious of having concealed from one another our actual convictions, nor compromised them away for the sake of a consensus more amiable than real.

Where major differences have seemed to require explicit notice, we have tried to make that fact plain. That these differences (especially as between pacifist and non-pacifist members of the Commission) exist inside a more fundamental context of shared Christian faith, and of mutual understanding, mutual confidence, and readiness to learn, became clear in the course of our debates. That fact is itself one of our primary findings. Less important differences that might have led some of us to prefer one form of words here, another there, in the final draft of the report, have naturally been taken in stride, without separate mention.

The perspective and the results of our study are primarily theological. This is in accordance with the assignment indicated in the title of the report. We have not excluded moral questions where these are essential factors in the theological problem posed for us: the problem of trying to interpret the Church's present task in the light of the Christian faith. We have tried, moreover, to keep in view the actual questions of all sorts, theological and moral, that are being raised inside and outside the Church today, and the actual positions taken by the Church or by its major constituent bodies at various times, respecting moral as well as doctrinal problems of a society at war. Yet our primary concern is theological. We are trying to help clarify the bearing of the Christian faith upon the Church's problems, institutional, intellectual, moral, religious, in this time of global war.

The Christian Church and its gospel must always stand in a double relationship to human history. On the other hand, they are deeply involved at every moment in the actual events that make up the earthly career of human persons and peoples. The gospel is no mere ideal picture of what would be excellent if only it were true. It is a declaration of what has actually happened to men in history through the actual life and death and resurrection of Jesus Christ, and an avowal of faith in the saving Power that was disclosed through him as a sovereign help in every time of trouble. The Church, likewise, is so embedded in history, for better and for worse, that in every part of it are visible the marks of historic developments and crises now long past, and of the actual fierce pressures that unite and divide men today. The Church and the gospel, then, are involved in every new human situation.

On the other hand, both the Christian gospel and the Church that proclaims it must display in every age the sort of freedom that comes from being oriented not only to present and passing events of human history but to present and permanent reality and truth that are in God. Such freedom from complete entanglement makes the Church and its gospel view history in a different perspective from that of national patriotism, capitalistic or communistic class interest, or any cultural loyalty alone. A living Church is aware of all these secular loyalties, and reflects them in its actual behavior. At the same time, it must see beyond them, criticize them and itself with them, and affirm as an ultimate court of appeal for all human thought and life the sovereign presence of God. In a word, the Church and its gospel must be at every moment both in the midst of human history and beyond it.

This means that to every historic situation, the Church has a dual word to speak. On the one hand, it must try to bring clearly into view the distinctive character of each new situation, neither blurring its uniqueness with generalities, nor losing sight of its continuity with other historic events past and future. The Church must try to speak directly to the actual needs of each new time. On the other hand, it must try to hold clearly before every age, with changing detailed insights but with steady central conviction, what Christian faith believes to be abiding truth concerning God and man, sin and salvation. The Church must try to speak steadily a word of faith that is for all times.

These two phases of its preaching and teaching involve a third. From the effort thus to apprehend a new situation in the light of an abiding faith, specific guiding judgments should emerge that illuminate Christian action. Such judgments are not a code of rules, but a body of working insights in which the meaning of Christian faith for individual and social conduct in the existing historic crisis is made more explicit. What courses of action will then actually be followed by the Church and by individual Christians must still be determined by conscientious conviction. No body of Christians, large or small, can undertake to replace enlightened conscience by prescribed rules.

There are thus three phases of the word the Church must speak to our time: diagnostic, doctrinal, and practical. The three parts of this report attempt to deal successively with these interrelated demands. The first part is diagnostic: an attempt to make clear what seems to us the character of our present situation, and some of the major problems it raises concerning the relation of the Church, its gospel, and its members to the war. The second is doctrinal: a statement of those primary Christian affirmations that seem to us normative for any attempt to deal with the problems of the Church in war-time. The third is practical: a glance at the major attitudes toward war, past and present, that have actually been maintained in the Church as fitting expressions of Christian faith, and a summary of the attitudes that seem to us to accord best with that faith in our own day and for the near future. Supporting documents will work out certain portions of the report in more concrete detail.

I. OUR PRESENT SITUATION AND ITS PROBLEMS

Diagnosis of the situation in which we stand has two natural parts: an attempt to discern the character of the present crisis, and a brief notice of some particular problems it raises for Christian faith.

A. THE CHARACTER OF THE PRESENT CRISIS

There is general agreement that we are in the midst of one of the great transition periods of human history. The war that broke out in 1914 and has continued, with temporary and local interruptions, to the present moment—a thirty years' war the end of which cannot yet be clearly seen—is the outward and visible sign of a vaster conflict, by no means identical in its battle-lines with the war between Axis and United Nations. Around the globe, in the home of every civilized people, belligerent or neutral, and in places hitherto but little concerned with the modern world, a life and death struggle is going on between various old ways of living and various new ones. Long after the present phase of organized armed warfare has been succeeded by some sort of armistice or declared peace, unorganized struggles both armed and unarmed will continue, until some worldwide equilibrium not yet discernible may be worked out. So inclusive has this pattern of armed warfare and unarmed conflict become that for magnitude there is no close analogy to it in all previous history. By comparison, the fall of the Roman empire in the West or the rise of the Mongol empire in the East were local in scope, however great in cultural import. And surely no lesser events than these, it now appears, can serve as yardsticks to measure the dimensions of our time. It poses problems of unprecedented magnitude, and no small-scale answers can be regarded for a moment as fit to command our assent.

When as Christians, aware in some degree of the extent of the present crisis, we ask what kinds of factors enter into it and give it a distinctive character, we find ourselves at the outset sharing many insights with secular and non-Christian observers. This crisis, including the war and the still larger struggles revealed and sharpened by *the war, is in one aspect a dynamic readjustment of impersonal forces,* not without likeness to an avalanche or an earthquake, of planetary scope. We recognize in it the violent threshing of physical, biological, and economic forces long out of balance—the impersonal tensions of unequal population pressures, unevenly distributed natural resources, accelerating technological advances, undisciplined mass production methods—released in destructive spasms during the past thirty years, after accumulating during a century of comparative quiet. We recognize in it also a *world-wide power struggle* of the familiar type between loose coalitions of nation-states, each seeking its own advantage, putting first its own national interests in security, prosperity, and prestige. We recognize in it *a revolutionary attempt by each of the chief Axis powers to move toward world conquest* and the establishment of a totalitarian "New Order," and *a resolute struggle by their opponents to prevent such totalitarian conquest* and to keep the way open for more humane modes of life. We recognize in it, cutting across the boundaries of national self-interest and of military alliance, *a clash of forces—psychological, cultural, political—that seek strongly to maintain, to restore, or to extend the old patterns* of privileged minority rule, unrestricted national sovereignty, and colonial imperialism, *against other forces that tend, much less deliberately and concertedly, toward a wider distribution of privilege and power, a more effectively and equitably organized world, or both.* Armed civil wars are in progress within the framework of international war. Unarmed economic and social class struggles, racial and cultural conflicts, and political hostilities zig-zag across all the fighting fronts. All these are essential factors in the war and in the underlying struggle. Together they help make the existing situation a revolutionary crisis, confused, dynamic, charged with opportunity and with dire peril for the life of generations to come.

In the confusion of this crisis, two factors appear to us to need especial notice, although neither must be separated, even in thought, from its roots and total setting. One is an apparent reversal, sudden and violent, of a long trend toward political democracy in the West. In less than two decades, popular governments were overthrown in Italy, Germany, and Spain. Under the pressures of Nazi aggression even the French republic collapsed. Reaction was strengthened, parliamentary government destroyed, and popular leaders and parties harried in all of Germany's satellites and in the countries occupied by her power. At the same time, among her opponents the strongest in military force has been the Soviet Union, that began its career by rejecting political democracy virtually without a trial. The case for democratic government, so long regarded as established beyond challenge in the West, has thus suffered a sudden and very destructive assault. But the experience of European peoples with the newer despotisms has already provoked a powerful counter-movement toward political freedom.

Still more dangerous in some respects has been a closely related but distinguishable assault on the growth of social democracy. In Russia, political dictatorship has itself been used to spread economic and social benefits far more widely among the people. There social democracy has made substantial gains under political despotism. But everywhere else, dictatorial control has been devoted to the advantage of a privileged minority at the expense of subjected groups. In Germany this despotism has assumed, of course, a form almost fantastic in its virulence and ruthlessness: the form of a demonic and terrible religion, laying claim to rule every side of the lives of its devotees, bent on military conquest, and ready to treat as subhuman victims the more helpless of those who stand in its way. Resistance, armed or unarmed, to this Nazi cult of intellectual and moral perversion and to the more primitive Japanese militarist despotism has become a major trend in both East and West.

All these insights must contribute to, but they do not constitute, a distinctively Christian understanding of our situation. In such understanding, the war is an event in the providential reign of God whom we know best through Christ crucified and triumphant. For Christian faith the whole cataclysm, having all the characters just noticed, is a tragic moment in God's work of creating and redeeming man, and in man's long struggle with himself and his Creator. In this perspective, the opportunity and obligation implicit in the crisis appear more commanding, and its dangers not less real but less disheartening than they might well seem apart from Christian faith.

Both the promise and the appalling danger of our situation are in important respects new in human history. They are inseparable from our present stage of political and industrial development. On the political side, our most characteristic achievement is the sovereign national state. To a degree unmatched in the ancient and medieval world, the great modern nation combines large territory and populace with effective political unity. Its emergence from the localized, personal, insecure political fabrics of feudalism has been a triumph of social unification and a great gain for stability. It provides greatly expanded and more effectively unified arenas for modern men's quest of freedom under law, and powerful new motives in the form of national loyalties that have helped to give both vitality and direction to that quest.

But this very consolidation of national consciousness, government, culture, and trade within national boundaries has tended no less strongly to accentuate the plurality and the diversity of nations. In feudal Europe there was at least in theory an over-all unity of Christendom under the emperor and the pope. Today each nation claims ultimate political sovereignty for itself, as regards its own territory and subjects, with no effective international or supranational authority to which appeal can be made. National interests, i.e., demands for security, prosperity, prestige, territorial and cultural unity, are superior in the actual practice of world politics to every other consideration. There is an extensive body of international law that exists on paper, but there is no political agency to enforce it, and in a serious collision with the national interests of the great powers, international law now stands little chance of having the last word. Even moral and religious principles, that in theory are widely held as binding upon men of different nations, are not now able in practice to hold in check their dynamic and often conflicting self-interest; and as for the national state itself, the sovereign political authority in each nation, much modern theory and practice frankly declares that upon the State, moral principles are not binding. Expediency, it is held, must be the primary guiding principle for the national state in its dealings with other states.

To this patchwork of modern nationalism, a great deal of modern church life and thought conforms. In theory, the Christian Church is one over all the earth. In practice, both individual Christians and organized churches, Roman Catholic, Orthodox, or Protestant, have become so deeply involved in national or cultural loyalties that when serious conflicts arise, their loyalty to a universal Church and to fellow Christians of other countries or cultures is often subordinated, if not temporarily extinguished. Indeed, there have been times when organized churches or their clergy have behaved, in practice, as departments of a national community and agencies of its government, rather than as witnesses to a universal gospel for all mankind. Such churches can scarcely speak convincingly about worldwide obligations, and especially about concern for the welfare of enemies, to a nation fighting for its life. And if the churches cannot so speak, there is little chance that any other group in the nation will do so. Modern national states, especially when at war, do not welcome moral challenge from any of their constituent members. Their claim to ultimate sovereignty is jealously maintained.

At the same time that we have developed a vigorous and tenacious political nationalism, our technology and industry have reached a stage at which physical isolation of one people from another is no longer possible. Both in peace and in war, new methods of transport and communication have tied the world inescapably together. New methods of production, moreover, pour out floods of economic wares that cannot under present conditions be dammed up within national boundaries without either violent economic crises, rigid governmental controls, or both. The worldwide depression of 1929-32, and the rise of international cartels and of expansionist totalitarian programs bear eloquent testimony to the inability of nationalism in its traditional form to cope with the expansive pressures of modern industry and finance. These pressures are by no means to be regarded as capable of producing, by themselves, a new world order. They demand it rather than provide it. But they demand it in language that cannot be ignored.

Our present world situation is distinguished, then, by the clash of divisive national interests in a world physically entangled in the web of modern industry and commerce. There is no chance to restore the physical isolation of nations in time past. The only conceivable way out is to seek, by all suitable means, to transform our interlocked society into world community, in which great nations may have contributive rather than destructive roles. The Industrial Revolution has made us involuntarily a world society, tied together by many sorts of physical bonds, natural and manufactured. But a society thus physically united in space and time may be only the body necessary for a living community, a body that is indispensable but not sufficient. Living community needs also spiritual bonds of the sorts that now exist only within limited areas. It needs common interests, laws, loyalties, traditions, standards, goals. These at once presuppose and promote mutual understanding and appreciation, shared language and experience, joint efforts and achievements. World community, in short, needs on a larger scale not only physical but spiritual interrelations comparable to those that now mark national life at its best.

For the first time in history, our generation has at least the physical means needed for progressing beyond the limits of the modern nation toward a fully inclusive human community. Hitherto, our larger political units have been empires, made up of ruling and subject peoples. A free and full sharing of life throughout such a unit has been not even physically possible. Today, with new means of production, communication, and transport at hand, we have the opportunity to develop a new kind of world order which, like a democratic nation, can become a society not of masters and subjects but of fellow-citizens and good neighbors.

The obligation to move toward this goal is fearfully urgent. For the alternative is prolonged international anarchy, widening and deepening hatreds, recurrent major wars of increasing destructiveness, and perhaps eventual exhaustion of many peoples. Therein lies the monstrous peril of wrong decisions in our time. The very factors that make it a day of unprecedented opportunity make it also a day of judgment for generations still unborn. The chastisement of our mistakes now will be upon them years hence. It is vital that we do not fail them.

B. PRACTICAL PROBLEMS AND PROBLEMS OF CHRISTIAN FAITH

Our difficulties are of two sorts. There are grave practical barriers that stand in the way of needed action, and there are problems of faith and reason that must be faced if we are even to see at all clearly what action is demanded of Christians in war time, and why.

1. Practical Problems:

First among the practical problems is one rooted deep in the nature of man and of human community, and the character of modern war. Genuine community must be an expression of the common life of free and responsible persons and groups, not a thinly disguised form of paternalism or servitude. But the necessary restraints upon freedom that become habitual in war, and the profound, demoralizing fatigue that a major war brings, make unusually difficult the extension of responsible freedom when organized fighting gives place to the new stresses of victory, defeat, and a struggle for recovery. The temptations then are exceedingly strong for both victors and vanquished to seek relief from the pains of responsible social life in dictatorial control without clear and present effort to promote freedom, in irresponsible relaxation and self-indulgence, or in recklessly destructive social explosions—the vengeful and unprincipled "revolution of nihilism" that appeals to frustrated, desperate men. This mood of irresponsible craving for escape from the hard way of growth toward community is sure to be widespread and deeply ingrained when the fighting has burned itself out. If it should be permitted again to dominate the decisions of the victors and the reactions of the vanquished, whatever chance our time may have offered for growth in shared freedom will be postponed to an indefinite future.

A second practical difficulty compounds and complicates this first one: present divisions within and among the United Nations. The best pattern for growth toward world community would seem to be some version of social and political democracy. Hitler's totalitarian pattern for "a new order" had obviously failed even before his armies were driven out of conquered territory. Community of peoples is not to be had on such terms, no matter by what power they are proposed or enforced. But the understanding of man and his freedom, of personal integrity and social interrelations, of the role of minorities, and of the social importance of such moral factors as nonpartisan justice and good faith that has developed in the democratic tradition is by its very nature a demand for universal growth in responsible freedom and community. The more democratically organized great powers among the United Nations, then, might be expected to stand out as the most effective champions of such growth. In principle, and to some considerable degree in fact, they do have this role. They have themselves made substantial progress in achieving and maintaining freedom of thought, speech, and worship at home, and in proving that loyal cooperation among diverse groups for social and political ends is feasible on a large scale without totalitarian control. As things now stand, however, their effectiveness as champions of world democracy is hampered by a deep-going ambiguity in their present status and practice. Their history has forced them at this juncture to defend abroad as well as they can the free democratic way of life when they have achieved it very imperfectly at home and in subject territories. Both the popular will and the national governments of the greater democratic powers are inwardly divided between seeking to extend the freedom, security, and opportunity of ordinary people everywhere, and seeking to maintain special privilege for chosen families, classes, and peoples. Refusal of equal opportunity to persons of Negro, Jewish, or Oriental ancestry, to various colonial peoples, to landless farmers, unorganized laborers, and certain social radicals has long marred the domestic behavior and helped mould the foreign policy of even the most democratic of the United Nations. At the same time, their persisting democratic tradition ensures that even in war time the policies of both those who seek and those who distrust the spread of democracy and of international community shall be openly debated. The net result is at present a partial devotion to worldwide community, with inconsistency of apparent aim and uncertainty as to future policy respecting both the domestic affairs of allied, liberated, and vanquished countries and the pattern of world society for years to come.

The policy of Russia, the chief totalitarian power among the United Nations is set, with much less ambiguity, toward the practical goal of its own national security. Realistic pursuit of this policy involves the encouragement of radical popular movements in all the countries of central and eastern Europe and of central Asia, on condition that these popular movements, in turn, remain friendly to their great neighbor. Happily, it also involves consistent preference at present for the more democratic and cooperative forces in other countries, and in so far a strong support for the quest of a more peaceful world. In practice, moreover, the Russian people and its present government seem to have held their own in the fulfillment of international pledges and in realistic fairness even toward some of their foes. Yet because of differences both past and present, in theory and in practice, a basis for more complete confidence between Russia and her western allies, on the one hand, and between each of these powers and China, on the other, needs still to be more fully established. Until that result has been achieved by patient intelligence and good will on both sides, the future of world community will continue in doubt.

There is scarcely need to speak here of the multitude of problems— technical, economic, political—that beset the reconversion of a world mostly organized for combat to the pursuits of competitive production and trade, without losing whatever common devotion and mutual trust may be achieved in alliance for war. *But two problems that especially concern us as Christians need at least brief mention. The first is the unprecedented and appalling extent of calculated ruthlessness, both before and during the present phase of the unfinished revolution, and of the hatred engendered thereby.* Terrorist methods of GPU and Gestapo, brutalities of Japanese, Italian, Spanish, and German troops in the field and in conquered territories, food blockades and obliteration bombings by the United Nations in rejoinder, commando tactics and improved flame throwers, mass murders and robot bombs—all these mere incidents in the global struggle—have brought back on a larger scale the hardness and the vengefulness that must have filled numbers of decent people in the seventeenth century, during the earlier Thirty Years' War. The extent of such implacability today, among victims of the Axis powers and among their own peoples, can only be conjectured. It is hard to doubt that it will prove a major obstacle to the making of genuine peace, and there can be no doubt that it is a peculiar concern of the Christian churches everywhere.

The second of these special problems is posed by the divided loyalties, the human weaknesses, and the secular involvements of the churches themselves. It is neither possible nor desirable that they should stand outside the agonies of the peoples to whom they minister. A Church aloof from sinning, suffering men and nations could not be the Church of Jesus Christ. Its life and its ministries must bear the marks of full humanity, and without intense loyalty to a particular place and folk there is no such thing as full human living. The needs, the sorrows, the sins, and the hopes of particular men and nations, not simply of mankind at large, must be woven into the life of a Church that seeks to be the body of Christ. But its ministry to particular men and nations can be performed with faithfulness only if, like its Master, the Church speaks to them unceasingly, by word and deed, of the judgment and mercy of God that are for all men alike. In as far as the Church embodies and proclaims this saving Word, it can serve at once particular men and nations and all mankind, displaying among them imperfectly but genuinely a common life in which acute differences are composed, deep wrongs are judged with the penetrating wisdom of love, human wounds are healed, and the true God of all the world is worshipped. In as far as the human existence of any church denies or distorts this universal Word instead of proclaiming it, in so far that church fails to be the Christian Church or a faithful member thereof. When through self-interest, or fear, or forgetfulness, through preoccupation with nearby human loyalties, a church or its ministers and members becomes so fully identified with the success of human group or institution—itself, a class, a nation, a civilization—that it cannot speak any save a partisan or a platitudinous word, then the salt has lost its savor. We rejoice that the churches of our day, with a growing awareness of ecumenical membership and mission, and with new understanding of conscientious differences among their members, have come to see this truth with new clarity. Yet we cannot close our eyes to our own failures and those of many fellow Christians in all lands to find and to speak clearly the words of judgment and of reconciliation that hold true at once for our own folk and for all men. Such words are being spoken superbly here and there, in both East and West. They need to be spoken everywhere with more unanimity and power. From this obligation that rests on us and on all Christians there must arise a concerted demand that in our time the way toward world community—not an expanded imperialism and not continued anarchy—be chosen. Christian conviction, for all our own weaknesses, can be and must be made a source of guidance for peoples and their governments today. It can help produce and it can help nurture the spirit for a genuine community of mankind, whose body has been growing faster year by year.

2. *Problems of Christian Faith:*

But to claim thus for Christian faith and for the Church a crucial role in the world struggle is to throw into more vivid relief the problems posed especially for Christian faith and reason by the struggle itself. It is with these primarily that the next part of this report deals.

They fall easily into four main groups. There are questions, first of all, concerning the grounds of Christian faith and knowledge. If there be indeed a distinctive Christian understanding of the war, it is right to ask upon what foundations that understanding can be affirmed, and what measure of authority it may properly claim.

There are questions next concerning the relation of God to the war. In such a time it seems to many that God (if indeed there be a God) is aloof from His tortured world. To others the war seems rather a direct and fearful act of divine judgment upon human wickedness. To still others it may seem a stunning defeat for God's purposes, at the hands of successful human rebels. Which view is right? or is some other view required?

Thirdly, questions arise concerning man's part in the war. Whether fatally bound or free and responsible, men act in this war time as though issues of better and worse are clearly at stake, and as though their own decisions can make a real difference in the working out of God's will and of men's destiny. Acknowledging more freely than in any other recent war the involvement of both sides in blame for the outbreak of armed conflict, they fight or refuse to fight still with some hope that in so doing they serve God and men. Is this belief in human freedom justified?

Lastly, how does all this bear on the place and tasks of the Church, and of its members, in the war-torn world? A whole array of questions here are pressing: the nature of the Church as universal community, the meaning of its ministry of reconciliation, the obligations that lie upon its members. Perhaps above all this question: Is there any common life in which all Christians in war-time can and should take part together as Christians, alike devoted in their several ways to the Kingdom of God and the salvation of mankind?

These are a few of the problems we have had before us in preparing this report. There are many more, as the following paragraphs will show, and we make no pretension to full knowledge of the answers. But in the Christian faith, reaffirmed in the next part of our report, we believe there is light for the guidance of all who will follow it.

II. THE CHRISTIAN FAITH AND THE WAR

We turn now to those Christian convictions that we have found most directly relevant to our problems. The statement that follows is organized around the four main subjects just indicated: the grounds and conditions of a Christian's understanding of the war; God's relation to the war; man's part in the war; the Church in a world at war.

A. GROUNDS OF A CHRISTIAN UNDERSTANDING OF THE WAR

The primary ground for a distinctive Christian understanding of any situation is the revelation of God in Jesus Christ. This is not to be separated from continuing revelations of God through the work of the Holy Spirit in the history of the Hebrew people and of the Christian Church, recorded in the Old and New Testaments, and in the whole literature of Christian life. Moreover, to the eye of Christian faith and understanding, there is revelation of the same God in the histories of all peoples, in the existence, order, and growth of the whole world of nature and man, in the rise of conscience, and in every struggle for truth and freedom. But revelation of God in Jesus Christ is the crucial disclosure, from whose light these other areas derive new meaning.

1. Revelation in Jesus Christ:

Revelation of God in Jesus Christ takes place whenever and wherever human persons find themselves effectively confronted, through the Gospel record or some spoken word, through personal contact or social heritage, inside or outside the institutional Church, by the person Jesus of Nazareth as an embodiment of unqualified moral judgment and of regenerating power, "God's power and God's wisdom." Effectively confronted: that is to say, compelled to acknowledge him as stubborn reality, as summons to repentance, and as source of drastic spiritual renewal. The person Jesus of Nazareth: the actual subject of that unique actual human life and death and triumph over death from which the Christian Church and the so-called Christian era of history, a new age and a new mode of life for mankind, have their beginnings. An embodiment of God's power and God's wisdom: one in whom, for Christian faith, the initiative of God for man's redemption uniquely assumed individual human form, so that uniquely and definitively "God was in Christ reconciling the world to himself."

In speaking of the revelation of God in Jesus Christ to us, we speak of a situation in which two stages of disclosure are involved. There is first the need that the man Jesus of Nazareth be disclosed to us, men of the twentieth century. This disclosure comes mainly in two ways. On the one hand, there is the written record in the New Testament of his words and deeds. There are recorded also the reactions of others, in his earthly lifetime and later, to the impact of his personal existence in history. As the record of events that are normative for Christian faith, the New Testament, though it must be interpreted by the Christian community, is itself normative for the life of that community. On the other hand, there is the Christian Church, a living community in which his spirit is still present and active. The written record and the living community cannot be separated. Each involves the other and neither can be reduced to simple dependence on, nor to simple parallelism with the other. Through both at once, the person Jesus of Nazareth makes his impress and finds his interpreters in our day, not perfectly but in the manner of all vital communication in history.

There is hidden within this historical disclosure another that gives it an added dimension of meaning and efficacy. In Jesus of Nazareth, known to us through written word and living church, was present, we believe, the redemptive Word and Will of God. Factual evidence for this conviction has been briefly indicated. Human history then and there entered a new era, became subject to divine judgment and mercy in a new way. But the conviction itself involves not only recognition of a publicly observable state of affairs. It involves a personal reorientation of the one who believes. What is meant by saying that God was in Christ is, in essential part, that Jesus Christ has been able through the centuries and is able now to awaken in men the profound personal response we call faith. Herein is made concrete and contemporary the revealing of God in Jesus Christ to us.

Like love, such faith is a personal response too inclusive and profound to be simply an overt act of either thought or will. It is a basic response of the whole self to the presence of a reality that appears overwhelmingly great and good. It is unreserved commitment in response to a Presence from which one cannot hold oneself back, any more than the eye to which light is present can withhold itself from seeing. Through this commitment, and within the personal life pervaded and conditioned by it, both knowledge and will proceed upon lines not open before, yet so related to the past life and the persisting nature of the believer that he finds in his new orientation a powerful expansion and correction of all that he has been. Through faith, as through love, he becomes a new person, in whom new insights and energies come to life, though never in simple escape from the old self nor from essential human limitations.

In a word, Christ crucified can appear as the embodiment of God's power and God's wisdom, the crucial and unique revelation of God, only to those who actually are moved by him to religious faith and who find that faith actually an enduring condition of new insight, devotion, and regenerate life. *For those who are thus responsive, a basis is provided for a distinctive Christian approach to every situation that calls for understanding. As the natural scientist approaches each phenomenon, no matter how distasteful or threatening it may appear to him personally, with the confidence that in it the great regularities of the natural process will be exhibited, so the Christian comes to each event in his or mankind's history with the confidence that he is dealing with something that contains divine meaning, that is intelligible, if not in every detail yet in essence, in terms of the faithful working of God.* As the former expects to have his previous understanding of natural process not only verified but also corrected and enlarged, so the latter anticipates that in each new event, loyally accepted and responded to, his understanding of God's way and will, received first in the revelation of Christ, will be corrected, widened, and particularized while it is being confirmed.

2. Basis of Christian Confidence:

To describe in these terms the nature of revelation and of Christian faith is to make clear at once the basis for confidence and the need for caution in Christian affirmations about God and man in any complex situation, such as this war. The basis for confidence is the discovery that for oneself, for other Christians, and for the Church as enduring and expanding Christian community, the dynamic life of Jesus Christ as revelation of God has become a vital premise for all thought and action that have in view the ultimate significance of human living. Inasmuch as the actual life of Jesus must have had the specific character required to account for the actual historic results that followed and for the present personal regeneration its impact still produces, the more precisely we learn to know these historical and personal realities, their relations to the rest of nature and history, and the demands they lay upon us, the more accurately and profoundly we may hope to discern the truth and the will of God for us men. We are not dealing simply with human ideals, wishes, wistful hopes that shift like cloud-shapes, from culture to culture and from century to century. We are face to face with an actual expanding range of events in history that arise from and bear witness to an actual center, at which we believe a crucial act of God made manifest His presence and essential aspects of His nature. We affirm, then, an actual specific revelation of the abiding truth and goodness that are in God.

The revelation itself, moreover, both as an historical reality uniquely realized in space and time and as a continuing source of regenerative energy and insight for men at grips with evil today, is an ultimate objective factor in human living. As given fact, the impact of Jesus Christ on human history is not derivative from nor dependent upon some more primary presupposition such as a certain culture or a particular philosophy, within which alone it is valid. The personal commitment to which this revelation gives rise, also, is ultimate for each person who finds himself under its sway. Faith in and love for the God and Father of Jesus Christ is an ultimate inner standard, real though not external, to which the believer's life at every moment and in every decision is amenable. He cannot choose at will to be judged now by this standard and now by some other—by the standard, for example, of unqualified obedience to some national sovereign, or ultimate devotion to some racial group. Christian faith affirms that God is absolutely good, just, merciful, and that the revelation of God in Jesus Christ and the commitment which it awakens are ultimate realities and norms for every Christian. It affirms too that all these are realities and norms even for non-Christians, in the sense that human life carried on without acknowledgment of them and participation in their meaning lacks a dimension for which there is no equivalent. Thus far Christians can speak confidently.

3. Need for Humility:

But in two obvious facts there lies a need for clear-headed humility in Christian judgments about God and human affairs. First, our apprehension of the central revelation in Jesus Christ is in many respects conditioned by our own failings. Our very faith itself, though an ultimate inner reality and norm for each of us, is variable and corruptible. Human devotion to God, though life-giving in principle and in truth, is hard to practice. Devotion to oneself is easier, and faith and insight suffer from that fact. Our understanding of the Scriptures and other records and of the living Church is conditioned in all sorts of ways by the time and place in which we live, the traditions we inherit, the lacks in our individual heredity and training, the blind spots made in us by special interests, desires, and fears. Furthermore, the written records through which the Word of God is transmitted to us, and the Church as historical community in which the spirit of Jesus Christ is alive, themselves leave room for honest differences of understanding. In the Scriptures, the Word of God is mediated through very diverse witnesses, who wrote in the midst of historical situations, known to us only in part, that helped to shape their insights and their words. The institutional Church has come to be not one community but many, and its witness in both word and deed is often confused and contradictory.

Secondly, the specific implications of the revealed truth for human understanding and conduct in a particular present situation can be discerned only by processes of thought that are liable at every step to the risk of error. Sincere Christians who agree on the primary demand for love of neighbors and enemies can disagree on its meaning for statemen, citizens, and victims of belligerent powers. To confident assertions about the details of Christian duty, as though human judgment could ever claim the infallibility of God, are presumptuous and self-refuting. There is need then for humility on the part of every Christian.

But to recognize clearly these limitations, and to welcome rather than to evade or suppress the criticisms they invite, can hold the way open for correction of human errors and for emergence of fresh visions of the truth. If our minds are twisted this way and that by undisciplined wishes and fears, so that we can see in the witness of Scriptures and Church only what serves our special interests, then in candid fellowship we need the more earnestly to practice self-denial and openheartedness for the sake of the very truth we profess. Though our faith can never be made perfect in this life, it can by just such persistent correction become less bound by our cravings for safety or self-justification, and more responsive to the truth that is in God. If the Scriptures and the other Jewish and Christians records of God's dealings with our fathers, through which He speaks also to us, cannot be detached from the complexities of human history, the more need for devoted, clear-eyed Christian scholarship to help us see more plainly the truth that shines through them. If the churches speak with a confusion of tongues, more patient exploration of their past and present existence is bringing to light a persisting deeper unity, and increased recognition of mutual need can make that unity still more vital and more reassuring.

In all this acknowledgment of human limitation, and hope for more light, we trust confidently in the gracious wisdom of God, who has not permitted men to rest in error, nor suffered the light of His gospel to be quenched or confined. Through the centuries of turmoil, in spite of human weakness and the opposition of demonic powers, Christian faith has grown around the globe. Herein we see the gracious Spirit of truth, in whose presence our darkness is lightened and our faith confirmed. We have no ground for claims to full knowledge of the truth that is vital to all human living, but we are assured that the Holy Spirit will continue to overrule our errors and guide us into more light.

B. GOD'S RELATION TO THE WAR

In this mood, we venture to affirm next our belief that God's relation to the war is defined in broad terms by His essential unitary activity as Creator, Redeemer, Life-Giver. These are not three activities, but one, as the Father, Son and Holy Spirit of Christian teaching are not three Gods but one. In seeking, then, to discern God more clearly by such distinctions as these, we must never suppose that creation and redemption, or judgment and mercy, can be so separated that in a given act of God, one is present without the other. It is true that for minds like ours, some areas of history are far easier to interpret as stark fact than as regenerative action, as displaying ruthless judgment rather than forgiving mercy. But Christian faith in one God forbids taking the appearance of separate, mutually exclusive segments of divine activity as the truth. God is one, and His essential activity with respect to us men and our world is one. The infinitely diverse power and range of that activity as revealed to us we try to apprehend more concretely by attending now to one aspect, now to another, and by seeing all those manifold aspects of divine action as displaying God in three primary roles: creation, redemption, renovation. In the war, God is active in all these personal ways.

1. God as Creator:

The doctrine of God as Maker of heaven and earth forbids any assertion that He is aloof from the war. In the first place, that doctrine holds that the existence of every situation depends on the creative energy of God's will, put forth not merely in some past moment of time but throughout all time. In the next place, it holds that as God's energy transcends and pervades all time, all history, so likewise it transcends and pervades all that we call space, in such wise that from no portion of the existing world is God absent. He is the living and present Creator of all men and all nations. Thirdly, it holds that the presence of God is never static but always active presence, not merely form or law but energy. God then is present, active, creative, in every part of nature and history, and so in this war.

But the manner of God's omnipresence as Creator is further defined by the fact that what He creates is existent as other than Himself. God is not identical with the world, nor with any part of it. If there is no event from which God is absent, equally there is no event in which God alone is present.

In as far as creation is effective, it brings into existence and maintains in existence subordinate centers and fields of energy that are at once yielding and resistant to the continuing energy of their Creator, as well as embodying attraction and repulsion, partial harmony and partial discord among themselves.

This comment applies with especial pertinence to human history, and to the war, in which natural and impersonal forces are complicated in their working by the continuous cross fire of personal human decisions, and by the consequences of past decisions. The latter may go on long after the initial act, in large part as impersonally as widening and mingling ripples in a pool, so that there is always some temptation to regard them simply as natural entities devoid of moral significance. Slums can look much like swamps, caste systems like terraced hillsides, wars like hurricanes; and both popular and learned opinion has often regarded them as facts of nature or "acts of God." In protest against such easy reduction of important segments of history to natural mechanisms, other interpreters have insisted that slums, caste systems, and wars are all moral realities through and through, the direct and continuous manifestations of human choices and especially of human sins. *The truth as it seems to us is that the war is neither simply a natural fact nor an act of God nor a sinful choice of man. It is a complex event in which all of these factors are present, and need to be duly recognized.* God, then, acts in the war as the creative ground that continuously keeps the warring world and its members in existence, and enables them to act in accordance with their respective natures or decisions. God does not act as an all-inclusive "One-for-All," nor in any way that excludes or nullifies decision and action by His creatures. Moreover, God does not act as a world Ruler who has willed the outbreak of the war, nor all those specific antecedent conditions that made the war inescapable. Some of these conditions God directly wills, we believe—the freedom and the interdependence of men, the inseparability of moral decisions from natural consequences, and the like. Others are the resultants of natural forces that operate in relatively uniform causal networks, perhaps without complete mechanical fixity but presumably without the foresight or decision characteristic of persons: natural forces that operate, then, often in ways that enhance or destroy values, even perhaps in ways that further or hamper the will of God, but that are not themselves amenable to moral judgment. Some are the personal decisions of men, together with their antecedents and consequences, some personal, others more or less impersonal, but all identified more directly with responsible human action than with the irresponsible forces of extra-human nature, and all involving a crucial factor of human difference from, and often of opposition to, the will of God.

We notice next another aspect of God's creative action in the war. As Creator He is not only the source of existence in all creatures. He is the ground also of their respective actual natures and primary relationships.

His world is a world of order, not caprice. Those causal and moral inter-relations noticed in the foregoing paragraphs are established and maintained by His creative power. The particular combinations that arise within these fabrics of ordered existence and action are, in every instance, the resultants of both divine and creaturely activity, as we have seen. But the over-all persistence of order, both natural and moral, in spite of local spasms of natural and personal conflict, and in the closest union with human freedom and with whatever natural fluidness this freedom may imply, is referable directly to the sovereign presence of God. There is indeed a divinely established "order of creation," a universal "law of nature" that has both natural and moral aspects, though as we have seen it will not do to assign to this order without more ado such human institutions as slums, caste systems, slavery, claims of racial inequality, or any particular social, political, or ecclesiastical pattern in history. War is not divinely ordained, any more than these other historical emergents. But in war, as in all of these, divine law and order are present and in the long run controlling, even when human law and order are damaged or demolished by human action.

Lastly, God as Creator "is good, and the Author only of good to men," as Greek wisdom affirmed long ago. His creative will and His providential rule are set to favor not all sorts of action equally, but those that make for the realization of truth, beauty, justice, mercy, good faith, devoted love, and all else that accords with His perfection whether it be known to us or not. The God revealed in Jesus Christ is not a neutral Force but the infinitely perfect Father. His goodness is indeed of a different order from that of most good men. He cares for the unthankful and the evil. He gives sun and rain alike to the just and the unjust, and lets the tares grow along with the wheat. His valuations often are puzzling to sincerely righteous men, who not unnaturally suppose that unequal work in the vineyard deserves unequal pay and gold pieces in the alms box weigh more than a widow's coppers. He lets His best beloved Son be crucified between two men of violence because He loves them. But in spite of all appearances, He is a God of order and righteousness, who makes even the wrath of men to praise Him. For He is God above all other gods.

In this war, then, He is not neutral, and not helpless. He is maintaining invincibly an order that men cannot overthrow. Moreover, He is taking sides throughout the struggle, not with the Axis powers nor with the United Nations, nor with any government nor any institutional church or churchman, but with the impulses toward good and against the impulses toward evil in every man and every group in both camps. God is not a combatant, nor a neutral onlooker, nor a helpless victim. First of all, He is, in war as in peace, the Creator and Sovereign whose power sustains and governs, but does not annul, the activities of nature and of men.

2. God as Redeemer:

At the same time and for the same reason, His own perfect goodness, God is in the war as Redeemer. Divine redemption of the world appears to us men under two aspects, that can be distinguished but never separated. Redemption embraces both judgment and forgiveness. So we speak of divine justice and mercy, and we seek both in this war, remembering that nowhere ought we expect to find the one without the other. As Calvin wisely noted, even a human judge cannot pronounce an equitable sentence without mercy; nor can mercy work in opposition to justice, nor wait until merciless judgment is first wreaked upon the offender, and be redemptive. No doubt in human action, because it is imperfect, what is called justice is often separated from what is called mercy; but in the perfect redemptive love of God, the two are inseparable at every moment of time. We believe that this is always true as regards the divine intent and action, however difficult it may be at times for men to discern both aspects.

Divine judgment in the war can be plainly seen at two levels. First, as we have noted, there is a natural and moral order of creation that God maintains against all man's wayward efforts in peace and in war. For human persons, that order has especial significance in these respects: that every man is in his essential nature a responsible person, as well as a natural being; that all men are interdependent, as well as dependent upon their natural environment with its network of causal processes; and that the primary demand upon every man in this situation is love, for God, for men as children of God, and for nature as man's temporal home. Man may act, in both peace and war, as though these primary conditions of his life did not exist, but they hold fast and his denials in thought and act bring calamity upon himself, his fellows, and his natural home. *Divine judgment is not vengeful. It is inexorable. And in war, more vividly than in quieter times, men can see its fearful majesty.* In times when human conflict operates below the threshold of armed warfare, men sow with busy hands the winds of private and public aggression or negligence, of headstrong ignorance or cunning treachery. In times of open warfare, they reap the hurricane of outraged human life and divine power. In a terrible way, the fury of war vindicates the existence and inescapability of divine law.

Secondly, God's judgment in war time negates not merely the selfish conduct of men, but also their inadequate ideals for living. There are many of our accustomed ways of action that we are ready to acknowledge to be wrong, even though usually we hope that the fitting penalty for them may somehow be escaped. But other ways of ours seem to us surely right, and the ideals we hold often seem to us beyond criticism. It is hard not to think we know what is right even when we do otherwise. Service to one's country, or to one's church, for example, seems surely right, and the ideal of patriotism or of church loyalty that moves us in our most devoted moments seems wholly good. Precisely at these points of human self-confidence the judgment of God cuts deep. The very group loyalty in which we take pride and find a basis for self-righteousness is shown up in the fierce light of warfare to be tinctured with deadly poison. For uncritical group loyalty is a potent source of war, it helps to intensify hatred while war goes on, it is most characteristic of the more aggressive and tyrannous nations in the present war, and it can retard for generations our attempts to establish a peaceful world when this war has run its course. The judgment of God writ large in war-time says: "Patriotism is not enough." Human righteousness at any level thus far achieved is not enough. That is true in times of comparative quiet. It becomes glaringly evident in times of war.

Is then war itself to be called "a divine judgment," or an instrument thereof? Does God decree war to punish the waywardness of men? We have said no. War is not divinely ordained, any more than slums or slavery. God's will is always that men shall live at peace with one another and with Him. This is true at all times and without any exception. This refers not simply to armed warfare. It is not God's will that men shall carry on covert strife with one another, and with Him, under the name of peace. When that is done, His will is already being violated, and the outbreak of open war makes that fact plain. It is not God's will that war shall come upon mankind, at any time, nor that it be regarded as a suitable instrument for good. It is God's will that the primary order of natural and human life be maintained, and in presence of that order some sorts of human conduct bring war. The order itself is confirmed and vindicated. The specific decisions that make war break out are man's decisions, not God's. Moreover, the specific decisions we make thereafter, in seeking to do "the right as God gives us to see the right," are still our decisions, not God's. War is not, then "a judgment of God" in the sense that God wills it as a punishment for men. It serves to reveal and vindicate the judgment of God that upholds inexorably the order of His world even though in the presence of that order some combinations of human decision and natural causation, in resistance to God's will for peace, bring war.

God's judgment, in a word, is never merely punitive. Man brings down punishment when he acts in violation of God's law made dynamic by God's will. Yet that very law is even in its vigor a gift without which neither natural nor personal life could go on, and the will that maintains it is even in its unyield-ingness a will to more abundant life. Divine judgment is redemptive in purpose, and it becomes so in effect, as far as men are brought by its unceasing pressures to respond in repentance and faith.

To make this clear to ourselves, *we seek in the war for evidences also of divine mercy. First, we find such evidence in the fact that in the midst of the terrifying bitterness and hatred, deceit and disruption of war, there are signs of recreative forces at work it would seem continuously.* In part these have a character so drastic that mercy may seem a strange word for them. If that be true, there is need to remind ourselves that divine mercy means not softness but healing, not passivity but regeneration. If divine judgment is not without mercy, divine mercy is not without rigor. Its distinctive character lies in its positive purging, renovating, and reconciling power. This power is discernible in war, on the social side, in the successive breaking down of refuges for human self-sufficiency, and the positive affirmation of interdependence. Every country at war is compelled to seek internal unity, even at the cost of many vested privileges. This is not by the will of men. Self-interest is not displaced in war time. Willful resistance to rationing laws and pressure groups tactics for winning private advantages, sharpening of racial, regional, and class jealousies, and departmental factionalism bear witness to the contrary. Likewise, competition and distrust between allied nations even in the face of a dangerous foe make it clear that war does not wholly purge men and nations of divisive self-interest. Yet in spite of these symptoms of continuing illness, the very necessities of war time compel the redoubling of efforts to extend the scope of effective cooperation. Old barriers give way here and there. The self-confidence of a ruling class or the provincialism of a self-satisfied folk group is shaken by new contacts. A new sense of the meaning of wastage of natural resources for human life takes shape. So halting, reluctant, but inescapable awareness of the fact of human and natural interdependence and the need for better cooperation is forced upon men by their very struggles. This is not the purpose of warfare, but it happens in time of war and by reason of some of the special conditions of such a time. Similarly, the pressures of belligerent needs help to stimulate intellectual and technical enterprise, and to force pooling of information and resources, in such fashion that results are quickly achieved (in medicine, in the mechanical arts, in communication and in social organization) that may be of great value when more peaceable life is resumed. These achievements may be morally neutral in themselves, but the devoted effort spent in reaching them and the new patterns of human cooperation they make possible are not neutral. And in so far as knowledge is better than ignorance, such discoveries have worth that cannot be denied a place among the gifts of God.

Secondly, to some individual men in war time there come searching insights into the meaning of human life and the will of God. Undisciplined wastrels may find new responsibility, snobbish aristocrats or proletarians new respect for their fellows, complacent worldlings a new humility in the presence of engulfing tragedy. Such change may come to men either in or out of uniform, and find expression in words and acts that long outlast the fighting. Particular episodes can be highlighted in the prevailing darkness of war so that they become more effective witnesses to the perpetual beauty of righteousness than the routine of more peaceable living is likely to provide. There must be no exaggeration of these gleams of light, and no minimizing of the horrors against which they are visible. There must be no hint that war is justifiable as a source of human betterment. The point here is rather that, for all its ghastliness, war bears the marks of a Power that works in it for good.

Underlying the two sets of detailed evidence just reviewed, and more impressive than all of them together, we are able to discern what may be called *a residual health of mankind that resists and survives the fevers of war.* Herein is the active mercy of God to be seen, quietly and invincibly at work. We affirm in this specific sense Augustine's judgment, "Nothing can be evil except something which is good." Disease can exist only in a living body, and the very forces of life work to resist disease and to restore health. It is so in national societies, when a despot more powerful than any Caesar cannot prevent Germans from reading the Old Testament or befriending Jews. It is so in international warfare, when the exigencies of war itself cannot altogether prevent men from acting humanely and applauding decency. This we affirm is good evidence that God is in the midst of the struggle as healing power.

Shall we say also as the victim of a new crucifixion? Is war itself a Golgotha, and suffering humanity a new embodiment of the crucified Redeemer? In particular, can we say that the men killed in battle, or the refugees driven out to wander and starve, or the children who die in bomb shelters or blockaded famine areas are vicarious redeemers of our time? We share deeply in the desire of bereaved parents and comrades, and of chaplains and pastors to say these things, but they must not be said carelessly. *War is in a general sense a crucifixion of both man and God, but it is not the crucifixion of Jesus Christ, and it is not a chief source of man's salvation. What made the tragedy on Calvary uniquely redemptive was the Man on the middle cross, and the unmixed revelation of love and power that was in him.* There were crosses on either side of him, and there have been many before and after. In a sense men have been crucifying one another, and in a different sense crucifying God, from the beginning of human history. But only one crucifixion has become a central spring of light and grace for mankind. Let the Church, then, say that in the light of that Crucifixion we see more deeply and clearly the meaning of this present struggle. We see that in our world, the burden of suffering is not distributed according to guilt and innocence, but that all suffer, even the best. We see that the spirit in which suffering and death are confronted can make them vehicles of life for many rather than merely of loss. We see that as the cross of Jesus Christ demonstrated the power of God to overcome evil in its very moment of victory, there is good ground to hope for a like conquest continuing today and tomorrow. We and our brothers are not the saviors of mankind. The Savior is God, who suffers for us, with us, at our own hands, yet in such a way that the outcome is life perpetually made new. Our part is to bear witness to this saving work of God.

3. *God as Holy Spirit:*

One more dominant role must be ascribed to God in the war, as in all human history: His special work as Holy Spirit, Sanctifier, Sustainer, Life-Giver. This aspect of His presence and action, once more, is not to be thought of as separate from His presence as Creator and as sovereign Redeemer. God is one, and His work is indivisible. Hence, in what has already been said of universal creation and providence, divine judgment and mercy, the work of God as Holy Spirit has been often in view. Yet it is right to recognize along with these more general activities a special range of peculiarly personal relationship between God and those men who actually respond to His presence in conscious trust. Through such men, God is able to perform works of power that are not possible in lives ruled by unbelief. This is in a special way the distinctive work of the Holy Spirit.

The chief of such miracles has already been referred to in the discussion of divine mercy: the actual remaking of persons hard hit by the war, yet quickened into faith and devotion so that they become new and better men and women. This is the Spirit's work of sanctification, springing from God's redemptive love, and issuing in human life transformed, redirected, with new dimensions in which to grow. Nurturing such growth, likewise, toward the full stature of the manhood whose norm is Jesus Christ in the work of the same Spirit, whose impulse is one and whose gifts are many. The impulse is devoted love for God and man, for all that is good, true, and right. Among the gifts are reinforced strength and courage, sharpened insight and self-forgetfulness, steadfast patience and serenity and joy, invincible security, and others too many to name. Including them all is an abiding experience of heightened, deepened, broadened fellowship with men and nature, and with God.

The undivided Source of such new life, and the abiding Sustainer of communion among men and communion of men with God, the Holy Spirit is the living Ground of community as personal fellowship and as corporate life. Where the Spirit works, there diversity becomes enrichment of a common good rather than mere conflict or mutual destruction. We see this Spirit working wherever men are faithful to one another and to the best they know, wherever recognition of human kinship is maintained in spite of separation and strife, and especially wherever men are united in devotion to the one eternal God of heaven and earth. Upon this ground rest our understanding of the existence of the Christian Church itself, and our hope that its members and constituent bodies everywhere will find themselves increasingly pervaded by one shared and growing life.

A striking way in which this divine work comes to be affirmed in war time, with varying degrees of Christian insight, is the report from many quarters of a new sense, that comes to sorely tried men, of the fellowship of the Holy Spirit in hardship and peril, a sense often of supernatural help and protection. In this war, as in earlier wars, there is first-hand testimony, much of it startling, some of it very moving, with respect to the survival of hard-pressed pilots or mariners through unforeseen and powerful aid beyond known human powers. To the minds of many, these are palpable miracles in our time, like the "mighty works" that first century Christians took as signs and gifts of the Holy Spirit. Our problem now, like St. Paul's then, is to keep clear the right lines of Christian conviction across an area in which human cravings and emotions are uncommonly strong. It seems to us right to affirm that to every devoted person in war time, Christian or non-Christian, combatant or non-combatant, the presence of God offers an accessible source of power and spiritual security. Especially through genuine prayer, however inarticulate, a human spirit is opened toward God who is never absent, and strengthened to bear rightly whatever burden must be borne. That fresh energies, beyond the shallows drawn upon in ordinary living, can be tapped under conditions of great stress has long been known, and fresh testimony to the fact is welcome. Such energies, and such guidance as the hidden perceptions within men's bodies and minds may provide in times of extreme peril or exhaustion, can indeed manifest the watchful care of the God who neither slumbers nor sleeps.

But as in St. Paul's day, so in ours it is vital to insist that no marvel of force nor of physical guidance, not even a rescue from impending bodily death, is in itself a sufficient evidence of a special working of the Holy Spirit. The crucial test is still the old one: Is the spirit of man, in the presence of these marvels, brought closer to the pattern of the spirit of Jesus Christ? Of two men confronted by the same event, one may be moved to self-searching, humility, and new devotion, the other to self-satisfaction and arrogance. It seems not too rash to say that one has heard in rescue from peril the voice of God, the other only a magnified echo of his own.

The difference becomes very clear in the differing attitudes of those who pray in war-time. It is good that men are moved to pray in times of especial stress, far better if they pray continually in good times and bad, both in words and in unspoken cravings and grateful impulses. We believe that the half-involuntary, unaccustomed cry for help and the calm reaffirmation of a lifelong trust are alike understood and accepted by an infinite Father. But they can scarcely be answered alike. Prayer is a mutual relationship between personal spirits and its significance and results are necessarily dependent on the characters, attitudes, and actions of both participants. We are assured that God will unfailingly provide, in answer to every one who turns to Him sincerely in prayer, the utmost of good that the attitude of the petitioner and the whole situation permit. But that good will often be very different from what the petitioner seeks. In particular, there is no warrant for expecting that God will protect from physical harm all those who call upon Him however sincerely, nor that prayers are enough to assure military victory or avert another war. Prayers for all these things can be offered, with or without Christian insight and faith. The one kind of petition, we believe, that God cannot accept as genuine prayer at all is a presumptuous and self-righteous effort to use Him and His power for human ends, chosen without regard to His will. Humble prayer for safety or for bread can be real prayer. Yet we believe that those soldiers pray best who pray in the spirit of the young officer who wrote to his family from Bataan: "My prayer each night is that God will send you His strength and peace. During the first few days of the war, I prayed also for personal protection from physical harm, but now, that I may be given strength to bear whatever I must bear, and do whatever I must do, so that those men under me will have every reasonable chance." The models for prayer in time of trial are still the prayers in Gethsemane and on the cross: "Abba, Father, all things are possible unto thee; take away this cup from me; nevertheless not what I will, but what thou wilt." "Father, forgive them; for they know not what they do." "Father, into Thy hands I commend my spirit."

C. MAN'S PART IN THE WAR

In speaking of God's action in the war, we have spoken continually of man's action also. This is neither accidental nor avoidable. No sharp line can be drawn through the world nor through any part of it with God's acts on one side, man's on the other. In every historical event, both God and man are actively present though neither can at any point be simply identified with the other. Now we seek to view the same war situation from another angle, and ask what man is doing to himself and in relation to God in the struggle. In Christian terms, our concern here is man as creature, as sinner, and as subject of redemption.

1. Man as Creature Enjoying the Status of Responsible Freedom:

First, then, we recognize the existence of man as created personal being. We think of man as emergent in the midst of nature, called into being by the creative power of God, to become a personal self. His natural status is not thus denied, but a further range of life is opened out for him: a status we know as responsible freedom. Man's freedom is visible most simply in his ability to judge his environment and himself, intellectually and morally. In perceptual judgment, in memory and anticipation, and in reasoning to new conclusions such as he has never hitherto experienced, man asserts his partial independence of the physical situation in which at any moment he stands. In self-consciousness he brings even his own thinking under review, and in moral self-criticism he compares himself with standards that he neither has attained nor can attain. In making and carrying out practical decisions, he alters what would have been the natural course of events, and makes both the world and himself different from what they would have been. In this sense, *man affirms his freedom in every act of critical awareness, and especially in self-consciousness, moral judgment and personal decision.*

This freedom is not negated but complemented by the fact that as person, a man is a responsible being. For responsibility is first of all ability to respond to factors for which many living things have no capacity for response. Truth, justice, humbleness are duties for man because the meanings, the patterns of life, for which these words stand are discernible by him and awaken acknowledgment in him. The presence of other persons as persons, moreover, not as means to his pleasure but as ends for his devotion, and the presence of God beyond all natural and human goods—to these also he is capable of appropriate response, and to them he is thence responsible. *Herein is his more-than-animal freedom the more concretely defined. In being thus obligated, as irresponsible creatures are not, he is the more genuinely free—free, as they are not, to be a person intent upon freely chosen good, whose constraint upon him is not compulsion, but obligation, that can be denied though not escaped.*

This paradox of freedom and constraint runs throughout man's existence as social being. Not only is he under obligation to the law of God—the ingrained patterns of the world and his own being that require of him willing affirmation of what is true and right—but he is bound up so intimately with the lives of his fellow-men that apart from them he cannot be himself. Only in community can persons be persons. Yet in human community, growing individuals achieve maturity as persons only through both yielding and resistance to the demands of fellowship. Tension between individual and group, between person and person, between group and group is a constant pattern of growing human life. Group loyalty and individual self-assertion are both indispensable to such personal life as we know, even at its best. This dependence of each person upon the social groups in which he is a member obviously limits his freedom by committing him in advance to specific folkways, in which he is nurtured and which enter into him as presuppositions for action. He becomes a child of his people, his nation, his culture, with his decisions partly predetermined by this social parentage; yet without some such determinations he could not achieve the freedom of personal living at all.

In rigidly authoritarian societies or groups, this sort of moulding through conscious training and the pressure of custom can make it extremely hard for individual persons to act, or even to think freely in relation to the nurturing group. So it is in our day for the young people of both Germany and Japan. Among them group loyalty has been stressed and personal dissent discouraged until the very meaning of critical independence, one may suppose, has still to be learned. Yet under extreme conditions, there are two ways in which a person can find a new lease of freedom with respect to his nation or people. One way is through human contacts that make him realize that his nation is one member of a world society in which diverse national and cultural patterns exist in a wider human context. He is himself, therefore, a member of that world society as well as of his smaller group, and the scope of his loyalty is widened, the details of it modified, by this realization. He can still be a devoted patriot if the well-being of his nation is clearly seen to be inseparable from the well-being of the wider society and its other members. But this is different from the patriotism of the unawakened nationalist. A second way to such liberation is through direct conscious dependence on God and His universal laws. This is "the liberty of a Christian man," that sets one free from any cultural, political, or secular absolutism, though not from the demands of God.

In still another way man's freedom is restricted: by his dependence upon nature and history through his particular place in space and time. That he can transcend this location in some fundamental respects we have seen. He has power to think his way out beyond any specifiable limits of spatial or temporal extent. But he cannot escape the actual impacts and restraints, the defects and frustrations that are part and parcel of the world-scene into which he is born. In war time, he cannot escape the special impacts and frustrations of such a time; nor in any given age of history can he live as though the conditions that help to bound his life were not real. Attempts to escape from reality, in this sense, can lead indeed to an irresponsibility of weakness and false comfort but not to an increase of personal freedom. On the other hand, loyal acceptance of the actual place in nature and history into which one is born and grows, and at the same time persistent effort to discern the truth and right that are God's law for human living, can extend one's freedom even though one's finiteness is never left behind. The fact of bodily death is the perpetual reminder that one is finite. Yet even in the presence of death, men can be free moral selves.

Man who is thus at once finite and free becomes a genuine person, then, growing in wisdom and stature, in awareness and integrity, by accepting his responsible status and willingly affirming as his own good the truth and right that are involved in God's world-order. The law is at once around him and within him. He is summoned to obey God and thus to become more fully himself. Through love toward God and his fellow-men, and appreciation of his natural home, his own life is widened, deepened, and carried on toward fulfillment.

2. *Man as Sinner:*

Conversely, man is a sinner when he denies his responsibility to God and men, and so violates his own nature and his own good as personal self. Such violation is always wrought by personal decision. It is never the automatic result of natural impacts, as bodily injury or disease may be. In these latter instances a person does not actively identify himself with the corrupting change and make it his own. But in asserting his interests without due regard to his neighbor's, in seeking pleasure or profit or power in defiance of equity, in treating persons as things or the will of God as though it were the will of man, a person affirms as his own the falsehoods that such conduct involves. This is sin, and through such commitment to falsehood a person becomes bound in a different way from the ways that mark his finiteness. As sinner he has corrupted his own powers and become less fully a person than before, less able to see truth and right clearly, and less resistant to the pressures of nature and human society that continually threaten his integrity and personal freedom.

What men thus do as individuals, they do also in groups. Human society as we know it is organized on the understanding that both loyalty and disloyalty are to be expected. We build vast credit systems that presuppose general good faith, and parallel them with police courts and prisons to deal with expected violations. We form voluntary associations for business, education, research, communal worship, held together mainly by voluntary ties, and we organize elaborate coercive machinery in the name of the State to keep the peace when quarrels arise. Within the modern nation, most disputes can be settled either by agreement or by legal coercion. But since no effective government yet runs beyond the frontiers of a state, when international disputes arise, with major collisions of national interests, the stresses and conflicts of ordinary times are likely to deteriorate sooner or later into war.

If we ask how man's sinfulness is manifest in this war, our answer can only select from the appalling tangle a few typical threads. Without minimizing the fateful consequences of the policies and decisions of the Axis governments, we can say that war came not because the peoples on both sides deliberately willed it, but because enough people on each side willed, half-gropingly, half-wittingly, their own apparent advantage without due regard to the obligations of human community and divine order. This involved both deep-seated lack of trust in God and neighbor, and faithlessness to promises given or implied, each act of faithlessness itself prompted in part by suspicion of the others' good faith. To this mesh of distrust all peoples have contributed through all history to the present outbreak, and the weaving of the web still goes on. Bad faith between men presupposes, in large part, men's distrust of God. Instead of seeking security and fullness of life through acceptance of His ways, they have tried to seize and hold these good things by defrauding or subjugating other men. And other men have sought to secure themselves against loss by more subtle deceptions or more powerful retaliations.

Add to faithlessness the kindred sins of pride and idolatry. In pride men seek to achieve fulfillment through the exercise of power above their fellows. During ordinary time the means are economic, intellectual, social, political, ecclesiastical. The unending struggle for preferment, and assertion of superiority, develops in each people a tradition—almost an ethic—of ambition and domination, a half-articulate *Herrenmoral* in which children are reared believing that life can have savor only through the exercise of lordship. In this context, lesser dominations lead to striving for greater ones. Success already won must be protected against the resentful victim and the envious rival. Success for oneself becomes identified with dominance for one's business house, or class, or church, or nation. Small nations fear larger neighbors and make alliances against them. Large nations fear encirclement, build up armaments, and seek to use small neighbors as outposts against larger ones. Trade rivalries grow into diplomatic contests, and irredentist minorities become symbols of inferiority to be put right. And so at last to war, to which there is no self-confessed aggressor but only aggrieved defenders of imperiled security.

Another way of saying much the same thing is to say that in seeking unrivaled dominance and impregnable security, men are seeking for themselves, their church, their country the status of God. Idolatry thus underlies and aggravates human conflict, in peacetime and in war. In the degree to which one's own finite objects of devotion are treated as absolutes, the crusading temper against which Christian insight within the Church has turned, in recent years, tends to reappear on secular grounds. Defense of home and country, of capitalism, imperialism, of democracy, can become defense of "the faith."

The counterpart to pride and self-seeking, present also in all peoples in varying degree, is moral lethargy and that effort to escape irksome responsibility to which we have already referred. The very persons who are jealous of their own security and privilege are too often unconcerned about the security and freedom of others, and unwilling to share with them the task of seeking opportunity for all. *Aggression and irresponsibility, tyranny and anarchy, two major forms of social sin, feed one upon the other. Deliberate wrongdoing and ignorant unconcern are a human soil in which the dragon's teeth take root and grow.*

Wars, then are not the outcome of wicked acts of particular men, in isolation from a great body of shared social evil. They grow out of that massive moral and religious wrongness which is the seed-bed of all our specific transgressions, and to which all of us and all our forbears have contributed. For in affirming as our own these war-breeding attitudes toward God and men, we have identified ourselves with the drift toward war, whether we have deliberately sought war or simply a more privileged place in the sun.

Once open war begins, under modern conditions, the malignant propagation of sin becomes a kind of perverted virtue. Systematic lying to both foes and friendly peoples becomes an implement of statecraft. Atrocious cruelties are practiced in hot blood and with cold deliberation. Reports of such cruelties are kept on file, and coined at the proper time into righteous fury and support for counter-measures. Young men are schooled into fighting methods derived from the jungle and improved by cool intelligence and careful experiment. Hatred and ruthlessness are approved, mass exterminations of enemy troops are sought and of civilians are practiced, military necessity tends to become the supreme guiding principle of conduct.

What thus comes to horrid fruitage in the war had its roots, once again, in the behavior of men and nations before the war broke out. Hideous brutalities, cold-blooded treacheries, cowardly evasions, callous stupidities—all these and more we must charge against our present enemies, our allies, and ourselves in varying proportions during the years of miscalled peace. There is no warrant for blurring the differences of situation, behavior, and objectives of the various powers during that armed truce. Some were concerned chiefly to keep the advantages already won; some were more bent on revenge and the seizure of increased power at the expense of their neighbors. Some were prepared to maintain, chiefly for their own peoples, such measures of freedom and equity as they had inherited and developed; some were intent on destroying both freedom and equity for the sake of greater power at home and abroad. Though all were involved in sin, their ways of sinning were not identical in the sight of God, we believe, nor in their portent for the common life of men. *In the actual course of events, dominance by the Axis powers would have fastened upon their own peoples and upon conquered lands a reign of tyranny and terror full of danger to humane living everywhere. Resistance to such rule, whether by armed force or by more peaceful means, became imperative. We speak here with keen awareness of the confusions of human motives, the mingling of good with bad intents, the differences among striving human groups that mark each new situation in history. We have in view at the same time the certainty that our own judgment of all these matters is biased and incomplete. Yet one judgment concerning the years of uneasy truce seems clear. Every nation then was concerned more for the immediate advantage of self than for the larger welfare of mankind and for the glory of God as Lord of all. Every nation, moreover, thus jeopardized even its own well-being, along with that of its neighbors, since none can long prosper alone.*

To the sins of the pre-war years, also, the conduct of the war itself has added greatly. It is not to be thought that with the outbreak of war, the distinction between sin and suffering temporarily disappears, so that all who are involved become helpless victims of unmoral necessity because all chance for significant decision is ended until hostilities cease. War is not hell, save in metaphor. It displays horrors, indeed, that are worthy of hell, but they are in essential part the results of continuing decisions of men who are at once bound and free in exactly the same sense in which men are bound and free in the intervals before and after a war. The specific decisions open to them are not the same nor, of course, are the specific conditions—the intellectual barriers and social pressures—under which they must decide. These become much more restrictive, and the range of choice more narrow. But as long as persons are living persons, there is no situation in which their decisions cease to be significant before God.

The view that the war is, for the persons involved in it, a morally neutral though spiritually horrible interlude in human history may seem to find a certain plausibility in another consideration: the distortions of human goodness in war as we know it. *On the one hand, spiritual excellences of many sorts are intrinsic, not accidental, to the conduct of war. This war is the outcome and the scene not only of sin and of natural necessity, but also of impulses to good among many plain people.* Besides the faithlessness that leads to the breakdown of peaceable ways, there is the loyalty that keeps men together under fire. There are promises honored at heavy cost as well as promises broken. There is concern for one's own country and children, and also for weaker peoples abroad, with whose security one's own is involved. This kind of faithfulness of men to one another is characteristic of all armies not demoralized into mobs. Without it war could not go on. There is courage of many grades, up to the lambent heroism of soldiers who smother grenades with their bodies in order that the men beside them may live, or the quiet faith of chaplains who give their life-belts to others and go down with a sinking troop ship. There is love and self-sacrifice and generosity— even at times toward the enemy. The spirit of man is not simply bad in war.

But the good that men do in war has to be done mainly at the expense of genuine elements of good in what other men are seeking. Moreover, the good that one seeks for one's own part is likely then, even more obviously than at other times, to be so entangled in evil that it produces Dead Sea fruit. It is almost never possible to will good in war-time without seeing the good that one wills bring evil in its train. Neither fighting in defense of the weak, nor refusing to fight while abuse of them goes on, can provide a way that is unambiguously good. *The active participant, the pacifist, and the victim in war all may seek recognizable goods and all help to propagate different sorts of evil.* Herein is man's misery. But though in time of war this moral plight is most acutely felt, it is in essence the same at all other times as well. War intensifies the tragedy of imperfect personal living. It does not annul its personal character, nor obliterate the permanent difference between evil and good while the fighting lasts.

3. *Man as a Subject of Redemption:*

A practically urgent question arises from all that has been said about man in war: whether war itself is inevitable, by reason of human nature or of the corruption to which it has already been subjected. We believe that it is not. Particular wars become inevitable only by reason of a particular series of decisions and causal processes within the framework of the divine order. Given the freedom and interdependence of men, either aggression or neglect of obligation by national governments can result in dangerous tensions. In the absence of international community and effective means for maintaining international order, wars eventually result. But in two ways this situation can be changed, by human decisions and divine grace. On the one hand, the human sources from which war-making tensions develop can be altered by the slow processes of personal regeneration and re-education. *It is an essential article of Christian faith that the hearts of men, though corrupted, can be renewed through the power of God; and only because this is so dare we hope for the ultimate elimination of war. But this hope, especially if it be held for the calculable future, requires that personal regeneration go forward in vital union with institutional change.* As in widening areas through medieval and modern history, effective government and living community have been developed, the danger of armed conflict within such areas has decreased. For the world society now crowded into an uneasy physical entanglement, a similar need is evident. World society must become world community, and a way must be found to maintain lawful order and equity as a common trust. What men under God have achieved on the smaller but enlarging scale of provincial and national life we believe is not impossible on the international scale required by the conditions of our time.

Meanwhile, one other question demands an answer. Supposing that a more peaceful time for a future generation is not impossible, what shall we say of the men who are killing and being killed now? Is death for them an ultimate frustration, or does the Christian faith see for them some fulfillment?

There is for us no easy answer. We have felt the shock of untimely death, the pain of broken ties, the loss of unique and irreplaceable companions in our human lot. We have known the cruel disappointment and the lingering regret over powers undeveloped, promises unrealized, when young lives are cut short. We grieve with the parents, wives, and children of all countries who are suffering such pangs today. Their sorrow is not to be quieted by words of ours. It will be quieted, we believe, wherever trust in God becomes the basic premise for understanding life and death alike. For some, the death of a beloved may be the first real doorway to such faith. For some it will long be like a blank wall that only time can dissolve. For some, there is vivid assurance that resurrection or eternal life means restoration and fulfillment of all that has been lost. For all, it is good to be assured that the souls of the righteous are in the hands of God. Christian faith provides no secret knowledge and no promise of immunity from sorrow and loss. It does provide a wisdom and a power in whose presence even death can lose its sting. For we are assured that in the everlasting mercy of God, no faithful servant will have died in vain.

D. THE CHURCH IN A WORLD AT WAR

We come finally to the Church in a world at war. The context within which the Church has its place in history is human society, partly organized into communities of many sorts, of which the Church itself is one. A community, as we understand the term, is a group of persons in dynamic interrelation, who display both unity and diversity of fairly specific sorts. The unity of such a group may be conditioned in part by such external factors as geographic locale and environmental pressures of various kinds. But its more important conditions are internal. There must be a common ethos: a set of common working presuppositions, whether articulate or not, a body of common traditions, and a sense of shared living. There may be common language and literature, rites and festivals, perhaps a common founder or ruler, ancestors or heroes. At all events, the unity of such a group exists in important part in its imaginative life, its memories, feelings, thoughts, and purposes. Diversity within it may have many phases. In a small communal group, this may consist of little more than individual differences among its members. In a large community, this inner diversity will include not only various interest groups, but distinct institutions—domestic, economic, educational, political—embodying major patterns of community life.

1. The Nature of the State:

Among such institutions, two are of especial concern to us here, the State and the Church. The State is the seat of political power in a complex community. In it are concentrated the means for making and recording law, and for interpreting and enforcing it. Law and coercive force are the twin pillars of government, and the State is the enduring custodian of both. Its distinctive task is to maintain order, among the diverse members of the inclusive community—for our present purpose, the modern nation. As far as possible, this is to be done by reason and persuasion, by appeal to community loyalty, and by similar measures. But coercive power, greater than that commanded by any member of the community, is always at the disposal of the State (acting at any given time through the government then in office), and such power can be used for the common good, in accordance with the laws understood to be in force for the whole community. *The State as the chief earthly custodian of law is regarded by most Christians as in principle a pattern of life divinely ordained to safeguard social order against anarchy, justice against injustice. On these grounds it has a just claim to the loyal support of Christian citizens in the performance of its proper duties. It has no just claim to absolute or unconditional authority even within its own territorial bounds. In relations both to its own subjects and to other states or persons, it is bound by the demands of that divine order often denoted by the terms natural and moral law, that is binding upon all men and human institutions. The modern secular theory of ultimate sovereignty for each existing state cannot be justified to Christian faith.*

In a democratic community, the State makes no pretense to exercise political control over all the interests and phases of community life. Homes, schools, business, the press, churches—all have large areas of independent activity, not invaded by the State as long as they do not interfere with the maintenance of public order. In a totalitarian community, on the contrary, the State is in theory entitled to regiment all community interests and groups under complete political control. State and community in theory are coextensive. Such theory is antithetic to Christian belief.

2. The Character of the Church:

The Church is a community of very special character and of complex status at once within and beyond each nation. The indispensable basis for a doctrine of the Church is recognition of the will of God evoking responses among men. The will of God must be thought of, for this purpose, as the steady power of superhuman wisdom and love, the wisdom and love revealed in Jesus Christ, to which all men are at all times subjected, and to which they are at all times responding in divers ways, whether they know it or not. The will of God is not in any simple way coercive, nor the responses of men automatic. Rather, the infinite variety and the intrinsic freedom of personal appeal and response are maintained on both sides. In consequence, though the love of God is constant because God is unchangeable good, the responses of men are highly variable and always fall short of the whole-souled trust and love which God requires. Yet there is a crucial difference between the orientation of life which in fact (not merely in wish or intent) is moving toward such trust and love, and that which in fact is moving away from it. There is a human craving, much more basic than conscious desire or deliberate intent, which is in effect a hunger and thirst for the true God, a seeking above all things His kingdom and His righteousness. *Wherever the presence of God quickens this deep craving into faith and love toward Him, there exists the "commonwealth of God," civitas dei.*

The living core of the Church, the true Church, is this actual communion of men with God, and with one another in Him, never static and never definable by counting heads, in which the regeneration and reformation of human lives by the power of God is going on. In this communion, divine grace and human response are in vital interplay, and from it there springs perpetually (though by no means uniformly) new life—intellectual, moral, religious, individual and social, human and divine. To this spiritual life-giving intercourse between men and God, the term *communio sanctorum* can most appropriately be applied. The true Church, then, cannot be identified with any organized company of people but it is in a strict sense the fellowship of the Holy Spirit—the living spring of Christian life.

This living communion of men with God and with one another which defines the true Church must find historical embodiment in appropriate corporate form, the institutional Church, the outward and visible sign of the invisible fellowship of grace. Full Christian life is not to be lived by lone individuals in separation from their fellows. As in other areas of human behavior, so in this, the living movement of spirit frames itself in social patterns and institutions which may be compared with the habit-patterns of individual life. In spite of the plurality and diversity of the patterns of shared Christian living and of the persons and things in which they are concretely embodied, it seems legitimate to believe that amidst all the diversity there is a unitary and inclusive though not a static pattern which makes it possible for members of one particular church body to recognize kinship with members of other church bodies. This inclusive pattern is then *ecclesia catholica,* the actual Church Universal. No particular one among the church bodies today can fairly claim by itself a full title to that name. On the other hand, just in so far as members of any one or two or more of these bodies do actually find themselves enlisted in one common movement with fellow Christians of past and present, acknowledging allegiance to one Lord, and recognizing positive shared values rather than mere stumbling-blocks in their diversity, just so far the realization of positive catholicity in behavior (as distinguished from simple tolerance, or even spiritual affinity) can be affirmed. This actual Church Universal, in which the several church bodies are coming more and more to find their common existence, is the proper body of the true Church, not to be sundered from it but to be more fully actuated by it. Herein a sacramental relationship, unfinished and creative, is to be recognized.

In this existence of the institutional Church as a universal body of many members, needing to be actuated by one spirit, we recognize both power and peril. Here, at its best, is a conservator and bulwark for the sensitive life of the spirit; and more specifically, for groups within the Church who are ready to stand forth in a more dangerous sort of witnessing than the members of a secular community or of a cross-sectional Church by and large will risk. Here too is a massive object of loyalty and love, which can more than hold its own in steadfast endurance against even the modern State, freeing men by so much from the grip of totalitarian politics. On the other hand, this very massiveness fosters vested interests within and without, and the formalisms, inertias, and tyrannies that these so easily involve. It fosters also a subtler misdirection and perversion of loyalties by slipping too smoothly into an identification with "the world": the cultures and the social, economic, and political ambitions among which it lives.

To define justly the due relation of Church and world is notoriously hard. One may begin, perhaps, by distinguishing between the world and its worships. A sound doctrine of creation, providence, and grace will not fall into the pessimist's frequent error, and despise the world which God so loves. It will give full recognition to the secular orders of life—domestic, economic, and so on—as homes and proving-grounds for life and love. But it will attack with full force the idolatrous worldliness that confuses love and worship, and renders to Caesar the things that are God's. "The devil's commonwealth," *civitas terrena*, is defined not by secular status but by power-lust and pleasure-lust, egoism and irresponsibility. Against "the world" in this sense of *civitas terrena* the true Church does, and the institutional Church should, maintain a struggle of clear-sighted love, to the end that God's world may the more fully acknowledge Him, and have more abundant life.

This means that the Church, in both peace and war time, as we have said more than once, stands in a double relation to the State and to the community of civil affairs. On the one hand, members and constituent bodies of the Church are members also of civil communities and citizens of particular states that have emerged in history, and as such are obligated by the law of God to render loyal service aimed at promoting the welfare of their respective nations. On the other land, the Church being universal is not a subject of any state, nor a constituent body in any civil community. It is itself, in principle and to an increasing degree in actuality, an ecumenical community having members in all nations and owing direct allegiance to the God and Father of all mankind. Its proper service to civil life can be rendered only while its ultimate and direct obligation to proclaim the Kingdom of God is kept clear. Its service to the world must be a ministry, not a vassalage nor a partnership.

This double relation of the Church and its members to civil society takes on in war time a phase of exceptional tension. For in any war, the Church as ecumenical community has members in both camps, and as a ministry of God must seek the spiritual welfare of all who are involved in the war. In this war, the Protestant Churches alive with a new sense of ecumenical membership and obligation find themselves compelled to realize this status of the Church far more acutely than quasi-national churches in the past have had to realize it. In this war, moreover, as we have seen, a civil issue of desperate moment for human history and spiritual health is at stake: the issue of establishing or failure to establish an effective international community of civil life. In presence of this imperative laid upon all nations by the law of God at this juncture in history, the Church and its members must seek to discern and to perform their duties to God and to mankind.

III. CHRISTIAN ATTITUDES AND DUTIES IN WAR TIME

Rightly to conceive and to perform these duties in war time has long been the task of Christians who agree in primary affirmations and differ in some important derivative judgments. It is agreed that the perennial task of the Church and of its members is to bear witness incessantly to the judgment and the mercy of God revealed in Jesus Christ, and thus to carry on through peace and war its ministry of reconciliation. There has long been difference of conviction as to whether in war time this primary task calls for renunciation, by the Church and its members, of all voluntary support to the military efforts of any belligerent group. This difference of conviction is represented among the signers of this report, as later paragraphs will make plain. To a far more profound and far-reaching concurrence among us, both those paragraphs and the report as a whole bear witness.

To set both agreement and differences in their right perspective, we have examined together the occurrence of similar convictions in the developing life and thought of the Church from the beginning, and of some of its constituent bodies in more recent times. A brief survey of this development is presented in a supporting study.[2] Its major findings can be summarized still more briefly here, and the greater part of this section devoted to the problem of defining our Christian duty today.

A. ATTITUDES TOWARD PARTICIPATION IN WAR

Three main attitudes toward participation in war have developed in the life of the Christian Church. With some exceptions and qualifications, and for various reasons, *the general attitude of the Christian communities until the time of Constantine seems to have been renunciation   by Christians of military service in war time.* When the Church, hitherto a disapproved fellowship within the Roman empire but not of it, now came to have a privileged and more responsible place in the world of Greek and Roman culture, *a second attitude developed: a readiness to distinguish between just and unjust warfare, and to approve active participation by ordinary Christians in a just war.* Monks and clergy still refrained from bearing arms, though not from exhortations and prayers for victory. For other Christians, it came to be regarded as a civic duty to share in armed defense or attack in a just cause. The just war was carefully defined, in such terms that only one side could be regarded as fighting justly, and strict rules were laid down for the treatment of enemies, prisoners, and non-combatants. Still later a third attitude arose alongside the first two. When the empire in the West disintegrated under successive waves of warring barbarian peoples, who became the citizenry of a new medieval Christendom, the rules of just warfare became much harder to enforce. After many vain attempts to get them enforced, the Church—now claiming theocratic authority over civil as well as ecclesiastical life—turned the fierce energies of her bellicose children toward the Holy Land and the infidel Muslim who held it. The crusades that resulted were proclaimed not by a secular prince but by the pope, the "vicar of Christ," for defense not of homeland and civic order but of "the faith," as a religious duty to God and the Lord Christ himself. Many monks and clergy, as well as laity, were now in the fighting ranks, the ordinary rules of just warfare were largely disregarded, and religious benefits were proclaimed for all who took part. *A third attitude was here manifested, not supplanting the first two but taking shape alongside them: an attitude of unrestrained commitment, under the Church's auspices, to a divinely ordained war as a religious duty and privilege.*

All three of these attitudes in changing forms continued within the Church during the rise and the struggles of modern nations, the discovery and colonizing of new continents, the massing of new industrial forces, and the arousing of ancient civilizations to dynamic new life. *The most prevalent attitude in the West, in Roman Catholic, Orthodox, and Protestant churches alike, has been approval of combatant service by laymen in wars regarded as just, that is, decreed by lawful authority for good cause, and conducted without official sanction for slaughter of prisoners or non-combatants, or similar barbarities.* Both renunciation of war and religious zeal for war have almost always been minority attitudes in the churches in modern times.

During the present war, a further development seems to be taking place. Crusading enthusiasm seems to be much diminished, if not wholly lacking this time, among Christians. At the same time, in certain important respects Christians willing to fight in a just war and Christian pacifists have drawn closer together. Many Christian pacifists are acutely aware of the monstrous dangers let loose upon the world by the Axis governments, the self-sacrificing heroism of men and women who are giving their lives in an effort to check the spread of such tyranny, and the inescapable ambiguities of their own moral and religious position in war time. Especially in a social order which refuses them most natural outlets for their readiness to work in relief of war-made suffering, the shortcomings of the ways that remain open to them are kept constantly before their eyes. They act as they must under the dictate of conscience, seeking to be guided by God's will yet always conscious of their failure really to fulfill its demands. Many Christians who are willing to support one side in this war are no less clearly aware of the depth of evil both in the conduct of modern war on either side and in the national behavior on all sides that made this war at last inevitable and a stable peace after the war uncertain, the inadequacy of military victory in itself to bring nearer the Kingdom of God on earth, and the grave compromises into which Christians are forced into military service. They know, in short, that there is no such thing as a wholly just war, that decision to fight on either side is at best a choice among mixed evils in the hope of choosing the least. They also seek to follow the will of God in so choosing, but without exultation and often with heavy hearts. *Under such conditions, there can be more profound mutual understanding and community among Christians of both groups, and better hope than ever before that both may contribute to the deepening and widening of the faith and life they share.*

B. THE PRESENT OBLIGATIONS OF THE CHURCH

Their common faith and life includes some fundamental convictions about the Church and its ministries and present obligations. *First of all, the true Church cannot and the institutional Church ought not to act as a belligerent, nor even as an unarmed co-belligerent, in any war.* The ecumenical character and the spiritual task of the Church alike forbid today its participation in the war as though it were a civil community, or a constituent part or a partner of such a community. In this sense, "the Church is not at war." *At the same time, since the Church is never simply separate from the civil orders, and its membership largely consists of persons who are citizens or subjects of nations at war, it cannot exclude from its own life the tensions that their divergent or opposing activities as citizens involve. Some as conscientious objectors are in alternative service or in prison. The Church must keep room for all these its children, not merely tolerating their differences but seeking to understand them more profoundly, to correct them where correction is clearly needed, and to apprehend more concretely through them all the will of God that they all seek to follow. The Church must continually relate them all, with their various special loyalties and personal stresses, to the Kingdom of God in which they all have their heritage and their best hope.*
1. In Worship of God:
For the Church's primary task, once more, is its ministry of reconciliation. It must continually serve as vehicle for the reconciling of man with God and of man

with man. This means, first, the continuing worship of God. In Christian worship, the way is kept open for all sorts and conditions of men to seek renewal and inward light in God's presence. Through prayer and meditation, through hearing and expounding of the word of God in the Scriptures, and through participation in the sacraments that attest and renew the communion of the faithful with one another and with God, the Church functions for its members and before all men as a true Body through which the Spirit works. In such worship there is no condoning of human wickedness and no forgetting that the God of our Lord Jesus Christ is kind to the unthankful and the evil, that the Lord himself came to call not the righteous but men of sin to repentance. In such worship men are brought before God on one common footing, as wayward children of one Father, so that in all their strength and weakness, their good and their evil, they stand together beneath His judgment and within His everlasting mercy. Both general and specific prayers for the triumph of good and the defeat of evil in every heart and in every land, for the correction and healing of friend and foe, for the curbing of tyranny and the establishment of justice and freedom, for the calming of grief and the renewing of hope, for the cleansing of nations and the establishment of peace—such prayers we believe are acceptable before God. Prayers of self-glorification, for vengeance, or for the establishment or maintenance of partisan advantage at the expense of justice, freedom, and community we believe are an offense to the Father of all men. So too the preaching of the word of God must have as its constant aim the proclamation of His kingdom, that is not one of the kingdoms of this world nor any league of earthly kingdoms, not even some far-off government of all mankind, but that eternal present sovereignty of divine law and grace by which earthly kingdoms and their subjects are both judged and renovated from age to age. In worship the Church must bring men face to face with the One God of heaven and earth.

2. *In Services to Men—Interpretation:*

Its worship of God must issue continually in distinctive services to men. By spoken and written word, the Church must seek to make clear the meaning and urgency of divine judgment and the hope of divine mercy in each new situation. This involves first and always preaching and teaching the principles of Christian faith. Our conception of the way these bear upon the problems posed by the war has been set forth as fully as we can present it in a brief statement. The content of that faith, however it may best be conceived, comprises the primary message of the Church for our time. Yet not the whole message. For, as we have said in the opening paragraphs, the Church is called upon also to interpret in the light of its own faith each historical situation that involves the lives of its members and the well-being of mankind.

Such interpretation includes two phases, explanation and criticism. In seeking to help make clear what each new phase of history involves for both present and future, the Church will not seek to substitute some quite separate account of its own for the analyses of experts in history, government, psychology, or practical affairs. It will seek to bring their findings into the light of its own unique perspective: the history of God's creative, redemptive, and life-giving work with man. In this perspective, the significance of economic or psychological realities is not diminished but rather deepened and made more concrete, in as far as through such realities the working of God can be discerned. Again, our conception of the way in which a human situation can be illuminated by distinctively Christian judgments has been suggested very briefly in the preceding sections. Other Christians will find very much more that needs to be said.

Beside such effort to help explain a current situation, the Church is called upon also to help criticize it. There is need to urge in war time the vital import of conscious personal devotion to the will of God and to the common good, as far as Christian faith and reason, manifested in Christian conscience, make each person aware of these controlling ends. The Church must approve such devotion wherever it appears, among soldiers or civilians, and seek to resist the uncritical submergence of personal decision in mass impulses. It must honor courage and faithfulness, patience and fairness, truth-speaking and generosity, especially where they are displayed under the the greatest difficulties and at the greatest cost. Such qualities of spirit displayed under fire or in the face of powerful oppressors mark human life at its best. The Church must condemn cruelty, ruthlessness, and power-lust, especially when they are provoked in large part by the very helplessness of potential victims. In such behavior man appears at his worst, and the Church dare not connive at such evil. Its victims must be aided and its perpetrators steadily opposed in all ways appropriate for an ecumenical and spiritual community. At the same time, even while it understands with deep sympathy the rise, among victims and liberators, of hatred for the oppressors and vengefulness toward them, the Church must resist no less steadily the spread of these self-propagating poisons. We rejoice that in so much of Christian judgment and popular will, especially in Great Britain and in certain occupied lands where civilian suffering by direct action of the enemy has been very great, and also in the United States where civilian life has been almost entirely safe from direct attack, there has been so much moderation and so little blind hatred toward enemy peoples. The Church of Jesus Christ has a primary obligation to voice and to support such generosity toward the peoples of Germany and Japan, in spite of the evil they have done and are doing, as one indispensable factor in restoring the spiritual health of all peoples in the hard days ahead. Forgiveness, we remember, is a Christian duty; and though forgiveness does not exclude severe correction, it does exclude vindictiveness and retaliation.

In like manner, the Church must approve in war time those influences in the shaping of public policy that best keep the way open for community among men and free worship of God. It must resist, by open criticism and persuasion, the theory and the attempted practice of "total war," and its counterpart, a Carthaginian *"peace."* Total war is suited only for a totalitarian society, which as we have said is irreconcilable in principle with Christian faith in the sovereignty of God and the responsible freedom of man. No matter what the provocation, however great the extremity of military peril—even to the imminence of military defeat—the Church dare not approve a supposition that military expediency or necessity can ever rightfully become the supreme principle of human conduct. We are acutely aware how difficult it is to apply in practice this principle of resistance to claims for the supremacy in war times of military demands and to the elevation of war even temporarily into a status of unconditional domination of human behavior. All of us agree that in war some practices cannot be regarded by the Church as justifiable: the killing of prisoners, of hostages, or of refugees to lessen military handicaps or to gain military advantages; the torture of prisoners or of hostages to gain military information, however vital; the massacre of civilian populations. Some of the signers of the report believe that certain other measures, such as rigorous blockades of foodstuffs essential to civilian life, and obliteration bombing of civilian areas, however repugnant to humane feelings, are still justifiable on Christian principles, if they are essential to the successful conduct of a war that is itself justified. A majority of the commission, moreover, believe that today war against the Axis powers, by all needful measures, is in fact justified. Others among us believe that the methods named are not justifiable on Christian principles, even though they are now practiced or defended by great numbers of sincere Christians and patriotic non-Christians, and even if they be essential to military victory for the United Nations. If it be true that modern war cannot be successfully waged without use of methods that cannot distinguish even roughly between combatants and non-combatants, or between perpetrators and victims, that fact seems to a minority in the commission to raise the question whether in modern war even the more scrupulous side can meet the conditions hitherto generally held by the Church to define a just war. On these specific issues, then, the commission is divided. *On the basic principle that the Church cannot acquiesce in the supremacy of military considerations even in war time, nor in the view that modern war may properly, even in case of extreme peril to nation, church, or culture, become total war, we are agreed.*

In like manner we are agreed that the Church must oppose any plan to deprive the peoples of Germany and Japan of the basis for a normal, peaceable livelihood or of reasonable opportunity for peaceable intercourse with other peoples. We are not competent to judge what methods for ensuring military disarmament in these countries, and what selective restrictions upon their imports of critical materials and development of heavy industry may best aid the difficult transition from war to a more peaceful world. We are convinced that the doors must not be closed now, by decisions made in war time, upon the chances of young Germans and Japanese to live normally in the postwar world.

3. *Personal Services:*

Besides its ministries of preaching, teaching, and writing, the Church is committed also to more concrete, personal services to men everywhere in war time. Men in the armed services rightfully look to the Church for help in their hard, unaccustomed tasks. In camps, on their travels, on furlough, and on the fighting fronts the Church must serve them in ways too many to name here. Interpretation of their goals and duties as members of the armed forces, explanation and help in evaluation of the necessities and the opportunities they face, companionship with them in the worship of God and in dangers at home and abroad: these are among the services the Church must seek to provide. It provides them mainly through the chaplains who are its ministers to the men and women in uniform. We rejoice in the record of their devotion to their task and in the evidences they have given of thoughtful concern for the future as well as the present well-being of the men they serve. At the same time, we remember that the *Church is not a partner of any State, however loyal church members may be as citizens, and its ministries are offered not as civil duties but as the Church's witness to a spiritual Lord of all mankind. Hence, we believe the Church must persistently seek, on behalf of its ministers to men in the armed forces, both freedom from military restraints that hinder their work of Christian ministry, and clear recognition that they serve as clergy of the Church Universal rather than as officers of the several belligerent governments.* Many of us believe that from the standpoint of the Church, civilian status would be preferable to military rank for ministers with the armed forces.

To demobilized soldiers, to war victims, and to defeated enemy peoples the Church has obligations to which it has devoted time, energy, and resources from the beginning of the war. There is no need to urge that these obligations must continue to be met long after the fighting stops. The special responsibility of the churches in lands less severely hurt by the war to their fellow Christians in the fighting zones, on both sides of the lines, cannot be discharged without the establishment of new bonds of fellowship within the Church itself. Of this need, more will be said in a later section.

4. *Counseling:*

Meanwhile, the Church must face in war time the task of counseling its individual members with respect to their problems and duties as Christian citizens. The premise for all such counseling must be the dual status and complex loyalties of every Christian, who is at the same time a member of the Church universal and a member of a civil community, a citizen or subject of a belligerent or neutral state. The Church must teach that the primary determinative obligation of every Christian is to the Kingdom of

God, which can best find earthly expression through the growth every-where of community in which the Holy Spirit is at work. Love of one's country and devotion to its well-being is not to be displaced but rather to be validated by alignment with this primary obligation. As far as the two are clearly in accord, the way is plain. If at any point devotion to the Kingdom of God requires dissent from the present policy of a national government, or the present will of a popular majority, the Church must teach that such dissent can be itself a service to the welfare of the beloved country as well as to the Commonwealth of God. *The principle for each Christian must be: Devotion above all to God and His righteousness; full loyalty to country, friends, and home within the frame of this more ultimate devotion; support of established public policies, obedience to lawful demands of government, and concurrence in the accepted patterns of civic life as far as Christian conscience will permit.*

The positive duties of each individual Christian, like those of the Church, center about two foci: the obligation to bear witness by word and deed to the continuing judgment and mercy of God; and the active quest of justice, freedom, love, and fellowship among men. These duties are shaped in detail, for each person, by his specific vocation, family relationships, individual training, and many other conditions. In war time, moreover, they come to have an urgency and a particular direction that make them involve some special problems of conduct for every Christian. These are not separable in kind from the perennial problems of Christian living, but the particular forms they take in war time require special notice here.

In war as in peace, the key to all effort by individual Christians to serve the Kingdom of God is Christian conscience. In agreement with the tradi-tional thought of the Church, we recognize in every man both a general tendency to distinguish between right and wrong, and many specific insights into the rightness or wrongness of particular courses of action. We recognize that these specific insights are learned through personal experi-ence, at once individual and communal, that to every Christian the touch-stone for such particular responses is given in that revelation that centers in Jesus Christ, and that each Christian must necessarily apprehend and interpret this revelation in the terms made possible by his own individual existence, with all its resources and its shortcomings. Individual insights and decisions will differ because individual persons differ. Yet there is one obvious common requirement: *that each shall follow, in sober sincerity, what really appears to him as the present way toward fulfillment of God's will. In war time, with its drastic narrowing of some sorts of choice, especially for men of military age, one decision that must be made by very many Christian citizens is decision to participate in the war as soldier or war worker, or to bear one's part as conscientious objector in alternative service or prison. With many representa-tives of the Church's mind, we recognize that equally earnest Christians may decide for either course.*

There is no disposition among our members to weaken in any way the primary principle that every Christian is in duty bound to decide for that course which really seems to him right. At the same time, there is no disposition among us to hold that any course actually open to men of our day (or of any day) is wholly good. We are agreed that the objectively right course for any Christian in history is that course which actually will most contribute to, and least detract from, the manifestation of God's reign on earth. His duty as Christian is to choose and follow what seems to him to be that objectively right course; the course of his largest possible contribution, and his own conduct is morally right in as far as it does honestly seek to find and follow that way. His judgment as finite human being, however, can be mistaken as to the manner in which his greatest possible contribution might be made. There is room, therefore, in our imperfect human living, for agreement at this point also upon a primary Christian principle and difference as to the specific ways in which that principle may best be put into current practice.

A majority of our members, then, believe that Christian duty today is more adequately conceived by those Christians who voluntarily support the military campaign of the United Nations against the Axis powers. They are clearly aware that successful military action by itself can at best serve the subordinate end of breaking the present military and political dominance of the Axis governments in their own and in occupied lands. The larger ends sought, in terms of justice, freedom, human understanding and cooperation, require measures other than military force. Yet it seems to a majority of the Commission that these ends cannot, in the actual world situation, be hopefully pursued without the use of military force until full victory is achieved.

For those who take the way of the soldier or civilian war worker, and participate voluntarily in active prosecution of the war, we believe there is need for unceasing effort to keep clear the Christian perspective with regard to God and men. We recognize the heart-breaking strains to which men in combat are subjected, and the extreme pressures that may be imposed on every man in military or civilian war service to subordinate all other considerations to the demand for victory. We are mindful of the profound dangers to individual Christian character in a system of military training and service in which many of the accustomed patterns of Christian conduct are replaced by training for ruthless efficiency in destruction. *We are mindful at the same time of the vital need that the Church and all its members resist any temptation to acquiesce in the displacement of the primary Christian goals and standards by any others, in the lives of its young men. Conscience cannot be adjourned in war time without extreme damage to human personality now and to the chance for progress toward world community even in the distant future.*

A minority of our members believe that those Christians are judging more accurately the meaning of Christian duty who in time of peace preach the renunciation of war, and in wartime follow the way of conscientious objection. The dangers of this course also are present to our minds. There is the always obvious danger of inward dishonesty, of spiritual laziness wearing the mask of self-sacrifice, of preference for personal safety above needed service to fellow men. There is the danger of self-righteousness and the unwarranted assumption of superior virtue. There is the danger that in seeking to serve the advance of community among men the conscientious objector may actually lose touch with the larger communities of which he is already a member, and serve the cause of isolationism instead of more vital world fellowship. We cannot ignore the immensely wide influence that present comradeship in arms will have upon future social, political, and spiritual patterns of life. Besides all these risks to the integrity and actual influence of Christian pacifists, there is the social risk that seems to their critics far more important: the risk that such decision as theirs, if practiced by large enough numbers of Christians, would prevent effective military action by the United Nations, and open the way to control of the world by the totalitarian powers. Yet in spite of these dangers, a minority of the Commission, and a proportionately lesser minority in the churches, are committed to the way of Christian pacifism. To them it appears that resistance to the spread of totalitarian modes of life can best be maintained by Christians who renounce voluntary participation in war, and devote their full energies to practicing as consistently as possible the ways of peace. *They believe that widespread, consistent practice of Christian pacifism is the best way to proclaim now the Church's gospel of reconciliation, and therefore the best way that Christians can help to extend the growth of community among men and nations, and the development of methods other than war for dealing with conflicts of interest.*

Upon Christians who choose this course in war time, there rest special responsibilities of at least two sorts. They must assume voluntarily and wholeheartedly a real share of the burden that the war entails. Most Christian conscientious objectors today, we believe, desire to carry a heavier load rather than a lighter one. They cannot willingly support military action, but they could and would most willingly perform many sorts of arduous and dangerous work for relief of suffering, reconstruction of ruined territories, and ministry to human needs that now are closed against them. We believe that they would be actively grateful for more exacting and varied demands upon their personal resources for service, and that the Church that approves the principle on which they are acting should seek to have their devotion given more significant scope in action. *Meanwhile, it goes without saying that both conscientious objectors of military age and other Christian pacifists must make the most of such ways to serve as may be open to them.* A second responsibility, which they share with all Christians, is the maintenance of understanding, mutual appreciation, and profound fellowship among fellow Christians. This need Christian pacifists cannot meet alone.

Yet we believe that the especial risk of isolation which they run should call forth in them an especial, persistent avowal of common faith and hope with their brothers in the Church of Jesus Christ. Among all Christians there is one devotion to the quest for justice and peace. They set out from common premises, seek common goals, and even in their differences can experience together the fellowship of the Holy Spirit.

C. THE CHURCH AS A NUCLEUS FOR WORLD COMMUNITY

The most important task of the Church in wartime is, indeed, just to be as fully as possible the present embodiment of that fellowship. For in fulfilling this role, the Church can be, in principle and to some extent in fact, a present nucleus for the world community that must come to birth.

There is no warrant for overestimating the influence the Church has now, or will have in the post-war world. Secular forces more powerful than any that history has produced hitherto are alternately seeking to use the Church or to disregard it. A majority of men even in the so-called Christian lands pay it lip-service or none. The Church will not rule the war nor write the peace. In the steps already taken by the Allied great powers toward organizing the post-war world, the dominant influence of vested national interests and of traditional power politics is plain. It is inevitable at least in this stage of history that factors like these should have a major place in the effort to establish world order. Stable large-scale community is not to be had in isolation from large-scale economic and political power. But such power by itself will never produce the community we so desperately need. In fact, possession or quest of great temporal power and exercise of vested privilege tend always to distort any effort to achieve more inclusive unity and greater security. Such power, moreover, the Church itself does not and should not wield. For like every other social institution, the organized Church is liable to the corruption of motive and warping of vision that temporal power and privilege bring, and more than any other institution it can forfeit, through such warping and corruption, its effectiveness for its own proper task. *The Church's task in relation to economic and political power is not to exercise rulership. It is rather to help induce the peoples and governments who may properly wield such power to use it less for immediate gain and more to extend the range of justice, peace, and freedom.* The truth, as Christian faith and fully enlightened reason can see it, is that in thus serving mankind, the great powers of our time would be serving also their own essential interests. But this truth can be fully evident neither to unreflective secular enterprise, nor even to the partly enlightened self-interest of secular prudence. The full strength of powerful tendencies to seek first nearby, clearly visible goods for oneself and one's group always operates to deflect human eyes from more distant goals. The Church must here make common cause with spokesmen of social enlightenment and goodwill, in business, education, press, or political life, to urge the vital need for long-range vision and action.

This need and the difficulty of meeting it are augmented in our day by the brevity of time and by the probable aftermath of war. The demand we face is that power impulses be enlisted for the common good, on the huge scale of international society, within the few years' respite on which we may count after this war. Yet the way is thick with the specific hindrances that arise out of the war itself, some of them noticed in preceding sections of this report, many of them too familiar to need mention. The sum is a task far too great for unaided human powers. In effect, we are called upon to restore a shattered world and to transform it from widespread anarchy to ordered community within one generation—before another war, still more devastating, breaks upon us and our children. For such a task all our secular wisdom, strength, and goodness simply are not enough.

Among all existing institutions, the Church is best able to face this sobering truth without despair. For in the course of a long and growing life, it has shared in the collapse and the transforming of more than one civilization—the Roman empire, the Byzantine world, the feudal order of Christendom—and through such experience has been made all the more vividly aware of the sustaining, redemptive power of God. Today once again the Church can see, pervading and transcending the tumult of world-crisis, His invincible judgment and mercy. At the same time, the Church itself is sharing more inclusively than ever before in the crisis of mankind. In its membership today there are people of all nations and cultures. *The Church that began as a handful of unknown disciples has grown, tenaciously and irrepressibly, through the centuries. Its breadth now, around the globe, is under-girded with the depth and power of proved vitality.* The City of the World is mightier than ever in all the weapons of force, but the City of God still manifests in our time, and that more widely than ever, the unconquered Spirit of life.

Today and tomorrow, that Spirit is the best hope of our war-torn peoples. Their wounds of body and mind and heart the Church must acknowledge as its own, and it must seek to provide for them the healing energies that truth, love, and faithfulness alone possess. Their bewilderment, fear, and despair the Church will need to meet with that demonstration of under-standing, mutual forgiveness, and common hope that are its own heritage. *Within its walls, men of all races and cultures have their rightful homes. It will need to make their claims to brotherhood more evident and effective.* In a time when the hope of shared and creative life for all mankind is the one light that can lighten a dark future, the Church must hold that hope high.

With all its faults, the Christian Church in our time is an actual massive embodiment of growing community, and the only one whose organized membership is worldwide. Its long divided constituent bodies are astir today with hunger for closer communion. It seeks a new level of common life among its own people, and in the very quest, it finds an ampler unity-in-difference coming to realization in its own corporate life.

Thus it must come to be, too, in the world society now struggling to find a way of peace. *The Church*, with members now in every major part of that society, and with its faith grounded in the Ever-Living God whose Spirit moves still within His half-finished creation, *can by its very existence as faithful Church help the world to find that way.* The Church must seek to realize yet more fully its own growing unity of spirit, to bring into its communion of faith and love an ever more inclusive company of God's children, and to make its own awareness of divine judgment and forgiveness pervade, like widening daylight, the whole tortured life of our time.

---

[1] The members of the commission were appointed by the Federal Council's Executive Committee on March 16, 1943. Robert L. Calhoun was asked to serve as chairman. Members of the Commission chose John C. Bennett as their secretary. Four meetings were held, each one running from one to five days. Since another commission was actively at work on the problems of "A Just and Durable Peace," the Commission did not enter into this field, but concentrated on the theological and ethical issues involved. Their report was submitted to the Council in November, 1944.

Members of the Commission were: Robert L. Calhoun, Professor, Yale University; Edwin E. Aubrey, President, Crozier Theological Seminary; Roland H. Bainton, Professor, Yale University Divinity School; John C. Bennett, Professor, Union Theological Seminary; Conrad J. I. Bergendoff, President, Augustana College and Theological Seminary; B. Harvie Branscomb, Dean of the School of Religion, Duke University; Frank H. Caldwell, President, Louisville Presbyterian Seminary; Angus Dun, Bishop of the Washington Diocese of the Episcopal Church; Nels F. S. Ferre, Professor, Andover-Newton Theological Institution; Robert E. Fitch, Professor, Occidental College; Theodore M. Greene, Professor, Princeton University; Georgia E. Harkness, Professor, Garrett Biblical Institute; Walter M. Horton, Professor, Oberlin Graduate School of Theology; John Knox, Professor, Union Theological Seminary; Umphrey Lee, President, Southern Methodist University; John A. Mackay, President, Princeton Theological Seminary; Benjamin E. Mays, President, Morehouse College; John T. McNeill, Professor, Union Theological Seminary; H. Richard Niebuhr, Professor, Yale University Divinity School; Reinhold Niebuhr, Professor, Union Theological Seminary; Wilhelm Pauck, Professor, Chicago Theological Seminary; Douglas V. Steere, Professor, Haverford College; Ernest Fremont Tittle, Minister of First Methodist Church, Evanston, Illinois; Henry P. Van Dusen, Professor, Union Theological Seminary; Theodore O. Wedel, Warden, College of Preachers, Washington Cathedral; Alexander C. Zabriskie, Dean, Episcopal Theological Seminary.

[2] Bainton, Roland H., " The Churches and War: Historic Attitudes Toward Christian Participation: A Survey from Biblical Times to the Present Day," *Social Action*, XI, No. 1 (Jan. 15, 1945), 3-71.

WAR IN THE ATOMIC AGE;
"Atomic Warfare and the Christian Faith"*[1]

A Commission of Theologians, 1946

The atomic bomb gives new and fearful meaning to the age-old plight of man. His proudest powers have always been his most dangerous sources of peril, and his earthly life has been lived always under the threat of eventual extinction. Christians of earlier times have felt these truths more keenly than modern men, whose growing control over physical forces has led many of them to believe that science and technology would in time assure human safety and well-being. This hope has been dashed. Our latest epochal triumph of science and technology may prove to be our last. The scientists who know most about the nature of atomic energy have been the first to declare themselves frightened men. With admirable restraint, but with impressive urgency, they have sought to awaken both military leaders and civilians to the alarming realities which as scientists they see more clearly than laymen who lack their special knowledge. The new weapon has destroyed at one blow the familiar conceptions of national security, changed the scale of destructive conflict among peoples, and opened before us all the prospect of swift ruin for civilization and even the possibility of a speedy end to man's life on earth.

There is little doubt that as knowledge of the new weapon becomes more widespread, and the earlier talk of some technical defense against it is clearly seen to be unrealistic clutching at straws, fear of these possibilities will be shared by more citizens and statesmen. Whether universal fear, one of the most powerful of all human motives, will help to save us or to push us the more quickly to destruction depends on how it is directed. The fear of God and His laws can indeed be a source of saving wisdom, but the fear of fellowmen or life or death or any created thing can be disastrous.

---

*The use of the atomic bomb on Japanese cities in August 1945 greatly magnified the theological and ethical dilemmas of Christians facing the problems and threat of war. At the request of the Federal Council of Churches the Commission on "the relation of the Churches to the War in light of the Christian faith" resumed its deliberations and produced the following report the next year.

In particular, blind panic is premature surrender to the evil that is feared. It may result either in mental and moral paralysis, or in acts of suicidal desperation. Death is the outcome, in either case.

By contrast, a more clear-sighted fear not of dangerous forces but of unrighteous use of them or capitulation to them, and of the consequences of such violation of God's will, can lead toward a sustaining faith which misdirected panic is sure to lose. In the face of atomic bombs and radio-active gases, no less truly than in the presence of smaller perils, the rule is: Seek first the Kingdom of God, and His righteousness, as the only sure ground of ultimate security. In a continuously perilous world, as on the battlefield, brave men who refuse to make personal safety their primary goal have a safety that cowards never know. A major task of the Church in the anxious months ahead will be to demonstrate a courageous fear of God and faith in His invincible goodness, in place of either complacency or panic before the awful energies now accessible for human use. Men have found new strength and wisdom to face repeated crises in the past. It seems right to reject despair and earnestly seek such needed strength once more.

It is a fundamental Christian conviction that amid all the perils of earthly life, the Lordship of God will prevail and His purpose of judgment and mercy will not be frustrated. Moreover, it has always been in moments of supreme despair, when men have turned to God in an agony of trust, that spiritual redemptive power has been released which has changed the shadow of night into a morning of new hope. Today also the prospects of man's life on earth are intimately bound up with the measure in which, through the gospel of Jesus Christ, the worldwide expansion and integrity of the Christian Church, and the diverse workings of the Holy Spirit, the lives of men become centered in God. The reality of God-centered thought and action, which it is the supreme task of the Church to cherish, is the one hope of securing a world order in which man's release of atomic energy would be employed for human welfare and not for world suicide. To develop such world order is a task of fearful urgency for both Church and State, for Christians and non-Christians alike—a task in which we must engage with mind, heart, and strength as servants of God.

To that end, there is need first to face squarely the changes that the great discovery has made in our situation. The release of atomic energy brings new resources and a new kind of threat to civilized living. A new pattern of warfare has suddenly taken shape that may invalidate many traditional judgments about war. Certain theological problems have been set, almost overnight, in a new perspective. These changes must be examined briefly.

I. ATOMIC ENERGY AND TOTAL WAR

It is too early to weigh the possible benefits that may come to mankind from suitably controlled atomic energy; and a detailed appraisal would, in any event, be largely a task for physical scientists and engineers. Perhaps it is within proper bounds to notice that the chief benefits now regarded as immediately accessible are the opening of new avenues for research in the physical and biological sciences, and the provision of new tools for medical practice. Beyond these immediate benefits, it seems conceivable that constructive use of atomic energy could bring a more equitable distribution around the globe of labor-saving power, and the consequent freeing of additional millions of people from drudgery, with the chance for spiritual growth that is now denied to multitudes of human burden-bearers. This result would be the more likely (at the price of greatly increased peril) if ways should be found to release atomic energy from elements more plentiful and widespread than uranium. At all events, for the present it seems to be agreed that although power plants designed to utilize the heat liberated by atomic fission are not far away, the industrial benefits to be expected in the near future are pale beside the deadly threat to our tenure of life on earth.

The present fact is that neither the possible range of benefit from atomic energy nor the possible range of destruction to which we are henceforth exposed is accurately calculable. Even the physicists, chemists, and engineers who have developed the atomic bomb do not know how far the effects of a massive attack with such bombs, or with radioactive gases, might go toward making the earth uninhabitable. Some hold it theoretically possible, though highly improbable, that the entire atmosphere might be destroyed by atomic chain reactions. Somewhat greater, it would seem, is the chance that the atmosphere might be vitiated by radioactive gases, so that neither plants nor animals could live. Short of such total obliteration, we are quite certain at least that the industrial basis of civilized life is now largely at the mercy of weapons already in existence. Moreover, this threat is apparently permanent, beyond the reach of any technological defense now conceivable. As far as our best minds can see, the only promising defenses against atomic warfare are moral and political, not physical defenses. This momentous fact is fundamental in our present situation. The basis of any hope for the redemption of mankind simply through progress in the sciences and technology, always an unsound hope, has been permanently wrecked by the latest achievement in that very progress.

This judgment is underscored by the changes in the pattern of warfare as it can now be envisioned. The march toward total war, which this commission and other theologians have judged irreconcilable with Christian principles,[2] has been advanced a giant step further. For the new weapons are especially well suited to indiscriminate destruction. In purely tactical bombing of such targets as fighting ships, beach-heads, or fortifications, isolated from civilian areas, destruction might indeed be restricted to combatant units and equipment. But in the strategic bombing that has already become so large a factor in modern war, atomic weapons clearly belong with the tools for obliteration, not precision attack. A blast that incinerates four square miles of buildings at a time cannot be used to destroy a munitions plant or a railway yard and spare the city around it. Moreover, there is strong reason to expect that if another major war is fought, strategic bombing of key cities will have a still larger place from the very outset, and that rockets with atomic warheads, not piloted planes, will be the chief weapons for such attack. Since rockets and robots have even less precision than piloted bombers, whole cities and not simply factories or freight yards must be the targets, and all pretense of discrimination between military objectives and civilian homes would disappear. Even more all-inclusive would be attack with radioactive poison gases that were already known in 1940 as by-products of the work with uranium.[3] The logical end would be total war in grim truth.

THE PREMIUM UPON AGGRESSION

Further, the new weapons alter in two morally fateful ways the balance between aggressive and defensive war. If two nations are armed with atomic weapons, both the incentive to strike a crippling blow first and the possibility of doing so are incalculably increased. The first phase of a future *Blitzkrieg* would require not days but minutes, and the destruction possible in the first blow is of a different order of magnitude from anything previously know. A premium is therefore placed on swift, ruthless aggression by any power that may believe itself in danger. Moreover, wholly new advantages can now be won through successful treachery. The planting of bombs by trained saboteurs in the key cities of a non-belligerent country can lay an effective basis for blackmailing or assassinating a neighbor so reduced to helplessness before a shot is fired. Thus, practices most revolting to ordinary human beings can well become accepted tactics of the new warfare, and conscientious statesmen may feel called upon to adopt them to forestall such action by a possible enemy. Finally, the uses of atomic weapons that can now be foreseen would make war not only more destructive and treacherous, but more irresponsible than ever. On the one hand, an aggressor who first employs such weapons in massive volume will be taking action the total result of which, as already noticed, is not now foreseeable, and certainly not controllable within predetermined limits. The immediate effects of single atomic bomb explosions are indeed localized within a few square miles. But the lethal effects of radioactive poisons would be vastly wider,[4] and total destruction or vitiation of the earth's atmosphere, however unlikely, is believed to be not impossible. Where the destructive effects of a massive concentration of atomic discharges might end is, therefore in essential respects unpredictable. On the other hand, if a country were attacked with atomic bombs carried by rockets or planted by saboteurs, and attempted prompt retaliation, the reprisals might easily be directed against an offending third party, suspected but not guilty of the attack. In an atmosphere of general suspicion, atomic war would have, more than any previous form of combat, the characteristics of universal madness.

In this new perspective, both moral and theological problems raised by war assume new proportions and a new urgency. Hence, all men and Christians in particular are required to search their hearts and minds, to re-examine their principles and practices, and to seek with the greatest diligence for effective ways to abolish this diabolical horror. We can speak here only of some of the moral and social problems posed for the Church by atomic warfare: problems arising from the past and possible future uses of the new weapons, the need for international controls, and the distinctive moral and social role of the Church. We shall speak also of what seem necessary restatements of our convictions about man's part in history, God's justice and mercy, and the hope of eternal life.

II. THE PAST USE OF THE ATOMIC BOMB

We would begin with an act of contrition. As American Christians, we are deeply penitent for the irresponsible use already made of the atomic bomb. We are agreed that, whatever be one's judgment of the ethics of war in principle, the surprise bombings of Hiroshima and Nagasaki are morally indefensible. They repeated in a ghastly form the indiscriminate slaughter of non-combatants that has become familiar during World War II. They were loosed without specific warning, under conditions which virtually assured the deaths of 100,000 civilians. No word of the existence of atomic bombs was published before the actual blasting of Hiroshima. A prior demonstration on enemy soil (either in vacant territory or on a fortification) would have been quite possible and was actually suggested by a group of the scientists concerned. The proposed use of the atomic bomb was sure to affect gravely the future of mankind. Yet the peoples whose governments controlled the bomb were given no chance to weigh beforehand the moral and political consequences of its use. Nagasaki was bombed also without specific warning, after the power of the bomb had been proved but before the Japanese government and high command had been given reasonable time to reach a decision to surrender. Both bombings, moreover, must be judged to have been unnecessary for winning the war. Japan's strategic position was already hopeless, and it was virtually certain that she had not developed atomic weapons of her own.[5] Even though use of the new weapon last August may well have shortened the war, the moral cost was too high. As the power that first used the atomic bomb under these circumstances, we have sinned grievously against the laws of God and against the people of Japan. Without seeking to apportion blame among individuals, we are compelled to judge our chosen course inexcusable.

At the same time, we are agreed that these two specific bombing sorties cannot properly be treated in isolation from the whole system of obliteration attacks with explosives and fire-bombs, of which the atomic raids were the stunning climax. We are mindful of the horrors of incendiary raids on Tokyo, and of the saturation bombings of Hamburg, Dresden, and Berlin. We are mindful also that protests against these earlier obliterative methods were met chiefly by appeals to military necessity, whereas the eventual report of the Air Force's investigators has now admitted the military ineffectiveness of much of this planned destruction. All things considered, it seems necessary to include in any condemnation of indiscriminate, excessive violence not only the use of atomic bombs in August, 1945, but the policy of wholesale obliteration bombing as practiced at first by the Axis powers and then on a far greater scale by the Allies. We recognize the grievous provocation to which the Allied leaders were subjected before they adopted the policy, and the persuasiveness of wartime appeals by military leaders to the superior competence of soldiers to decide military policy. But we have never agreed that a policy affecting the present well-being of millions of non-combatants and the future relationships of whole peoples should be decided finally on military grounds, and we believe the right to criticize military policies on ethical grounds is freshly justified by the proved fallibility of competent professional soldiers in dealing with such problems in this war. In the light of present knowledge, we are prepared to affirm that the policy of obliteration bombing as actually practiced in World War II, culminating in the use of atomic bombs against Japan, is not defensible on Christian premises.[6]

III. POLICIES TO PREVENT ATOMIC WAR

We are agreed, further, on four major theses respecting future policy with regard to atomic warfare and other new methods of effecting mass destruction. First, these methods, more than the simpler combatant techniques of the past, lend themselves to belligerent practices that are intolerable to Christian conscience. They make it harder than ever before to give real effect to the traditional distinctions between combatants and non-combatants among the enemy, and between proportionate and excessive violence in conduct of the war. They tend to unlimited, indiscriminate destruction. They increase appallingly the problems of the aftermath of war, because indiscriminate destruction wrecks not only the military potential of the enemy but also his civil institutions, upon which depend the reestablishment and maintenance of social order. Hence, it is more than ever incumbent upon Christians to resist the development of situations in which these methods are likely to be employed.

Secondly, the only mode of control that holds much promise is control directed to the prevention of war. We recognize the probable futility, in practice, of measures to outlaw atomic weapons while war itself continues. Use of the newer weapons might indeed be temporarily restrained, on the part of some belligerents by concern for humanity, on the part of others by fear of retaliation. But experience indicates that in a struggle for survival one side or the other will resort to whatever weapons promise victory, and its opponent will feel constrained to adopt counter-measures in kind. War itself must go.

Thirdly, in pursuit of this aim, we believe the Churches should call upon the government of the United States, as present holder of existing atomic bombs and plants for producing them, to move more swiftly toward allaying distrust respecting their possible use. Such distrust on the part of former enemies, neutrals, and even allies of this country seems to us understandable under present conditions. At the same time its existence is a barrier to international good will, and a possible cause of future conflict. We therefore call upon the Churches to urge, first, that all manufacture of atomic bombs be stopped, pending the development of effective international controls. We urge, secondly, that the Churches call upon the government of the United States to affirm publicly, with suitable guaranties, that it will under no circumstances be the first to use atomic weapons in any possible future war. Such measures are to be thought of not as adequate means of control but as aids to the development of a better state of international confidence, in which effective measures for the prevention of war may the more readily be worked out.

For we believe, fourthly, that the only conceivable road toward effective control of atomic warfare and other forms of mass destruction is the road of international comity and joint effort. Whatever be one's judgment respecting the pattern of future world society, it is clear that the war-making powers of national states must be given up, and the maintenance of justice and peace among nations become an international responsibility. In the present situation, we are agreed that progress toward this end may best follow two lines: the adoption of such political measures as may strengthen and improve the existing United Nations Organization, and unceasing effort to further the growth of spiritual world community.

COOPERATION FOR INTERNATIONAL CONTROL

As to the former line of action, we are not competent to prescribe a political structure for international dealing with these problems. We are agreed, however, on two major propositions. First, exclusive trust in a political structure of any sort to solve the problems posed by atomic warfare would be a dangerous illusion. In particular, the hope for world government, useful as a guiding principle, cannot be turned into a program for immediate action without very serious confusion of aim. Although improvement of the United Nations Organization is imperative, world government in any literal sense of the term is not yet attainable, and rigid insistence on full world government now is in effect a vote for continued international anarchy. It might even tend to widen, not lessen, the distances among the Great Powers. Moreover, if world government could be imposed now, it would have to be by the overwhelming force wielded by a few powers in concert, and such forced rule would gravely imperil essential human liberty and growth. It is better to start with the imperfect accomplishments and promises of the provisional forms of cooperation that have actually begun to take shape, and earnestly to seek their improvement. For such improvement, the ideal of world government may indeed provide valuable guidance, to the end that as rapidly as possible reliance on force shall give place to reliance on common agreement and a growing body of law.

Secondly, international provision for the control of atomic research and its application to the problems of peace and war, should fulfill certain elementary conditions. Ultimate control should be assigned to civilian, not military agencies. The development and use of atomic energies should be steadily held in the perspective of concern for the enhancement of human welfare, and both promotion and restrictions should be directed to that end. A major concern of the supervising agencies must be to assure a wide and equitable distribution of whatever economic benefits may result from the use of atomic energy, and to prevent monopolistic exploitation by cartels or other minority groups. The policies of supervision and control, moreover, should be calculated to safeguard intellectual freedom, both among responsible scientists of all nations, and, as far as technical difficulties permit, among the peoples whose welfare is at stake. We can see only harm in a policy of attempted monopoly of either scientific research or political information by either national or international agencies. The only atmosphere in which growing rivalry and suspicion cannot thrive is an atmosphere of free and cooperative enterprise.

GROWTH OF SPIRITUAL WORLD COMMUNITY

These demands for attention to the general welfare suggest the need that political and technical measures be sustained, directed, and inspired by the development of spiritual world community. We know how vague and empty this term may seem, to many readers, without detailed elaboration for which there is no room here. We recognize also that the essential nature and basis of community call for much more profound study. Here we may note four requirements for such a spiritual common life as the welfare of the peoples urgently demands. There must be established, in the midst of hostility and suspicion, a basis for mutual confidence. There must be evoked in every people a deep humility before God and men, a genuine readiness to acknowledge present faults and to learn better ways, a habit of self-criticism and of self-restraint toward others. There must be encouraged and increasingly satisfied a hunger and thirst after truth: the truth about men, their needs, shortcomings, common hopes, the truth about the world in which and with which they must live, the truth about God as the Beginning and the End of all human life. There must be made known, by word and deed, the sure ground of hope that Christians find in the God and Father of our Lord Jesus Christ. Only when the profound kinship of common need, quest, achievement, failure and hope becomes a living groundwork of men's efforts to achieve a world order can such efforts endure the strain of repeated disappointment. The more fully we recognize that other men have the same needs, the same fears, the same weaknesses as we, the better we shall understand our common failures and the more patiently we shall seek to help one another rise above them.

IV. THE DISTINCTIVE ROLE OF THE CHURCH

The moral and social role of the Church in world affairs clearly is to help this spirit grow. This is not a political task. In essence it is a work of reconciliation among men, carried on in the spirit of Jesus Christ, in dependence on the power of God—a work that no political agency, partisan by its very nature, can perform as well. Precisely because the Church is ecumenical and supra-national in its being, worldwide in its membership and mission, it can speak directly to men and women of any nation in the name of one divine Father and one universal humanity.

Its first word in our present situation must be a call to active penitence, addressed to friends and former enemies as alike. There is no useful place among us for sentimental self-accusation. But there is acute need for such humility as not many among victors or vanquished have yet shown: the humility of clear-headed, honest men who see how grievously they have squandered resources inherited from a long, laborious past and jeopardized what should have been a more enlightened future. We shall not rehearse here the sorry record of sin and misery of the years just ended. But we must note with urgent concern the continuing abuses of power by the victorious great nations and the demonstrations of irresponsibility among both conquerors and conquered. That such faults are natural after an exhausting war is obvious. That they are excusable, not to say negligible, on that account is untrue. They call for genuine, effective repentance, in which Christians ought to take the lead.

The most appropriate and convincing expression of such repentance must be determined resistance to public policies of the victors that seek to cripple former enemy powers. Military disarmament, as competent critics have insisted, is not the same as economic dismemberment. Destruction of the industrial basis of German and Japanese livelihood, already far advanced by strategic bombing and other military action, cannot now be completed on political grounds without adding heavily to the injustice already committed in the name of the Allied peoples. Against such compounding of injustice the Church must steadily protest, in the name of God and of the common sonship of all men.

Within the setting of Christian resistance to unjust public policies, there is need also for continual urging of more active provision for relief and rebuilding of devastated lands. Plainly the largest part of this load must be carried by governments, but the Christian Churches have a special duty to urge upon their members, their neighbors, and all appropriate public agencies the honoring of our obligations as victors. This is not optional generosity but plain justice. If it is right that aggressors be held to account for reparations, then it is only right that we make some specific amends for damage that has resulted from our wanton acts of destruction. We are well aware that to some of our fellow Americans, the matter appears very differently, and that any curtailment of the plenty to which we are accustomed is looked upon with resentment, even if it be for the benefit of needy or starving allies. Such callousness we are bound to view with shame. It is unwelcome further evidence of our corporate failure in human understanding or decency, and of our deep need for repentance.

We are well aware also of the inadequacy and the dangers of proposing specific acts of restitution: the inadequacy of singling out a few victims from among millions, the dangers of displaying in that way complacency, hypocrisy, or misunderstanding. To rebuild Hiroshima and Nagasaki, the victims of our most spectacular offenses, would be to restore only a small fraction of what our strategic bombings needlessly destroyed. To provide special aid for the survivors of those two murdered cities would be hardly more than a token of repentance. Yet we believe either would have lasting value for future human relations. The former task would require public funds or a large popular subscription. The latter could be undertaken by the Churches of the United States, and we hope that at least so much may be done. We do not forget that the fire-bombing of Tokyo and the area bombing in Germany entailed a greater mass of suffering, and we have no thought of suggesting that token reparations now can overbalance the harm done by excessive violence in wartime. Whatever we can do will be at best a belated effort to make some amends for past failure. All of us are too deeply in debt to appear as simple benefactors. A more realistic view of our role is essential to the growth of healthy community life. But even a small effort to right injustice, if the effort be sincere, can have reconciling value far beyond its intrinsic weight. Our refusal to accept a share of the Boxer indemnity has had that effect. Relief or remembrance for the first victims of atomic warfare might be misunderstood, or might be cherished as long as men remember the first atomic bomb.

One other task the Church has been performing throughout the war. It has maintained fellowship among Christians on both sides of the fighting lines, and around the globe. Now that the shooting has stopped, the evidence of persisting unbroken relationships within the Church is accumulating steadily. There have been, of course, large and painful losses, and these must as far as possible be made good through patient knitting up of broken threads, reestablishment of understanding and confidence, shared worship, and initiation of new common tasks. It is too early to judge how well the Church's ecumenical fellowship has come through the storm.

It may prove to be in better case than anyone dared hope. And if that be so, Christians will give thanks first to God, who is not helpless in the presence of human strife.

V. ULTIMATE PROBLEMS FOR FAITH

To speak thus of God is to raise the final group of questions we have had to reconsider in relation to the new warfare: questions of Christian faith, which is the Church's ultimate recourse in times of extreme pressure. First, we have had to recognize important new light on man's part in history. The release and utilization of atomic energy has given a quite fresh view of the scope of the effects that may result from his freedom. For on the one hand it would appear that by suitable directing of this new resource, man may be able to prolong the period during which the earth will sustain human life. If this be so, if man can actually extend earthly history beyond its natural term, then he can, in principle, transcend natural limits more fundamental and significant than any physical barrier he has hitherto surmounted. On the other hand, it seems at least as likely that by misdirection of atomic energy, man can bring earthly history to a premature close. His freedom, then, is more decisive and dangerous than we had suspected. In making man a little lower than the angels, God seemingly has laid on him a weight of responsibility that has not only personal but cosmic import.

This startling disclosure of the true dimensions of man's freedom raises again, in new perspective, the question of God's power, justice and mercy. We have held steadily that all these aspects of God's sovereignty are discernible in war as well as in peace. We reaffirm that view here, with a somewhat wider frame of reference to match the wider scope that now seems ascribable to human freedom. We believe in God still as Creator and Sovereign of heaven and earth. We believe also that His judgment and His mercy are present inseparably in every moment of history. But our conceptions of divine judgment and mercy in history need to be carried a step further. Divine justice and judgment, we still believe, are to be seen in the steady maintenance of a natural and moral order such that men can live and thrive in it only on condition that they yield to it an adequate measure of voluntary obedience, as well as a great hidden body of unconscious adaptations. This order, with the obligations it entails for man, stands fast in peace and in war. If man should violate its demands so grievously as to destroy civilization or even to extinguish all earthly life, the inexorable justice of God would thus be vindicated, not impugned.

For divine justice is not the "distributive" or "retributive" justice of a human law-court, balancing claims and counterclaims, but primarily the unswerving maintenance of natural and moral law for mankind and the world as a whole. This, we believe, is the necessary basis of human learning and moral betterment. As such, it is intended as a manifestation also of divine mercy, which we believe is not to be separated, in the purpose of God, from divine judgment. Suppose then that in a sudden tempest of atomic warfare human civilization or even all earthly human life were extinguished, by the acts of some men. The fatal decisions would be human decisions, not divine fiats. In as far as divine justice contributed to the outcome, it would be through the active preservation of dependable order. Nothing else than this could be regarded as consistent with the dependability of God. But the persons thus suddenly ending their lives on earth would come to the end of very different roles, some as active aggressors, and others as relatively innocent victims. This contrast is always present in massive man-made disasters, and poses in itself no new problem. But the inclusiveness and finality of a possible global annihilation puts the old problem with fresh urgency. How, in the face of such a cataclysm, is the mercy of God—nay, even the justice of God, in any personal sense—to be seen?

THE JUSTICE AND MERCY OF GOD

First of all, it must be remembered that the possible cataclysm is foreseeable, and such foresight can help to prevent the end from coming to pass. Such annihilation is possible only because of extraordinary gifts granted to man. Even if these gifts should be perverted, it is still right to recognize divine bounty in the grant itself, and in the opportunity to turn the gifts to good account rather than ill. Secondly, the saving power of God is such that from otherwise desperate situations in the past—the crucifixion of Jesus Christ and the scattering of his disciples, the persecution of the early Church, the submergence of the Roman Empire in a flood of barbarism—new life has been called forth. It is essential to remember that the new peril we confront today is not the impersonal closing down of an Age of Ice but a possible man-made disaster that will come, if at all, because of specific human decisions. These fateful decisions in turn will be made, if at all, because of underlying attitudes of fear, vengefulness, pride, or rashness. We know that the one good ground for hope that such human attitudes may be profoundly changed is the redemptive activity of God, and we are confident that as long as human life on earth goes on, there will be clear signs that His providence is steadily at work to change men's hearts and win them back from the edge of impending ruin. Finally, men of faith will find, even as time grows short, that strength is given them to live without panic—nay more, with quickened force and earnestness. In a word, until the possible disaster actually occurs, there is no great difficulty in seeing divine favor as well as divine rigor in our new situation.

If, in spite of all, through human malice or blundering a worldwide disaster should come, there is at least a fair chance that not all human life on earth would be destroyed. Urban civilization, dependent on heavy industry and on complex networks of communication and transport, would almost certainly be ended for a long time. The greater part of any survivors would most probably be agricultural or nomadic people in out-of-the-way places, who might not even know that a catastrophe had occurred. They could not, with straining terms, be regarded as a "faithful remnant," saved by reason of obedience to God, even though civilization were thought of as destroyed because of fatal disobedience. They would be ignorant rather than obedient. Yet there is no reason to doubt that God could make them also become great peoples, and bring to realization through them new stretches of history, perhaps new levels of spiritual community.

At any rate, there is no need to question whether, as long as man's life of earth continues, the justice and mercy of God surround him and can sustain him. We confidently affirm again that they do. But if a premature end of history should come, then plainly the nature of the problem posed is different. The problem then is whether beyond the end of history God's justice and mercy are still a ground for hope, or whether the stultification of human life by a premature end is to be feared.

To this final question we can answer partly in terms of experience, partly in terms of our Christian faith and hope. First of all, even while earthly life lasts, men by God's grace rise above it in many ways: in devotion to truth and honor, in love for God and neighbor, in self-sacrifice, in martyrdom, even in Christlike life. Thus they achieve a dimension of living that is different in kind from sensation, natural impulse, and prudential selfinterest. Such living is not stultified even if—as in martyrdom—it comes prematurely to a close. The quality of life so attained has become, we believe. a permanent gain, not subject to destruction by passage of time. This is true, secondly, because God lives and holds in eternal presence the life of His children in time. His creating and redeeming work will not end even if the earth be destroyed, and whatever men have done, whatever of human existence has been good, He will cherish forever. Finally, it is a part of our Christian faith that not only the high moments of men's lives but their very existence and fellowship as personal selves is safe in God's hands; that death is swallowed up in the victory we call resurrection, so that death is not the last word. How such triumph over death is best to be conceived, we do not know. No more than we can define or picture the being of God are we able to picture what He has in store for us. But we are confident that in it lies the answer to the final question concerning His justice and mercy. We trust in God, and look toward the future with sure hope.

---

[1]In the note accompanying the published report the officers of the Federal Council point out that the document "Was not intended to be adopted by the Council and was therefore not considered for adoption. Its publication is authorized as an expression of the opinion of the signers." The report was published in March, 1946.

[2]See Appendix B: "The Relation of the Church to the War in the Light of the Christian Faith"; *Cf.* also John C. Ford, S. J., "The Morality of Obliteration Bombing," *Theological Studies*, V, 261-309.

[3]H. D. Smyth: *Atomic Energy for Military Purposes* (1945), 2.32, 4.26-4.28, 4.48. *Cf. Science News Letter*, 48:121 (Aug. 25, 1945).

[4]Professor M. L. E. Oliphant, leader of the British physicists in the joint research program, is represented as declaring that a single gas attack with these poisons would destroy life over an area 1000 miles in radius. *Cf. The Christian Century*, 62:1341 (Dec. 5, 1945).

[5]Smyth, *op. cit.*, 13.3.

[6]Some who concur in the foregoing judgment find their grounds primarily in the circumstances under which particular raids were carried out rather than in the practice of obliteration bombing or in the nature of the weapons employed. They agree that what has been done is wrong, and that it would be wrong for any nation in the future to take the initiative in using such measures for its own advantage; but they believe the way should be left open to regard the use of atomic weapons under some circumstances as right. For they believe that in the present state of human relations, if plans for international control of aggression should fail, the only effective restraint upon would-be aggressors might be fear of reprisals, and that this possible restraint should not be removed in advance. Others hold that even if belligerent action be regarded as, in extreme circumstances, unavoidable and justifiable, obliteration bombing and the atomic bomb as utilized for that purpose cannot be justified. Still others hold that the atomic bomb has revealed the impossibility of a just war, and has shown the necessity for repudiation of all support of war by the Church. They judge that since in fact belligerent powers are virtually certain to use any means that seems needed to insure victory, condemnation of obliterative bombing or of surprise attack with atomic weapons entails condemnation of all war.

APPENDIX D

WEAPONS OF MASS DESTRUCTION
"The Christian Conscience and Weapons of Mass Destruction"*

Report of a Special Commission, 1950

We are a company of Christians called upon to look with open eyes at our human situation and at the powers of mass destruction now available to our nation and to other nations. We are asked to seek under God for a Christian word that might guide or strengthen our fellow Christians and our fellow men in the darkness we face together.

We are Christians who are also citizens of the United States. We cannot and would not escape from the responsibilities and the limitations of this destiny which we accept as God's purpose for us. Of necessity we must look out upon our world from where we stand. We cannot see with the eyes of Chinese men or men of India or men of Europe or of Russia. At the same time, we are called to lift up our eyes and try to see ourselves and our world in the light that comes from Him who hath made of one blood all nations of men to dwell on the face of the whole earth. And by His commandment of love we are called to identify ourselves with men of other lands in order that we may in some measure see through the eyes of those others. We are grateful for the growing opportunity which membership in the United Nations gives us as a nation, to act with other nations in the service of general human welfare and in the promotion of international justice and order. As Christians, we are grateful that we are helped by the world-wide Christian fellowship to look beyond ourselves, however imperfectly.

When we look out upon our world we see an ugly and unclean thing hanging over all the brightness and the good and even the shared sorrows

---

*The following is the report of a special commission appointed by the Federal Council of Churches in March 1950 to study the moral problems confronting the Christian conscience as a result of the increasing availability and use of military weapons of mass destruction. Statements from two of the 19 members of the commission who dissented from the report are also included.

and shared failures that make precious our human existence. It is not Christians alone or Americans alone who see this darkness or whose lives and homes and children and cities and laboriously built structures of common life are threatened by it. It is mankind that lives under this cloud. We Americans think in dread of what could happen tomorrow or five years from now to Chicago or New York or Washington. Frenchmen think of what could happen to Paris; Englishmen of what could happen to London; Russians of what could happen to Moscow.

Because in our human wrongness we are self-centered, we think first and most often of what others might do to us and ours. And so it is with those others. Some of them think first and most often of what we might do to them. But as Christians we are compelled to think of what we might do or have done or even now are doing to others. For we cannot get out from under that commandment, "Thou shalt care for those others as thou carest for thyself."

THE NEW DIMENSIONS OF WAR

This ugly thing, which we call war, hanging over our common humanity, is not something new. Through all man's tragic history he has suffered locally and periodically from war, family feuds, tribal wars, civil wars, religious wars, international wars. In Korea, as we have wrestled with this report, there have been fighting men and helpless, driven people whose whole existence has been flattened into shapelessness by a conflict to which we are parties. But the dimensions of the evil in any major conflict are now so heightened as to face us with something new.

It is as though the One who said to us, "They that take the sword shall perish by the sword," were pointing with inexorable logic to a Dead End towards which man's way of violence leads. Each stepping up of the powers of violence calls out more demonic ingenuity in matching destructive power with destructive power. Resistance to the use of more brutal weapons is broken through in a struggle for existence that at last threatens all existence. The means we have found of blowing up whole cities reveal mankind as in an inescapable community of danger and fear. The only real escape from these evils of war is the prevention of war.

Serious Christians of every name now see in war a grievous disclosure of man's lostness and wrongness. War destroys what God creates. It hurts those whom Christ came to heal. It mocks the love of God and His commandment of love. It is the stark opposite of the way of reconciliation. It breeds hatred and deception and cruelty.

Even in the face of that judgment we have to recognize that the overwhelming majority of Christians, after the earliest days when the Christian community was a little persecuted minority in a pagan society, without political responsibilities, have held that there are times when Christians should take the sword and fight as very imperfect servants of God's justice.

They have acknowledged their responsibilities not only for peace within the Church, where the persuasions of love are most readily effective, but also for the maintenance of order and justice in civil society. There they have recognized the tragic necessity for coercive restraints on "the unruly wills and affections of sinful men," including their own. They have fought for what they believed was justice or good order or freedom, and against wanton aggression or enslavement. Often they have been swept heedlessly into the conflicts of the nations of which they were a part. The best among them have, like Abraham Lincoln, held fast to a recognition that God's justice and mercy stand high above all our human warfare; they have sought to show mercy even in conflict; and they have pressed for the speediest possible reconciliation when actual warfare ended.

Faced with the terrible ambiguities and compromises of fighting to serve even in so crude and soiled a way the more elementary demands of God's justice, sensitive Christians have sought to bring war itself under some restraints. In this they have certainly been joined by other men of good will. They have struggled to reduce or eliminate the savagery and sheer sadism that are set free by the madness of war. They have condemned the killing of prisoners and of hostages or the use of torture to gain military information. They have condemned the massacre of civilian populations, especially of women and children and the bombardment of "undefended" towns. They have sought to bring the radical lawlessness of war under some law.

Plainly what we now face in war and the threat of war and our involvement in it is an overwhelming break-through in the weak moral defenses erected to keep war in some bounds. At no point is this break-through more evident than in the widespread acceptance of the bombing of cities as an inescapable part of modern war. The industrial and technical potential of strong nations is now concentrated in cities. Their factories and power plants and fuel stores and transportation centers are their arsenals of war. It is forcefully argued that to destroy or cripple them by tons of "conventional" bombs or by raining fire upon them or by one atomic bomb is to strike at their fighting power as surely as to destroy an army or a fleet or an air force. In the harsh light of history, the best hope of preventing a global atomic war lies in preventing the recurrence of global war itself.

If global war comes, and with it a resort to still more powerful means of obliteration bombing, all of us will be caught up in it, men, women and children, believers and unbelievers, soldiers and civilians. Even those in the hills and on the plains may be drafted into it. In all soberness this is the grim possibility that hangs over us in rough proportion to the power and privilege of the people to which we belong. The safest places to be, as far as this threat is concerned, are the "backward" parts of the "backward" continents. It could well be that "the meek" will inherit the earth in an unexpected sense.

It is in this time and situation that we who profess and call ourselves Christians must make our decisions, for ourselves and as Churches, and that our nations and those who govern must make their decisions. And those of us who are Church people cannot divorce ourselves from those who carry for us the heavy burdens of political and military decisions.

I. WAR AND WEAPONS OF MASS DESTRUCTION

What are the decisions open to us?

The clearest and least ambiguous alternative is that urged upon us by our most uncompromising pacifist fellow-Christians. They believe that the refusal of all kinds of military service and an unqualified witness against war and for peace is for them the will of God. They would summon all Christian people and all Churches to unite with them in their witness. For them the infinitely heightened destructiveness and the morally catastrophic character of modern war confirm their conviction that followers of Christ can make no compromise with so great an evil. They find themselves called to follow the way of love and reconciliation at whatever cost and to accept the historical consequences of a repudiation of armaments and of war. For those who make this radical decision need for debate as to the choice of weapons is ruled out by a repudiation of all weapons.

Pacifist and non-pacifist Christians can probably agree that, as men are, responsible political leaders could not take the pacifist position and continue to hold positions of effective political leadership. But that fact does not relieve those of us who are Christians from making our own decisions in the sight of God and urging what we believe to be right Christian decisions on those who govern as our representatives.

The large majority of professing Christians are not pacifists. But Christian non-pacifists share with their pacifist brethren abhorrence of war and with them see in it a sign of man's Godlessness. They agree that in all human conflicts the most righteous side is never so righteous as it thinks it is. They acknowledge that whatever good may ever come out of war, incalculable evil always comes out of it, too. We believe that God calls some men to take the way of nonviolence as a special and high vocation in order to give a clearer witness to the way of love than those can give who accept responsibility for the coercions in civil society. We rejoice that God has called some of our brethren in the universal Christian fellowship to bear this witness and are humbled by the faithfulness of many in bearing it. Without minimizing the moral heroism it can require, we are even envious of the greater inner simplicity of that non-violent way.

But most of us find ourselves called to follow a course which is less simple and which appears to us more responsible because more directly relevant to the hard realities of our situation. And we believe it is the way in which most Christians must go.

There can be no justice for men and no responsible freedom without law and order. When men confront one another with their contending egotisms, without moral or spiritual bonds, they take the law into their own hands and work what is at best a very crude justice. They reach beyond that only when they have achieved some substantial moral community and a sovereign law rooted in moral community. This we have reached, however imperfectly, where we find ordered society. Even then the law which gives any just order must be sustained by power, and, when necessary, by coercive power.

The world we live in, the world of states and of great masses of men struggling up towards nationhood, is without strong uniting moral or spiritual bonds. It possesses no overruling law and in the United Nations an institution which marks only the beginnings of common order. In large measure our world is a "frontier" of self-regarding, mutually distrustful human masses. God's will for justice and for mercy broods over this disorder in which we find ourselves. We Christians believe that we are called to be the servants of His justice and His mercy. But can we be just to men if we do not struggle to maintain for them and for ourselves some order of justice in which good faith and freedom and truth can find a dwelling place? And can we extend the beginnings of this order in the United Nations, if we do not undergird it with effective power?

So most Christians, faced with the lawlessness of our world of nations, see no way of serving the righteousness of God in the presence of brutal and irresponsible violence save by taking responsible collective action against aggression within the framework of the United Nations. That we must do in fear and trembling, as those who know how our own self-interest blinds us. We must take upon ourselves the dreadful responsibilities of conflict, if we are to accept even the imperfect justice and freedom which others have painfully won and for which others fight and die even now. In the last resort we are in conscience bound to turn to force in defense of justice even though we know that the destruction of human life is evil. There are times when this can be the lesser of two evils, forced upon us by our common human failure to achieve a better relationship.

The deep disorder within men and among men, which Christian faith calls sin, leads to both brutal dominion and conflict. Today, two great dangers threaten mankind, the danger that totalitarian tyranny may be extended over the world and the danger of global war. Many of us believe that the policies most likely to avoid both dangers inevitably carry the risk of war.

Does this mean that for those who take this position the love of God and the judgments of God and the commandments of God cease to have meaning? We know that Christ died for our enemies as well as for us. We know that we are bidden to pray for our enemies as for ourselves. We know that we stand with them in need of forgiveness. We know that our failures to find another way of dealing with our deep differences and conflicts of interest and distrust of one another is a judgment on us and our forefathers as well as on them. But this does not extricate us from the hard realities of our situation.

We cannot lightly assume that a victory for our own nation, or a victory for the United Nations, is in itself a victory for God and His righteousness. Even in war we cannot rejoice that more of the enemy are killed than of our own people. Even in victory we can rejoice only if, from the sacrifices of so much life, some little gain is made for order and freedom, and renewed opportunity is found for mercy and reconciliation.

CONCEPTS OF TOTAL WAR

Christians who have decided that in the last resort they may be compelled to accept the terrible responsibilities of warfare are now confronted with these questions: Does that mean warfare without any limits? Does that mean warfare with any weapons which man's ingenuity can provide?

War has developed rapidly in the direction of "total war" in two meanings, which it is important to distinguish.

In the first meaning total war refers to the fact that in a conflict between highly industrialized nations all human and material resources are mobilized for war purposes. The traditional distinction between combatants and non-combatants is far less clear. Only small children and the helpless sick and aged stand outside the war effort. It is practically impossible to distinguish between guilty and innocent. Certainly men who are drafted into uniform may be among the least guilty. Total war, in this sense of the involvement of the whole nation in it, cannot be avoided if we have a major war at all.

Total war, in the second sense, means war in which all moral restraints are thrown aside and all the purposes of the community are fully controlled by sheer military expediency. We must recognize that the greater the threat to national existence the greater will be the temptation to subordinate everything, all civil rights, the liberty of conscience, all moral judgments regarding the means to be used, and all consideration of postwar international relations, to the single aim of military victory.

Christians and Christian Churches, if they admit that occasions can arise when the use of military force by a nation or a group of nations may be less evil than surrender to some malignant power, cannot deny that total war in the first sense may be inescapable.

But Christians and Christian Churches can never consent to total war in the second sense. The only possible justification for war is that it offers a possibility of achieving a moral result, however imperfect, to prevent an overwhelming moral evil and to offer a new opportunity for men to live in freedom and decency and in just and merciful relationships.

Christians certainly, and humane men of any faith, if they find themselves driven to hurt, will hurt as little and as few as possible; and if they find themselves driven to kill, will seek to restrict killing within the harsh necessities determined by their total goals, military, political, and moral. Military victory is not an end in itself. Just as death is preferable to life under some conditions, so, too, victory at any price is not worth having. If this price is for us to become utterly brutal, victory becomes a moral defeat. Victory is worth having only if it leaves us with enough reserves of decency, justice and mercy to build a better world and only if it leaves those we have conquered in a condition in which they can ultimately cooperate in the task of setting forward God's purpose in creation. Hence the way we fight and the means we use are of crucial importance. And these will be determined by the spirit in which we fight and the purposes for which we fight. Military expediency, therefore, cannot be the sole test, but must be subordinated to moral and political considerations.

Any people who in savagery of war kill and destroy without reckoning will stand under the condemnation of our common humanity and surely under the condemnation of God. The concept of "atrocities" does not lose its meaning, merely because all war is brutal. Torture and killing of prisoners is more inhuman than wounding and killing in combat. The fact that industrial workers and women and children live in the areas surrounding major industrial plants compels us to reckon with the death and maiming involved for them in striking at industrial targets. And we cannot forget that the destruction of the industrial fabric of a human community can make almost impossible the recovery of decent and ordered existence, after victory in a military sense has been won.

THE WEAPONS OF MASS DESTRUCTION

What then of the weapons we shall or shall not be prepared to use?

Can we find some absolute line we can draw? Can we say that Christians can approve of using swords and spears, but not guns; conventional bombs or jellied fire, but not atomic bombs; uranium bombs, but not hydrogen bombs? Can we say that Christians must pledge themselves or seek to pledge their nations not to stock this or that weapon, even though the enemy stocks them; or not to use some weapons, even though the enemy uses them?

We find no "clean" methods of fighting, but some methods are dirtier than others. Some cause more pain and maiming without commensurate military decisiveness. Some are more indiscriminate.

We have no more—nor any less—right to kill with a rifle or a bazooka than with an A-bomb or an H-bomb. In the sight of Him, "to whom all hearts are open," the inner quality of an act is to be distinguished from its consequences. There may be more hatred and less penitence in the heart of a man who kills one enemy with a rifle, or in the heart of a frenzied super-patriot in his arm chair, than in the heart of an airman who devastates a city with a bomb. Sin in its inward meaning cannot be measured by the number of people who are affected. But a reckoning of consequences is also a part of a Christian's decision. It is more dreadful to kill a thousand men than one man, even if both are done in the service of justice and order. We cannot, therefore, be released from the responsibility for doing no more hurt than must be.

Here a distinction can be drawn between precision weapons, which can be directed with reasonable control at primary military objectives, and weapons of mass destruction. But we are compelled to recognize that the increasing distance from which bombs or projectiles are released and the speed of planes and guided missiles are likely to offset all gains in precision. If, as we have felt bound to acknowledge, certain key industrial targets are inescapably involved in modern war, we find no moral distinction between destroying them by tons of T.N.T. or by fire as compared with an atomic bomb, save as greater precision is possible in one as compared with others. But this recognition that we cannot isolate the atomic bomb or even the projected H-bomb as belonging to an absolutely different moral category must not blind us to the terrible dimensions of the moral problem they present.

With a single atomic bomb, destruction is produced that is as great as that from a large fleet of airplanes dropping conventional explosives. If the H-bomb is made, it will be destructive on a still more horrible scale. If such weapons are used generally upon centers of population, we may doubt whether enough will remain to rebuild decent human society.

But the abandonment of atomic weapons would not eliminate mass destruction. Conventional or new weapons may produce comparable destruction. The real moral line between what may be done and what may not be done by the Christian lies not in the realm of the distinction between weapons but in the realm of the motives for using and the consequences of using all kinds of weapons. Some measures corrupt the users, and destroy the humanity of the victims. Some may further the victory but impair the peace. There are certainly things which Christians should not do to save self, or family, or nation, or free civilization. There seems to us, however, no certain way to draw this moral line in advance, apart from all the actual circumstances. What may or may not be done under God can be known only in relation to the whole, concrete situation by those responsibly involved in it. We can find no moral security, or moral hiding place, in legalistic definitions. The terrible burden of decision is the Christian man's responsibility, standing where he does before God.

Nevertheless, real distinctions can be made to illumine and help the conscience in its trouble. The destruction of life clearly incidental to the destruction of decisive military objectives, for example, is radically different from mass destruction which is aimed primarily at the lives of civilians, their morale, or the sources of their livelihood. In the event of war,

Christian conscience guides us to restraint from destruction not essential to our total objectives, to a continual weighing of the human values that may be won against those lost in the fighting, and to the avoidance of needless human suffering.

Unhappily we see little hope at this time of a trustworthy international agreement that would effectively prevent the manufacture or use of weapons of mass destruction by any nation. This should not deter us from the search for such an agreement, perhaps as a part of a general disarmament program, and for a restoration of mutual confidence that would make an agreement possible and effective.

As long as the existing situation holds, for the United States to abandon its atomic weapons, or to give the impression that they would not be used, would leave the noncommunist world with totally inadequate defense. For Christians to advocate such a policy would be for them to share responsibility for the worldwide tyranny that might result. We believe that American military strength, which must include atomic weapons as long as any other nation may possess them, is an essential factor in the possibility of preventing both world war and tyranny. If atomic weapons or other weapons of parallel destructiveness are used against us or our friends in Europe or Asia, we believe that it could be justifiable for our government to use them with all possible restraint to prevent the triumph of an aggressor. We come to this conclusion with troubled spirits but any other conclusion would leave our own people and the people of other nations open to continuing devastating attack and to probable defeat. Even if as individuals we would choose rather to be destroyed than to destroy in such measure, we do not believe it would be right for us to urge policies on our government which would expose others to such a fate.

Having taken the position that no absolute line can be drawn we are especially concerned to emphasize checks on every step towards the increased destructiveness of war.

To engage in reckless and uncontrolled violence against the people of any other nation is to reduce the possibilities of peace and justice and freedom after the war's end and even to destroy the foundation of ordered society. Military judgment must not yield to the vengefulness that too often possesses civilians in wartime; nor must the national government yield to the military its own responsibility for the immediate and the postwar consequences of the conduct of the war.

We have recognized that indiscriminate mass destruction may be caused by atomic bombs or by a fleet of armored tanks or by a ruthless army laying waste cities and countryside. We have found no moral distinction between these instruments of warfare, apart from the ends they serve and the consequences of their use. We would, however, call attention to the fact that the first use of atomic weapons in another war, even if limited to sharply defined military targets, would open the way for their use in retaliation. Because of the very power of these weapons, it would be difficult to prevent their use from extending to military targets that would involve also the destruction of noncombatants on a massive scale. If the United States should use atomic weapons, it would expose its allies to similar attack. The nation that uses atomic weapons first, therefore, bears a special burden of responsibility for the almost inevitable development of extensive mass destruction with all its desolation and horror.

Even more fundamental, the dreadful prospect of devastation that must result from any major war illuminates with special clarity the immorality of those in any country who initiate an aggression against which the only effective means of defense may be the resort to atomic weapons, and which may thus be expected to lead to an atomic war. If general war comes it will probably be a war for survival, not only for the survival of a free civilization, but for the physical survival of peoples. In such a war the temptation will be tremendous to forget all other considerations and to use every available means of destruction. If this happens, physical survival may be bought at the price of the nation's soul, of the moral values which make the civilization worth saving.

II. PEACE AND A POSITIVE STRATEGY

Just because the choices open to us on the plane of war appear so tragic and offer so little hope, we are firmly convinced that the way out of our darkness must be sought, not *primarily* by limiting some one or other weapon, but on the political and moral plane. The weapons already in our hands and in the hands of others heighten immeasurably our fear and distrust and grievously complicate our political problem. But war itself and the malignant sickness of our human relationships are at the center of our trouble.

By dread of the death that threatens us and ours, and equally our fellows in other lands; even more, by dread of the moral catastrophe before which we stand, God calls us Christians and us Americans to a deeper self-searching than we have yet known and to a more bold and imaginative, even adventurous, seeking from Him of the way of life.

Though certainly we shall not be saved by weakness, we shall not be saved by military power alone. A one-sided concentration on military measures can easily lead to disaster.

The avoidance of global war without surrender to tyranny is the one great issue overriding all others.

THE REJECTION OF PREVENTIVE WAR

To avoid the physical and moral disaster of global war we must put behind us as a satanic temptation the dangerous idea of a "preventive war," which is closely bound up with the faithless and defeatist idea that war is inevitable.

Since we are in a situation of acute international tension well described as a "cold war," there are those who suggest that it is neither important nor possible to distinguish between that situation and overt conflict. "We are already at war in fact," they say. "Let's have it out and have it over." This appeals partly because it offers a release into action from a wearing state of anxiety and day-by-day irritation. But there is this great difference between open conflict and our present tensions, namely, that the latter do not involve the mass destruction and the moral debacle of global war. Just because that difference is so great no nation which subordinates national policy to moral purpose can think of beginning a general war, however uncomfortable and frustrating the present situation is.

There are those who argue that "cold war" must lead inevitably to "hot war." With modern methods of mass destruction the striker of the first blow may have a great advantage. "Let us," they say, "choose the time most favorable to our cause and gain the advantage of striking the first blow."

To accept general war as inevitable is to treat ourselves as helpless objects carried by a fated tide of events rather than as responsible men. The fact that many things in history are probable does not make them inevitable. One reason why fascism and nazism gained their dread power over great nations was because otherwise decent people bowed before what they regarded as "inevitable" and allowed a "wave of the future" to inundate them. Just because the probable results of general war with atomic weapons are so terrible no God-fearing people can take the responsibility for initiating a war which cannot be fought successfully without their use. "Woe unto the world because of offenses: for it must needs be that offenses come; but woe to that man by whom the offense cometh."

A fatalism and defeatism which assumes the inevitability of war with world Communism deflects us from the very strategy which offers us the greatest hope of any real victory; namely, the building up of the economic and social and moral health of the areas in our world not already under complete Communist domination. For Communism is more than the tyranny and imperial ambitions of the Soviet rulers. It is also a political religion, whose promises of a universal, classless society, tragically perverted though they have been, still carry a dynamic appeal to those oppressed by harsh and unjust conditions. To overcome such conditions requires positive non-military measures.

Thus to accept the inevitability of war is strategically wrong. It is morally wrong because it is a surrender to irresponsibility. It is religiously wrong because it involves a pretension on the part of man to know the future with an assurance not granted to man.

A second argument for a "preventive" war is based on the idea that Communism is an evil so monstrous that the evils even of a general conflict are not too high a price to pay for its elimination. If Communism should press hostilities against the non-communist world we would undoubtedly continue to resist, even though we could not measure the ultimate consequences. But precisely because this is true, we must insist the more that we have no right to initiate, by our own act, a struggle with such incalculable consequences. But consequences which will be horrible according to responsible calculation, and may be more terrible than any calculations, cannot be morally justified, if the decision rests with us.

A further reason for rejecting the idea of a preventive war is that even if the Soviet Union were defeated in such a war, that would not necessarily mean the defeat of communism, much less the successful defense of democracy. The world in the aftermath of such a war would be ripe for anarchy or for totalitarian movements promising men bread and security, rather than for the freedoms we seek to extend.

THE NEED FOR DEMOCRATIC STRENGTH

To build up and maintain adequate strength in the free world—yes, military strength, but military strength undergirded as it must be by economic and political and moral health—will make tremendous moral demands on the people of the United States and other members of the United Nations. For America even to maintain over a long period adequate military strength, let alone support bold strategies for strengthening economically and socially our less fortunate neighbors, without the obvious incentive of war itself, will call for self-discipline and resolution and a tightening of our belts such as we have never achieved. It is futile to argue with those who urge a desperate try for a quick decision because they do not believe we can rise to such demands, unless we are prepared to support the policies of armament and preparedness and of taxation and consumption restraints required for the maintenance of adequate strength in the free world. Whether or not we can avoid atomic devastation of the world in which we and our children dwell can well depend on the readiness of Americans to have fewer washing machines and television sets and automobiles for the sake of an all-out girding for the responsibilities laid upon us.

We should not and we do not rule out the possibility of an ultimate stability in the world situation. But we are quite clear that no significant agreements can be made with world-wide Communism so long as it assumes that it can violate the decisions of the United Nations with impunity and success. We believe in a moral approach to our problem, but a moral approach is one which accepts responsibly the full burdens imposed by the situation in which we find ourselves.

Since we believe that peace in the world, like peace in major human communities, must be sustained by power, we believe that peace in our world can be preserved only by the strength of the free world. This includes military power. But moral and political strength is ultimately a larger factor than military strength. Military strength is simply the hand, and the hand belongs to an arm and a body. Political and moral strength are the arm and body. If the moral and political struggle with Communism is lost, no military strength will avail.

Therefore the faith that sustains American life and the moral vitality of our society and the enthusiastic commitment that we can win from our people are of supreme importance. In the trials of our time every American who lives irresponsibly, who seeks his own gain without counting the cost to others; every politician who plays recklessly for partisan advantage or his own advancement; every injustice in our common life, every hypocrisy in our democratic professions, weakens us and makes us less ready to fulfill the role laid upon us by reason of our power.

If we are to maintain and renew the political and moral health of our nation, Christians must stand firmly against public hysteria and against all attempts to exploit the fears of our people in these critical days. The sensational or self-righteous distortion of truth, the slanderous defamation of men in public life, the attacks upon hard-won freedoms and the safe-guards of our Constitution—these divide and weaken our nation in the face of grave external dangers. They point in the direction of the police state methods we oppose. They rob us of the steadfast will to carry through our world responsibilities. They tend to make impossible a far-sighted and constructive strategy for peace. In the midst of the fears and frustrations of our new insecurity, the Churches of Christ must stand as guardians of freedom, as well as of faith.

Christians must never allow themselves to become complacent about America or the Western societies. It would be a fatal mistake to defend every aspect of our institutions, merely because they are under violent attack by Communist propagandists. Democratic strength requires self-criticism, a willingness to confront the facts with open eyes, and a deter-mination to improve the application of democratic principles to our common life.

Above all, our Churches must be concerned for the spiritual foundations of democratic strength. Ultimately the strength that avails is the power of the Lord, and we are ill prepared for the evil day unless we have the armor of God. With freedom in worldwide jeopardy, the Church must lead men and women to the true source of freedom, that He who makes us free may be our constant guide.

And next to the quality of the common life we bring to the issues of our time is the role we are able to play in helping other nations to gain physical well-being and moral vigor in freedom. The life-giving qualities of the free world, if vigorously renewed, can provide the surest human defense against tyranny and war. If the vitality, integrity, and neighborliness of the democratic societies can be developed and demonstrated in convincing ways, the Soviet rulers may find a modification of their expansionist aims, or at least of their intolerant methods, to be expedient. That would provide new opportunity for bridging the gulf between the Soviet and Western worlds with understanding and more reliable agreements.

Only a bold and imaginative strategy, supported by self-discipline and devotion, has a chance of success. There are no sure patterns of action to enhance the inner and outward strength of the non-Soviet world. Rather, there must be a willingness to try new and uncharted courses of constructive action which offer reasonable promise.

The policies pursued need to be convincing on two basic points. They must carry conviction that the non-Soviet societies are morally impregnable to totalitarian infiltration, as well as militarily strong enough to make overt aggression too hazardous. On the other hand, they must also carry conviction that the goal of the West is peace and not the conquest or forcible conversion of the Soviet Union. This means that the dominant motives of peace strategy should be positive and creative, and that every opportunity to develop friendly contacts with the Soviet peoples, or to draw Soviet representatives into the constructive activities and fellowship of the non-Soviet nations, should be utilized. On this, most Christian pacifists and non-pacifists can agree.

ELEMENTS OF A POSITIVE PEACE PROGRAM

In the forefront of a positive peace program is the plan to provide technical assistance and help secure financial assistance for the development of underdeveloped nations. This plan to attack in a concerted way the ancient enemies of ignorance, hunger, and disease, by concentrating available scientific and material resources on areas of greatest need, has aroused new hope around the world. Its scope and creative purpose have stirred the imaginations of men and enlisted their support.

We recognize the many and stubborn difficulties which beset, and will continue to beset for many years, a program such as this. But we believe it provides a means for combatting the conditions in which totalitarianism finds fertile soil. It provides an opportunity for joining the efforts of nations in a common interest which promotes international fellowship. It invites, although it does not require, the cooperation of the Soviet Union. This United Nations program should be supported vigorously by our government, and be reinforced at every appropriate point by our Churches and mission boards.

We are grateful for the pioneering work done by missionaries. Educational missions seeking the enlightenment of entire peoples, medical missions bringing health freely to all in need, and preaching missions offering a Gospel which gives meaning to life and death—these are the best values of our culture. These are treasures the Christian fellowship can contribute to a positive peace program.

In all the confusing complexities of our world-political problems we can discern some broad outlines. The hard core of our grievously disturbed relationships is in the constantly mounting tension between ourselves and

Soviet Russia and her satellites. All can agree that this is the hardest to change. But Russia and the United States do not stand alone. The power of either to hurt the other decisively depends greatly on the direction taken by other communities of men, in the East as well as the West.

In Eastern Asia and the Pacific area there are millions of men struggling up out of poverty and ignorance. The failure of Communism to capture Western Europe has accentuated its activities in the East. There vast social confusion, due to the disintegration of the colonial system and the impact of technical civilization on backward economies, and the resentment of colored peoples against the white world give Communism a fertile field in which to sow its false promises to desperate peoples. In dangerous measure the Communists have captured the leadership of this revolution of depressed masses against ancient privilege. Rice and land they can call their own and a chance to stand among men in their own right mean more to them than our slogans of freedom or free enterprise. We have to offer them something better than "free privilege" or unrestricted freedom for gain. We need to make it clear that our democratic constitution is Christian in background just because it is founded upon restraints, not upon doctrinaire freedom.

These peoples have suffered for generations the indignity of being treated by white men as "inferior breeds." Just because man is a spiritual being, the indignity of treatment as an inferior rankles more bitterly that physical deprivation. These peoples find it hard to trust us. Their resentments are awakened by every indignity imposed upon Jews or Negroes or Orientals or Mexicans or American Indians. A chance to live as equals and the millenial promises of Communism for rice and land have fired the awakening hopes of the Asiatic peoples. It is not enough to say complacently that we are working to eliminate discriminations against racial and religious minorities and that it will take time. It will take time, but we need to work at it harder, determined to succeed in the shortest time possible. Renewal of our own way of life and sustained effort to help the peoples of other lands achieve a better way of life than is possible under totalitarianism—these must be the goals of our strategy.

In Western Europe and the Atlantic area there are the peoples out of which our own inheritance has come most directly. With them, in spite of all strain and even past wars, we have a fuller basis for understanding and greater moral community than with any others. They have suffered the impoverishment and devastation of two world wars fought over their fields and cities. They now stand between the two great centers of power. They fear that if they must be rescued by us they shall be a waste land. And ordinary men will take their chances with much tyranny if the only alternative they can see is a waste land.

In our common peril, we desperately need the friendship of these peoples, too, and their strength. To win that we must give them the confidence that we understand them and how they are placed and that in full truth we make common cause with them. We shall not win that confidence if they can reasonably suspect that we seek to build them up to be buffers between us and the great center of power we fear, instead of seeking the welfare of their peoples for themselves. Our pride and our assurance that we know so much better than they how things should be done and our impatience are constant threats to the winning and holding of this confidence. We and they share a common destiny. Together we are called to meet it in comradeship.

Even in the case of Russia, in the face of the crass effrontery and the baffling falsity of her spokesmen, we cannot afford to accept the assumption that there is nothing human and good and real there to which we could speak. The Russian people share our common human needs and fears and hopes and sensibilities. They too, we are sure, want peace, if for no other reason than that like us they have such a dread of war. We must ask ourselves again and again, "Have we exhausted every means of speaking to them and of saying to them that we do not desire to destroy them or to take their land from them or to convert them by force? Have we repudiated in ourselves the things we have done or the things said in our name that could make it plausible to the people of Russia that we will their destruction?"

We have no clever new political stratagem to offer. But in the sight of God we are persuaded that our desperate times call for a mighty and costly drive for the political and moral revival and uniting of the free world and beyond that for reconciliation. That must accompany and even speak louder than our resolve to be strong. Are we conscripting the best intelligence and the most disinterested good will that America possesses for this supreme task? Are we Americans willing to spend and be spent for peace even more than for war?

The special task of the Churches in our time as in every time is to cry out to men, "Behold you God." It is in beholding Him and in standing in penitence before Him that we can gain and regain our moral stature as responsible men. In Him alone we can find the forgiveness without which our moral burden would be intolerable. And in receiving His forgiveness we can win the power to forgive those who trespass against us. Beholding Him, we can be delivered from the ultimate fears and the hysteria out of which no wisdom can come for meeting the terrors of our time. Before Him we dare to believe that we have a citizenship which no human weapons can destroy. From Him who "would fold both heaven and earth in a single peace" there comes even in our darkness that strange word, "Be not anxious."

***

Statements by Two Members Of The Commission

The chairman and my other colleagues have graciously suggested that I add a brief note to indicate why I cannot join them in signing the statement on which we have worked together. With much of it, needless to say, I am in hearty accord. Most of what is said in the introduction and second main section seems to me sound and admirable.

But on the most central issue, the statement seems to be still involved in deep-going confusion. On the one hand, it is repeatedly affirmed that "victory at any price is not worth having," that "military expediency" is not an adequate test for conduct in wartime. But in fact this turns out to be the only practically effective test that is consistently urged; and the only wartime practice that is consistently condemned is wanton cruelty or destruction "without commensurate military decisiveness." Concern for social and political welfare after a war does not rule out military measures that may well preclude it. Christian conscience in wartime is assigned the negative inhibitory role of suggesting "restraint" on destructive procedures. But the norm for practically effective inhibitions turns out to be, after all, military decisiveness; and beyond ruling out wanton destruction, Christian conscience in wartime seems to have chiefly the effect (certainly important but scarcely decisive) of making Christians do reluctantly what military necessity requires. The ruling assumption throughout, it seems to me, is that if "we" are attacked, we must do whatever is needed to win.

This perspective may be defended on political and cultural grounds. It can scarcely be regarded as distinctively Christian. Still less is it ecumenical. It represents a majority view, not an inclusive common mind. We who have worked together on this statement have not failed in earnestness, candor or charity. But I think all of us have failed, thus far, to achieve the wisdom and clearness needed to make our statement a valid whole.

Robert L. Calhoun

I assent to the introduction and second main section of the statement but feel obliged to withhold my signature from the intervening section on "War and The Weapons of Mass Destruction." My reasons are: (1) Christian pacifism as an attempt to eliminate war through international reconciliation is less simple and more responsible than is here suggested. (2) Under conditions of modern warfare the restraints proposed are largely inapplicable. To say that our government might justifiably use atomic weapons in retaliation "with all possible restraint" seems a contradiction in terms. (3) Although the general tone of the document is deeply and movingly Christian I do not find in this section such distinctive moral guidance from the Christian Gospel as I believe to be both possible and necessary.

Georgia Harkness

The report was signed by seventeen of the nineteen members who actually served on the commission. These were Angus Dun, chairman, Edwin E. Aubrey, Chester I. Barnard, John C. Bennett, Conrad J. I. Bergendoff, Arthur H. Compton, John R. Cunningham, Peter K. Emmons, Theodore M. Greene, Walter M. Horton, Benjamin E. Mays, Albert T. Mollegen, James H. Nichols, Reinhold Niebuhr, George F. Thomas, Paul J. Tillich, William W. Waymack. Two members of the commission, Robert L. Calhoun and Georgia Harkness, dissented from certain portions of the report and their statements are appended to the report. When the Federal Council received the report of the commission [on November 27, 1950], it did so with the following resolution: "(1) That the Federal Council of the Churches of Christ in America express deep appreciation to Bishop Dun and his colleagues for their report on 'The Christian Conscience and Weapons of Mass Destruction.' (2) That the report be printed by the Federal Council and commended to the Churches for careful study. (3) That the document be also referred for consideration to the National Council of the Churches of Christ in the U.S.A., when it comes into being."

AGENDA OF ACTION FOR PEACE
"Toward a Family of Nations Under God"*

The NCCC General Board, 1960

Christian faith requires us to take initiatives for peace, and against such ancient enemies of man as: human want, denial of individual freedoms, war-breeding international tensions. We believe in the sovereignty of God's love in the life of mankind. We respect the dignity and worth of the individual. Both as Christians and as citizens of a democracy, our duty is to find and support practical programs of action toward peace and justice.

INTRODUCTORY STATEMENT

In 1943, while armies were still locked in battle, a "Statement of Political Propositions" was formulated by the Commission of the Churches to Study the Bases of a Just and Durable Peace. Known as the "Six Pillars of Peace," this Statement has provided standards for expressing the relevance of the Christian faith to United States foreign policy.

The Commission predicted in 1943: "Appalling moral, social and material aftermaths ... will arise to perplex and divide the United Nations."

Two years later, the Atomic Age had its fiery dawn. The Second Great Age of Exploration was about to lure into space the residents of a shrinking planet. The war-time coalition even then was crumbling, and the communist systems had begun a march for power and empire. Colonialism was in disintegration on all the restless continents. A score of new states would soon be born, having little except hope with which to clothe and feed themselves. Science provided means to improve the welfare of mankind, and expectations grew with knowledge that fulfillment was possible.

These developments have crowded the years since the end of the war. They have brought in full measure the perplexity and division forecast by

---

*The following is a policy statement of the National Council of Churches of Christ in the United States of America adopted by the general board on June 2, 1960 as a message for use in the churches on World Order Sunday, October 23, 1960 and for general use after that date.

the Commission.

Now, the future of our nation and world peace rests heavily upon our nation's capacity and will to translate its traditions into realistic programs of action.

Faithful to the duty of the Christian Churches to weigh moral aspects of political, economic and social affairs, in the light of their faith in Jesus Christ as Lord and Saviour, the National Council of Churches sets forth the following Proposals for Action. They are intended to serve as guides in the search for truth and for responsible action.

PROPOSAL FOR ACTION—ITEM I

Our nation shares with all mankind both a common danger and an opportunity under God to define and serve the common good.

Christians need to seek new insight as to how moral power can be made an effective element of national strength and international action, rather than a moralistic excuse for inaction. National self-interest in a disordered world often calls for practical action which appears to conflict with moral objectives. Although hard choices must be made, a nation's obligation to the society of mankind is governed by the moral law as are the duties of the individual to society. Our responsibility as Christians involves learning the facts, appraising them fearlessly, seeking humbly to apply to them the moral principles which our faith inspires.

PROPOSAL FOR ACTION—ITEM II

The United States must persevere in the quest for enforceable agreements to eliminate weapons of death and to reduce the burden of armaments. At the same time, the need for alternatives to the use of military force requires the development of institutions for collective security and the strengthening of peaceful processes.

War has never been a morally acceptable instrument for the pursuit of national policy, even though the capacity for self-defense has been recognized as necessary to survival. The dilemma of defense is sharpened by the existence of ultimate weapons, which threaten victim and aggressor alike with mutual suicide.

What, then, are the alternatives to appeasement or surrender? The quest for enforceable disarmament clearly is part of the answer. We have sought, and must continue to seek, enforceable agreements pertaining to the production, testing and means of delivery of weapons of mass destruction, as well as more inclusive agreements.

"Disarmament" in reality means the reduction of national military power and acceptance of limits upon the use of such power. No nation will voluntarily agree to weaken its relative strength, if it lacks confidence in existing processes for security and for orderly change.

The objective of general disarmament can, therefore, be achieved only in relation to a relatively stable international order. This, in turn, depends upon strengthening institutions to build the foundations of peace and more effective use of processes to keep the peace and assure justice.

The United Nations and other international processes cannot be wished into maturity. They grow only with use, encouragement and support. They atrophy when neglected or by-passed in the areas of their greatest service to humanity: mutual economic and technical assistance, promotion of human rights, development of the atom for peaceful uses, cooperation in the use of outer space, and faithful use of international juridical, political and economic agencies.

The United States should respect the competence of the International Court of Justice, without self-appointed powers of reservation, such as the Connally Amendment. Until the Amendment is repealed, we should use the reserved power with utmost restraint.

PROPOSAL FOR ACTION—ITEM III

Improvement of standards of life of our fellow-men is a privilege the United States shares, not a benefit it confers. Moral principle even more than concern for our own national welfare impels an abiding interest in our neighbors on a crowded planet. Their growth is part of our growth and their partnership for peace is essential to all security.

The arithmetic of world poverty can be simply expressed: more than half of mankind are undernourished all their lives, cannot expect to live over forty, and cannot read or write. Yesterday, some thought them strangers who could be used, isolated or ignored. In a jet age, they are seen to be our neighbors across narrow waters.

Increase of population in many places thwarts efforts to raise living standards even to bare subsistence levels. When governments concerned request information and scientific aid for responsible parenthood, we believe our government should comply with such requests.

The United States has, similarly a responsibility with respect to the new states. It is a responsibility not only to them, but to ourselves. In accordance with our own tradition of self-determination, we hail their emergence from colonial rule, and welcome them into the United Nations. Yet we must go further to strengthen the ties which enable them to join a community of freedom.

We tend to think too much in terms of military posture, with economic assistance closely related to it. Political, cultural and economic relationships must be given higher priority. Repeated demonstration shows that international development and technical assistance can be soundly administered by multilateral programs and that those have an important place alongside of bilateral programs. Nevertheless, we resort to the United Nations in little more than token proportions. Our country must do more for world economic development through the United Nations and its specialized agencies.

PROPOSAL FOR ACTION—ITEM IV

Promotion of human rights and fostering freedom throughout the world are duties of citizenship, as well as mandates of the Christian faith. United States leadership in support of these efforts must be renewed and invigorated.

Free institutions can survive only in societies of free individuals.

The Charter of the United Nations expresses an international interest in the promotion of human rights and fundamental freedoms. But the Charter does not itself define human rights, nor does it specify methods by which states will achieve practical recognition of these values. The Universal Declaration of Human Rights does set forth standards for achievement which have already had significant influence.

The responsibility for action is left to the member states. It remains one of the major uncompleted tasks of the member nations, including the United States.

Rapidly shifting social, political, economic and cultural forces within the emerging societies impede orderly transition to stability. Authoritarian and democratic systems compete to fill the need. More than slogans about freedom and justice are required. "Freedom" must be translated into the rights to exercise religious liberty, to vote, to learn, to assemble, to speak, to protest and to act. "Justice" can be realized only in terms of fair legal and administrative systems. Without these, the restless societies will seek alternatives born of despair rather than of free choice.

For these practical reasons, as well as the mandates of our faith, we believe that the United States Government should renew and invigorate its leadership in the promotion of human rights. It should support the United Nations as a forum for airing grievances. The Genocide Convention, which the United States signed in 1948, should be ratified without delay. The United States should restore its leadership by supporting the Covenants of Human Rights.

PROPOSAL FOR ACTION—ITEM V

Communications of ideas, exchanges among peoples, and willingness to negotiate at all levels, assume greater urgency, the more ideas clash or political tensions mount. Communication does not imply approval, exchanges do not corrupt men of principle, and negotiation need not mean appeasement. The basic Christian concept of reconciliation must be persistently pursued.

The necessity for coupling power with responsibility imposes upon democratic societies a duty to maintain channels of reconciliation, of communication and of influence with the community of mankind, whatever the form of government to which peoples are pledged or subjugated.

Godless and lawless doctrines of communism are abhorrent to the Christian. Nevertheless it has never been Christian doctrine that evil can be overcome by ignoring it or pretending it does not exist.

Principles of freedom and democracy have universal appeal, and their highest values are realized in the sharing of them. The free exchange of ideas and persons contributes to the spread of these principles and the development of open societies. These, in turn, are a necessary precondition for the sound growth of institutions of international order and cooperation.

Appeasement consists in the surrender of principle, not in the discussion of differences. Our government should, therefore, be ready to confer at all levels with all governments, on any issues which affect our national interest or international order, including disarmament, the prohibition of nuclear tests, and the peaceful uses of atomic energy, all of which require cooperation of the major powers, including those which are not officially recognized by the United States.

PROPOSAL FOR ACTION—ITEM VI

Leadership toward world community requires justice in our own national community. Full respect for the United States rests upon our own respect for the dignity and equality of all our citizens before the law.

All social structures, being human, have built-in weaknesses. Although authoritarian forms may display outward solidarity, societies which are morally-based and self-disciplining are capable of an inward strength of purpose denied to other forms. The Christian is concerned primarily with the moral force and vision requisite to generate such inward strength.

One essential element is vigorous action to secure equality of opportunity for all citizens in education, in civic and economic rights, and before the law. The national interest in building a community of freedom is paramount to local action inconsistent with that interest. States rights are entitled to respect in our federal system. Nevertheless, states owe a duty to respect the human rights which the federal system guarantees and the international standards affirm.

These moral requirements have a direct and practical application to United States foreign policy. New states and emergent peoples are engaged in a struggle for social stability, without undue loss of human diversity and freedom. The traditions of the United States classically embody this universal aspiration. But our present national patterns of behavior profoundly affect our international power of persuasion.

We, the people of the United States, owe it to ourselves to grasp the opportunity—perhaps the last we shall be accorded in foreseeable history—to help lead mankind toward a universal dominion of justice and peace.

INDEX